# THE POWER OF POSITIVE PARENTING

## A Wonderful Way to Raise Children

# THE POWER OF POSITIVE PARENTING

## A Wonderful Way to Raise Children

Glenn I. Latham

Utah State University

Original Cover Design: Michael Smith
Revised Cover Design: Jason Holladay

**P&T** *ink*

**1668 No. 1515 East
North Logan, UT 84341**

**P&T** *ink*

To contact P & T ink or Parenting Prescriptions:
1668 North 1515 East
North Logan, UT 84341
E-mail: lamlatham@aol.com
Phone (435) 752-5749, Fax (435) 750-5715

**Eighth Printing 2003**

PRINTED IN THE UNITED STATES OF AMERICA
**8 10 9**

**ISBN: 1-56713-175-1**

P & T Ink books are published by P & T Ink

"P & T Ink" and the "P & T Ink" logo are trademarks of P & T ink.

This book is written for parents who care enough to learn the skills necessary to raise children well in these difficult times.

It is more a manual than it is a book; hence, it must be read, then reread, then read some more. Wide margins have been provided for note taking. Use it as a tool with which to build your family.

So far as the author has been able to determine, the book has been subjected to more independent, scientific scrutiny than any parenting book in print today. In every instance, it has been shown to be an effective parenting tool. For that reason, it has been adopted by parent training programs, schools, university professors, early childhood and head start programs, and governmental programs as the basic text for teaching parenting skills. Summaries of studies conducted on the book, the documented impact the book has had on families, and unsolicited testimonials from parents are available from the author.

# Also By Glenn I. Latham

Parenting With Love: Making A Difference in A Day

What's a Parent To Do?
Solving Family Problems in a Christlike Way

Christlike Parenting

Parenting Prescriptions (2 audio cassettes)

An Angel Out of Tune (2 CDs or 2 audio cassettes)

The Making of A Stable Family (A 2 video tape training program for parents)

Behind the Schoolhouse Door: Eight Skills Every Teacher Should Have

Keys to Classroom Management

Management NOT "Discipline". A Wakeup Call for Educators

Managing the Classroom Environment to Facilitate Effective Instruction (Teacher training & inservice materials. Six videos, user's manual, teaching aids, & technical report)

# Acknowledgments

This book is a product of the efforts of many wonderful people who deserve to be acknowledged. First, my family. My lovely wife Louise; our six precious children, Karen, Philip, Laura, Roxanne, Allen, and Julie; our nineteen grandchildren and our great grandchild have given life to the body of this book. Many of the illustrations are drawn from their lives, and to some extent constitute an invasion of their privacy. Nevertheless, they have supported this effort willingly, and for that I am especially grateful.

Several of my associates have spent long hours typing, proofreading, and organizing draft after draft of the book. They have been wonderful. They are (in alphabetical order), Cindy Budge, Julia Burnham, Shauna Crane, Conna Dudley, Adrian Glover Fluckiger, Sydney Peterson, Jana Roberts, and Paulette Sip.

Dr. Sidney Bijou, his extraordinary wife Janet, and my good friend and colleague Dr. Carl Cheney deserve special mention here. They have been ready—indeed eager—respondents every time I needed their help, which was frequent.

A special thanks to all of these very special people!

Glenn Latham

*Cover photo by Art Reid. Cover design and Logo by Michael Smith.*

# Foreword

As they have in the past, parents today are still asking: How can I deal with my child's tantrums? How can I get my kids to do their chores promptly and without complaining? What can I do to help my family members live together more harmoniously? And on and on.

Here is a book that should go a long way in helping parents to resolve such problems. *The Power of Positive Parenting* is a unique book for many reasons, with the two that follow heading the list.

First, the practices advocated by Dr. Latham are based on solid psychological principles, "solid" because they have originated in research done over the past 60 years. In contrast, books dealing with child rearing practices are generally based on personal impressions or convictions, fragments of a psychological theory, or a mixture of psychological theories.

Second, the principles are applied to parenting practices by an educator who is not only well-versed in the principles and in the research on their application but has also used them with his own six children and in counseling parents and adolescents with a wide variety of problems. Also noteworthy is the skill of the author in conveying his message in an easy-to-understand style coupled with a flair for recounting compelling instances and examples.

Now about the content of the book. The strategies for dealing with the problem behavior of a child center on an indisputable fact: Whatever a child (or anyone else) does or says has consequences which influence the way that child will behave in future similar situations. With repetition, those behaviors become part of a child's personality. In other words, the consequences of a child's behavior, whether the behavior is considered by the parents to be desirable or undesirable, shape a child's traits—abilities, habits, manners, attitudes, etc.

Whether parents realize it or not, they, by virtue of being parents, provide most of the consequences of a child's behavior during the child rearing years. Hence, the essential ingredient in dealing with problem behavior and in child rearing practices in general, is the management of consequences in ways that increase desirable behavior and decrease undesirable behavior. One other essential stipulation: To be maximally effective, as Dr. Latham puts it, consequences must be positive, constructive, and growth-supportive. Although negative consequences, that is, physical punishment and coercion, unquestionably stop undesirable behavior, it is not advocated because research has repeatedly shown that in the long run, the use of aversive consequences is detrimental to a child's development and to the relationship between parent and child.

To tell parents that the way to deal with a child's problem behavior is to manage the consequences of the child's behavior in a positive, constructive manner is equivalent to telling them to change their own behavior. Without a doubt such a prescription will be difficult for some parents to follow. Yet it will be eminently worthwhile considering that to do so will make for a happier, better focused child and for a more harmonious family situation. And, in so far as a family's standards and goals are consistent with those of society's, positive parenting will help reduce many of the juvenile problems facing us today: violence, even in the early years; teenage promiscuity; alcohol and drug abuse; poor school achievement; and so on. True, other factors, such as unstable marital relationships, inadequate medical and educational services, and excessive TV watching, contribute to these problems. However, ineffective child rearing practices and low standards of conduct are at the heart of most of them. Hence the power of positive parenting cannot be overstressed.

*S.W. Bijou, Ph.D. Distinguished*
*Distinguished Professor of Psychology,*
*University of Nevada Reno*

# Reviewers

Though written in non-technical language, and illustrated using everyday events and circumstances in home and family settings, the content of this book is solidly anchored in science. To assure both its technical and practical accuracy, the book has been critically reviewed by parents and professionals, with revisions made on the basis of those reviews. The reviewers, with a brief observation from each, are listed below in alphabetical order. To each one, I owe a special debt of gratitude.

"We first met Dr. Latham nearly 30 years ago, listened to his counsel and tried to incorporate his very sensible help into our child rearing and other relationships. His ideas have seen us through tough and troubling times as well as normal toddler to teenage challenges, and now we're using the helps to become better grandparents. Parents throughout the world would do well to listen to Dr. Latham and do as he suggests. Homes would be happier, children would be given the opportunities to grow as they deserve, and the world would be a much happier place in which to live."

*Doug and Elaine Alder*
*St. George, Utah*
*President of Dixie College and Freelance Writer*
*Parents of four children, grandparents of three*

"Dr. Latham's book, *The Power of Positive Parenting*, has been a blessing to me as a parent. In a world with so many confusing messages being sent to children as well as parents, it is refreshing to hear such common sense, clear cut, advice. These techniques for parenting have been proven to be successful in my own family as well as many others I have shared this book with. Two different times, I was "at the end of my parenting rope", feeling like there was no solution to my particular problems. It was through using some very simple behavior changing techniques Dr. Latham suggested that incredible changes occurred. These didn't happen overnight, and it wasn't always easy, but with patience and time, the situation resolved. Many other times I have used this book as a quick reference to remind myself of what is just plain "normal" for a child!

Best of all, I have discovered there really is more power in positive parenting and that it is never too late to change. It really is possible to discipline a child and still maintain the dignity of both the child and the parent! I am convinced that every human relationship we have can be enhanced through these principles. *The Power of Positive Parenting* should be required reading for all parents!"

*Cecelia J. Benson*
*Utah Young Mother of the Year*
*Mother of eight children*

"In this book Professor Latham shows that he is an expert in applying the principles of behavior science to family management. His book is a wonderful tool for parents who want to understand how to foster appropriate behavior in children and at the same time maintain a happy and loving relationship. The techniques for establishing and maintaining discipline with children are those proven to be effective and acceptable from extensive laboratory and field research. Dr. Latham takes scientific and data-based procedures and makes them understandable and applicable for every parent. This book is a rare example of how parents can put behaviorological science to use in the home. Dr. Latham knows his business, has practiced what he preaches, and has now made that experience available for everyone. I recommend this book very highly."

*Carl D. Cheney, Ph.D.*
*Professor of Psychology, Utah State University*
*Father of four children, grandfather of three*

"This book is so positive and practical—a great handbook for parents of any age. The material is reinforcing for parent and child and would be a key to making all families happier and better, if only parents would try Dr. Latham's suggestions and never give up. The book has so many descriptive sections that parents can learn from every page, even without formal training or classes in parenting."

*Elise A. Clark, Orem, Utah*
*Teacher and mother of two children*

There is one thing we have to tell you about this book: IT IS AN EXCELLENT BOOK.

We did not find a thing to criticize or disapprove. It was hard to suggest improvements and to stop ourselves from marking all over good! We often felt that what we were reading was written just the way we would have done it. We also like the way you wrote so that *ordinary people* can benefit from what has been learned about human behavior. The frequent and real behavioral episodes that you use with your explanations make the text very comprehensive and practical."

*Linda Armendariz, for*
*Comunidad Los Horcones*
*Hermosillo, Sonora, Mexico*

"A book like Dr. Latham's vividly portraying the practical application of scientific laws, principles, and rules to real-life parent-child interactions, is long overdue. The book describes a myriad of relationship scenarios every parent can relate to, and by consistently utilizing behavioral principles parents change from being *reactionary* to being proactive.

Such a wealth of treasured behaviorally engineered parent-child interactions at all age levels could only come from a person with deep empathy and understanding stemming from a lifetime of family experience and a scholarly pen as expressive as Dr. Latham's."

*Jack Rudio, Ed.D*
*Research Associate Professor*
*Utah State University*
*Father of five children*

"*The Power of Positive Parenting* gives parents the principles and strategies to be good parents in ways that are very easy to understand and implement. This book is for all parents who feel the need for more positive interactions with their children. Only as a suffering parent, watching a beloved child go astray did I come to understand the importance of the principles in this book. It has enabled me to continue parenting with a perfect brightness of hope."

*Sydney Peterson*
*Mother of four children, ages three to seventeen*

"I continue to read your book with a good deal of enjoyment. It does not compromise either the science or its language, nevertheless the book makes its points clearly and with anecdotes that have an immediacy to any parent."

*Ernest Vargus, Ph.D*
*Professor of Behaviorology,*
*West Virginia University*
*Father of two grown daughters*

# NOTE

**PLEASE READ THIS SHORT MESSAGE
BEFORE READING THE BOOK**

As you read this book you might feel that at times I am overly redundant in describing the application of basic principles and strategies. The fact of the matter is, I am redundant—purposefully—for three reasons:

1. I want to impress you with the fact that these principles and strategies apply to children of *all* ages and in *all* settings. Just as basic medicine is applicable to people of all ages and in all settings, so is basic "behavioral medicine". I hope that by describing its application in a variety of applied settings, its generalizability will become progressively more apparent.

2. People have a hard time generalizing from one situation to another; from one age to another. Parents are forever saying to me, "Well, that's okay for a 5-year-old, but what about my 16-year-old?" A mother, after watching me role play a strategy with a father, responded dourly, "Now let's talk about some *real* behavior." What she was saying, of course, was, "The behaviors of my kids are the only real behaviors." I role played the same strategies with her, but tailored them to her children's "real behaviors," and sure enough, the principles applied. When we analyzed what I had done and suggested, she realized that I had simply tailored a basic set of principles and strategies to her problems. That tailoring (or, put another way, generalizing) of principles and strategies from one situation to another is not always easily done; consequently, in this book I illustrate how that is done in many, many settings, and with a wide range of ages. Please be alert to how the basic principles and strategies apply in *all* of the examples and situations.

3. Single-trial learning is rarely effective. Sometimes it works quite well. For example, not many people will repeatedly thrust their hands into the whirring blade of a band saw. That only has to happen once for a person to learn never to do it again! But when learning things like behavioral principles and strategies—well, that takes multiple learning opportunities. As a renowned

American business and religious leader said, "A genius is a person who does what he's been told to do after having been told to do it 12 times." By restating the basics again and again and again in a variety of settings, the probability of learning them well is proportionally increased.

Recently while working with a set of parents and rehearsing what we had discussed repeatedly in previous sessions, the mother said, almost with alarm, "Dr. Latham, how many more times are you going to have to tell us this before it sinks in? When we do what you tell us to do, it works, but then we get tired and careless and sloppy. We do what we think is the most expedient thing. We holler at the kids, give them a swat on the bottom, plead with them to behave, and it all goes to pot!"

In this book, I tell you the same things in many different ways using many different settings. I do it with the hope that by the time you've read (and reread) this book, you won't be saying, "Dr. Latham, how many more times are you going to have to tell us this before it sinks in?"

☆  ☆  ☆

The essence of this book is found in the following statement of Dr. Sidney W. Bijou. For that reason, it is presented at the end of every chapter.

**Research has shown that the most effective way to reduce problem behavior in children is to strengthen desirable behavior through positive reinforcement rather than trying to weaken undesirable behavior using aversive or negative processes.**

*The International Encyclopedia of Education, 1988*

# Table of Contents

*"Mrs. West, I am so excited. I am spending the weekend with my real father and my brother is spending the weekend with his real father and my sister is spending the weekend with her real father. My mother is spending a relaxing weekend at home alone—unless her boyfriend comes by."*

*A preschool child to her teacher,*
*Somerset, England*
*1987*

# ONE
# The Changing Family, and How To Change for the Better

The human family will never be the same—and that's not all bad. Perhaps the best thing we have going for us today is that so much is known about how to raise a happy family.

Without doubt many of us grew up in families that reflected the best in Currier and Ives tradition. Over the river and through the woods to grandmother's house we went, and when we got there we were joyfully greeted by loving, gray-haired saints, arms outstretched, warmly welcoming us home to the aroma of freshly baked bread and a jar of chocolate chip cookies.

Despite this pleasant stereotype, social research has taught us that the family woes of today were probably as prevalent in generations past. Had it not been for a demanding life of survival that kept their noses to the grindstone (and their hands in the milking shed), our parents and grandparents would have been every bit as beside themselves about the behavior of their children as parents are today.

> *In earlier generations circumstances in the environment helped parents manage most behaviors. But not now! Parents must have parenting skills.*

Parents today tend to be too hard on themselves by buying into the myth of the ideal family. They make simple comparisons between themselves and their parents, between their families and families past, without considering changes in society and the effects of those changes on children's behavior. In earlier generations, circumstances in the environment helped parents manage most behavior. As a boy, I knew that if the wood boxes weren't full, Mom couldn't fix supper and there would be no heat to warm the house the next morning. I had chores that really meant something! I knew what my dad did for a living. I worked beside him from childhood through young adulthood. Furthermore, he was the boss, and like the other men who worked for him, I knew that and behaved accordingly. If I was going to be delinquent, I was going to have to do it on my own time!

My responsibilities, the clear-cut roles of my parents, and the *need* to perform to survive combined to make parenting relatively easy. Shortly before my 89-year-old mother died, I asked about her approach to parenting. She looked at me quizzically and said, "I never had an approach to parenting. I never thought about it. I had too much to do just to keep you kids clothed and fed."

For most families, those days are gone forever. I have six children, all well educated. Not one of them knows for sure what I do for a living. They grew up in comfort and security, and never had to turn a finger to help achieve that. One of their biggest problems was trying to figure out what to do with all the time they had on their hands. How many times I heard, "Dad, I'm bored! What can I do?"
My wife and I learned early on that, unlike the past, it wasn't circumstances that were going to raise our children—it was us! In fact, a new set of circumstances in society had now become the problem. The environment was no longer on our side. Tragically, it was working against us. Dramatic evidence of this state of things was reported in 1988 by the Fullerton, California Police Department and the California Department of Education. This side-by-side comparison of problems facing our society today, compared with those of 50 years ago, is dramatic:

> **The environment is no longer on our side.**

| 1940 | 1988 |
|---|---|
| Talking out of turn | Drug abuse |
| Chewing gum in school | Alcohol abuse |
| Making noise in class | Teen pregnancy |
| Running in the halls | Teen suicide |
| Getting out of line | Rape |

In her book *The Working Mother's Guilt Guide*, Mary Hickey draws a cogent comparison between what our mothers worried about and what we worry about:

| THINGS YOUR MOM WORRIED ABOUT | THINGS YOU WORRY ABOUT |
| --- | --- |
| Washing whites/darks in same load | Race relations |
| Ring-around-the collar | Drug rings |
| Napping | Kidnapping |
| The heating bill | Global warming |
| Cavities | AIDS |
| Grass stains | The greenhouse effect |
| The nuclear bomb | The nuclear family |

It is nearly impossible to escape the bombardment of social statistics that describe the human environment today, characterized by one author as "a catastrophe": e.g., marginally functional families, the insanity of child and spouse abuse, the ever-enlarging grip of poverty, a welfare system that has "contributed to the deteriorating state of the family," "throwaway" kids in the hundreds of thousands being fed upon by the lusts of the lowest of the low-life, and the list goes on and on and on. It has been estimated that 90% of the children of today are growing up "under vastly different circumstances than children did just one generation ago." A survey of elementary teachers conducted for the National PTA and the American Academy of Pediatrics identified psychological and emotional problems, unhealthy lifestyle of parents, and family violence and abuse as the three biggest health problems of children today. As one author noted, "We have to spend more time just doing battle with our own culture."

In large measure, that battle is being lost, not because parents don't love or care about their children, because the great majority certainly do care. A report issued in 1992 by the Center for the Study of Social Policy noted that "American parents care about their children. They spend most of their time at work or taking care of family matters. They want to give their children the right start in life and a better chance than they themselves had. But many families live in situations that make it difficult to reach these goals."

This book speaks to one of those situations, and though it's only one, it is perhaps the most important one: parenting skills. Yes, *skills*, as contrasted with intuition, common logic, and conventional wisdom, none of which forms a good basis for parenting. As we study stress and conflict in homes and families, it becomes immediately evident that these stresses and conflicts exist and persist because parents lack basic parenting skills; they haven't been taught a better way to deal with their own behaviors nor the behaviors of their children. They tend to raise their children as they were raised, and by and large that leaves a lot to be desired! When people become parents, they bring to that new role in life models and experiences about parenting, but rarely skills. Recently I was in the home of a young couple—struggling college students, the parents of a 2-year-old boy and a baby girl—who said, "We want to raise our children differently than we were raised. We swore we would never shout at or hit our children as our parents did with us. But we find ourselves doing those very things! We find ourselves hitting and spanking and screaming at our children, and doing all of that negative stuff. We don't want that. We just don't want that in our home!"

There is so much "negative stuff" going on in families, and it exists because parents don't know a better way. They have no skills! I'm reminded of the father who called the police into his home to arrest his 6-year-old son for refusing to obey him. I remember reading of the grandmother who locked a 3-year-old child in a 5-foot-by-5-foot wooden cage because "she was an active 3-year-old and her family couldn't handle her." Of the parents who chained up their 15-year-old daughter to keep her away from drugs because they were "desperate." Of the father who shook his 3-month old son to death because "…he got frustrated when the baby wouldn't quit crying." And of the parents who put their 4-year-old daughter in scalding water as punishment for soiling her pants. Of course, that is not punishment, it is brutality. Mindless, out-of-control brutality! Parents with no skills.

> *Not knowing a better way, parents turn almost immediately to coercive methods to control their children's behavior.*

"Desperate" and "out of control" are terms I hear continually from parents. Not knowing a better way of parenting, they turn almost immediately to coercive methods to control behavior. They try to control by hitting, spanking, screaming, threatening, hurting (Oh, I could tell you some terrible stories in this regard!), and abandoning. Louis Sullivan, President Bush's Health and Human Services Secretary, said, "We are raising a generation of young males who measure their manhood by the caliber of their gun and by the number of children they have fathered—a generation for whom the camaraderie of a gang has replaced the love of a family." Dr. Sullivan is sadly correct, but it can also be said in truth and in fact that we are raising a generation for whom the *camaraderie* of a gang has replaced the *coercion* of a family; where children seek the acceptance of the gang as an escape from the coercion of the home. Well, there is a better way, to which this book is dedicated.

Happily, research in human behavior has given us a lot of help. In this book, that help centers around three dominant themes: parent-child interactions, ignoring inconsequential behavior, and parents' responsibility to teach their children how to behave appropriately.

First, parents must go out of their way to have positive, pleasant experiences and interactions with their children. As we study parent-child interactions in the home, we are alarmed to find that these interactions are far more likely to be negative than positive. In fact, parents are typically five to six times more likely to have negative interactions with their children than they are to have positive interactions with them. A study conducted in 1984 revealed that whereas in 1930, contact between parents and their children averaged 3 to 4 hours per day, by 1984 the amount of contact was 14 1/2 minutes per day, of which slightly more than 12 1/2 of those minutes were spent in one-way (parent to child) negative communication! Nowadays it seems that parents are so anxious to set their children straight (perhaps out of fear of what might happen if they don't!) that they feel compelled to "nip trouble in the bud" by getting after their kids every time they do something wrong. Unfortunately, this ultimately produces just the opposite of what is desired. Since behavior is typically strengthened by parental attention (positive or negative), by attending to inappropriate behavior we are far more likely to increase its frequency and intensity than we are to "nip it in the bud." In other words, we make matters worse. We strengthen the very behaviors we want to eliminate! We create a coercive environment from which children want to escape, or in which they try time and again to get even.

> **Parents are typically far more likely to have negative than positive interactions with their children.**

The far better way is to give positive attention to the things our children do appropriately. By attending to the good and desirable things our children do, we dramatically increase the likelihood that those good and desirable things will increase. My friend and colleague, Dr. Joseph Cautela, advocates a high "general level of positive reinforcement" as the best way to establish a healthy home environment. (How this is done is addressed repeatedly throughout the book.)

There is an old adage in our society that admonishes us to "leave well enough alone." That is good advice where things like live ammunition, angry rattle snakes, and scabs on sores are concerned. But it is *terrible* advice where human behavior is concerned. I advise parents to go out of their way to have dozens of positive interactions and no negative interactions every day with *each* of their children who are living at home. And it's easy to do. It takes some effort and practice, as is discussed at length later, to get into the habit, but it *can* be done. And when it is done, oh, how wonderful things become! Parents are always complaining to me that their kids never hear a thing they say. Well, just try praise. You'll be surprised how quickly children's hearing improves (and adults', too!).

Negativeness at home is killing the family! I recently gave a talk about parenting to a group of high school students and stressed the need for a positive environment in the home. During some role playing to demonstrate how to be positive during stressful situations, the girl I was role-playing with burst out laughing, and said, "If my father said those things to me I'd pass right out. I can't imagine him saying those things to me!" Later the teacher asked the students, "Let me see by a raise of hands how many of you are regularly and predictably criticized by your parents for the things you do wrong." Every hand went up. She then said, "Let me see the hands of those who are

> Negativeness at home is killing the family.

regularly and predictably praised or complimented by their parents for the good and appropriate things they do." You guessed it: not one hand went up! A few months ago my wife and I were judges at a county contest among teenage girls. While being interviewed, the contestants were asked, "What makes you really happy?" Twelve of the 15 girls answered, "When my parents compliment me." In this regard I was interested in a conclusion drawn by a family researcher (Dr. Brent Miller, Utah State University, College of Family Life) who wrote, "Female teenagers involved in sexual activity are more likely to have strained relations with their families in the form of less open communications with their parents, receiving less praise for their achievements, and viewing their parents' marriage as being less close and warm."

Secondly, and certainly related to the first, parents must learn to ignore most of the age-typical, "junk" behavior of their children. (When I use the term "behavior," I am referring to things people say and do—including what kids say and do, given that they are people!) Easily 95% of the things kids do that drive their parents crazy should not be given any attention at all. Just turn and walk away. Just ignore it. It is simply age-typical behavior; it goes with the territory. It is the "heat of the kitchen." Behavior that does not get attention soon weakens and dies. When kids argue and scrap with one another, just walk out of the room. Most of the time they are simply performing, and if an audience gathers, it just encourages (that is, reinforces) the performance.

> *Unless what you are about to say or do has a high probability for making things better, don't say it and don't do it.*

I know, parents get frustrated and don't know what to do or say. Out of frustration they feel compelled to say and do something! My advice is this: Unless what you are about to say or do has a high probability of making things better (both for the moment and in the long run), don't say it and don't do it! For every ounce of frustration we get off our chests by screaming at and beating on our kids, we put a pound of trouble on their shoulders and ours!

By looking for opportunities to have happy, positive interactions with our children, and by just ignoring the "junk" behavior, it is possible to transform an otherwise unhappy home into a pleasant, more stable environment. Try it. You have nothing to lose but a lot of unhappiness and a lot of unpleasant behavior.

Third, parents have the ultimate responsibility to *teach* children how to behave appropriately. Yes, *teach*. How often parents say to me, "My child won't behave," "My child can't stay out of trouble," or "My child will not mind." Statements like these describe what the child can't or won't do in terms that suggest the child is to blame: it's the child's fault! If parents better understood their role as teachers, they would say, "I haven't taught my child to behave well," "I haven't taught my child to stay out of trouble," or "I haven't taught my child to mind." When a child fails to behave properly, that is evidence the child has either not been taught to behave appropriately, or the child is more often reinforced for behaving inappropriately than for behaving appropriately. Therefore, inappropriate, improper behavior *must* be recognized as a reason and an opportunity to teach, not as an excuse to punish. When children behave badly, rather than say, "That child needs to be punished for behaving that way,"

> *Misbehavior of children must be recognized as a need to teach appropriate behavior, not an excuse to punish. Punishment is a terrible teacher. It only teaches children how not to behave.*

say, "I need to teach the child how to behave appropriately," or, "I need to be more responsive to appropriate behavior." If you will look at behavior this way, you are well on the way to successful parenting. In this book, you learn how to do that.

Much is said and many examples are given about how to be positive and how to respond to behavior, both appropriate and inappropriate, in an instructive way rather than in a punitive, coercive way. It is quite possible you might have a child with a behavior problem that is so serious that it will need individual and specialized treatment.

I understand all too well how serious some behaviors can be. My wife and I have raised six children! Serious problems often need specialized attention. What I suggest in this book are proven, sound ways of preventing problems in the first place, or of keeping problems from becoming serious, and of making the home a more pleasant, facilitating environment in which to raise children. No matter how serious a behavior problem is, to one extent or another, the information contained in this book, appropriately applied, will make things better.

> **Even slight modifications in parent-child relations can produce remarkable changes in the home.**

When I advise parents on the use of the methods described in this book, they often have difficulty relating to what I tell them. Some can't even imagine their children behaving in any way other than has been the case in the past. It is hard for them to realize that by slightly altering events and circumstances in the environment, remarkable changes in behavior can and do occur. Children fight less, are more apt to do as told, feel better about themselves, and are generally happier and more enjoyable to be with. Parents often say to me, "Dr. Latham, that might work for some kids, but you don't know *my* kid!" In saying that, they assume that despite environmental changes, the behavior of their children will continue on totally unaffected. Please don't read this book in that frame of mind. As I illustrate time and again, with even slight modifications in the home, typically as they affect adult-child interactions, remarkable changes can and do happen.

I'm reminded of an experience I had a few years ago working with the dormitory parents of a Bureau of Indian Affairs off-reservation boarding school. A 17-year-old boy in one of the dorms was particularly troublesome. He was moody, sometimes violent, and "always" obnoxious and non-compliant. Referring to methods discussed in this book, I made a few simple and very basic suggestions. The dorm attendant actually laughed out loud at what I had proposed. He said, "Man, if I did that, he'd kill me. He doesn't understand anything but brute force. The *only* way you control that kid is with this!" as he displayed a clenched fist and a bulging muscular arm. I said, "Has that improved his behavior? Is he a nicer boy, a happier boy?" The dorm attendant, supported by responses from the other 64 people in the group, assured me that things weren't any better, "But at least it keeps him in line." I appealed to him: "Look," I said, "If what you've been doing hasn't worked or hasn't made things any better, do me a favor and just try what I've suggested. You have nothing to lose. Humor me. Okay?" He agreed.

The next morning as the group was convening, the dorm attendant was uncharacteristically early. He made a beeline for me and said, "Let's get started right away. I have something to tell these people." I had hardly gotten the group to order when, without invitation, the fellow jumped to his feet and said, "Hey, you guys. Be quiet. I have something to tell you. I did what Dr. Latham told me to do. What I really wanted to do was kill the kid, but I didn't. He waited around for me to get mad, or something. But I didn't. I just waited for an opportunity to be nice to him when he did something good. When I did, he looked at me kind of funny and just stood there—looking at me. I didn't know what else to do, so I just stood there looking back, then I put my arm around his shoulders and gave him a hug. I told him there were some things about him I really liked. Tears came into his eyes, and there was no expression at all on his face. Then he said, 'Do you mean there is some hope for me after all?' and he put his arms around me and we just stood there holding each other. Man, it was like a miracle. I couldn't believe what was happening." No miracles, just good "parenting."

Parents often ask me, "What characteristics are common to strong families? What should we do to increase our chances of raising happy, productive children?" These are questions of immense importance that I have tried to address in this book. To organize your thinking for what follows, as it relates to these important questions, carefully read and ponder what is included on the remaining pages of this chapter. Also, I recommend that you read an excellent article written by Dr. Robert Epstein, "Getting Your Child to Say Yes," published in the January, 1992 issue of *Reader's Digest*, pages 151–154.

Now, on to the development of important parenting skills!

> *Research has shown that the most effective way to reduce problem behavior in children is to strengthen desirable behavior through positive reinforcement rather than trying to weaken undesirable behavior using aversive or negative processes.*
>
> *S.W. Bijou*
> *The International Encyclopedia of Education, 1988*

**Characteristics of Low and High Risk Families: A Summary of Research[2]**

| Characteristics | Low-Risk Families | High-Risk Families |
|---|---|---|
| Leadership | There is a leader in the home who supervises studies and has the last word in health practices, major purchases, and the like. There is less freedom of choice for younger children (below 16). The children are self-controlled and learn to take 'no' for an answer. | Children have greater freedom to come and go pretty much as they please. The children feel they are externally controlled. |
| Work | Young children (age 2 and above) have chores and are expected to perform to criterion. | Have few, if any, required chores. |
| Religion | Regular church attendance with their families. Taught to believe in God and to participate in the activities, services, and conventions of their religion.[3] | Tend to allow children to wait until they are older to decide for themselves about religion. |
| Decision Making | Until children are 12–14, parents make most of the decisions in their lives. By age 16, the children take the primary role in making their own decisions, and are allowed to live with the consequences. | Children are left to make their own decisions, frequently being spared the opportunity to learn from them. |
| Frugality | Children are taught to turn off unused lights and water, to wear their clothes long after the first signs of wear appear, to avoid impulse buying, or the purchase of convenience items. | Spend money at will and tend not to be accountable for their own decisions. |
| Achievement of Success | Reject the idea that success is mainly determined by luck, chance, or by who you know, but rather see success as a function of how much effort one puts into his/her work, and how much one knows. | See success as a matter of luck, chance, or who you know. |
| Culture | Parents provide their children with culturally enriching experiences; they read to them regularly from good books, including the "classics"; they play good music in the home; they visit museums and take the children to plays and concerts. | Parents are satisfied to leave their children to be entertained by TV and contemporary music and literature. |
| Service | Children are given opportunities to serve others through community activities, helping the elderly or disabled, cleaning up a local park, etc. | Children tend to be takers not givers; exploiters not builders. |
| Self-Improvement | Children are taught to be health conscious, to take care of their bodies, to acquire new skills, and to control their appetites (taught to distinguish between needs and desires and to behave accordingly). | Children are basically committed to satisfying their appetite for what makes them feel good at the moment; they are less able to defer gratification. |

[1]Meaning risk of experiencing behavior problems.

[2]The structure for this summary, and much of its content, is credited to Dr. David Cherrington, Department of Organizational Behavior, Brigham Young University, from a paper he wrote entitled, "The Development of Work Values in the prevention of substance abuse."

[3]In her monumental study "Children of the Garden Island," Emmy E. Werner reported, "Personal competence and determination…and a strong religious faith were the shared qualities that we found characterized resilient children as adults." (*Scientific American,* April 1989, p. 110.)

Research reported in the August, 1992 issue of *Child and Adolescent Behavior Letter,* published by the Brown University, revealed sexual identity was complicated by a lack of religious beliefs.

---

From behavioral research, we have learned that adults who, as children, were conscientious, and learned discipline and self-control, are happier, are more creative, productive, and expressive; are more able to work well with others; are more socially acceptable; live longer; and are the most secure and adventurous. It's a whole lot easier to build the child than to repair the adult.

> *It is a lot easier to build the child than to repair the man.*

Following are characteristics we as parents should possess to eliminate stress, build physical and emotional endurance, and promote personal happiness:

1. **Conventional in life style.** Individuals who surround themselves with controversy and who strive for unconventional life styles tend to experience less satisfying lives, characterized by unhappiness.

2. **Less introspective.** Happy adults tend not to be quite as likely to spend large quantities of their time focused upon themselves, how they feel, what they are thinking, etc. (We tend to take ourselves too seriously.)

3. **Physically active.** Exercise is a miracle worker that cures all kinds of ills — including stress.

4. **Ability to share burdens.** There is real value in selectively sharing the problems we face with people who are truly trustworthy and caring. Emmy Warner, in her study "Children of the Garden Island," used the term "kith and kin"

to describe such people. Just telling someone that you are uptight can often act as a release. Don't become a crybaby, however.

5. Knowledge of one's limits.

If a problem is beyond your limits, admit it and accept that there is only so much that you can do. This often frees you to find solutions which would otherwise be hidden.

6. Self-respect.

You are special. Treat yourself that way. Eat properly (fewer potato chips and more carrots), set yourself a regular routine for sleep, dress upbeat, groom well, etc. It does wonders.

7. Relaxation.

People under stress tend to avoid relaxing. Take time to play, alone and with others. You need to let your hair down from time to time, but without losing your respectability. This is not an invitation to be a fool.

8. Involvement.

One way to deal with stress is to focus your attention on other people. Get involved in the lives of others. Help your neighbor in some way. Join a service club. Volunteer to be a fund raiser. Do it! Serve others.

9. Organization.

Make lists of what you need to do, and then check them off one by one. Lists give order and make complex tasks appear possible. Lists give hope and reduce tension. It's also very reinforcing to put a check beside an item on the list that has been accomplished.

10. Ability to be wrong.

Being right all the time is an impossibility. Learn to do your best and accept that you will fall flat on your face from time to time. Just get up, smile, laugh at yourself, and move on.

11. Sense of humor.

Read the funny papers, the jokes in magazines, etc. Interact with joyful people and learn to laugh with them. Laughter is wonderful medicine, as documented by Norman Cousins in his work, "Anatomy of an Illness."

12. Ability to express emotion.

If you are sad, shed a few tears. Don't feel as if you need to keep a stiff upper lip all the time. Cry and then get back to the business of living. Laugh a lot, particularly at yourself. Don't take yourself too seriously. It's okay to feel afraid, to be angry (in a nonhurtful way).

13. Getting away.

It is always well to take time-outs. Find a peaceful place and go there for nothing else but to get away and forget the troubles of the day. Go fishing, shopping; just get away by yourself doing something *you* want to do.

14. Avoiding self-medication.

The last thing in the world you should do is attempt to escape stress by "popping" pills. That is dumb and seldom helps. The suggestions given above are all far better than pills.

## ADULT BEHAVIORS
## JUDGED BY YOUNG PEOPLE AS:

| POSITIVE | NEGATIVE |
|---|---|
| 1. Calm, pleasant voice tone | 1. Shouting |
| 2. Offers to help | 2. Unfriendliness |

| | | | |
|---|---|---|---|
| 3. | Joking | 3. | Unpleasantness |
| 4. | Compliments on their performance | 4. | Talking only about mistakes |
| 5. | Fairness | 5. | Lack of fairness |
| 6. | Explaining why, how, or what | 6. | Accusing/blaming statements |
| 7. | Concern | 7. | Overt displays of anger |
| 8. | Enthusiasm | 8. | Unpleasant physical contact |
| 9. | Politeness | 9. | Bossy, demanding |
| 10. | Getting right to the point | 10. | Mean, insulting remarks |
| 11. | Giving specific examples | 11. | Giving no opportunity to speak |
| 12. | Eye Contact | 12. | No eye contact |

Used by permission,
Professor Richard West, Ph.D.
Utah State University

# TWO
# How Behavior Develops:
# Some Important Principles

Science is a wonderful thing. A really wonderful thing! From it we can learn so much if we will only listen to what it has to teach us. Nowhere is this more true than with human behavior, the things people say and do. As with physics, chemistry, or any of the other so-called "hard sciences," human behavior is lawful. It is predictable. Furthermore, as with physics, chemistry, and the hard sciences, research in human behavior has taught us about laws that govern human behavior and how to predict human behavior given a description of the environment within which it will occur. For example, in chemistry we know that under certain environmental conditions hydrogen and oxygen molecules will always form water. The laws of physics assure us that a heavier-than-air object will fall in a straight line towards the center of the earth at predictable speeds. Given the conditions under which the object is dropped, its behavior in space is absolutely predictable.

> *Though human behavior cannot always be predicted with absolute certainty, it can be predicted at high levels of accuracy.*

Human behavior is also predictable in light of the environment within which it occurs. It is not as absolutely predictable as is the case with chemical reactions, gravitational phenomena, and heavenly bodies in space, but it is predictable enough for us to know generally what will happen under given conditions. There is, indeed, a science of human behavior. Human behavior is lawful and as is the case with other sciences, we can predict events—not, perhaps, with the same level of certainty, but certainly at high levels of accuracy. With knowledge about human behavior, we can improve the quality of the environment within which we live. We can build a better world for all, including ourselves and our children—and grandchildren!

There is no need to be afraid of science, nor to be frightened away by the suggestion that we can use science to improve the quality of our lives and the lives of the members of our family. When I speak to parents about the science of human behavior, I sometimes see them flinch and become anxious because of the difficulty they had in school with their science classes. What I am talking about here is not to be confused with *doing* science or *studying* science in the traditional sense. What I am talking about here is using what we know from science to improve our lives. We do that all the time and quite effortlessly, in fact even comfortably. For example, though it might be frigidly cold or torridly hot outside, we can create a comfortable environment within our home or our car by simply manipulating a device on the wall or on the dashboard that controls the environment to our liking. That is a wonderful option over heating our house with an open fire, or hitching up a team of horses to take us to our destination through the heat or the cold. This option has been made available to us by science.

Science has made options available to us in the realm of human behavior which, if used properly, make it possible for us to create wonderfully comfortable human environments in our homes and families, in the work place and the community, or wherever human beings dwell or interact.

Just as the climate-control devices in our homes and cars can be used badly resulting in our discomfort, the "climate-control devices" available to us in managing the human environment can also be used badly, thus creating a good deal of discomfort there. To help assure the development of effective parenting skills so that the behavioral climate in the home can be correctly controlled, it is important to understand some basic principles of that science.

> Science has taught us a great deal about how to behave well, and we would be wise to listen!

In this chapter I discuss four principles of human behavior, which, if well understood and applied, make it possible for us to skillfully create and predict positive behavioral events in our environment. In Chapter 3, I discuss five strategies for effectively applying these principals in the family setting. The understanding of these principles and the skillful application of them will remarkably improve the quality of the environment in the home.

There is nothing mythical nor magical about what happens when behavioral principles are skillfully applied, though parents often tell me "a miracle has happened in my home" when they apply these principles well. Indeed, it might seem miraculous, but, in fact, it is simply a lawful, predictable, cause and effect relationship that can be repeated time and time again in an infinite array of settings.

I recently gave a talk to a group of parents during which I assured them that if they applied these principles correctly, they would have good results. A few days later, I met one of those parents in a grocery store. He said, "You know, we tried what you suggested and it worked!" (There was considerable surprise in his voice.) Then he stopped, and with a kind of funny look on his face added, "But I guess I shouldn't be surprised. That's what you said would happen." "Yeah!" I said, happy he'd gotten the message.

## PRINCIPLE 1:
## Behavior Is Strengthened or Weakened by Its Consequences

Though you might not think of the development of behavior in these terms, we are all very familiar with this principle as we experience it in our everyday lives. Everyday, members of the work force pull themselves out of a comfortable bed, put themselves back together, and even endure long hours in an unpleasant work place, and why? The answer, of course, is obvious: an array of pleasant, though delayed, consequences beginning with a paycheck and the goodies it provides. When driving through traffic we observe traffic rules, and why? Consequences in the form of continued driving privileges, a car that is free of scratches and dents and expensive repair bills, the avoidance of discomfort and the loss of money resulting from being stopped by a police officer and fined for breaking the law. A child will ask nicely for something he or she wants or will even have a tantrum to get what he or she wants, and why? Consequences, in the form of getting what is wanted.

If you ever wonder why individuals continue to behave the way they do, you needn't wonder for long. Just observe the events that follow their behavior and you will know why the behavior

> *Consequences shape behavior far more than do genes.*

persists. And by the same token, if you ever wonder why a behavior ceases to exist, wonder no longer. We call the events that follow behavior consequences. Behavior is strengthened or weakened by its consequences. This is a primary principle of human behavior and will be referred to repeatedly throughout this book.

A recent experience of the power of this principle provides a classic example for the point I want to make. I have the pleasant opportunity to work closely with about 90 young married couples attending the university, many of whom have small children. Recently I attended a program which featured several of these children as they sang and performed for their parents. After the program, I made sure to give all of the children a hug for the good job they had done, and to tell them how much I enjoyed the program. As I left the room where the children had gone after their performance, I heard a child's voice calling to me. I turned and there in the dimly lit hall was a little boy hurrying toward me. With his arms outstretched he said, " I didn't get my hug." Somehow I had missed him and he wasn't about to let that go unnoticed. I frequently give these little ones hugs for the many good things they do. They have come to value these hugs—consequences!—and they behave well in good measure because of them. Even the anticipation of a hug will greatly influence how they behave.

For centuries, the controversy has raged over the origins of human behavior; the persisting nature-nurture debate. Popular theories about one or the other guide the work of practitioners. In recent years, particularly due to advances in the study of human genetics, it has become popular to explain human behavior in terms of internal events and conditions, some of which are reported to virtually render an individual a victim of his/her genetic makeup. The genetic role in hyperactivity, eating disorders, sexual preference, schizophrenia, youth violence, depression, suicide, alcoholism, temper, crime, phobias, cancer, and so on are frequent topics in the popular and professional literature today.

Despite all that is being said about the genetic origins of human behavior, I caution you to not be too quick to cave in to the notion that just because there may appear to be a relationship between some genetic phenomenon and human behavior that there is, in fact, a close cause and effect relationship. Many, if not most, of these studies are *co*rrelational studies; that is, they simply reveal that some individuals with a common problem behavior also share a common genetic condition; hence; they are *co*-related. But since others who share that same genetic condition do *not* have the same problem behavior, and vice versa, we must not assume that some kind of a powerful cause and effect relationship necessarily exists.

For the most part, the behavioral literature speaks far more clearly and eloquently to the cause and effect relationship between one's environment and behavior than does genetic research speak to cause and effect relationships between one's genetics and his/her behavior. The lesson to be learned from this is that regardless of the behavior, and regardless of its origins, behavioral treatment which focuses on the careful arrangement of consequences (and, as is discussed later in the chapter, the equally careful arrangement of the environment) will ultimately have a much greater effect on behavior than does genetics. For that matter, being too preoccupied with internal events, genetic or otherwise, can and does rob people of the kind of treatment they need most. If a school counselor, teacher, psychologist, or a doctor tells you your child is "hyperactive" and suggests drug therapy to compensate for a supposed genetic disposition to be "out of control," regard that diagnosis with great suspicion and pursue with vigor behavioral treatments that we *know* to be effective. In fact, even if there is a bonafide genetic problem, behavioral treatment should also be a *major* part of therapy. Drug therapy alone is *never* adequate in the treatment of behavior problems. Be very careful about diagnoses and treatments that focus only on so-called "internal" events or conditions.

> **Drug therapy alone is never adequate in the treatment of behavior problems!**

The preoccupation of finding out what's going on inside a kid typically leads to a plethora of needless testing, endless and expensive and needless therapies, and a desperate search for answers to questions which, even if found, give little or no direction to treatment. One is much better off to begin with an analysis of the consequences of behavior. That *is* a cause and effect relationship. That *is* the relationship that most likely answers the question "Why does the kid behave that way?" That kind of an analysis also gives specific direction to treatment. Be careful of drug therapy as the treatment of first and only choice.

## PRINCIPLE 2:
## Behavior Ultimately Responds Better to Positive Consequences

My eighth-grade educated mother understood this principle very well and said it to me many, many times as a boy: "A cup of honey will draw more flies than a bucket of gall." Despite this age-old truth, the tendency of parents is to use negative, coercive, punitive means of stopping or eliminating behavior rather than positive, pleasant, reinforcing means of strengthening behavior. Why they do this is easily explained by the first principle of behavior we just discussed: consequences. A child misbehaves, the parent immediately scolds, spanks, or screams at the child, and the inappropriate behavior stops. The immediate *consequence* of the scolding, spanking, or screaming was exactly what the parents wanted: the child immediately quit misbehaving. Furthermore, the parents' behavior (that is, scolding, spanking or screaming) is also strengthened because it seems to be effective; hence it will certainly reoccur in the future when the child misbehaves again. And the child will misbehave again because the scolding, spanking, or screaming will have only a short-lived effect on the child's behavior. Unfortunately, parents don't see the reoccurrence of the child's behavior as being a function of the scolding, spanking, or screaming. Rather, they will recall only that the scolding, spanking, or screaming stopped the behavior before and it will stop it again…and again and again and again and again and again. Get the point?

> *The more parents scold, spank, and scream to control their children's behavior, the worse the children behave. You can be certain of it!*

The more parents scold, spank and scream to control their children's behavior, the more their children's behavior will invite scolding, spanking, and screaming because negative consequences are ineffective ways of controlling children's behavior. Similar studies in classrooms have revealed exactly the same thing. The more teachers scold and scream at students to sit down and be quiet, the more the students will be out of their seats and rowdy. It is predictable. It is lawful. (As well as awful!)

The better way, the way that has more lasting and beneficial results, is to take advantage of the many opportunities that occur every day to attach a positive consequence to an appropriate behavior. That positive consequence can come in the form of a hug, a kiss, a pat on the back, a word of encouragement and praise, a smile, a wink, a token in a jar or a point on a good behavior record, and the list goes on. But what is really wonderful about this approach is that when used appropriately and consistently, the incidence of inappropriate behavior goes down dramatically while the incidence of appropriate behavior increases dramatically and maintains. It is predictable. You can bet on it. It is lawful. It is a well established matter of fact that in homes where parents smile at their children, laugh with their children, have lots of positive and appropriate physical interactions with their children (hugging and kissing and patting), and talk to their children a lot in pleasant, supportive, nonjudgmental ways, the frequency of problem behaviors in those families goes down, down, down, and the frequency of pleasant parent-child relationships goes up, up, up!

Here is a telling case in point. Recently I was in the front yard of a friend's home playing with my 15-month-old grandson. As 15-month-old babies do, he made a dash for the street. I gently picked him up, and said, "No, you may not play in the street." As I put him down on the sidewalk, I said, as I patted his back, "Play here," and I touched the ground. As expected, he headed right back for the street. (Later, when I talk about multiple trial learning vs. single trial learning, this will make more sense.) Again, I gently picked him up, and repeated the same corrective teaching strategy. After four learning trials, he went to the edge of the sidewalk, stopped and looked up at me. I smiled, knelt down beside him, gave him a hug and kiss, and said, "Thank you for playing here," as I touched the ground. He went up and down the sidewalk for a few minutes, then, as to be expected, headed for the street. I repeated, word-for-word, action-for-action, exactly what I had done earlier. He played for a few minutes, headed for the street, stopped at the edge of the sidewalk, pointed to the street and said, "No. Don't." Of course, that behavior was rewarded with a loving, tender consequence.

As we headed back into the house, I heard a terrible noise coming from next door. The child of the family living there, also about 15-months-old, went into the street. The boy's father screamed,

> *Coercion teaches children to avoid, escape, and get even (counter coerce).*

"Get out of that street, you little brat!" Then in anger he grabbed the boy's arm, gave it a terrible jerk, swung the child into the air at the same time giving him a swat on the bottom, then harshly put the boy down on the lawn. The boy, by now, was crying in pain. You bet, the boy didn't return to the street, nor did he seek out his father for comfort. My heart aches for that boy, but it aches even more for him and his entire family when he is 15 years old! The child had been taught nothing about where he *should* play, but he was learning a lot about the distasteful effects of coercion, aversion, and pain. Since human beings behave to avoid coercion, aversion, and pain, imagine how that boy will behave when he has the opportunity to exercise avoidance behaviors. Imagine who he will avoid. Imagine what environment he will escape as soon as he can.

As parents, we must not be seduced into believing that because we get immediate results from scoldings, spankings, and screamings, that these are appropriate ways to respond to inappropriate behavior. They are not. In the long run, behavior responds better to positive than to negative consequences. Don't be blinded by immediate, short-lived results, or by immediate, short-lived gains. There is an economy in child rearing, a price we must pay. Either we remain solvent with positives or we are forever in debt and even bankrupted with negatives; positives that produce low-risk families or negatives that produce high-risk families.

> Insanity: Doing the same thing again and again and expecting different results.

If negative, aversive, coercive methods of control are not working (and they never do for long!), try a better way. I recently read a wonderful definition of insanity: "Doing the same thing again and again and expecting different results." This is much like the concentration-camp-behavior-management-philosophy that "the flogging will continue until behavior improves." Well, behavior seldom improves with such consequences. Rather, plans to escape, despite the risks, are continually being devised. And so it is with children and coercion: they desire to escape, which they do at the rate of millions a year—running away from home, dropping out of school, committing suicide, and just giving up!

## PRINCIPLE 3:
## Whether a Behavior Has Been Punished or Reinforced Is Known Only by the Course of that Behavior in the Future

Parents tell me repeatedly, "I punish the child for that rotten behavior time and time again everyday and the kid continues to do it!" In light of this principle of human behavior, what is the matter with that analysis of the child's behavior? The answer is simple and clear: The parent isn't punishing the child at all. Rather, the child's behavior is being reinforced. What the parent thinks he or she is doing is one thing but what the parent is really doing is another. The only way one can know what the parent is really doing to the behavior is by observing what happens to the behavior subsequently, as illustrated in Figure 2.1. If the behavior persists, no matter what the parent thinks he or she has done to it, the behavior has been reinforced. Punishment has not occurred in the least. Rather, the behavior has been strengthened, and a behavior that has been strengthened is a behavior that will probably reoccur. Conversely, if the behavior gets weaker, or stops, then it has been punished.

The lesson for parents to learn from this is that they must carefully observe the course of their children's behavior over time. If inappropriate behavior persists, parents must be prepared to change the way they have been responding to that behavior. If appropriate behavior persists, the parents must be prepared to continue what they are doing. Parents must be prepared

> "When used effectively, positive reinforcement is the most powerful teaching tool we have."

to change if they hope to improve an otherwise unpleasant situation. I heard it said, "If you're always going to do what you've always done, you're always going to get what you've always gotten." The changes that need to be made are revealed to us by how children respond to what we do.

## Figure 2.1—The Effects of Consequences

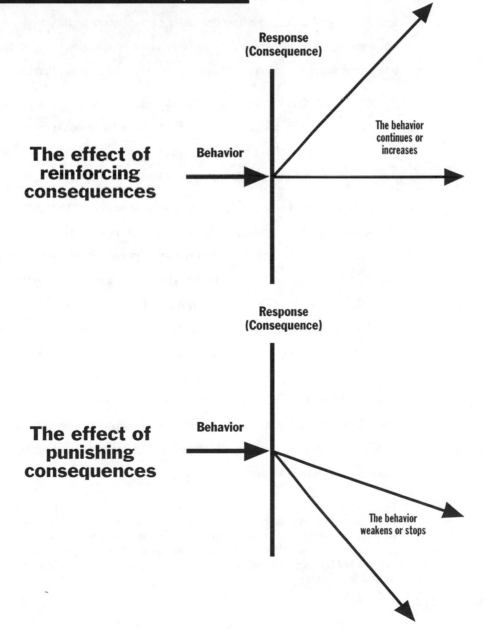

It is the child's behavior which should determine the course of our action, not what we feel logically or intuitively should be done. What we do can be thought of as a form of treatment, and if the behavior improves, then we know the treatment has been effective. If the behavior persists or even gets worse, then we know the treatment is ineffective and needs to be changed. The best treatment known to humankind is to respond in a positive way to appropriate behavior. As noted by Dr. Murray Sidman (1988) in his wonderful book *Coercion and Its Fallout*, "When used effectively, positive reinforcement is the most powerful teaching tool we have" (p. 249). Nothing is known to work better nor to have a more lasting effect. How to do that will be addressed repeatedly throughout this book in common everyday situations familiar to parents around the globe. As a constant reminder of the power and importance of positive responding, every chapter in this book ends with this quotation from Dr. Sidney Bijou, one of the world's greatest contributors to the study of human behavior:

> Research has shown that the most effective way to reduce problem behavior in children is to strengthen desirable behavior through positive reinforcement rather than trying to weaken undesirable behavior using aversive or negative processes.

Before going to principle 4, let's look at the treatment of behavior in light of what has been discussed so far. Look at Figure 2.2 on the next page. I call this the treatment curve and it illustrates something that is very important for parents to know. First, I'll explain a few of the terms on the figure. The term baseline simply refers to a measure of a behavior over time. For example, if we were to measure the number of times or the length of time a child spent throwing tantrums every day and plotted that behavior on a graph for several days, that graph would be a baseline measure of that behavior. We could assume that if nothing was done to change the behavior, it would continue on in the future pretty much as it occurred during the days when it was being measured[1] since past behavior is the best predictor of future behavior. Baseline data are often collected to help us determine how best to treat a behavior, and to know whether our treatment of that behavior has been effective.

---

[1]In this regard, one of Isaac Newton's laws of motion applies very much to human behavior: A body set in motion will remain in motion in the direction and at the velocity it was set in motion unless acted upon by some other force. And so it is with human behavior. Unless it is acted upon in some "other" way, it will continue in whatever direction it is going.

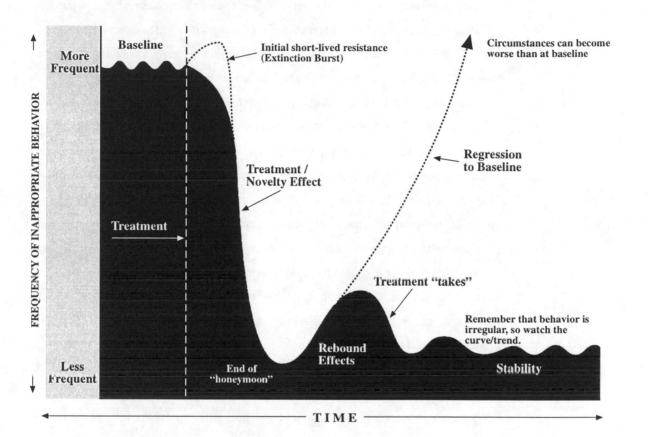

Figure 2.2—The Treatment Curve

The line labeled Treatment simply refers to that point in time when treatment of some sort was introduced to change the behavior. In this instance, the treatment was intended to decrease the amount of inappropriate behavior, for example, tantrums.

It is important to understand that treatment might not have the immediate effect we want it to have. In fact, in some instances the behavior might get worse for a short period of time. For example, when eliminating tantrums, it is not at all unusual for the severity of the child's tantrums to increase immediately following the onset of treatment. This is called an extinction burst. If and when this happens just remember, things might get worse before they get better. As I explain in Chapter 14, "Eliminating Tantrums," this is to be expected for a number of well known reasons. However, if the treatment is correct and correctly applied, regardless of what behavior is being treated, the probability is very great that the behavior will eventually improve as illustrated by the curve.

This improvement is accounted for by at least two things. First, the treatment is having the intended effect, and second, there is often a certain novelty associated with treatment. Parents often will tell me their kids get quite a kick out of what their parents are doing differently and seem to be willing to go along with it, at least for the time being, because it is somewhat novel and fun. One mother told me how amused she was when her children said to her, "Mom, you and Dad are acting really weird!"

However, after a while, usually two or three days, the "honeymoon" ends and the behavior moves back in the direction of baseline. We call this regression to baseline. It does this for at least two reasons. The first is that parents get careless and are sloppy in their management of the treatment. They become inconsistent, or they give in, or they slip back into their old habits of being punitive, coercive, and negative. When this occurs, the behavior will most certainly regress to its earlier level of inappropriateness. Second, as the novelty effect wears off and children tire of this "game" their parents are playing, they will challenge the system by going to extreme measures to get their way; or better put, to get the reinforcers (sick as they were!) that were available to them in such abundance before treatment was put into effect, and which maintained behavior at the baseline level. They are still under what we call the reinforcement control of their old ways of behaving (that is, during baseline), and since that is where all of the reinforcers have been in the past, and since past behavior is the best predictor of future behavior, that is the direction in which the behavior will go; it will regress. As I noted earlier, in scientific terms it is called regression to baseline.

Nevertheless, despite the tendency to regress to baseline, if treatment is administered correctly and consistently, the behavior will come under the immediate reinforcement control of the treatment and in time a new baseline will be established. When this occurs, you know that you have successfully administered the treatment. If the behavior returns to baseline, or even exceeds it, you know the treatment was either ineffective or ineffectively administered. But the only way you can know whether the treatment (that is, your response to the behavior) was effective is by looking at what happens to the behavior after treatment. Whether a behavior has been punished or reinforced is determined only by the course it takes in the future.

> **Past behavior is the best predictor of future behavior.**

Ultimately, of course, we hope that our children will perform and behave well because of "natural reinforcement," sometimes referred to as "intrinsic consequences," since such consequences are immediately reinforcing. That is, the child doesn't have to wait for someone to administer the reinforcer. As noted by my good friends at Comunidad Los Horcones, Sonora, Mexico, in an article entitled "Natural Reinforcement. A Way to Improve Education," "Natural reinforcers are available for all students at the same time. With contrived reinforcement it is about impossible for teachers to reinforce every behavior of every student at the most appropriate moment; with natural reinforcement, that is possible." And so it is with children at home. Once they find that behaving well is naturally reinforcing, the need for extrinsic (contrived) reinforcers diminishes rapidly.

## PRINCIPLE 4:
## Behavior is Largely a Product of its Immediate Environment

Invariably, when perplexed by a child's inappropriate behavior, parents will ask, "What's the matter with that kid?" They will even look for answers in their spouses genes ("The kid got it from his father"). They will explain it away using meaningless terms: "He's hyperactive," "He has a short attention span," "She's spoiled," and so on. None of these explanations, or excuses, or reasons, give *any* clue whatsoever about what to do with the behavior.

The only thing parents can agree on is that the kid needs to be fixed. We hear it not only at home with parents, but in schools with teachers, psychologists, and principals, in the court system with judges and juvenile justice people, and in virtually any situation where children are behaving inappropriately: fix the kid. Well, there is a better way, and this fourth principle of human behavior teaches us what that better way is: fix the environment and you'll fix the behavior. That's what fixes the kid! In its simplest, purest sense, a disciplined child is a product of a disciplined environment.

It is not possible to make sense out of a child's behavior without first making sense out of the environment within which that behavior occurs. Think of it this way. If you are repeatedly

> *A disciplined child is a product of a disciplined environment.*

spending money on costly automobile repairs made necessary because the road you travel is in such bad condition as to be forever destructive to your car, no amount of money spent fixing the car is going to have any lasting benefit on how well the car operates unless the road gets fixed or you go a different way. How well the car operates isn't a function of how much time it spends being repaired. How well the car operates depends upon the condition of the road over which it travels every day. Fix the road and you "fix" the car. And so it is with children. Their behavior is simply a response to forces in the environment that get their behavior going (we call these cues and prompts), and forces in the environment that keep them going (we call these consequences). So the question isn't, "What's the matter with that kid?," the question is, "What's the matter with the environment?" Fix the environment and you fix the behavior.

> *Fix the environment and you'll fix the behavior.*

This is almost too simple for some people to accept. As I pointed out earlier, we have become so conditioned to believing that the answer to children's problem behaviors lies somewhere within them, it is hard to imagine that by simply fine-tuning the environment we can have a remarkably positive, remedial effect on the behavior. As difficult as that may be to believe, that's the way it is. A recent experience illustrates this point. Parents of two small boys, a 4-year-old and a 2-year-old, came to me distraught because the older boy was repeatedly attacking his 2-year-old brother. As I listened to the parents recount their agonies over this situation, I heard what I typically hear from parents: "We can't imagine what's going on inside this boy of ours. We fear that we are raising a monster. It worries us so to think that he is going to grow up and be a menace to society. What can possibly be going on inside of this kid's head that causes him to do these things?" These expressions of quandary were then followed by predictable expressions of guilt and inadequacy: "We must be doing something terribly wrong. We must be terrible parents. Sometimes we wonder if we should have ever had any children in the first place. We feel so awful, so ashamed." Then the tears began flowing. As is typically the case, it was very intense.

After I was sure the parents had gotten their feelings out on the table and emotions were under control, I began to systematically analyze the relationships that existed between the child's behavior and his environment. (We call this a behavior analysis.) My first question was, "What happens when your 4-year-old hits his little brother?" The mother answered, "His little brother begins to cry. I mean, he really gets hurt!" My next question was simply a repeat of the first one, "Then what happens?" "Well," answered the mother, "I make my 4-year-old stop it." I then asked, "How do you do that? What do you say or do to your 4-year-old that makes him stop? Let's pretend that I am your 4-year-old and I have just hit my little brother. Say and do to me what you usually say and do to your 4-year-old when he hits his little brother."

The mother's response to this simple role-playing activity provided the answers to both why the 4-year-old repeatedly hit his younger brother, and what needed to be done to bring that behavior under control. She said she scolded the child, asked him why he hit his brother, reminded the boy that they go through this time and again every day, and said, "I'm getting sick and tired of it, so stop it! Stop it right now!" She spanked the 4-year-old, then gave affectionate comfort to the little brother. Simply stated, the mother gave the boy immense amounts of attention every time he hit his little brother. Parental attention is a powerful, powerful reinforcer of children's behavior.

More than anything else, children want the attention of their parents, and if they can't get it behaving appropriately, they will get it behaving inappropriately. As a young mother recently told me, recalling her childhood at home, "If I couldn't get my parent's attention by behaving well, then I behaved badly. Even that's better than no attention at all." One way or another, they will get it because it is so reinforcing to them. I often make this point by using an analogy. Profits are to business what attention is to behavior. People go into business to earn a profit, and people behave to get attention. In this instance, the 4-year-old child was getting a ton of attention, even though some of it was, by adult standards, not very pleasant. He was being scolded, sometimes spanked, frequently abruptly lifted up and carried to another area of the house, and questioned at great lengths about why he continues to do this kind of thing and how many times is he going to have to be told to stop it before he stops it, and so on. I then asked the mother what she did in response to the younger child's crying. She told me she picks him up and comforts him, holds him close, and assures him that she loves him, and that everything will be okay.

> *Profits are to business what attention is to behavior.*

Can you see what is happening in this environment to encourage and maintain this hitting behavior by the 4-year-old? The 4-year-old gets huge amounts of attention for hitting and the 2-year-old gets huge amounts of attention for crying. It is in the best interest of both of them, from a behavioral perspective, to persist in these behaviors since the consequences available in their environment are so heavily reinforcing to them.

Knowing this, treatment became quite obvious and began with this question to the parents, "What do you do when the children are playing nicely together?" The answer was typical: "Well, we just leave them alone to play. We don't want to disturb them when they are happy." Though, at first blush, it appears to be the logically appropriate thing to do, it is, in fact, the absolutely wrong thing to do. Here is what I had the parents do. First, I told them to have at least 20 positive interactions with their children every hour while they were behaving nicely and playing appropriately together. As illustrated later in this book, I demonstrated how that was to be done. It's called raising the general level of reinforcement.

I pointed out that these interactions should be very brief and natural, and how they could have 20 positive interactions per hour without it taking more than a minute per hour, by using a wink, a smile, a pat on the back, or by simply saying, "You boys are playing so nicely together." All of it was to be done in a very natural way in the course of the parents' comings and goings in the home.

> **Use prosthetics to remind yourself to have positive interactions with your children.**

To help remind the parents to do this sort of thing regularly and frequently, I encouraged them to arrange *their* environment to give them the reminders they need. We call this creating a prosthetic environment. A prosthetic device is something that helps us do something we can't otherwise do alone. For example, a pair of glasses is a prosthetic that helps us see, a hearing aid is a prosthetic that helps us hear, and a crutch is a prosthetic that helps us walk. The prosthetics I suggested were to help the parents remember to have lots and lots of appropriate positive interactions with their children when they were behaving well. For example, I suggested to the mother that she tilt a picture on the wall so that it was enough off level to catch her attention. When she saw it, it would remind her to have a positive interaction with her children when they were behaving appropriately. I suggested that a plant or a knick-knack be moved to an unusual place as a reminder. Parents I've worked with have put a rubber band around their wrist, or a bandaid around their thumb, or a penny in their shoe as reminders to acknowledge their children's appropriate behavior. I assured the parents that if they did these things the probability was extremely great that appropriate behavior would rapidly increase and inappropriate behavior would rapidly decrease. "After all," I told them, "why should the children behave inappropriately when they are getting all of the attention they want by behaving appropriately? Remember, it's your attention they are after. They would far rather have your attention for behaving appropriately than for hitting and crying."

I then showed them how to respond in the event that the 4-year-old hit his 2-year-old brother. This, too, was a simple matter. I told the parents to unemotionally and immediately stop the hitting by removing the 4-year-old to a safe distance, looking him squarely in the eye and saying, "No, you may not do that to your brother," and to maintain eye-to-eye contact for a few seconds after he was told to stop. I instructed the parents to then redirect the boy's behavior to something that was appropriate: "Now sit over here and look at your book," or "Go play with your toys in the other room" or something to that effect. Remember, it isn't enough to simply stop the behavior. The behavior must be stopped then *redirected* to an appropriate behavior. This is important for two reasons. First, it gets the child doing something positive and worthy of attention. Second, after the child has been behaving appropriately for a minute or so, the parent has an opportunity to acknowledge that behavior, thus reinforcing appropriate behavior. I call this the stop, redirect, reinforce strategy.

As will be noted repeatedly in this book, it is not sufficient to simply stop inappropriate behavior. As parents, we must *teach* appropriate behavior. Parents are forever telling their children to "stop that!", but not providing them with replacement behaviors by

> *Rather than just stopping a behavior, redirect it, then reinforce the appropriate, redirected behavior that follows.*

which they can learn a better way to behave. The only thing children learn when they are told to stop behaving is what not to do. In effect, we leave it up to the child to figure out how to behave well, and the probabilities of the child doing that are very, very slim! Very slim indeed. The better way is for the parent to direct the child's behavior toward something that is appropriate, then briefly acknowledge the better behavior in a positive, descriptive way: "Thanks, Honey, for getting that chore done."

Now, regarding the behavior of the 2-year-old who was left crying, I instructed the parents to gently touch the child and in comforting words say, "You will feel better soon," then, in a very natural, unemotional way, go on to other things that need to be done around the house. This is called purposeful or planned ignoring. I cautioned the parents that as they walk away, they should not have any expressions of despair or frustration on their faces, they are not to be abrupt in their movements, they should not roll their eyes to the ceiling, nor do anything that would suggest that they are the least bit upset by the hitting and the crying. I told them that as they walk away, they should look at their watch and make note of when a minute to a minute and a half has passed, at which time they are to revisit their children, and if they are behaving appropriately, to have a positive, brief, reinforcing interaction with them. For example, "Thank you, Billy, for being so kind to your brother."

After role playing this in a simulated setting, I sent the parents on their way with the instructions to call me in two or three days to tell me how things were going. Usually parents don't call, but that is often a good sign meaning things are going well. (People don't typically call their doctor or their therapist to tell them that things are going well.) As chance would have it, I ran into the family about a week later. What I experienced during that brief visit was what I experience so often. The parents said to me, "We can't believe what has happened in our home. It's like a miracle!" Then the mother said, "I guess the children just weren't developmentally ready before." Even in a situation as dramatic as this, the parents couldn't imagine that such simple adjustments in the environment could possibly produce such remarkable improvements in their boys' behavior. To the parents, it could only be accounted for by some maturational phenomenon going on inside the children. I asked, "What effect do you think the *treatment* had on the children's behavior?" The mother replied, "Oh, I'm sure it helped some. We were lucky that it happened at a time when the children were developmentally ready." It wasn't until a few weeks later when the parents were back in my office with their original concerns that they became convinced that inner forces didn't have a single thing to do with the improvement in their children's behavior. As illustrated by the treatment curve, (Figure 2.2), the children's behavior had begun regressing toward baseline and the parents were beside themselves again.

As I suspected, the environment had gotten out of tune and the behavior was responding in kind. In a word, the parents had reverted to their old ways of doing things. Their behavior had regressed to baseline; consequently, so had the children's. We repeated the role-playing exercises, reviewed these important principles of human behavior, and the parents have subsequently shaped up the environment. Consequently, the behavior of the boys is just fine. In fact, a short time ago I happened to meet the mother's father and even he commented on how much better the boys behaved. Happily, the parents now have a functional understanding of this important principle of human behavior: behavior is largely a product of its immediate environment. They also know that it doesn't always take remarkable changes within the environment to produce remarkable changes in children's behavior. They know that it is essentially a matter of simply fine-tuning events in the environment. A radio doesn't have to be very far out of tune to produce static, noise, and annoying sounds.

*Good parenting requires constant tuning and retuning the environment of the home and family.*

Although the illustration I used here involved small children, what I have said is equally relevant to adolescents and adults. It might take longer to get the desired results, but if the environment is well tuned—and kept well tuned—the odds are great that the desired results will eventually come. Remember, behavior is largely the product of its immediate environment. Fix the environment and you fix the behavior. As parents, our responsibility isn't so much with modifying behavior as it is with modifying the environment. The environment will modify the behavior. Luther Burbank, one of history's preeminent horticulturists, in his book *Training of the Human Plant*, wrote:

> If you are cultivating a plant, developing it into something finer and nobler, you must love it, not hate it; be gentle with it, not abusive; be firm, never harsh. I give plants…the best possible environment. So should it be with a child, if you want to develop it in right ways. Let the children have music, let them have pictures, let them have laughter.

This discussion of principles of human behavior is important because it takes behavior out of the realms of myth, magic, and tradition, and anchors it squarely where it ought to be—in science. Parents who have a working knowledge of these principles are no longer victims of despair and hopelessness aroused by the behavior of their children. It doesn't mean that knowledgeable parents won't be upset by the behavior of their children or annoyed by it or concerned about it. Certainly all conscientious parents have these feelings about their children. Nor does having a working knowledge of these principles guarantee parents that their children's behavior will always be wonderful. Kids are kids, and age-typical behaviors are real. But with a working knowledge of these principles, the probabilities increase dramatically that children's behaviors will be more wonderful because we as parents will be more skilled.

As I pointed out earlier, the "hard" sciences, like physics and chemistry, allow us to predict events precisely and exactly. The study of human behavior like medicine, is a less exact science; hence, we can only predict events in terms of probabilities, not certainties. But we know for sure that if certain conditions exist within the child's environment, the probability is great that the desired results will occur. Our job as parents is to create the environment in our homes that will remarkably increase the prob-

> **Behavior can be predicted only in terms of probabilities, not certainties.**

ability that children will behave appropriately and that they will be happy, productive, and contributing members of society. Unfortunately, since behavior is the product of its immediate environment, the older children get the greater number of environments they find themselves in, most of which are outside parents' sphere of influence. Therefore, it is important for us to equip our children at home with those behaviors that will make it possible for them to defend themselves against the harmful yet reinforcing effects of those other environments. To a large extent, we can do that, but we can't expect to be absolutely successful in every instance.

From time to time, children will come upon "unhealthy" reinforcers operating in other environments that encourage inappropriate behavior. None of us makes it through life completely undamaged by the slings and arrows of other environments. The school, the work place, places of entertainment, and even the church can encourage and reinforce junk behavior. But that's to be expected. Even the most expensive car ever built, given the best care imaginable, will occasionally need repairs and tune-ups. Our job isn't to create perfect, risk-free children. That's impossible. Our job is to create in our homes, and within those spheres of our influence, environments that will teach children and reinforce children for behaving appropriately; to create an environment which brings joy to them for behaving appropriately. A working knowledge of the principles of human behavior makes it possible for us to do that, but not totally without risk or without some failure. My wife and I have six children, six lovely children all grown and married. Every one of them is a well educated, contributing, productive member of society. If I were to describe the circumstances of each of our children at the time of this writing, you would consider me a braggart. You would think I was showing off my kids. But bound up in the lives of those six wonderful children is a litany of nearly every imaginable rotten behavior short of homicide and grand larceny. When they were behaving in those dumb ways, they were, unfortunately, under the reinforcement control of environments beyond our influence as parents.

Happily, those environments have not had long-term negative effects, and our children are well established in the family fold and within the family value system

*Parenting is inherently risky.*

because that is where the long-term reinforcers were always pre- dictably available. They all had their fling with idiocy and selfish- ness (i.e., age-typical behavior) as they made their way through the treachery of adolescence (the age of raging hormonal imbalance). In time, a new set of reinforcers came into play in their lives. They suddenly realized that home and family were the best of all places. They came to that realization because of a history of its long- term and predictably reinforcing effects in their lives. I received a Father's Day card from my oldest son, a father of three, who wrote: "It seems the older I get and the more my family grows the more I appreciate all the time and sacrifice you and Mom went through on our behalf. We really love and appreciate you for who you are and for all you've done for us." While reviewing my materials in preparation of this chapter, I ran across a note I made a few years ago as I listened in on a conversation between my wife and youngest son. He said with alarm, "Mom, you know what I find myself doing? Things I said I'd never do! I'm doing things just like Dad. I'm growing up to be just like Dad!"

Human beings seek out and gravitate toward those environments that are pleasant and positively reinforcing, and they avoid and flee those environments that are coercive and punishing. A working knowledge of these principles makes it possible for us to create a positive, pleasant, reinforcing environment that our children will crave. But even then, they will do things that we as parents find annoying and distasteful. But that should not prompt us to reject them. As I point out in Chapter 25, When All Else Fails, we must do all we can to create the most pleasant, positive, reinforcing environment possible within our homes irrespective of our children's behavior. To one degree or another, *they* might be out of control, but *we* must not be out of control. If a *child* is out of control, a *child* is out of control. If the parents are out of control, the *family* is out of control. As I point out in Chapter 7, Proactive Responding To Reactive Adolescent Behavior, as parents we must be proactive

> *Science is a wonderful thing!*

rather than reactive. We must be teachers of behavior, not punishers of behavior. When we learn to do that, we see behavior in an entirely different light. The husband of a couple with whom I worked put it this way:

> At first this stuff almost scared us off. We went to you with parenting problems and you said, "Here are some tools and skills. Learn to use them and you will be able to solve your own problems." That's not what we wanted to hear. What we wanted to do was give our parenting problems to you and have you solve them. But when we learned to use these tools skillfully—when it clicked—we were in a whole different mode. We now look at behavior entirely differently.

The intent of this book is to help you see your behavior and the behavior of your children and others entirely differently, and then to respond to it appropriately; that is, in a scientifically sound way—analytically and clinically. Indeed, science is a wonderful thing!

## NOW TO REVIEW

Human behavior is lawful, and can be managed and predicted given a keen understanding of the principles of human behavior. Especially for parenting purposes, the following principles are important:

1. Behavior is strengthened or weakened by its consequences.

2. Behavior ultimately responds better to positive consequences.

3. Whether a behavior has been punished or reinforced is known only by the course of that behavior in the future.

4. Behavior is largely a product of its immediate environment.

> *Research has shown that the most effective way to reduce problem behavior in children is to strengthen desirable behavior through positive reinforcement rather than trying to weaken undesirable behavior using aversive or negative processes.*
> *S.W. Bijou*
> *The International Encyclopedia of Education, 1988*

# THREE
# Applying Behavioral Principles in the Home and Family

Knowing the principles of human behavior is one thing; applying them well is quite another thing. The two together constitute what I have referred to earlier as a working knowledge of the principles of behavior. In this chapter I discuss five strategies which, when used appropriately, will help parents create and maintain a happy, supportive home environment. I talk about managing—even controlling—behavior. Such a discussion sometimes offends people. Some people take the position that we have no right to control the behavior of others. This is true if our intention is to control the behavior of others simply to satisfy ourselves, if our intent is basically selfish. (That's manipulation.) On the other hand, particularly as parents, we have a responsibility to manage, and sometimes control, behavior, and it is foolish and irresponsible to think otherwise. The following quote from Murray Sidman's book *Coercion and Its Fallout* helps make this point:

> "Should behavior be controlled?" is...a meaningless question. Be-
> haviors are always being controlled; we have no option. But the

question of who is to control remains a matter of concern to everyone, particularly when coercive control predominates. (page 193)

Denying the existence of control provides no reassuring answer to the question of who will do the controlling. Such denial will only leave control in the hands of those who would coerce the rest of us for their own advantage. (page 194)

Everyone's behavior is continually under the reinforcement control of something in its immediate environment. Our job as parents (to say what I have said time and time again) is to create the kind of environment that will exercise positive control over the behavior of our children. (That's management). Dr. B. F. Skinner, world renowned psychologist, said it well when he said, "I've created a world where everything I do is positively reinforced. I've redesigned a world in which I can behave well." That is our responsibility in behalf of ourselves and our children, to create a world where we and our children receive immense amounts of positive reinforcement; to design a world in which we can all behave well. My wife, Louise, recently observed, "You're not controlling kids. You are making it easier for them to behave well." That is such a wonderful way to put it.

> We must design a world in which we can behave well.

When I begin my work with parents, I often ask this question: "For whose good are you wanting to change your children's behavior—yours, the children, or both?" It isn't unusual for parents to want to change the behavior of their children simply to get their kids out of their hair! The well-being of the children may not be the main consideration. In such instances, it is not the children's behavior that is questionable; rather, it is the parents' motives. Another question I ask parents is, "Are you prepared to be consistent and exact in your approach to shaping your children's behavior?" Parents are often looking for a quick fix, something that will turn a monster into a dream child overnight and with a bat of an eyelash. That's not what I'm talking about in this book. I'm talking about a gradual, methodological, systematic approach to organizing an environment that will reinforce children for behaving well. But as parents, we must be honest about our motives. We must first accept as fact that in the course of growing up, children will behave in ways that annoy us. Most of these behaviors are simply age-typical, garden variety, weed behaviors that go along with growing up. They are just part of the territory, the heat

> In shaping and managing behavior, there are no quick fixes.

of the kitchen: leaving a mess, sibling rivalry, moodiness, mouthing off, messy bedrooms, poor eating habits, sloppy and even bizarre dress and grooming, seeming carelessness and selfishness, refusal to comply, and the list goes on.

Typically, such behaviors are less important than how we as parents respond to them. An appropriate response would put the behavior in a proper perspective without doing damage to the child. A beautiful example of how parents should behave in such instances was published in Guideposts, February, 1983, in a brief article entitled "A Lesson Warmly Taught", by Jill Taylor. The author recalled an experience as a teenager when she failed to return home on time after attending a dance in a neighboring city. Anxious about her mother's reaction, she lamented to her date, "The minute I get home my mother'll lace into me. She'll be waiting at the door."

To the girls surprise, her mother had gone to bed, leaving a light on to welcome her daughter home. But the best surprise of all came as she slipped into bed between "the icy sheets." "Instead of coldness, I found a pocket of warmth." Her mother "had tucked a toasty-warm hot-water bottle" into the foot of her bed. Rather than being met with a scolding, she was met with warmth and security. "Suddenly, intensely, I didn't want to disappoint my mother with my laxity and lateness anymore. And you know what? I didn't!"

Earlier, I talked about age-typical behaviors, and gave several examples of them. In most instances, age-typical behaviors are not as inappropriate as they are uncivilized.

> As parents we must realize that children are in the process of becoming civilized.

As parents we must realize that children are in the process of becoming civilized. Our job is to civilize them, that is, teach them how to behave appropriately within the society of human beings. To judge children's behavior using adults standards is both inappropriate and unfair. (This is addressed in detail in Chapter 4, On Being in Control.) Parents who get angry at a baby for crying are the ones who are behaving inappropriately, not the baby. Parents who strike a child for accidently spilling his milk at the dinner table are behaving far less appropriately than did the child. For an adult to scream and holler at a screaming and hollering child is an example of an adult abandoning civility; hence, the adult is behaving far less appropriately than is the yet-to-be-civilized child. (This is illustrated in Figure 4.1 page 89.) As parents, therefore, we must be very careful that we understand the behavior the child is exhibiting before we respond to it, then respond to it in a mature, scientifically sound way.

Love, kindness, patience, understanding, and so on are all wonderful qualities parents should possess. Unfortunately, in these difficult times where there are endless distractions—" forbidden fruits" that are so tempting and seductive—parents need to learn to skillfully use tools to both build and fix the behavior of their children. The five rules of parenting discussed in this chapter give parents specific direction, including the very words they can use, to help create an environment in the home that will properly direct and strengthen behavior. In discussing these rules, I also call your attention to how the principles of behavior that were discussed in Chapter 2 apply to making these tools effective.

The five parenting rules are:

Rule 1:      Clearly communicate your expectations to your children. This includes a clear description of those behaviors which will get your attention. This is typically taught best in a role-playing setting.

Rule 2:      Ignore inconsequential behaviors.

Rule 3:      Selectively reinforce appropriate behaviors.

Rule 4:      Stop then redirect inappropriate behavior.

Rule 5:      Stay close to your children.

## RULE 1: Clearly communicate your expectations to your children. This includes a clear description of those behaviors that will get your attention. This is typically taught best in a role-playing setting.

At the outset, make certain your children understand exactly what you expect of them. I'm continually amazed, as I visit with parents and their children who are having problems, at how unsure children are of what their parents expect, and how those expectations change given the mood of the situation. When the child says to a parent, "I didn't know what you wanted me to do!" and the parent angrily responds, "What do you mean you didn't know what I wanted? What are you, stupid?," I know there is a serious communication problem concerning expectations.

*Rather than simply telling children what you expect of them, role play those expectations.*

Suppose, for example, that you expect your children to come to the dinner table when called. Rather than simply saying, "When I call you for dinner, I want you to come immediately. Now, do you understand that?", role play your expectations with your children. Here's how you could do that. Seat your children around the table and in a very calm, pleasant, controlled voice and demeanor say:

Parent: "Children, when I call you for dinner I expect you to be seated at the table within 30 seconds after I call you. Billy, what do I expect you to do when I call you for dinner?"

*Note*: Don't ask the children if they understand what you are saying. A yes or no answer is not sufficient. Be sure you get a substantive response so you know they heard you and understood you. Also, direct your question to an individual child, not to all the children at once.

Billy: "Ah, Mom, this is dumb! Don't treat me like a baby. I know what you mean when you tell me to come to dinner."

*Note*: If the child should respond in this way, be very careful that you are not drawn into an argument or an unrelated discussion about your intelligence or how mature the child is. Rather, simply restate your question.

Parent: "Billy, what do I expect you to do when I call you for dinner?"

*Note*: This is called the broken record approach. It instructs us that if a child's response is not in line with what we expect, ignore that response completely and restate, perhaps rephrase, the question. If you do this calmly and without argument, the probability is very, very great the child will give you an appropriate answer, typically requiring no more than two repeats of the question/direction. The child's response might be given grudgingly and sullenly, but don't attend to any of that junk behavior, as follows:

Billy: "Oh, this is stupid. You want me to come to the table when you call me!"

Parent: "Thank you, Billy, That is exactly what I expect. When I call you, I expect you to come to the table. Thank you for that answer."

*Note*: With this response the parent has cut through all of the extraneous junk behavior and has gotten immediately to the heart of the matter. The response the parent wanted was the response that got the parent's attention, and as we learned earlier, behaviors that are attended to in a positive way are behaviors that are strengthened. Remember, pay no attention to those inconsequential behaviors you don't want repeated.

> *Pay no attention to inconsequential behaviors you don't want repeated.*

Parent: (Turning to another child), "Mary, how quickly do I expect you to come to the table when I call you?"

*Note*: Since Billy didn't give the parent a complete answer (he didn't say "within 30 seconds"), it is necessary to pursue the expectation until all aspects of the question have been adequately addressed and responded to.

Mary: "I don't know. I forgot."

*Note*: Unless parents get substantive responses from their children regarding expectations, it is altogether possible that key components of the expectations will be left unaddressed only to cause problems in the future.

Parent: "Listen carefully, Mary. When I call you to the table I expect you to be seated within 30 seconds. Mary, when do I expect you to be in your chair

THE POWER OF POSITIVE PARENTING

at the table after I call you?"

*Note*: You will notice that the parent prompted the child to pay attention by saying "Listen carefully, Mary." This is a directing, sometimes redirecting, statement. Whatever you do, don't say some dumb thing like "For heaven's sake! Don't you ever listen to anything I say?" Sometimes, since children's minds wander, particularly in situations where they are not happy, it is helpful to prompt them to pay attention.

Mary:     "You expect me to be in my chair within 30 seconds after you call me. But Mom, that isn't fair! What if I'm busy doing something? Am I just supposed to drop it and come to dinner just because you called?"

Parent:   "Thank you, Mary, for listening carefully. You are exactly correct. I expect you to be seated at the table within 30 seconds after I call you."

*Note*: Notice, the parent did not get side-tracked by the child's resistance to the expectation. The parent complimented the child for listening carefully and repeated to the child what she said that was consistent with the parent's expectation. Everything else was left unattended. Don't give attention to any behavior you don't want repeated! (What principle of behavior applies here? Look back at principle #1: Behavior Is Strengthened or Weakened by Consequences.)

Once the parent is absolutely certain the children have a clear understanding of what is expected, it is time to discuss consequences for compliance and noncompliance. Remember, the consequences of behaviors are what maintain or eliminate them. (An extended discussion of consequences is found in Chapter 5.) Now, back to our example.

Parent:   "Good, I'm glad you listened carefully and understand what I expect you to do when I call you to the table to eat. When you meet these expectations, you will continue to have those privileges you enjoy so much. What are some of those privileges, Billy?"

> **Never tell children something they already know. Let them tell you.**

*Note*: Don't tell the children what those privileges are. In fact, never tell children something they already know. Let them tell you. It can be very instructional for you, and it engages the child in the discussion in a very dynamic way.

Billy:    "Do you mean to tell me that if I don't come to the table within 30 seconds after I'm called you're not going to let me watch television!"

*Note*: A response like this is very instructional. Now you know exactly what the child values most: watching television.

Parent:   "Thank you, Billy. Television is one of those privileges you really enjoy."

*Note*: The parent did not answer Billy's combative question. This is very important. Parents who allow themselves to be drawn off track to answer such questions simply yield control of the situation to the children. When that happens, the ball game is all over, and no one has won.

Parent:   "Mary, what are some privileges around the house you really enjoy?"

Mary:     "Well, I like playing with my Barbie doll, but you're not going to take my Barbie doll away from me just because I don't come to the table are you?"

*Note*: In both of these children's responses the parent was immediately made out to be a bad guy who won't let the children do things they want to do just because of some stupid rule. That is certainly the implication. Pay no attention to this. Rather, search the children's responses for those bits and pieces of information that are in line with your instructional intent and build on those. Ignore everything else.

Parent: "Yes, Mary, you really do enjoy playing with your Barbie doll. Billy and Mary, when you come to the table to eat within 30 seconds after you're called, you will have earned these privileges for the rest of the day. Mary, what privilege do you earn if you come to the table within 30 seconds after you're called?"

*Note*: The parent has put privileges in their proper perspective: as something children earn as a result of proper behavior. The availability of these privileges is entirely up to the children. It isn't a matter of whether the parent is a good guy or a bad guy. The ball is completely in the child's court and what he or she does with it is his or her business, as are the consequences.

Mary: "You'll let me play with my Barbie doll for the rest of the day."

Parent: "Thank you, Mary. That's right, you will have earned the privilege of playing with your Barbie doll for the rest of the day."

*Note*: The parent did not respond to the child's saying, "You'll let me..." The parent merely restated the consequence in terms of what the child had earned.

Parent: "If, on the other hand, you become distracted or careless and don't come to the table within 30 seconds after I've called, we will start eating without you and you'll have denied yourself the privilege of playing with your Barbie doll or watching television for the rest of the day. Furthermore, if you are more than a minute late coming to the table, you will have to wait until breakfast (or lunch or dinner) before you can eat. Billy, what will happen if you chose to not come to the table in time?"

*Note*: Since children will sometimes dawdle endlessly before coming to eat, its a good idea to put limits on how long they can dawdle before they lose the privilege of eating. And remember, if they do lose the privilege of eating, don't worry about it. I've never known an otherwise healthy, well-fed child to starve over night. (Of course, this strategy would be modified if there were compelling medical reasons why a child must not miss a meal.)

Billy: "This is absolutely the dumbest thing I've ever heard in my life. I can't believe you, Mom. What's so important about coming to the dinner table within 30 seconds or a minute? I can't wait until I'm old enough to get out of this dumb house and away from all these stupid rules that treat me like a baby!"

Parent: "Mary, what will happen if you fail to come to the dinner table on time?"

*Note*: The parent has completely ignored Billy's juvenile and defensive outburst. There wasn't a single thing Billy said that was worth a response. Not a single thing! Under those conditions, direct your question to another child. If there isn't another child, simply redirect the question to the one child. "What privileges will you deny yourself if you choose to come to the table late?"

Mary: "If we don't come to the table within 30 seconds, we won't be able to play with our toys or watch television for the rest of the day. If we don't come to the table within a minute, we won't be able to have supper either."

Parent: "Thank you, Mary. Now I know that you understand exactly what I expect. Thank you for listening carefully and answering correctly.

Billy, what can you expect if you don't come to dinner on time when I call?"

Billy: "I know what you mean, Mom. No T.V. or no supper! Brother, I can't believe this is happening."

Parent: "Thank you, Billy. I'm glad to know you completely understand what I expect, and that you understand perfectly what to expect if you do or do not come to dinner when called."

All of this shouldn't take more than a few minutes. Don't drag it out. Make it brief and make it crisp then let the children be on their way. Don't be concerned if the children don't agree with you. Agreeing is not that important, assuming that your expectations are reasonable. But their understanding of your expectations is important. Once you have that established, including an understanding of the consequences for compliance or noncompliance, terminate the discussion there.

Now, let's move on to the moment of truth: the children have been called to come eat.

Parent: "Billy and Mary, it's time to eat. You have 30 seconds."

> **Agreeing with parental expectations is less important than understanding them.**

*Note*: When the children are called, the parents should use a pleasant voice, even a lilting voice, during which time the expectations of the parent are restated in brief detail. As the children come to the table on time, be sure to acknowledge that.

Parent: "Thanks, for coming to the table when you were called. I really appreciate that."

Billy: (Muttering under his breath) "That's the dumbest thing I ever heard of."

Parent: (Changing the subject) "Mary, what exciting thing happened to you at school today?"

*Note*: At this point, any number of responses might be forthcoming from either of the children. In any event, it is important that the parent be certain to not attend to any of the mouthy, sullen, disgusting, age-typical, inconsequential behaviors. Rather, the parent should move the discussion along in a positive way, picking up on cues that are provided by the children as to which responses to attend to and reinforce and which responses to simply ignore and allow to die on their own. When handled correctly, with lots of reinforcement being given to appropriate behavior, even the most sullen, disgusted, out-of-sorts child will enter a discussion in an attempt to get a few of the goodies the parents are so lavishly handing out.

The example above involved younger children. Here is an example of how parents would state their expectations to an older adolescent child. The parents are expressing their expectations about when the child should be in at night.

Parent:  "Sid, it is very important for you to be home at night at a reasonable hour. Why is that so important?"

*Note*: Again, don't tell the child something that he or she already knows. Let the child tell you.

Sid:  "I know you want me in early, but I don't know why. There is nothing the matter with me being out late. I'm doing okay in school, I'm not getting into trouble, so what's the big deal?"

Parent:  "We know it annoys you when we talk about this, but it is very important. Why is it so important?"

*Note*: Rather than responding to the child's questions and getting side tracked, the parent showed empathy and understanding then came right back to the original question.

Sid:  "I really don't know why it is such a big deal. I suppose you think I need my rest or that I'm safer when I'm home."

Parent:  "Those are good reasons, Sid. You do need your rest, and home is certainly a safer place to be at night, particularly late at night."

*Note*: Here, again, the parent cut through all the extraneous, distracting, age-typical junk behavior and found those pearls of wisdom that were worth paying attention to. Everything else was just junk and was left alone.

> *Parents, don't be distracted by age-typical, garden-variety, weed behavior.*

Parent:  "All things considered, Sid, we have concluded that you should be home on school nights, and that includes Sunday nights, no later that 9:30, and on Friday nights and Saturday nights no later than midnight. Those are the times by which we expect you to be home."

Sid:  "What!: 9:30 on school nights and 12:00 on weekends![1] What do you want me to do, lose every friend I've got? That is just flatout unreasonable. I won't do it and you can't make me do it."

Parent:  "You are correct, Sid, we can't make you do it, but we expect you to do it anyway, and when you meet our expectations, you will continue to earn the privileges of this family that you really like. What comes to your mind when I use the term 'those privileges of the family'?"

Sid:  "I suppose that you are telling me that if I don't get home at night by these

---

[1]These times, of course, are only for purposes of illustration. They would vary from time to time and from family to family. Also, depending on the maturity and dependability of the child/children, conditions can be negotiated. Ultimately, however, conditions and expectations must be established.

ridiculous times, you are not going to let me use the car anymore. Is that what you are telling me?"

Parent: "You are correct, Sid, in assuming that the use of the car is one of those privileges that you will deny yourself if you decide to stay out later than 9:30 at night on school nights and midnight on weekends. What other privileges will you deny yourself?"

*Note*: The parent put the burden of responsibility squarely on the child's shoulders, acknowledged the child's accurate perception of the parent's expectation, and moved forward with the discussion without being drawn off course.

Sid: (Sarcastically) "Well, I suppose you could lock me out of the kitchen or out of my bedroom or even out of the house."

Parent: "No, we are not going to starve you into submission or invite you to leave home. You mean far too much to us to do a thing like that. Sid, we are sorry this kind of discussion annoys you, but it is because you mean so much to us that we feel it is important to have this discussion."

> **Use empathy and understanding, but stay on course.**

*Note*: Again, empathy and understanding were used while at the same time reassuring the child that he is a valuable member of the family unit. Though the child may appear to be disinterested in this expression of affection, and even say things to that effect, the probability is very, very great that he is glad to have heard it and is reassured by it. Never conclude that just because a teenager says something rude and ugly in response to a tender expression of affection the child didn't appreciate that expression of affection. Remember, he is still in the process of becoming civilized and has a lot to learn about how to respond appropriately to parental love and affection. Some kids will have learned this well by late adolescence. For others, it may take awhile. Everyone learns at a different rate whether we are talking about learning to read or do arithmetic or to deal appropriately with expression of parental affection. (Chapter 9, "Dealing with Hate and Anger," has more to say about this.)

Sid: "Frankly, I don't know if the use of the car is that important to me. After all, I have a lot of friends with cars and I'm sure they won't mind using their cars when we want to go some place. So it's really no big deal to me. If I don't get to use the car, so what! I have options, you know. I'm not the baby you think I am."

Parent: "You are certainly correct when you say you are not a baby. In fact, you are a very able young man and when you are ready to assure us that you will comply with our expectations, the privilege of using the car will be yours. Give it some thought, and if you would like to discuss it later, just let us know."

*Note*: The parent has once again assured the boy that he is valued and that the privileges that are under parental control will be extended to him as soon as he is ready to comply with parental expectations. The boy hasn't been told that he will not be able to stay out longer than the parents want him to. To do this is very risky and can persuade a child to do everything he can to make sure the parents' expectations are not met.

Unless children are willing to comply, either because of their respect for their parents or because of their wanting to enjoy the privileges of the home that are under parental control, parents of older children must not delude themselves into believing they can "make" their children do anything. Expressions to that effect are simply invitations to a child to rebel even further. Rather, parents should wait until the child wants the privileges of the home that are under their control and then make those privileges available (contingent) upon those expectations being met, all the while being on the lookout for opportunities to reinforce those behaviors that are consistent with parental expectations. For example, when the child does come home by the expected time, the parents should reinforce that with such statements as, "Hi, son. Glad to see you home safe and sound. And by the way, thanks for being home early." Then, if possible, accompany this with a hug, a pat on the back, or some other appropriate physical contact. Furthermore, if it's not awkward to do so, it's a good idea to engage the child in a pleasant, non-judgmental, non-moral-bound discussion about something that has happened during the day, or recently, which was of interest to the boy: events surrounding a ball game, something that was reported in the news, a family happening, something at school, or whatever. These discussions don't need to be long. A discussion of this type need last just a few minutes, and if pleasant can have a great effect in bonding the child to his parents and increasing the probability that he will continue in the future to comply with their expectations.

With older children, achieving the desired level of compliance takes longer and might even find the child engaging in what we call counter-control behaviors; for example, deliberately doing exactly the opposite of what is expected. A sort of extinction burst (see page 25). Don't be intimidated by this. Remain calm, proceed in a positive, direct manner consistent with your expectation, and carefully observe the direction of the behavior. Give the treatment time to work. Usually within a week to 10 days, you'll begin to see improvement. You won't likely "be there" in that length of time, but you'll likely see behavior moving in that direction. If you do, acknowledge it in a positive, reinforcing way. If you don't, restudy the consequences then make adjustments accordingly. Don't expect miracles. Be systematic.

## RULE 2: Ignore inconsequential behaviors.

As I noted earlier, many (in fact, most) of the annoying behaviors of children are not worth paying attention to at all. The question is, "Which ones should be attended to and which ones shouldn't?" Certainly, there is no way of identifying with absolute certainty and in every situation which behaviors should or should not be attended to. As a general rule of thumb, age-typical behaviors such as mild sibling rivalry, and when children are just being mouthy with one another, should be ignored. Occasionally, children will scrap with each other even to the point of pushing, shoving, grabbing, and hitting, more for the purpose of annoying than for hurting. These behaviors can usually be ignored. Just turn your back on them or completely walk out of the room. Say nothing about them. Don't even look at the children when they are behaving this way. Behave as though the children are not even there. Children who fuss over toys or territory or what's fair should generally be ignored. Children who argue with one another and exchange meaningless verbal blows should be left alone.

If the condition of a child's bedroom is creating a rift between a parent and a child, it is better for the room to be left a mess than for the relationship between the child and the parent to be a mess. This is not to mean that parents should make no effort whatsoever to teach their children neatness, orderliness, and care for their immediate environment. But in the long run, it isn't how neat, orderly, and careful children are with their bedrooms or bathrooms that determines how neat, orderly, and careful they will be with their own homes as adults. That is determined by the model set by their parents. As children grow into adulthood, they don't typically model or maintain their own childish or adolescent behaviors. Rather, as adults they tend to model the behaviors of the adults who were prominent in their formative lives as children—usually their parents.

Looking back over our child-rearing years, my wife and I can recall bedrooms that were nothing short of a menace to society and disgusting in about every respect. On the other hand, some of our children were very neat, orderly, and careful. Everything had its place and everything was in its place. Today, we can go into the homes of any of our six children and find there a level of neatness, orderliness, and care that very nearly approximates that of the home in which they were raised. To many adolescents, a messy room is a status symbol. One of our children once told us, "If you think I'm going to bring my friends into a clean bedroom, you're crazy. They'll think I'm some kind of weirdo." As I noted earlier, the first question we must ask ourselves when we set about changing the behavior of our children is, "For whom is this behavior being changed?"

If parents' attempts to teach their children reasonable dress and grooming standards have failed and their children have succumbed to the pressures and reinforcers of the peer group, parents are well advised to ignore all the junk behavior and look for opportunities to acknowledge and positively reinforce those behaviors which approximate reasonable dress and grooming standards.

This is tough, I know, but in the long run it is worth it. One of our sons came under the reinforcement control of his peer group resulting in a hair style that Louise and I found very distasteful. After we had made several fruitless attempts at getting him to change, we decided it wasn't worth losing our son over so we just lived with it. It wasn't easy, I'll admit. There were times when I wanted to chloroform the kid and shave his head as bald as a billiard ball! But we just gritted our teeth and continued to hug him and tell him we loved him and built the relationship, focusing our attention on bonding the boy to us and the value system of the family unit. As adolescence passed and the boy's behavior began to gradually moderate—responding to new forces within his adult environment (remember, behavior is shaped by consequences within one's immediate environment)—his hair got shorter and shorter until finally it became very becoming—even to us! Recently, he brought his family home for a vacation and his oldest daughter wanted to see pictures of her daddy when he was a boy. Our granddaughter flipped open the pages of the family photo album and staring back at her were pictures of her daddy in the bloom of adolescence. "Daddy! Is this you?" she asked in startled tones. Her father went over to see what she was looking at. "Mother!" he gasped, "How could you have let me wear my hair like that?" (Admittedly, my wife and I had a difficult time not touting this as a triumphant moment.)

> *Parent-child relationships are more important than grooming.*

A mother once asked me what she should do about her 17-year-old son. She said he had dyed the left side of his hair red and the right side green. She wanted to know what she should do and say to him when he got home. My advice to her was simple. I told her, "Say to him, 'Hi, Son, I'm glad you're home safe and sound.' Then give him a hug and a kiss and send him off to bed with an affectionate 'Sleep tight, Son. I love you.'" "But," she asked, "what about his awful hair?" To which I asked, "What about it?" "Well," she asked, "what am I going to do about his terrible hair?" In return, I asked, "What *can* you do about his hair?" To which she answered, "I don't know. I've tried everything. I tried reasoning with him. I pled with him. I even tried bribing him, but all to no avail. I don't know what to do. That's why I'm asking you." To which I said, "In that case, don't do anything about his hair, but do everything you can to establish a good relationship with the boy. Forget the hair." I felt confident then and would give the same advice today, that a good relationship between the parent and the boy will have a far better and more lasting effect on how the boy grooms himself as an adult than all of

> *Children will engage in junk behavior over which we as parents have zero control.*

the pleading, complaining, reasoning, and bribing will ever do.

I vividly recall an interview between a reporter and a young television starlet. Apparently during her teenage years, the girl had been quite rowdy and a terrible problem to her parents. During the interview she was asked, "How did your mother feel about your behavior. Did she try to crack down on you?" To which the girl replied, "My mother tried everything. It was something I had to outgrow. I was having a good time and it took me time to grow up. And I did. Now I eat health foods and I don't smoke or drink or anything. I guess I evolved in finding things in my life that were more pleasing to me than partying." She was then asked, "If you had a daughter, would you be a disciplinarian with her?" She answered, "I would chain her to her bed and lock her in her room. My greatest fear in life is spawning a daughter just like me. I couldn't go through the suffering, the wondering of when it was going to end, the way my mother did. I wouldn't be able to take it because I know what she'd be doing when she was out there. My mother didn't know." Lastly, she was asked, "Is there anyone to blame for that crazy period of your life?" To which she answered, "Me. It was a specific time and specific town with a specific girl. I wasn't mistreated or abused by my parents, I was loved. That's how I felt at the time. I blame me."

There are a couple of excellent lessons to be learned from this interview. The one is that kids *will* engage in junk behavior over which we as parents have zero control. It was the case with us when we were kids and it will be the case with our kids' kids. It just goes with growing up. Our responsibility as parents is to establish the best relationship possible with our children so they can survive those high-risk times and come out whole and intact. The second great lesson to be learned from this is that kids ultimately grow up and come to realize what they put their parents through. Although that is of little comfort to parents at times when their children are misbehaving, it at least might be a learning experience for the children as they enter parenthood. A couple of years ago, my wife and I were talking with a friend whose son had been a terror during adolescence and had gotten into all kinds of trouble. As a young adult, he turned out very well and had even achieved some rather remarkable accomplishments. While visiting with the boy's mother, my wife said, "You must be very proud of your son." To which the mother replied, "Yes, I am. But why did he have to put me through the meat grinder first?" Well, those are simply the risks we take when we have children.

> *Anyone who ever says parenting is easy, never had children.*

Anyone who ever says parenting is easy, never had children! When our children engage in behaviors over which we have no influence or control, we are best advised to ignore those behaviors and do everything we can to establish a solid bond with them, a point I address at length in Chapter 25, When All Else Fails. A short time ago I was watching a public service spot on TV about child abuse. An outraged father (i.e., a skill-less father) was justifying his abusive behavior by saying, "It's how I keep the boy in line—just like my father did with me." Think about that. Think about it really hard!

To sum up, I'm reminded of the biblical admonition to "Be slow to anger," and of the Chinese proverb, "If you are patient in one moment of anger, you will escape a hundred days of sorrow." Be slow to pay attention to behaviors which are basically age-typical and which left alone extinguish because of lack of attention. Behaviors that fall in this category tend to become apparent within a short period of time.

> *"If you are patient in one moment of anger, you will escape a hundred days of sorrow."*
> **Chinese proverb**

Also, as I noted earlier, ignore those behaviors over which you have no control and place the emphasis rather on building relationships between you and your children, a point I address in Rule 3, Selectively Reinforce Appropriate Behavior.

As parents, we are inclined to work ourselves into a tizzy over behaviors that just aren't that significant. I had an experience a few years ago after giving a keynote address at a conference for human service providers that illustrates this point. An anxious and dis-traught woman cornered me and insisted that I talk with her about

> *Be slow to pay attention to annoying age-typical behaviors that are sure to fade with time.*

her out-of-control daughter. The woman was in her late 30s or early 40s and I quickly envisioned a rebellious 15-or 16-year-old daughter who was driving her mother crazy. Finding a remote spot away from the convention hall, the mother began pouring out her anxieties to me about her daughter: "She is rebellious, refuses to do anything she is told to do, is absolutely demanding of every moment of my life," and on and on and on. The intensity with which the mother recounted the litany of her daughter's behaviors was such that it was exhausting to me. I suggested we find a couple of chairs where we could sit down. I had about become convinced, after years and years of working with distraught parents, that I had met the situation that would try me to my limit, and perhaps even exceed it. Finally, after the mother had poured her frustrations and despair out on me, for want of anything else to say, I asked, "How old is your daughter?" Her answer nearly knocked me off my chair: "Six months!" For an account of what I told the mother, read Chapter 11, A Word About Fussy Babies.

### RULE 3: Selectively reinforce appropriate behaviors.

Without a doubt, the key to developing high quality human behavior is through the selective, positive reinforcement of appropriate behavior. I've already said this several times in this book and it will be illustrated time and again in subsequent chapters. But it is of such importance that it demands to be revisited. When I talk about the selective, positive reinforcement of appropriate behaviors I mean simply that we as parents *MUST*(!!) be constantly aware of the behaviors of our children and to carefully select and skillfully reinforce those behaviors that should be strengthened. It is neither possible nor appropriate to attend to every "good" thing a child does every time he or she does it. To do that would be artificial and even punishing to a child. Instead, look for opportunities to pay attention, in a very positive way, to a few select, appropriate behaviors, and do it intermittently, i.e., at times children least expect it.

For example, it is important for human beings to learn to get along well with other human beings. This is so basic to our individual happiness and success that no aware person could possibly disagree with it. It is a given. This being true, when we see our children interacting appropriately with other children, we should seize this as an opportunity to selectively reinforce that appropriate interaction. This can be easily done by walking past the children while they are thus engaged and in a very natural way, taking only a few seconds and using a few descriptive words, say, "You children are surely having fun playing together so nicely." Those are ten words that took only about three seconds to say. And that's plenty. In the process you might even gently and affectionately touch the children. Certainly you would smile and perhaps even wink, then go on about your business without giving the children the slightest hint that you had planned the entire thing; that you were selectively reinforcing appropriate behavior.

Having a healthy relationship with good books and good music and good art has also been shown to be important in the raising of low-risk children: low-risk meaning children who are less likely to engage in delinquent behaviors, abuse drugs, become members of unhealthy peer groups, drop out of school, and so on. Knowing this, parents should be on the lookout for opportunities to selectively reinforce behaviors which indicate that the child is showing even the slightest interest in these things. For example, a child brings a book home from the school library and you say, "Hey, that looks like a neat book. When you've read it I'd appreciate your telling me about it." Or, in the case of younger children, you might say, "I'd love it if you'd read me part of your story before you go to bed tonight." You might even carefully arrange your environment to prompt behaviors you would then selectively reinforce. For example, check out from your public library a colorful book you think might be attractive to your children. Perhaps a picture book of animals. Set the book open in a conspicuous place at home and then watch to see if a child shows any interest in it. If he does, make sure you take a moment to share your interest in the book by saying something like, "Isn't that a neat book? I checked it out of the library. I was sure you would love those pictures." If the child shows an interest, take a few minutes to enjoy the book with the child, all the while saying things that let the child know that books are a lot of fun.

We know that success in life is largely dependent on success at school which is in turn dependent upon how well children apply themselves to their studies. Therefore, when children are doing their homework, parents should take the opportunity to acknowledge that in a very positive, reinforcing way. For example, the parent might say in passing, "Glad to see you're getting your homework done, Honey. That's great." And as the parent passes, he gently runs his fingers across the child's shoulders. The child might look up and say, "I hate homework. It's dumb. My teachers are dumb." If that happens, the parent shouldn't even look back or acknowledge that response in any way whatsoever. Just keep going, but a while later, a few minutes later, the parent should once again walk past the child, but this time without saying a word just gently touch the child and then walk off.

> **Behavior that receives parents' attention is behavior that is strengthened.**

It is not at all unusual for children to have a radio or stereo blaring away while they are doing their homework, or even doing their homework in front of a noisy television show. In such instances, it is not at all unusual for parents to say things like, "For heaven's sake turn that thing off. How in the world can you think with that thing blaring away!" I strongly advise parents against doing this because it selectively reinforces the wrong thing: having the stereo/TV/radio on. Recalling the point I made earlier, ignore all of the distracting, peripheral things going on and focus only on the behavior that is most desirable. In this instance, the homework. Just ignore the stereo, the television, or the radio, and acknowledge that the child is doing his or her homework and that is really wonderful. The more negative things parents say about the radio, stereo, and television, and the less positive things they say about the homework, the more inclined the children will be to attend to their radio, stereo, or television and to not attend to the homework. Remember the simple rule, behavior which receives parental attention is behavior that is strengthened.

We know that to succeed in life and to be personally happy we must learn to work. This being true, look for opportunities to selectively reinforce their behavior when children are working. For example, while the child is doing his chores around the house, acknowledge that work by saying something like, "Thank you for getting your work done. You're doing a fine job." Avoid criticizing the quality of the work. If the work is not done to an acceptable standard, rather than saying, "Come on, you know better than that. I'm not going to let you get away with doing a lousy job! Now get on the ball and do it right!", say something like, "You're almost there. With a little more work on this and this (be specific) you'll have it in shipshape. I appreciate you sticking with it until it is done right." It is likely the child will complain about having to do something over. Rather than getting into a long discussion about why it is necessary for the job to be done right, simply say, "A little more work on this and this and you will be done in good shape. Let me know when you are finished. I like seeing a job well done." Then be on your way. In time, living in an environment like this where reinforcement of appropriate behavior is swift in coming and precise, where gently-given directives are used instead of scoldings, complaints, and "When I was your age" stuff, it won't be long before appropriate behaviors outweigh inappropriate behaviors by a large margin and the quality of life at home will be remarkably improved. Remember to maintain a high general level of reinforcement.

Not infrequently a parent will be unable to acknowledge behavior immediately, and reinforcement has to be delayed. Perhaps the parents are working, are away at the time, or are not aware of what the child did. It's important to give delayed reinforcement in these instances. The following example illustrates very well how this is done. (I regret that I do not know the source of this example so am unable to acknowledge authorship.)

> Chip was typically uncooperative and slow about going to bed on time. At six years of age he would find all kinds of reasons for procrastinating, particularly when the baby-sitter was taking care of him. One evening when his parents returned home, the baby-sitter reported a slight improvement in Chip's going-to-bed behavior. His mother asked the sitter for a detailed description of what the boy had done.
>
> The next morning she was able to say, "Chip, remember last night when the baby-sitter was here and you were watching television? Do

you remember when the program ended and she asked you to get ready for bed? She told me that you got up and turned off the television set and scarcely complained at all. She also said that you got your pajamas on without dawdling as much as you did the last time she was here. Daddy and I are pleased to hear that. It sounds like you're really becoming more prompt."

The mother's words of praise were reinforcers for Chip. His mother was not there to praise him immediately after his improved behavior, so she did the next best thing. She reconstructed the behavior so that Chip could remember quite well what he had done. She then reinforced Chip with her praise immediately after the verbal description of his improved behavior. Although Chip's mother at first regretted she had missed the opportunity to reinforce him immediately, she found she was still able to capitalize on the situation.

Whenever immediate reward is not possible the child may be reminded of the circumstances and the details of his own improved behavior; the reminder may then be followed by either a verbal or a nonverbal reinforcer.

Virtually all children, in the course of the day, will do or say something that is worth selecting out for reinforcement. Soon, selectively reinforcing appropriate behavior will become second nature to you. It might seem a little awkward at first, but in time it will be as natural as driving a car, dialing a telephone, playing the

> *Virtually all children, in the course of a day, will do or say something that is worth reinforcing.*

piano, or whatever else a person does without having to think about it. It just becomes automatic. Parents have asked me, "But isn't that kind of artificial? Isn't it kind of phony?" My answer is clear and unequivocal: "No!" It is never unnatural for us to positively reinforce people for doing things well. In fact, it is a bright and refreshing switch from the typically negative and coercive interactions that so often take place between parents and their children. If parents find doing this awkward and unnatural, that's all the more reason they need to develop the skill of praise-giving!

Parents sometimes complain to me that their children *never* do anything that is worth praising. They *never* behave nicely. They are *never* pleasant to be around. Although I find this hard to believe, I still wouldn't throw in the towel even if it were true. Rather,

I suggest to parents that they look for approximations of desirable behaviors and pay attention to those approximations. I will explain what I mean by approximations by recalling an experience I had in a class for emotionally disturbed children. It was a class of five upper elementary grade children who had severe behavior problems. The class was staffed by a certified teacher of the emotionally disturbed and a teacher's aide. As my school district host and I entered the classroom, the place was in total chaos. Children were running helter skelter around the room. Just as we walked in, one child leaped from a book shelf as he tried to grab the ceiling light fixture. Fortunately he missed, but went crashing to the floor, knocking over a desk and creating quite a commotion. He ran out of the room as fast as he could with the teacher in hot pursuit. About that time another child ran out of the classroom through another door, followed close on his heels by the aide. It was sheer pandemonium. In that setting, I can honestly say I didn't see a single behavior I could select for reinforcement. My host was mortified at what was going on and when the teacher returned to the classroom, dragging a kicking and screaming kid behind her, he advised her to leave the classroom with him so they could talk things over.

> People never outgrow their need for positive verbal praise.

Remaining in the room were five wild children, a crying aide, and me. I walked over to the aide and asked if she would mind if I helped. Choked up and unable to speak, she nodded in the affirmative. As I looked around the room, I concluded immediately that the one thing I wasn't going to do was run after misbehaving children. Remember, behavior that receives attention is behavior that is strengthened. So far as I had been able to tell during the few minutes I was in the classroom, only misbehavior had been getting attention. From this, of course, I could only conclude that those behaviors were the ones that were being strengthened, which, of course, explained what was going on in the classroom.

Not being able to find any human behavior worth reinforcing, I began looking for something that would approximate appropriate behavior. I noticed a worksheet on the desk of one of the children. The worksheet was there but the child wasn't. I walked over to the desk and began to pay careful and undivided attention to what was written on the paper. Within just a few seconds, the boy whose desk I was standing by sat down. I said, "Thank you for sitting down," and I patted him on the back. I didn't say, "Well, it's about time you sat down. Why are you running around this room like a wild animal?" That comment would have been terribly inappropriate since it would have given all of my attention to the very behaviors I didn't want. So calmly and quietly I said, "Thank you for sitting down." I then asked the boy to explain to me his work, pointing out that he had answered several of the questions correctly. I complimented him on his performance. As he explained his work to me and began completing other problems, a boy who belonged at another desk took his seat. I said to the boy I was standing by, "Do these problems. I'll be back in just a second." I patted the boy on the back then turned to the other boy and quietly said to him, "Thanks for sitting down. Tell me about your work." The boy got a workbook out of his desk and began explaining to me a social studies assignment. Within slightly over a minute and a half, all five children were in their seats doing their school work. I never had to raise my voice above a whisper nor physically restrain a child. I simply selected an approximate behavior, gave that approximation my undivided attention, then as the opportunity arose, I positively reinforced appropriate behaviors as they became evident.

This same strategy can be used in homes. An unruly child leaves a comic book open in the living room. The parent picks up the comic book and begins looking at it. The child comes over wondering what his mom or dad is doing with his favorite comic book. The parent says, "These are different characters than were in comic books when I was a child.

> *Unfortunately, we tend to focus attention on what is wrong, not what is right.*

Tell me about them." The child responds and the parent takes it from there by selecting only those behaviors which deserve further attention. It is not a difficult thing to do, and for sure, it is infinitely better than trying to bring behavior under control through coercion, screaming, or any other desperate, negative, aversive means.

Unfortunately, the tendency of care-givers, be they parents, teachers, therapists, or even medical personnel, is to focus on what is wrong rather than what is right. A few years ago, a mother of an 11-year-old girl came to me simply beside herself. Her daughter was in the pediatric ward of a hospital stuffed to the gills with Ritalin. She had been exhibiting some bizarre behaviors at school and at home, and the immediate therapy of choice of the attending physician and the consulting psychiatrist was to hospitalize the child and put her on Ritalin. The entire attention of everyone was on what was wrong. Not the slightest attention had been given to things the child did that were right and could be selected out for positive reinforcement. The mother, a registered nurse, was frantic. The parents had already sustained thousands of dollars in hospital and physician costs, and all they had to show for it was a glassy-eyed girl in the hospital who was all stoved up with drugs.

The mother got the family physician to grant me professional visiting rights in the hospital. After talking at length with the mother, and carefully and systematically observing the girl, I was convinced that through the use of selective reinforcement of appropriate behavior, the child could best be treated with behavioral medicine, not drug therapy. After completing a "functional analysis" of the child's behavior (I carefully looked at what consequences were shaping behaviors), I developed a behavioral intervention that focused on carefully selecting appropriate behaviors that should be reinforced while ignoring all others. I taught the mother how to do that and 3 days later the girl was back in school, off drugs, and doing fine. That girl is in college now and has had no residual problems in the intervening years.

> *Reinforcing appropriate behavior is absolutely the best way to go!*

Looking for that which is right and appropriate and then attending to it using positive reinforcement while ignoring—whenever possible—inappropriate behavior, is *absolutely* the best way to go. You can spend the rest of your life searching the scientific literature for a better way and you'll never find one.

At this point, a word of caution is in order. Specifically, it is important (a) to not selectively reinforce inappropriate behavior, and (b) to make sure that by selectively reinforcing the behaviors of other children, we don't appear to be unfair or unequal in our giving of reinforcers.

Regarding the first caution, I recall an experience I had while visiting one of my daughters in her office at work. Two women were in the office, one with two small children, ages 2 and 4. As I entered the office, I immediately directed my attention to the children since they were playing so well together while their mother and my daughter were discussing a business matter. I said to the children, "My, what lovely children you are. You are smiling, happy, and playing together so nicely!" The children beamed with pleasure and satisfaction, smiling even more broadly, obviously gratified at this assessment of their behavior. Just then, their mother added, somewhat sharply, "Yes, and with sticky fingers!" In an instant, the 4-year-old took a piece of hard candy from her mouth and began rolling it across her fingers, all the while looking intently at her mother. What should the mother have said?

> *"Nothing is more inequitable than the equal treatment of unequals."*

Regarding fairness and equality in the giving of reinforcers, I refer to the excellent work of Beth Sulzer-Azaroff and G. Roy Mayer, published in their classic book *Behavior Analysis for Lasting Changes* On page 169, under the subtitle "Treating People Differently," they provide some clear advice in this matter, beginning with a question, "Won't...others become jealous or angered if someone else is receiving special reinforcers they themselves are denied?" Their advice is to "…explain to these involved that each of us is unique and that each has special interests, skills, and areas of weakness (yourself included). Often…[others]…will understand that focusing on different behaviors to change and using different methods makes sense." They point out that "…knowing that help is finally on the way can be a source of relief to peers who may have been suffering from the difficult behaviors of others…Peers also may recognize that they stand to benefit" from the improved behaviors of others, and "…peers have been seen to applaud the success of their fellows. In this way the reinforcement program causes the environment to become more pleasant and rewarding for everyone."

The authors continue, "You could point out that the person is receiving the special privileges, objects, or access to activities for making progress. Inviting others to design programs for themselves in areas in which *they* need to improve is also possible. Emphasis is placed on each individual's progress, not on competitive comparisons." They further suggest that programs can be developed so that individuals can earn reinforcers not only for themselves but also for the whole group. They conclude by emphasizing the important point that "nothing is more inequitable than the equal treatment of unequals."

## Rule 4: Stop then redirect inappropriate behavior.

Occasionally, children will exhibit behaviors that simply can't be ignored. These are behaviors which left unattended can result in serious damage and harm to person and property. Before going into a detailed discussion about how to deal with inappropriate behaviors that can't be ignored, I must emphasize again the importance of looking first for opportunities to positively reinforce selected appropriate behaviors. In 99 out of 100 cases, when this is done systematically and consistently, there will be little need to worry about inappropriate behaviors becoming so severe as to need therapeutic attention. There will be no need for children to behave inappropriately if they are getting all the attention they need by behaving appropriately. Having said that, however, there still exists the probability that a child at some time will behave inappropriately to such a degree that it must be attended to.

The first thing that must be done is to determine whether the behavior is a predictably reoccurring behavior or whether it is an unexpected, out-of-the-blue, behavior which has seldom if ever happened before, which is totally uncharacteristic of the child, and which will probably never happen again. It is important to make the distinction between these two kinds of behaviors since the approach you should use is different for the one than for the other. I will begin with the treatment of those rare, unexpected, out-of-the blue behaviors. Let's suppose that for no readily apparent reason one child uncharacteristically lashes out at another child either verbally or physically. Maintaining complete composure, but with firmness in his or her voice and a stern but controlled facial expression, the parent should immediately put a stop to the assault. This can be done effectively by stepping between the two children, and in a calm authoritative voice—while looking the children in the eye—saying, "Stop that now. You may not

> *Gently stop then redirect inappropriate behaviors that cannot be ignored.*

behave that way in this house!" The parent should continue to fix his or her gaze on the children's eyes for a few seconds then in a calm, more relaxed voice say, "I'm sorry you are upset. Go to your room for a few minutes and relax. Lay down on your bed, take several deep breaths, and tell yourself to relax. When you are feeling better and have control of yourself, if you want to talk about it, let's get back together." Say this slowly and deliberately and non-threateningly. Say it in a therapeutic, understanding, relaxed manner. This will give time for the heat of the anger to cool down and to be replaced by reason. Having directed the child as to what to do, you might even place your hand gently on the child's back and move him or her in the direction of the bedroom.

If the child resists this directiveness and angrily lashes back with something like, "He started it! I was minding my own business and he began giving me a bad time! I hate his guts!" Do not try to correct the child or set him straight. Don't say a single word in response to such an out-burst. For goodness sake, *don't* get into a discussion about who's at fault or who started it. Say simply, "I'm sorry you're upset. Something surely must have gone wrong, otherwise you would never have behaved this way. It is so uncharacteristic of you. Please, go to your room and relax. You'll feel much better in a moment."

Such a response will reassure the child that he or she might indeed have a compelling reason for having lashed out at the other child, but the parent realizes that this behavior is not at all characteristic of him. With this reassurance, the probability is very high that the child will go to his room as instructed by the parent, and the whole matter will end there. If, during all of this, the child who was the object of the assault complains about being the innocent victim of a mean brother/sister, the parent should be careful not to try to determine or affix blame, to act as a negotiator to seek redress, or to do anything else to try and set the record straight. Efforts of this nature invariably do nothing but complicate things and drag the conflict on indefinitely. A parent should simply say, "I'm sorry you feel you have been the innocent victim of your sister's anger. You'll feel better soon." Then leave it at that. Later, when everyone is feeling better and emotions have calmed down, look for opportunities to selectively reinforce appropriate behaviors, as we have already discussed. At such a time, it is also appropriate to discuss feelings, but DO NOT allow that discussion to degenerate into fault finding, searching for fairness, placing blame, and all that junk. Use the discussion to clear the air, develop skills, and build bonds. For example:

Parent: "Mary, one of the things I admire about you the most is your ability to control your emotions. That's why this morning when you lashed out at Bill with such anger, I was really taken back. You know, of course, that behaving that way is not at all like you. Are you troubled about something that has you on edge?"

*Note*: The parent has not scolded, accused, threatened, or even warned the child. In fact, the child has been given the benefit of the doubt: "...behaving that way is not at all like you." The total focus of the parent's concern is on the child's well-being: "Are you troubled about something?" Remember, failure to behave well is not a reason to punish and scold. It is an opportunity to teach.

Mary: "Mother, I'm sorry for getting so mad. I'm stressed out, and Billy does those dumb things. I can usually just ignore them but this morning he just got to me. He's such a brat!"

Parent: "I know what you're saying. When a person is on the edge it doesn't take much sometimes to lose one's balance. I'm glad you've got your feelings under control. What can you do in the future if he gets to you again that way? Which he probably will."

*Note*: The parent has shown empathy and understanding, but has ignored the reference to Billy as "a brat." She moved right into problem solving and skill building. She is now about to teach a better way.

Rather than simply stopping inappropriate behavior, teach appropriate behavior.

Mary: "I'll just have to ignore him, Mom. But that's *so* hard to do. I wish I could just vaporize him. You know, Mom, he is such a pain to me that I can honestly say that if he were out of my life completely, I would be sooooo happy. I know that sounds awful, but that's really how I feel!"

Parent: (Smiling) "I know what you're saying. I've had my share of experiences with brothers. Let's pretend that I'm Billy and I've just done one of those dumb, annoying things. Show me what you should do."

*Note*: The parent has put all the age-typical emotions into perspective ("I've had my share of experiences with brothers"), and moved immediately into skill-building.

Mary: "I know, Mom. I just have to walk away. I can do that."

Parent: "That's certainly an important part of what you should do. But in addition to that, I have a couple of suggestions that will help you let Billy know that he hasn't upset you at all. Just knowing that he's gotten to you can be very reinforcing to him. So in addition to just walking away, I'd suggest that when doing that, you remain as casual and undisturbed as can be. Don't look at him in disgust, don't roll your eyes to the ceiling, don't shake your head or use body language or anything that suggests you are the least bit upset. Walk away with a purpose. Let Billy know by what you do that you have other, more important things, to attend to. You might even say to yourself as you walk away, something like, 'Gee, I was supposed to call Tammy 10 minutes ago,' then hurry off. It's called purposeful or planned ignoring. Watch me as I demonstrate it. (Mother role plays the skill.) Now, you do it. (Mary does it.)"

Parent: "You did that very well, Honey. How did it feel?"

Mary: "It seems kind of dumb to go to all this bother just because of a bratty brother, but I can see what you're getting at. It felt okay. I think I can do it—though what I'd really like to do is punch his lights out!"

Parent: "I'm glad it felt comfortable enough that you felt okay doing it. You'll be surprised how well it works, and how much happier you will be knowing you have a skill to use when you're under stress and might otherwise explode. You're a sweet girl, Mary. I love you. Thanks for spending a minute with me on this. It's been fun." (Kiss, hug, smile, wink.)

Mary: "Thanks, Mom. I love you, too."

*Note*: Again, all the age-typical garbage language has been ignored and the focus has stayed on skill development. By having the skill demonstrated, Mary learned that her mother has skills. That's a big plus. Furthermore, Mother let Mary know that she is acquiring skills that can be used elsewhere: "…you have a skill to use when you're under stress…", implying "under stress" anywhere.

Isn't this much better than exploding and reacting in-kind? Too often parents assume, when a child misbehaves, that, "what that kid needs is a good lickin'!" If you ever feel that way, I hope you'll reassess the situation and conclude that "What that child

> *Never try to resolve a problem if a person is drunk, stoned, emotionally distraught, or out of touch with reality.*

needs is a good lesson—in how to behave well, and I'm just the person who knows how to teach it." And when you do that, give yourself a pat on the back, a hearty smile, some affectionate verbal praise, and a gold star on your forehead!

Let's suppose, while in a fit of anger, the child broke something. Again, the parent would immediately stop the violent behavior by moving close to the child and even perhaps holding the child's hands to his sides. (You would not do this, however, if the child was stronger than you and there was a possibility he would physically lash out at you. If that were the case, stick with the use of verbal restraints only.) Looking the child squarely in the eye, and with a stern facial expression and a calm, authoritative voice say, "Stop that! You may not do that. I'm sorry you are angry, but no matter how angry you are you may not destroy things. Now go to your room and relax. When you are feeling better, come back and we will discuss what must be done to make things right." Then send the child to his room. Do not try to resolve the matter when the child is angry. *Never try to resolve a problem if a person is drunk, stoned, emotionally distraught, or out of touch with reality.* Trying to resolve a problem under those conditions only makes things worse. Instead, wait until the child has calmed down and is able to deal with things rationally. At that time, sit down with the child and calmly discuss the problem. You might begin like this:

Parent:     "I'm sorry you were upset and became so angry that you broke the lamp. That was so uncharacteristic of you. Would you care to talk about it?"

*Note*: If a child wants to talk about it that's good, but during the discussion, make sure you are understanding and compassionate, not judgmental, preachy, or full of a lot of advice.

After the matter has been discussed, or even if the child prefers not to discuss it, proceed with what must be done to make things right.

> *Do not allow children to pull you off course over discussions of fairness, blame, and so on.*

Parent:     "As you know, you broke the lamp. We need to come to an agreement on how you will pay to have it replaced. Do you have any suggestions?"

*Note*: As quickly as possible, engage the child in the problem-solving process.

Child:     "Why do I have to pay for it? Other kids break things around their houses and they don't have to pay for it. Just because I broke it because I was mad doesn't mean that I should have to pay for it. This just isn't fair. And after all, that idiot brother of mine started it. You're always picking on me."

*Note*: It isn't unusual for a child to respond this way. People are always trying to figure out ways of avoiding responsibility for their own behavior. It is certainly no different for children. If the child says something like this, respond as follows.

Parent:     "Paying for our mistakes is certainly no fun. In this instance, what suggestions do you have for paying for this breakage?"

*Note*: As I have illustrated before, the parent totally and completely ignores any of the stuff the child says that is designed to relieve her of any responsibility or to pull the conversation off course. The parent simply responds with empathy and then restates the question.

Child:     "Mom, this just isn't fair! Why should I have to pay? No one else ever has to pay! I just don't believe I'm being treated fairly."

Parent: "I'm sorry you feel you are being treated unfairly. What suggestions do you have for paying for this breakage?"

Child: "I don't have any suggestions. I don't even know what it would cost."

*Note*: Now we are getting somewhere. In about 95 times out of 100, if parents will stay the course and not be dragged into an argument with the child over what is right or what is wrong or what is fair or what is unfair, after only two attempts at derailing the conversation, the child will begin to come around. However, if after the *third* time the child is still balking, the parent should terminate the discussion by saying:

Parent: "I can tell you are not ready to discuss this matter yet. I'm ready to discuss it anytime you are. In the mean time…" (At this point indicate a reasonable consequence that will remain in place until the child is ready to discuss the matter to resolution. That consequence might be having to stay home or being denied the privilege of using her bicycle or driving the car or whatever is age-appropriate for the child. When the child is ready to discuss the matter to resolution, proceed as follows.)

Parent: "I'm glad you are ready to discuss this matter and get it resolved. What suggestions do you have for paying for this breakage?"

*Note*: The parent does not scold the child for delaying the discussion or carrying on about what a terrible thing was done. Rather, the child is thanked for being ready to discuss the matter. Remember, attend *only* to those behaviors you want strengthened.

Child: "Well, I guess I could pay for it out of my allowance (or out of what is earned from a paper route, babysitting, a job, or whatever is consistent with the child's ability to pay).

Parent: "Good suggestion. I'll find out what it is going to cost to repay the breakage and then let you know. At that time, we will come to an agreement of some sort on a reasonable pay-back schedule."

> **Consequences should be reasonable.**

*Note*: If it is an irreplaceable item such as an heirloom, an object of art, a gift from another country, or whatever, *some* kind of replacement should be insisted upon. Whatever payment is selected, it should be reasonable and accomplishable by the child. Obviously, the child should not be expected to pay on the thing for the next 4 years of her life. And besides, that is not the point. The point is that this is an opportunity to teach the child a lesson in being responsible for her actions. That is the bottom line. It is more of a learning experience than it is an effort to replace value for value. In the long run, if handled correctly, the lesson learned will be of infinitely greater value than was the object that was damaged or destroyed.

Now to discuss how parents can effectively attend to inappropriate behaviors that are frequently reoccurring, even predictable. First, parents must be able to clearly describe for the child the behavior that can no longer be tolerated. Descriptions like, "You are too mean," or "You've got to shape up," or "We just can't stand the way you have been behaving lately" are not acceptable. You must be very specific. For example:

Parent:     "We've noticed, Son, that every day during the last two weeks you have been using swear words. This is simply not acceptable and must stop. Why is using profanity such an inappropriate thing to do?"

*Note*: The parent didn't ask the child to explain why he swore. Do not ask children to explain their inappropriate behavior. (In Chapter 8, Questioning Children About Their Behavior, I explain in considerable detail why you must never question children about their inappropriate behavior.) It *is* appropriate to ask a child why a behavior is not appropriate since that invites the child to become part of the problem-solving process.

Child:     "I don't know. Everybody at school does it. I didn't think it was such a big deal."

Parent:     "Just because others do it does not mean it is right or good. Think of one reason why you should not swear."

*Note*: The parent did not allow the child to sidetrack the discussion by getting into a discussion about the rightness or wrongness of swearing. The parent stayed on course and simply repeated the question.

Child:     "Well, I guess it is wrong to swear. That's what you've always told me."

Parent:     "Others may not believe it's wrong, but we do and we are happy you know that. And besides, it just doesn't sound good. It makes people think you don't know a better way of expressing yourself. What are some words you can use other than swear words to express yourself?"

*Note*: The child has been briefly reminded about a characteristic of the family value system. An occasional reminder to this effect is good. The child is then invited to further explore a solution.

Child:     "I guess I could say, darn and heck, instead of those other words."

Parent:     "Good answer, Son. Those words are better than swear words. There isn't a single swear word that can't be replaced by a better word. Can you think of anything else you can do other than use swear words?"

*Note*: You will notice that every time the parent spoke, it took only a few seconds to say what was said and ask what was asked. In this last instance, it took less than 15 seconds for the parent to say all that was said. It is very important for parents to keep the child actively engaged in the discussion. It isn't the amount of time parents talk to the child that produces the desired results. It is the amount of time

> *Make children active participants in problem solving matters.*

and number of opportunities the child has to respond and to be actively engaged in the conversation, and exploring solutions that are then reinforced that produce the best results. If children think they are in for a long lecture, they will turn a parent off like a light. They might be looking at the parent and even have a facial expression that suggests they are listening, but their minds can be a million miles away. The best remedy for this is for parents to speak for short periods of time using only a few words and then inviting the youngster into the conversation.

Child:    "Ah, gee, Mom and Dad. This is embarrassing. I know what you are telling me and I will try really hard not to swear around the house any more."

Parent:    "You're right, Son, swearing can cause embarrassment and we are happy you feel that way. We are also happy you have decided not to swear around the house. But we expect you to stop swearing everywhere. What do we mean when we say we want you to stop swearing everywhere?"

*Note*: The parent has selectively reinforced an appropriate response, then expanded on it: "We are happy you have decided not to swear around the house. But we expect you to stop swearing anywhere."

Child:    "Oh, I guess you mean when I'm at school and when I'm with my friends and wherever I am. But that's going to be hard to do! They all swear and I'm going to look weird if I don't swear with them."

Parent:    "We can understand you may feel uneasy at first, but we still expect you to control yourself and to use better language. To use the words you suggested would be good substitutes for swear words. You know what we expect, and that's great. We will just have to trust you to do that when you are away from home. Can we trust you, Son?"

*Note*: The burden of responsibility for cleaning up his language still rests with the child, where it should rest. The parents have acknowledged they can't control his behavior when he is away from home, but they still expect him to behave appropriately. Furthermore, they have committed him to respecting their expectations.

Child:    "Well, I'll try, but it's going to be tough."

Parent:    "Thank you for giving us that assurance, Son. Maybe at the end of each day you can write in a notebook about how successful you were in using better language. And in the morning before you leave the house for school as you go out the door, say to yourself, 'Today I will control my language.' Will you do that?"

*Note*: Self monitoring and self prompting are well established strategies for helping us improve our behavior. They work as well for children as they do for adults.

Child:    "Yeah, I can do that. Is that all you wanted to talk to me about?"

*Note*: Children will often use comments like this that cue parents it's time to stop. If the parents feel their point has been adequately made, well understood, and well responded to, then it probably is time to stop. Stopping before you are entirely through is not always bad. Remember, today is not forever. This is not the last time you will ever have an opportunity to discuss your expectations with your children. It's better to leave a situation with the door open for further discussions.

Parent:    "We are almost done, Son. We need to talk for a minute about what you can expect when you do or don't use swear words around the house. When you control yourself and don't use swear words, you'll be able to continue to enjoy many privileges that you really like around here."

*Today is not forever.*

*Note*: This would be followed by a brief discussion of what those privileges are, as was illustrated earlier. Again, have the child tell you what those privileges are. Once this discussion has been completed, proceed with the discussion of consequences. With predictable, reoccurring behaviors, you will likely need to include in your teaching a discussion of consequences. This is not so much the case with rare, out-of-the-blue behaviors since they are usually not so firmly under the reinforcement control of whatever it is that keeps reoccurring behavior going. For out-of-the-blue behaviors, a simple teaching strategy, as illustrated earlier with Mary and her mother, is usually adequate.

Parent:  "And if you lose control of yourself, Son, what privileges will you deny yourself?"

*Note*: Then follow this up with a discussion of the privileges the child will deny himself, and for how long they will not be available. For a more detailed treatment of this, read Chapter 5, A Word About Consequences.

Another wonderful and marvelously effective strategy for stopping then redirecting behavior in a positive, instructive way is the Teaching Interaction Strategy, also known as the Corrective Teaching Procedure. It was developed as a part of the Achievement Place model, University of Kansas, and is used at Boys Town (historically known as Father Flannagan's Boys Town) near Omaha, Nebraska. The procedure has six steps:

1. Say something positive.
2. Briefly describe the problem behavior.
3. Describe the desired alternative behavior.
4. Give a reason why the new behavior is more desirable.
5. Practice the desired behavior.
6. Provide positive feedback.

The procedure works equally well in school and home settings. The following two examples, provided by Dr. Richard Young of the College of Education, Utah State University, illustrate how the procedure works:

*Example 1:* Jim fails to follow his teacher's direction.

1. "Jim, I like having you in class. You always give good answers to my questions."
2. "Just now when I asked you to sit down and listen to the lesson, you continued to talk to Bill."

3.  "When I ask you to do something, you need to look at me, say okay or nod, and do it immediately."

4.  "When you follow my directions, our class is a better place to learn for you and for everyone else in it."

5.  "Jim, what are the three things you should do when I give you an instruction?" (Jim says, "Look at you, say okay, and do it.") If Jim doesn't respond, prompt him. If he responds inappropriately, repeat the question without displaying anger. Then say, "Let's practice. I'll ask you to fold your arms and look at me, and you show me the correct way to follow my instructions."

6.  Praise Jim's correct responses and prompt him to redo any steps omitted or done incorrectly. For example, "Jim, you did a great job. You looked at me and folded your arms immediately, but you forgot to say okay. Let's try it again, and this time remember to do all three steps." (Jim responds correctly the second time.) Teacher says, "Great! That time you looked at me you said okay and you folded your arms."

Although this procedure may appear cumbersome at first, it will soon become natural as it is applied consistently. This procedure is easily adapted to home settings, as the following example illustrates.

*Example 2:* Bill (age 13) calls Ralph (age 15) a derogatory name, and Ralph responds by knocking Bill down and hitting him. After separating the two young men, the parent teaches Ralph a better way to solve the problem with the following corrective teaching episode:

1.  "Ralph, I know that it really hurts when someone calls you a name,"

2.  "But you responded to Bill by fighting."

3.  "A better way to handle name calling would be to walk away."

4.  "By walking away, you won't get in trouble for fighting, and Bill will probably forget about it. Then it won't damage your friendship."

5.  "Ralph, next time someone calls you a name, how do you think you can handle it?" (Response, "I'll try to walk away.")

6.  "That's great, Ralph. Even though it might be really hard, it will be easier for you in the long run."

(Note: a similar episode would need to be conducted with Bill regarding name calling.)

The major difference between the treatment of occasional, one-time, out-of-the-blue behaviors and predictable on-going behaviors is the extent to which solutions are explored and consequences are clarified. However, the treatment is similar in one important aspect: In both instances, once a solution to the problem has been discussed, it is very important for parents to keep a keen eye open for opportunities to acknowledge and reinforce selected appropriate behaviors that indicate that parental expectations are being met. This gets behavior going in the right direction, and keeps it going in the right direction. We call that behavioral momentum.

> *Reinforce behaviors that reflect parental expectations.*

Several years ago, as Louise and I were watching our child-rearing years come to a close, we found ourselves living with three young adults still living at home—our three youngest children. They were all busy, dashing here and there, and eating on the run. It suddenly occurred to me that every day, without fail, Louise and I were gathering up and cleaning dishes and eating utensils from throughout the house. The problem was highly predictable, so I decided to take data on it. After 6 days, I was confident I had an accurate assessment of the problem, so I put my graph of the 6 days of data, accompanied by a note stating my expectations, on the kitchen cupboard where the kids were all sure to see it (see Figure 3.1). Aside from this, Louise and I never said a word to the kids. Each day thereafter for 19 days I plotted the data, intermittently leaving notes on the cupboard door by the graph (as shown below the graph on Figure 3.1). Notice what happened on June 13th. This was the predictable "regression to baseline" phenomenon discussed earlier on pages 24–26. I didn't allow that to deter me. We just stuck with the program, and you can see the results. Although the problem was never completely eliminated, it was reduced to a tolerable level. To have completely eliminated the problem would have required either eliminating my kids, or making home such an aversive environment that they would have fled (which is essentially the same as eliminating the kids!).

In addition to the effect the treatment had on the problem behavior, it introduced a lot of humor into the family. We got a lot of good laughs out of it. It is quite possible to solve problems in the home and have fun at it.

> *It is quite possible to solve problems at home and have fun at it.*

## RULE 5: Stay close to your children.

As children grow from infancy through childhood and into adolescence, we notice some interesting things happening in the way parents interact with them. What we notice

## Figure 3.1—Reducing Thoughtless, Untidy Behaviors

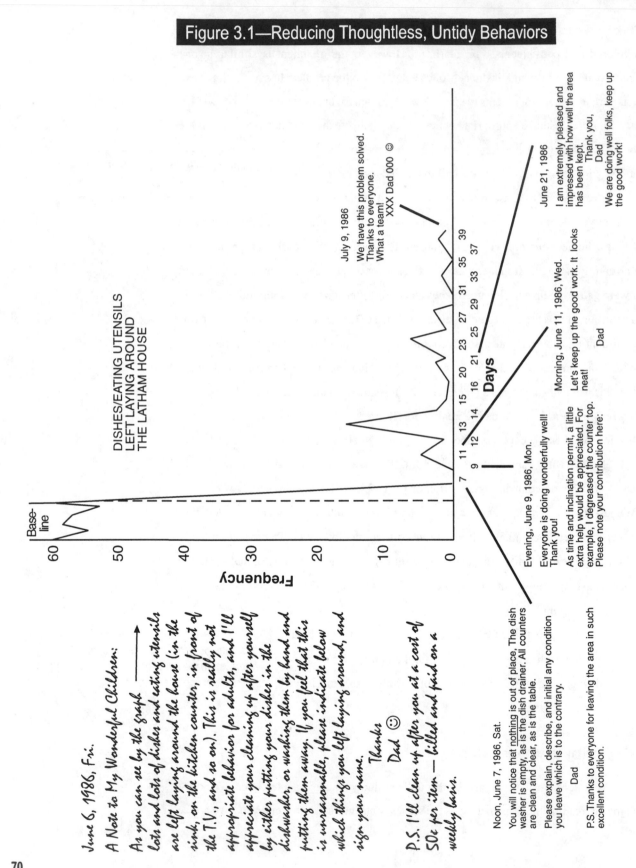

is a bit distressing, given the effects these things have on putting distance between parents and their children. Parents spend a great deal of time holding newborn babies close and cuddling them, stroking them, talking to them, looking into their eyes, poking them with their fingers, smiling at them, and trying to invoke smiles and laughter. But by the time children are adolescents, particularly boys, there is a remarkable decline in the frequency of touching, hugging, patting, or poking. There is very little shooting the breeze, chitchat, and casual talk, and in many homes, almost no laughter. The incidence of smiling has even taken a nose dive.

We know that how much influence a parent has on a child's behavior is directly related to the proximity of the parent to the child. In other words, the closer parents are to their children the greater the influence they can have on them. This, of course, is particularly true with young children who are still at home, but it is true, as well, with children who are raised and out of the home. In this section, I have several suggestions for how to remain verbally and physically close to our children.

## Remaining Verbally Close to Your Children

It wasn't until my children were nearly raised that I came to realize how important it is to maintain close verbal contact with them. It came on a winter day when my youngest son and I were returning from a day of skiing. It had been a wonderful day together. We skied and talked and skied and talked all day long. I was a bit surprised that my boy spent so much time on the slopes with me since he was so much better than I was and could certainly have had a more exciting time by joining some of his friends in the wilderness areas where I never dared to go. While driving home together that evening, my son said to me, "Dad, do you know why I asked you instead of a date to go skiing with me?" "No," I answered, "but I'm glad you did because I had a wonderful time being with you." "Well, I'll tell you," he said. "It's because I needed to talk to you about things I can't talk to a date about." I hadn't recalled talking about anything that was at all heavy. We just shot the breeze, laughed, and kidded around. We made a little ski jump out of packed snow, talked about the thrill he experienced jumping off it, and laughed about how I almost killed myself the one time I jumped off it. For the most part, I couldn't recall any particular thing we had talked about. But we did talk. Sometimes we talked loudly as we called to one another across the ski slopes. Sometimes we talked softly as we shot the breeze across the table during lunchtime in the lodge. But for the most part, it was just talk, small talk. At the time I had no idea how much that talk meant to my son. To this day, I'm sure he has no idea how much it meant to me.

As I have worked with families over the years, I have been impressed with concerns expressed to me by sons and daughters about how little they just talk with their parents about things that on the surface don't really seem to mean a lot. So often they tell me, "The only time my parents really talk to me is when they want to know where I'm going or where I've been or why I spent so much money or why I used up so much gas in the car or why I did this or why I didn't do that. We never just talk about things." Do you know what they mean when they say "just things?" Well, I'll tell you, Mom and Dad. "Just things" means talking to your kids without giving them advice, without teaching them something, without addressing some great moral issue, without being judgmental, or without setting the record straight. It means talking without telling, sometimes talking without saying anything.

A teenage boy was in my office recently and I asked, "What do you talk to your parents about?" He answered, "We don't talk much." I asked, "Why not?" He answered, "Because no matter what we start talking about, it always ends up in an argument about what I'm not doing right. It doesn't matter what we start talking about, it *always* ends up with a discussion about what I need to do better. I need to do better in school. I need to work harder around the house. I need to keep my room cleaner. I need to dress better and comb my hair better. It just isn't worth it to me, so we just don't talk." Parents, no matter how tempted or inclined you are to weave "talk" into a discussion about how your children could be better if they would just do this or just do that, don't do it. Carefully follow this advice (which is given full-page attention at the end of this chapter):

## Unless what you are about to say or do has a high probability of making things better, don't say it and don't do it.

> *Don't judge, sermonize, moralize, instruct, reason, or advise—just talk!*

Parents, just talk. Don't judge, don't sermonize, don't moralize, don't instruct, don't reason, don't advise—just talk. This doesn't mean there will never be times when you will advise or instruct, but make those separate occasions when that is what the occasion is for. The following situations illustrate what I mean. They give examples (in the left column) of how to just talk, and (in the column on the right) how to really mess up an otherwise good talk.

## Situation #1: Defending a Friend

| | **How To Just Talk** | **How To Really Mess Up An Otherwise Good Talk** |
|---|---|---|
| Daughter: | I really feel bad for Helen. She's pregnant and her boy friend doesn't want to have anything to do with her anymore. | I really feel bad for Helen. She's pregnant and her boy friend doesn't want to have anything to do with her anymore. |
| Mom: | She must really feel terrible. I'm certainly proud of you, Honey, for being so concerned about her. What can we do to help her? | Well, it was bound to happen. Just a matter of time. Play with fire and you get burned. I'm not the least bit surprised, nor do I feel sorry for her. She knew what she was getting into when she got mixed up with that loser. Just don't you get involved. Stay clear of her. It's her problem. Let her solve it. |
| Daughter: | I don't know, Mom. It's so complex. But I am going to keep being her friend. | Mom! How can you say that? Helen's a neat gal. She just made a mistake. No one is perfect! Not you *or* me. Don't be so hard on her. |
| Mom: | Good for you. A true friend is worth more than gold. Certainly that's so in situations like this. You're a good girl, Honey. I love you. | Neat girls don't go to bed with dumb guys. You bet she made a mistake, and she'll pay for it the rest of her life. As for you, young lady, don't you dare do a stupid thing like that. |
| Daughter: | I love you, Mom. It's so great talking to you—even about difficult things like this. You really understand. | I can't believe you, Mother! (as she leaves in a huff). |

## Situation #2: Defending Himself

| | How To Just Talk | How To Really Mess Up An Otherwise Good Talk |
|---|---|---|
| Dad: | That was quite a ball game last night. Your school really pulled it out of the fire in those last few minutes. | That was quite a ball game last night. Your school really pulled it out of the fire in those last few minutes. |
| Son: | Yeah. Squeaky, our point guard, was really hot. | Yeah. Squeaky, our point guard, was really hot. |
| Dad: | Indeed he was. And besides his ball handling skills, I understand he's a fine young man. | Indeed he was. And besides his ball handling skills, I understand he's an excellent student who hits the books like crazy every night. What kind of GPA does he have to maintain to stay on the team? |
| Son: | He really is. He's in a couple of my classes and he's super friendly. | He is a good student. I have some classes with him and he does well. He has to keep at least a C+ average to be on the team. |
| Dad: | The next time you see him, tell him what a great job I thought he did in that game. | I'm amazed he does so well with all of his athletic responsibilities. By the way, what's your GPA this year? |
| Son: | I'll do that. He'll be happy to hear it. | I don' know for sure. Somewhere between a C and a C+. |
| Dad: | Let me know when the next ball game is. Maybe we can go together. | Now, Son, you can surely do better than that. Surely you have more time to study than Squeaky does. I |

|  |  | mean with the amount of time you have, you should have a solid B average—or better! |
|------|------|------|
| Son: | I'll do it, Dad. Sounds fun. | I'm doing all right in school. I'm passing. What's the big deal? |
| Dad: | I'll look forward to that. | Just passing! I know you can do better than that. If a kid on the basketball team can do it, you can. You're just as smart as Squeaky. |
| Son: | Me, too. I gotta run, Dad. See ya. | Hey, what's this all about? What has Squeaky got to do with me. He lives his life and I live mine, and that's *just* how I want it! |
| Dad: | So long, Son. Have a good time. Take care. Love you. | I'll tell you what it's all about. It's about your life. Without decent grades it's the end of school for you. Just look at Squeaky. I'll bet he not only gets accepted to college, but he'll get an athletic scholarship as well. He's got his head on straight. You could use a little of that head-on-straight stuff, young man! |
| Son: | Love you, too, Dad. See ya. | Forget it. I'm outta here. I don't need this crap! |

I clipped an article out of my local newspaper that was titled "Unfavorite lines that parents say." Here are a few that several teenagers mentioned. Parents, avoid this kind of junk like a plague:

"Who said life was fair?"

"You just don't know how lucky you are!"

"Don't try to hide things from us because we're going to find them sooner or later."

"I pulled the same stunt with *my* parents, so it's not going to work for you."

"You want to try what?"

"There are kids in other countries who have it worse off than you do."

"Whatever happened to that nice, sweet, feminine girl you used to be?"

"Apologize to your sister!"

"When I was a little girl, I used to clean up the whole kitchen."

"This hurts me more than it does you."

"Do you want a smack?" To which the girl added, "I would love to say (sarcastically, of course): 'As a matter of fact, I want you to do me bodily harm!'"

To help parents increase the level, and improve the quality, of their verbal interactions with their children, here are a few do-able suggestions.

1.  Keep a 3 x 5 card and a pencil handy and make notes of the things you hear your children talking about or expressing interest in. When you hear them talking to their friends or to one another, quietly make note of the things they talk about. The topics they bring up on their own and spend time talking about provide you with the best clues available about what is of interest to them. If you need to, bone up on some of those topics so you can discuss them at least somewhat knowledgeably. Then when the time is right—at the dinner table, sitting around the living room, driving in the car together or whatever—casually bring up a topic and start talking about it. Remember, just talk. Leave the lessons for another time.

2.  Talk to your children in a very natural way. Make sure it doesn't come across as a formal discussion. The character of the conversation should be one of just shooting the breeze.

3.  Don't try to be too "hip" as you talk to children. Avoid the use of terms and language the kids use. Use terms that are most familiar to you and the most characteristic of you, but which the kids understand. Kids don't like it when their parents try to talk like kids. It turns them off, and it embarrasses them when

you do it in front of their friends.

4.  Watch for signs that tell you you've talked long enough. Ordinarily, conversations with children about "just things" don't usually last very long. For that matter, kids don't typically spend very long talking with their friends about such things. They bounce around from topic to topic, and thing to thing, never spending much time on anything or going into much depth. When you pick up cues that tell you the child is losing interest in the topic or in the conversation, gracefully bow out by moving on to other things.

5.  Keep the conversation dignified. Avoid gossip, profanity, off-color jokes, or turns-of-phrase that compromise your adult level of dignity and civility. Remain a cut above "just one of the guys." Children want their parents to have class. They want their parents to be someone to look up to. The quality of your conversations with them can go a long way in establishing that image of you in your children's eyes. An occasional, appropriate joke is a very good thing. While the family is gathered around the dinner table is a wonderful time to share a good joke and bring a little humor into the family. In my family, they are called, "Dad jokes," with "Dad" being somewhat equated with corny.

6.  Avoid ethnic jokes or any kind of joke or story that puts another person or another people down or that evokes humor at the expense of someone else. Maintain your dignity as an adult by showing respect for other cultures. Children really appreciate that.

7.  End the conversation with a brief up-beat parting statement: "It was fun talking to you about that, Son. It was really interesting." Or, "Thanks for visiting with me, Honey. It's always nice to just shoot the breeze with you." These kinds of statements help to assure the child you are a safe person to talk to and will keep the door open for subsequent conversations. But best of all, they will invite the children to come to you to talk about serious matters when they really need your help.

Regarding jokes, appropriate, clean humor is a characteristic of low-risk families. In such families there is a lot of smiling, laughing and lots of happy times. The curative effects of humor are well documented by the work of Norman Cousins and his "Anatomy of an Illness." A few good laughs every day is a great approach to keeping physically and behaviorally well. Come to the dinner table every night with a couple of good jokes. You'll learn in a hurry just how beneficial humor is for a family! During a hearty laugh, your throat goes into uncoordinated spasms, sending blasts of air out of your mouth at 70 miles an hour. Your body starts pumping adrenaline; your heart rate increases and your brain releases endorphins and enkephalins (natural painkillers). As your lungs pump out carbon dioxide, your eyes cleanse themselves with tears, and your muscles relax and lose their tenseness. It's actually pretty good exercise. Laughter is also good for your concept of self. Jimmy Durante, the great American comedian with the ponderous nose, who was known affectionately as "the Schnoz," was miserable as a boy because of his looks. He learned, however, that he was able, through humor, to turn what otherwise was a deficit into a great asset. Later in life he observed, "When I learned to laugh at myself, I knew I was safe from the world." What a great way to look at life, and at one's self!

In addition to the positive effects parent-child chitchat has on families there is some impressive research being reported in the study of verbal behavior that shows a direct relationship between verbal skills and social behavior. In other words, children who learn good verbal skills are more likely to also have good social skills, and the implications of that are simply immense!

Parents, spend time talking to your children. Model good verbal behavior. Teach your children through example and involvement how to express themselves, how to listen, and how to engage in conversation one with another. That is among one of the

> *Children who learn good verbal skills are more likely to also have good social skills.*

greatest skills you'll ever teach your children. It will keep them close to you for your entire lives. A young mother was recently in my office distraught over her relationship with her parents. "I go home to visit my parents and we just sit there looking at each other, or watching TV. We really have nothing to talk about. I'm not sure we even know how to talk to each other." (I might add, parenthetically, that she was also having trouble "just talking" to her husband.) Verbal skills are learned, and parents have the first responsibility to teach them to their children.

## Increasing Appropriate Physical Interactions

The skin is the largest organ of the body, unfurling to about 20 square feet for a person weighing 150 pounds. It weighs more than any other organ of the body and contains more nerve endings than all the other organs of the body put together. For a great majority of people, it loves to be hugged, rubbed, and scratched. Unfortunately, as children, especially boys, grow older, being hugged by parents, especially fathers, decreases dramatically. This is too bad. My number three daughter had the following sign on her bedroom wall:

**Four hugs a day for survival**

**Eight hugs a day for maintenance**

**Twelve hugs a day for growth**

If my wife and I did anything right at all in raising our children, it was that we took every opportunity to hug them. To this day, as adults, we still do a lot of hugging. Recently, our oldest son met me at the airport near the town where he lives. He's a big boy, standing a good 6 to 7 inches taller than me. Though the terminal was crowded with people, he hurried to me, unashamedly threw his arms around me, gave me a big hug and a kiss and told me that he loved me. That was pay day for Dad.

Not only does hugging feel good, but it's good for you. There is a growing scientific literature about the beneficial effects to our general health and well-being from hugging. Some parents have told me, "I just can't hug that kid. He looks so bad." To which I respond, "Then close your eyes while you're hugging." Others have complained, "I don't like to hug my kid because he/she smells so bad." To which I respond, "Then just don't breath in while you are hugging." There is not one, single, solitary, reasonable excuse for not hugging your

> *Not only does hugging feel good, it's good for you.*

kids, no matter how old they are, how bad they look, or how awful they smell. I read a really touching article that reported briefly on the work of Dr. Melvin Morse, a Seattle pediatrician, who has extensively studied the near-death experiences of children. One account involved a 7-year-old girl who, on the threshold of death, chose to return to mortality and to her family. "I decided I wanted to go back." She said, "I thought about my mom and about never being able to hug her again." Think about that one, Mom and Dad!

In addition to hugging, appropriate touching, tapping, rubbing, patting, scratching, and jabbing are wonderful ways of communicating with our children. Arm wrestling, playfully scrapping on the playing field, a good back and shoulder rub at the end of the day—this is the glue that binds. Of course, it goes without saying that all of this contact should be appropriate, proper, and wholesome *beyond any shadow of a doubt*. The U.S. Surgeon General recently published a 5,234 page report in which researchers concluded the following: "Hugging is non-fattening, naturally sweet, and contains no artificial ingredients. It is wholesome and pure and, most important, fully returnable." A study recently published by the University of Miami revealed that drug-addicted babies who were regularly massaged had a significantly higher survival rate, and were able to leave the hospital 6 days earlier than babies who had not been regularly massaged.

If hugging is something you haven't been doing with your children, ease into it. Rather than starting off with great big bear hugs, begin with a pat on the shoulder, a warm pat on the back, a stroking of the fingers across the shoulders, a gentle touch on the arm, or squeeze of a hand. It can become so wonderful. There is no feeling that I love more than the soft, smooth cheeks of my daughters', or the rough stubbled cheeks of my sons', against my cheek. It is altogether appropriate to accompany every greeting and every parting with a hug and a kiss. Make it a rule for every day you are with your children. It is a rule my wife and I have observed in our relationship with one another. Though at times our children would express embarrassment at our hugging and kissing in their presence, they loved it, and they still love it. It is a great model for your children and will serve them well for a lifetime of marriage and parenting. Recalling the observation of Dr. Brent Miller, College of Family Life, Utah State University, "Female teenagers involved in sexual activity are more likely to have strained relations with their families...and view...their parent's marriage as being less close and warm."

It is altogether appropriate to accompany every greeting and every parting with a hug and a kiss.

In this chapter I have addressed several very specific things parents can do to create a healthy environment in the home and to establish and maintain a healthy relationship with their children. Everything suggested in this chapter can be done without any formal training or special expertise.

For any number of reasons, however, some behaviors and some environments are so difficult that their treatment needs exceed the skills and resources of most parents; hence, they go beyond what I have covered here. For example, autism is a disabling condition that is very difficult to treat without professional help. (In fact, it is sometimes difficult to treat *with* professional help!)

In addition, abusive parents, years of deprivation, and psychological trauma are just a few of the plethora of conditions that can produce behavior problems so severe that professional, including clinical, treatment might be necessary.

What is discussed in this book, though altogether appropriate for children with severe behavior problems, might not be altogether sufficient in some particularly difficult situations. This is not a manual for the clinical treatment of severe emotional or behavioral problems. It is more a "well child"/prevention/first aid manual. Its first intent is to shape healthy behavior and to keep age-typical behaviors from becoming unhealthy. Figure 3.2 illustrates my point. On the left is the typical, well understood medical treatment model. On the right is a parallel behavior treatment model. As with medical treatment, we hope that behavioral treatment and first aid will be sufficient to keep our children well. But, for one reason or another, children sometimes get "sick" and treatment demands skills beyond our abilities as lay people. For example, if a child cuts his finger we clean it, put a bandage on it, show compassion, kiss it better, and the healing process is well on its way. However, if the child's hand is lacerated with an ugly wound, is bleeding profusely, and vulnerable to infection, a parent would be irresponsible to simply put a bandage on it, show compassion, and kiss it better. Providing professional medical attention would be the only responsible thing for the parent to do. And so it is with behavior. Applying the principles and employing the strategies discussed here are generally adequate for treating the age-typical, day-to-day behaviors of children. However, when children are threatening or attempting suicide, tampering with controlled substances, flagrantly defying parental expectations, repeatedly running amuck of the law, showing unusual signs of withdrawal and depression, or exhibiting neurotic and psychotic behaviors, parents should seek professional help—and the sooner the better! A behavioral injury or "disease" is no less worthy of professional treatment than is a physical injury or disease. Also, as with medicine, occasionally one's behavioral health will be so damaged that there will be no treatment effect, even after the best, most well-administered efforts. But this is rare, compared to the successes that can be expected when good medicine (including behavioral medicine) is skillfully administered.

## NOW TO REVIEW

By strategically applying sound principles of behavior, parents can greatly increase the probability that their children's growth and development will progress in the right direction, and life in the family will be remarkably better. The following parenting rules are recommended:

1. Clearly communicate to your children those behaviors that will get your attention.
2. Ignore inconsequential behaviors.
3. Selectively reinforce appropriate behaviors.
4. Stop then redirect inappropriate behaviors.

## Figure 3.2—Parallel Treatment Models

| Medical Model | Parenting Model |
| --- | --- |
| **Good Health Practices** (Prevention) | **Good Parenting Practices** (Prevention) |
| **Medical First Aid** | **Behavioral First Aid** |
| **Professional Attention of a Physician:**<br><br>• by phone<br><br>• in the office<br><br>• out-patient care<br><br>• hospitalization | **Professional Attention of a Therapist:**<br><br>• by phone<br><br>• in the office<br><br>• out-patient care<br><br>• hospitalization |
| **No Treatment Effect** | **No Treatment Effect** |

5.   Stay close to your children verbally and physically.

The remaining pages of this chapter contain items I encourage you to pay careful attention to. There are some wonderful, wonderful messages there. I encourage you to use the last one as a cue to you to have lots and lots of positive interactions with your children. Make a copy of it and tape it to your bathroom mirror as a constant reminder.

> *Research has shown that the most effective way to reduce problem behavior in children is to strengthen desirable behavior through positive reinforcement rather than trying to weaken undesirable behavior using aversive or negative processes.*
> *S.W. Bijou*
> *The International Encyclopedia of Education, 1988*

## Code for Parents

The boys at a youth correction center were asked for clues as to why they had ended up in that institution, and were then asked to draw up a code for parents. Here it is:

- **Keep cool.** Keep the lid on when things go wrong. Kids need to see how much better things turn out when people keep their tempers under control.

- **Don't get strung out** from too much booze or too many pills. When we see our parents reaching for those crutches, we get the idea that nobody goes out there alone and that it's perfectly okay to reach for a bottle or a capsule when things get heavy. Children are great imitators. We lose respect for parents who tell us to behave one way while they behave in another.

- **Bug us a little.** Be strict. Show us who's boss. We need to know we've got some strong supports under us. When you cave in, we get scared.

- **Don't blow your class.** Stay on that pedestal. Don't try to dress, dance, or talk like your kids. You embarrass us, and you look ridiculous.

- **Light a candle.** Show us the way. We need to believe in something bigger and stronger than ourselves.

- **Scare us.** If you catch us lying, stealing, or being cruel, get tough. Let us know why what we did was wrong. Impress on us the importance of not repeating such behavior.

- **When we need punishment**, dish it out. But let us know you still love us, even though we have let you down. It will make us think twice before we make that same move again.

- **Call our bluff.** Make it clear you mean what you say. Stand up to us, and we'll respect you. Kids don't want everything they ask for.

- **Be honest.** Tell us the truth, no matter what. Be the straight-arrow about everything. We can take it. We can smell uncertainty a mile away.

- **Praise us when we deserve it.** If you give us kids a few compliments once in a while, we will be able to accept criticism a lot easier!

---

# NOTE:
## Unless what you are about to say or do has a high probability for making things better, don't say it— don't do it.

## An ounce of *don't say it* is worth a pound of *I didn't mean it.*

*Glenn Latham*
*1994*

---

When Laura gets her home-
work done,
tell her what a good job she
did.

Tell Karen how much you appreciate her
kindness to others.

Don't wait
until children misbe-
have.

Give Roxanne a hug
for working so hard.

Describe what Philip
did well.

Verbally
praise Allen.

Catch Julie being good.

*"Triumph over nature and over oneseslf,
yes. But over others, never."*
  B. F. Skinner

# FOUR
# On Being In Control

As children grow older, and as the number of children in a family increases, parents tend to feel a gradual, incessant loss of control. Scarcely a week goes by but what a parent doesn't tell me in emotional, agonizing, desperate tones, "My kids are out of control. I'm helpless. I don't know what to do!" I consider this to be one of the major problems in families today: the feeling among parents that they are standing on the sidelines, helpless, as their kids romp helter-skelter over them.

Although a certain amount of disorder and lack of control is to be expected—after all, kids shouldn't be puppets on a string, and there is something to be learned from making poor decisions—parents do have a great responsibility to exercise reasonable control in the home. If the parents aren't in control, there is typically no control. Without a reasonable level of control, kids are left to the mercy of the worst that society has to offer. It's no wonder parents feel desperate when they say to me, "My kids are out of control. I'm helpless. I don't know what to do!"

> **If the parents aren't in control, there is typically no control.**

The bright side to this otherwise gloomy scene is that parents *can* be in control. They aren't necessarily the hapless victims of a naturally hopeless situation. It's always thrilling to me to see the change in parents when they learn the skills that put them in control in their homes. I recall the parents of a family of four children who described to me one desperate situation after another. The mother was crying, and the father's brow was wrinkled in agony. After about 45 minutes, the parents had pretty much covered everything. As they finished, they seemed to be surprised—at least curious—that I wasn't caught up in the same grip of hopelessness. What I heard was anything but a hopeless situation. Easily 90% of what was described to me was garden-variety, growing-up weed behavior that should have simply been ignored. The remaining 10% was easily manageable. By the time the visit ended, the parents were happy, hopeful, and after a few days of working with their children—using a better way—the parents were well on their way to having an environment in the home that was under their control. Not only are the parents happier, the kids are happier, too. Whereas before the parents were desperate and without skills, in the end they had skills and were in control.

In this chapter, I describe very specific things parents can do to create a home environment that is under their control—not under the control of children. I call it *proactive* management. Notice, again the emphasis is on parental management of the environment, not simply the control of kids. When parents learn to proactively manage the environment of their homes—which is really all they can be expected to manage—behavior of the children will respond accordingly. That's not to say that influences outside of the home will not affect the behavior of children. They will! But managing those out-of-home influences can be next to impossible. You have your hands full managing the environment inside your homes. But when you accomplish that, when you manage the home environment with reasonable means, you have created a proactive environment. My wife, Louise, said it all recently when she observed, "First, we must control our own behavior. Next, we must control the environment in our home. After we've done this, the children control themselves."

> *A proactive environment is a positive, supportive, reinforcing environment that is under parental control.*

A proactive environment is a positive, supportive, reinforcing environment that is under parental control. Most home environments, as illustrated by Figure 4.1, are reactive. That is, members of the family react in kind to one another's behavior, the result being that the moods that are brought into the home by members of the family, moods that are driven by outside influences, tend to be the moods that *control* the environment because they are what family members attend to. For example, a member of the family comes home and is upset. Being out of sorts, that family member does and says things that annoy others. Rather than simply ignoring that inappropriate behavior, family members react to it in kind. They say things that are negative, condemning, judgmental, sarcastic, and so on, things that are on the same low level of civility as what set them off.

## Figure 4.1—Parents' Reactive vs. Proactive Responding

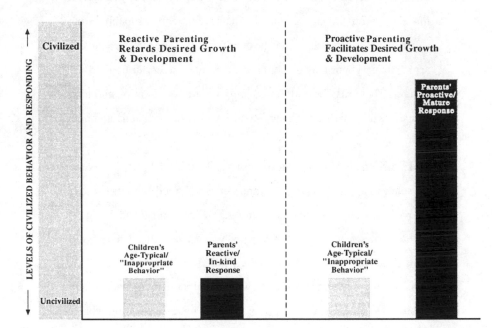

These negative reactions get attention and the cycle continues until before long there is a terrible explosion of behavior in the home and people are screaming, hollering, crying, and stomping around and the whole environment has been destroyed. It doesn't need to be that way! By creating a proactive environment, the negative and out-of-sorts moods that members of the family bring into the home soon yield to the positive, stable mood that is established by the parents. Since behavior typically follows that which pays attention to it, the inappropriate, undesirable behaviors are left unattended and soon die away. On the other hand, since a proactive environment is a positive and supportive one, appropriate behaviors are the ones that get attention and are the ones that grow, thrive, and increase.

Homes tend to be reactive because parents don't really know a better way of establishing and maintaining a positive, supportive, constructive home environment. Most people have been raised in homes that were reactive and that's the model they follow in their own homes. In this chapter I describe four things parents can do to maintain a proactive environment in the home, and how to protect the home from the negative behaviors that are so threatening to the harmony parents want there. A beautiful example of being proactive is described in "The Pause That Refreshes:"

> I am the father of a large family. I go home tired from the routine of busy days. Before I cross the threshold I pause. I reflect for just a moment to remember what may be inside. Someone probably broke a dish. The carpet sweeper may be out of order. There may be a broken arm. The neighbor may be phoning us about a paper our boy did not deliver. There may be children to jump on me for attention and love (maybe with jam on their hands) to tell me the important happenings of the day.

> So I pause and repeat a prayer something like this: "Oh, Lord, may my presence in this home bring faith and a cheerful good evening to those I love. May my homecoming strengthen this home and bring us together, not tear us apart. Keep my voice even, that I may build confidence and respect in me as their father and their friend."

> This is the "pause that refreshes." I walk in prepared to act, happily and positively—not to react in an unbalanced way. It is amazing what it will do for me. We can try this not only in the home but also in a meeting that promises to be tense in which human relations are bristling.

> The "pause that refreshes" is the priceless moment when we root the center of emotional gravity within us where it belongs, rather than in the social climate into which we are going.

> Let us try the "pause that refreshes" plan. It will give us power and influence as fathers, mothers, and leaders.

> Author Unknown

That's so great!

So often—too often!—as I observe parents interacting with their children, I see them reacting in ways that are totally out of

> The plaster need be no wider than the sore.

balance with the behavior that is being reacted to. I see little, essentially inconsequential behaviors being reacted to with a degree of intensity that is completely out of proportion to the behavior. A child will do the slightest little thing and the parent jumps all over the child screaming, hollering, and carrying on in a way that is far worse than anything the child did. A child at the grocery store steps the slightest bit out of line and the parent grabs him by the arm and harshly jerks him back, while at the same time giving him an undeserved tongue lashing. It's like using cannons to kill gnats. It's this unevenness and lack of balance that has to be eliminated. Think of it in terms of treating a physical wound. If a child scratches his knee, you don't put a cast on it. You put a little medicine and a bandage on it. The medicine and the bandage are equal to the size of the sore. A small scratch will require only a small amount of medicine and a small bandaid. The use of a cast is reserved for a more serious injury. There must be balance in the treatment.

To control and be in control we must carefully think in terms of prevention, endurance, and treatment.

Table 4.1 summarizes what follows.

## Table 4.1—Comparing the physical and the behavioral self

| Caring By | The Physical Self | The Behavioral Self |
|---|---|---|
| Prevention | Eat well, get plenty of rest, exercise, think well, follow the basic rules of good health. | Be positive, acknowledge good behavior, laugh and smile a lot, follow the basic rules of "proactive" living. |
| Endurance | Don't allow yourself to rush after professional treatment with every ache, pain, and discomfort common to everyday living. Ignore them and go on with life. The aches and pains will likely get no worse and might even go away and life will be none the worse because of them. | Don't allow yourself to chase after every annoying bothersome, age-typical behavior of children. Ignore them and go on with your life. Ignored, they will likely go away and life will be none the worse—in fact usually better—because they were simply left alone. |

| Caring by | The Physical Self | The Behavioral Self |
|---|---|---|
| Treatment: As first aid | If the malady persists, attend to it as simply and directly as possible. Whenever possible, stick with common household treatments: aspirin, cold medicine, bandages, salves, and ointments. Use sparingly. | If the behavior persists attend to it as simply and directly as possible. Be in complete control, be positive, have a plan, be proactive. |
| As outpatient care | Treatment might require a temporary restriction of life activities (e.g. crutches, casts, canes, bed rest). Prescription medication might be required, as well as a daily measurement of vital signs. | Treatment requires record keeping, and a more intensive application of contingencies and consequences which might be temporarily restrictive: use of the car, watching TV, riding one's bike, being in time-out, and so on. |
| As intensive care | Treatment requires a fully controlled environment (such as hospitalization) where the patient/child is subject to the requirements, conditions, and contingencies of that environment. There is a regular monitoring of vital signs, and changes in behavior, with treatment adjusted accordingly. | |

## PREVENTION

Physical ills and misfortunes can be largely prevented by eating well, keeping out of our body those things which would harm it, getting plenty of rest and proper exercise, following the basic rules of safety, watching for important danger signs, thinking well of ourselves, and so on. These are all very positive proactive things, and when we practice them, we heighten the probability that we will be in good physical health.

By the same token, there are preventative things we can do which remarkably heighten the probability that we will have a healthy home and pleasant, even delightful, relationships with our children. We do this, as I have noted earlier, by going out of our way to be positive in our interactions with our children, by acknowledging their good behavior, and by clearly communicating to our children what it is we expect of them; then, when they meet those expectations, we pay attention to that behavior. There is *no* better way to establish a positive, supportive, constructive environment in the home than by being positive, supportive, and constructive in our interactions with one another in

> *You will never beat, scream or shout your children into good behavior!*

the family. There Is No Better Way! You will never *beat* goodness and good sense into your kids. You will never be successful at shouting and screaming happiness and compliance into their lives.

These are all counterproductive, coercive, reactive, destructive behaviors that will, in time, breed sick countercoercive behaviors in the lives of family members, behaviors which will one day require intensive and costly treatment. Here are what I call my four "Rules of the Day." I have found them to be effective ways to be in positive control of the home environment. I call them "Rules of the *Day*" because each one of them should be practiced every day.

1. Catch every member of your family doing something right, appropriate, or pleasant. Keep a keen eye out for opportunities to acknowledge good behavior. Never let a day go by without saying something pleasant, complimentary, positive to every member of your family (adults as well as children).

2. Each day have an appropriate, positive physical interaction with your children and spouse. Hugging is a wonderful way of communicating love and tenderness to members of your family. There is research which indicates that hugging actually changes body metabolism for the better, and improves the functioning of the immune system. As I said earlier, the skin is the largest organ of the body with more nerve endings than all other organs of the body combined. Hugging it, stroking it, and caressing it appropriately is a marvelous way of establishing a positive relationship with our family members. In recalling my daughter who kept a sign on the wall in her room which read "four hugs per day for survival, eight hugs for maintenance, and twelve hugs for growth," if she didn't get them, she would come to me and say, "Daddy, I need my hugs."
Every physical interaction doesn't have to be a hug or a kiss. It can be a pat on the back, rubbing one's back, wrestling and scuffling around. Even a playful poke in the ribs or tap on the shoulder can be useful and effective in communicating love and affection. Fathers, don't be afraid to hug your boys.

It is not a sign of weakness. An appropriate touch can communicate much more love and warmth than you could ever communicate with words.

3.  Never say degrading or demeaning things to your children or spouse. When inclined to do so, leave the room and put time between your anger and a badly chosen word that you would later regret. Bite your tongue, keep your mouth shut, and turn your thoughts to other things until the drive to be verbally negative weakens and you are in control of *it* rather than *it* being in control of you. There isn't a shred of evidence in behavioral research which speaks to the value of using negative, degrading, demeaning language. To behave this way is a serious sign of weakness, and weak behavior is out-of-control behavior. Just don't say it! Keep your mouth shut! Cool off! Bring your emotions under control, then wait for an opportunity to say something nice, something that will build a person up rather than tear a person down. Again, remember to follow this admonition:

Unless what you are about to say or do has a high probability for making things better, don't say it, and don't do it.

4.  Where both the husband and wife are in the home, openly show affection to and for one another. A great American religious leader observed that the greatest gift a father can give to his children is to love their mother. What wonderful advice! Parents, don't be hesitant or embarrassed to express your affection toward one another in the company of your children. Husbands, tell your wife you love her, and let the children hear it. Wives, you do the same to your husband. Appropriately show physical affection to one another in the company of your children: a kiss, a hug, holding hands, and so on. I can remember vividly the mock expressions of embarrassment of my children as I would hug, kiss, and say loving things to their mother in their company: "Aw, Dad, you're crazy." Well, they were right. I am crazy—about my wife!

If these kinds of interactions are not a part of your home life, begin to make them a part of it, daily! You might have to ease into them. You might even have to practice them. A short time ago I was working with a mother of a 16-year-old daughter. The mother had completely lost the ability to say nice things to her daughter. She had said uncomplimentary and negative things to her for so long and so often, it became the dominant behavior. The mother had become trapped by her own reactive behavior! As we talked about the need for her to say positive things to her daughter, the mother told me she couldn't think of a single thing about her daughter that was worth saying something nice about. Of course, it wasn't true that the daughter was totally devoid of things to say something nice about, but that's all the mother could see because that's all the mother had responded to. Before the mother was able to say nice things to her daughter, she had to learn how to do it. Through role playing and practice, she finally reacquired the ability to say nice things to her daughter. I was pleased recently when I saw them together downtown engaged in happy, pleasant, animated conversation.

While working with a group of parents of adolescents, a mother—as with the mother I just described—assured me in no uncertain terms, and with colorfully descriptive language, that there was, indeed, *nothing* about her son that was in the least complimentary. She asked, challengingly, "What am I supposed to say to a kid like that?" I answered, "When you see your son, say 'Good breathing, Son.'" Though she was quite amused at this, she did it, and a few days later told me what happened. The boy came home looking, behaving, smelling as bad as ever. The mother (after practicing before a mirror on which her son's picture had been taped) said, "Hello, Glad you're home safe and sound. Good breathing." He looked at her quizzically and said, "What!?" The mother replied, "I said, 'Good breathing,' Son." The boy began to laugh and she began to laugh. They hugged. They talked about inconsequential things. A new world of healthy mother-son relationships opened up, and the mother was simply delighted. One must not assume from this that the boy immediately became a Jack Armstrong all-American boy type. That's fantasy. But it ripped away every gate that had kept them off the road to compatibility. Things began getting better and have been steadily improving.

## ENDURANCE

Aches and pains are a part of life. We don't rush off to the doctor or to the hospital seeking treatment for every ache and pain and discomfort. These are just natural parts of life. We ignore them and go on about our daily business. When left alone, most aches and pains (over 90% according to one report I read!) will likely go away and life will go on none the worse, and often better, because they were simply left alone.

Such is the case with many, even most, of the discomforting and painful behaviors of our children. Rather than chasing after every annoying, inappropriate, common, growing-up, garden-variety weed behavior of our children, we are better advised to ignore them and go on with our lives. A kid comes in the house and is grumpy, out of sorts, and says something rude or inappropriate, ignore it! Walk away from it. If one child is behaving appropriately, while another (or other children) is behaving inappropriately, just ignore the inappropriate behavior and turn your attention to the child who is

behaving appropriately. Remember, behavior follows that which pays attention to it. If we ignore a behavior, whether it is appropriate or inappropriate, it will likely cease. If we pay attention to a behavior, whether it is appropriate or inappropriate, it will likely continue and even increase in frequency.

> *Behavior follows that which pays attention to it.*

Before you think about paying attention to inappropriate behavior, carefully consider the seriousness of the behavior. We know that most inappropriate behaviors of children (like most of our aches and pains) are simply not serious enough to treat. They are not serious enough to pay attention to. They don't deserve our attention. Just endure, which is defined by Webster as "remaining firm under suffering or misfortune *without yielding*; to undergo hardship *without giving in*" (emphasis added).

## TREATMENT

If aches and pains persist, physical or behavioral, and the danger signs of serious problems continue, then it is time for treatment. But this attention to distress, disease, or injury is done reasonably, carefully, and systematically. It might even require restricting some of life's activities. For example, with a physical problem a person might have to use crutches or be in a wheelchair or even confined to bed. A careful analysis or diagnosis of the problem is made to be sure the treatment fits the illness. If taking four pills a day does the job, the doctor isn't going to prescribe 12 pills a day on the false assumption that more will hurry the healing process along. The doctor knows that even with the best of treatment, the body will heal only so fast, so treatment is carefully measured to be consistent with the seriousness of the illness and the body's ability to recover. It is not unusual for the first prescribed treatment to not work. The best and the most effective treatment might not be immediately evident to the doctor, so a chance is taken and an estimate is made at what will hopefully be the best treatment. But it might not work, so after a reexamination involving another measurement of the body's vital signs and so on, another attempt is made at prescribing a treatment that is equal to the illness. And so it is with behavioral ill health.

## DIAGNOSIS/ANALYSIS

Treatment generally involves the doctor sitting down with the patient and explaining what the matter is, why the treatment is necessary, and what the patient can expect as a result of treatment. In this explanation, the doctor might even go so far as to tell the patient that some of his or her activities will need to be more carefully controlled. The patient might have to go to bed for rest and recovery. Changes in diet might have to be made. Privileges that might otherwise be enjoyed might have to be curtailed or even eliminated for awhile. The doctor explains all of this to the patient so that he or she knows exactly what to expect. The doctor might also explain to the patient what might happen by ignoring the prescription. The patient might complain and say that he can't stay in bed to recuperate or that he doesn't like to take pills or he doesn't want to alter his diet. The doctor isn't going to scream and holler at him and argue with him over these points. The doctor will simply reiterate the diagnosis and treatment, then leave it up to the patient to make his own decision and to experience the natural consequences of those decisions.

When the patient comes to the doctor for treatment, the doctor doesn't scream and holler at him and give him the dickens because he is in ill health, even if he did something stupid that caused him to be in ill health. Let's say the patient broke his leg riding a motorcycle. The doctor doesn't launch into a long tirade about the foolishness of riding a motorcycle, or get into a long exposition about the fact that motorcycles are the most dangerous vehicles in the world to ride. He/she doesn't question the patient's wisdom and intelligence, or berate him for doing something that was so risky. By the same token, if the patient refuses to carefully follow the prescription and ignores the treatment, upon returning to the doctor, the doctor wouldn't rant and rave about this noncompliance and remind the patient of his stupidity and ignorance and so on. The doctor would allow the consequences to speak for themselves, while reminding the patient of the potential danger to one's health should treatment be ignored.

As with the body, there are times when behavior needs treatment; for example, when behavioral aches and pains persist and

> **Treatment should be equal to the problem.**

danger signs continue that suggest that the individual's normal growth and development are being threatened. When the behavior becomes more than annoying, it is necessary to treat the behavior, but this treatment must be prescriptive and carefully applied so that it is equal to the behavior that is being treated.

Before treatment begins, as is done by a medical doctor, it is necessary that the parent measure the vital signs of that behavior. The parent should take some time to observe the behavior to see how often it occurs, how long it persists, or the conditions under which it occurs. It is not unusual at all for parents to use sweeping statements to describe their children's behavior: "My kids *always* fight," "My son is *always* picking on his sister," "The kids *never* pick up after themselves," "My daughter is *never* home before one o'clock in the morning." However, when I have parents go back home and spend a week making notes that describe the behaviors that are troubling them, they invariably return with a totally different perception of the behavior. In some instances,

> Parents! Learn to systematically analyze behavior.

in fact not infrequently, parents will tell me they don't need any more help, that having looked at the behaviors carefully, they realize what the problem is and are perfectly able to handle the situation themselves by simply practicing being positive with the children and ignoring inconsequential behavior. Just as you would have no respect for a doctor who started filling your body with pills or putting serious limitations on your life without first examining you and measuring vital body functions, you should not begin to treat the behavior of your children, or let anybody else treat the behavior of your children, until the behavior has been carefully diagnosed and measured.

To help parents systematically analyze their and their children's behavior, I suggest the use of the form found in Figure 4.2. Before describing how to use the form, I want you to know that I understand very well how unpleasant it can be to take data on our own, and our children's, behavior.

Still, as the need arises, I strongly encourage you to do it. It's a pain at the time, but in the long run it relieves more pain than it causes because it gives you the information you need to treat the problems that beset you.

Behavior, like so many other things we deal with daily in life, is very complex and we must respect that. If your car is not functioning properly and you are explaining the problem in non-technical terms, it's all right to use terms like doodad, thingamabob, whatchamacallit, and "it's on the fritz." But when it comes time to actually fix the car, technical terms will have to be used to precisely describe problems, identify replacement parts, and prescribe repair procedures.

And so it is with human behavior. Terms like frustration, anger, hyperactive, depression, hate, obsessive-compulsive are okay as gross indicators that something is the matter, but without a clear diagnosis of cause and effect relationships, such terms have no treatment value whatsoever.

By using the form in Figure 4.2 you can discover cause and effect relationships that

## Figure 4.2—Analyzing Behavior

| Prompt | Behavior | Consequences |
|---|---|---|
|  |  |  |
|  |  |  |
|  |  |  |
|  |  |  |
|  |  |  |
|  |  |  |
|  |  |  |
|  |  |  |

would otherwise escape you completely. I've used it with thousands of parents and invariably, in wide-eyed amazement, they came to realize what is causing problem behaviors to arise in the first place, and what is keeping them going. In the study of behavior, this is called a "three-term contingency," and is used regularly as a tool for analyzing behavior problems. When using this tool, begin with a precise description of the problem behavior. For example, "Billy hit Susan hard on her back with his fist." Avoid description like, "Billy was mean to Susan," since "mean" can be interpreted in so many ways. Describe

> *Precise analyses lead to precise treatment.*

the behavior so clearly that anyone reading it would know exactly what happened. Next, if possible, identify what prompted Billy to hit Susan. For example, "Susan called Billy a scumball," or "Susan grabbed a book away from Billy," or "Susan just walked in the room and was minding her own business." Don't be too concerned if you can't identify the prompts. Sometimes they aren't obvious at all. But if you can, do so since it is information that can assist problem solving. Last describe what immediately follows the behavior. This is the consequence, and since behavior is shaped by consequences, it is very, very important that these be clearly identified. For example, "Susan went crying to Mother," or "Susan hit Billy back," or "Mother/Father scolded Billy and gave Susan a lot of attention in the form of hugs, kisses, and verbal comfort."

To illustrate how this information can be used for analyzing a behavior problem, consider the following three examples:

## Example 1:

| Prompt | Behavior | Consequences |
|---|---|---|
| Susan grabbed the book Billy was reading. | Billy hit Susan hard on her back with a closed fist | Susan ran crying to Mother/ Father who gave her a hug, kissed her on the cheek, and told her Billy should not be so mean to her. |
| Mother/Father is angry at Billy. | Mother/Father spank and scold Billy and send him to his room. | Susan taunts Billy and says, "Ha, ha to you, you meany." |

## Analysis:

It is altogether possible that Susan prompted Billy on purpose just to get him into trouble and to get a lot of parental attention.

## Treatment:

Either ignore both Susan and Billy completely, or use the Stop, Redirect, Reinforce strategy described on Pages 59–62, or the Teaching Interaction Strategy described on Pages 67-69.

## Example 2:

| Prompt | Behavior | Consequences |
|---|---|---|
| Susan walked in to the room, minding her own business. | Billy hit Susan hard on her back with a closed fist. | Susan cried out in pain and called for parental protection: "Mom/Dad, Billy is hitting me and hurting me and I didn't do anything to him!" |
| Mother/Father are in the room with Billy and Susan. | Billy quits hitting Susan. | Susan seeks the protection of her Mother/Father. |

## Analysis:

It is not clear why Billy hit Susan, only that he did and such behavior is intolerable. There appear to be no ulterior motives on Susan's part. She was simply an innocent victim of her brother's angry outburst.

## Treatment:

a.  Briefly comfort Susan: "I'm sorry Billy hit you. I'm sure it must have hurt. You'll feel fine in a minute." Note: Don't carry on longer than is necessary to show your genuine concern, otherwise it could condition Susan to invite hitting so she can get a disproportionate amount of parental attention.

b.  Take Billy aside and use the Teaching Interaction Strategy. Also, discuss the positive consequences of Billy controlling his behavior and the negative consequences if he chooses to hit Susan again. (For a detailed discussion of how to use consequences, see chapter 5, A Word About Consequences. Additional examples are provided on the following pages of this section.)

## Example 3:

| Prompt | Behavior | Consequences |
|--------|----------|--------------|
| Susan called Billy a scumball. | Billy hit Susan hard on her back with a closed fist. | Susan cries out in pain and says, "I hate you Billy, I wish you'd die!" |

## Analysis:

I would classify this as inconsequential, garden variety weed behavior, a classic example of no-account sibling rivalry.

## Treatment:

Put the entire thing on extinction. If Susan comes crying in pain in search of comfort, the parent should say simply, "I'm sorry you chose to make Billy angry at you and got hurt. You'll feel better soon." The parent should then leave it at that. If she continues to seek attention, the parent should just ignore it and if possible get out of Susan's company entirely: leave the room, go into the bathroom and lock the door, or whatever. Without the parent present, the crying and carrying on will not last long, typically less than 2 minutes.

If Billy seeks redress, "Susan always calls me bad names and I hate her! How come you don't make her stop that!?", the parent(s) should briefly restate their expectations, comfort the boy and leave it at that: "Billy, in this house, we don't hit each other. I'm sorry she upset you. Still, no hitting."

I realize that these are examples of fairly simple behaviors. Still, over time, parents can become proficient in recording, analyzing, and treating very complex behaviors if they will just take the time and put forth the effort to do so. I know a lot of parents who, if they spent as much time, concern, effort, and money analyzing and working on their children's behavior as they spend analyzing and working on their golf game, bowling skills, bridge playing, and TV game show quizzes, would soon become behavior analysts and therapists of the first order, to say nothing about how much more skillful they would become as parents, and how much happier, healthier, and more productive their children would be. As with achieving proficiency in any skills, parenting skills are typically achieved with some effort, but it is surely worth whatever effort it takes!

After the behavior has been carefully diagnosed, measurements have been taken of it, and it has been carefully described in terms of how it relates to its environment, treatment can begin. As with the doctor, that treatment might begin by visiting with the child and explaining your concern as parents. Assuming that the child is old enough to understand what you are saying (usually four or five years of age and older), you would begin by telling the child that you are concerned about the behavior and that something needs to be done about it. Again, if the child is old enough to understand, you would be very specific by referring to the information that you have collected. For example, it might go

> *When stating expectations, remember to engage the child in the conversation.*

something like this: "Mary, we have noticed during this past week, that you have hit your little sister 12 times, and this has hurt her. We could tell by the way she cried that she was really hurt. Now you must never do that again. Hitting people and hurting them is not allowed in this home." When saying this, you are calm, kind, and in complete control. Like the doctor, you aren't going to rant, rave, and carry on at this inexcusable, horrible behavior!

Let's suppose, however, that Mary argues and says something like, "I did not hit that little brat 12 times this last week, and if I did she deserved it!" The parent should not react to that in kind. The parent shouldn't argue: "Oh yes you did, young lady! And we have the data right here to prove it!" And so on. This accomplishes nothing of value. Instead, you respond calmly, unemotionally, and in complete control: "We can understand you might be upset; nevertheless, you must not hit your sister any more." And at this point, you lay out in clear, careful, and understandable terms the prescription: "Mary, so long as you control yourself and are kind to your sister, you will continue to enjoy the privileges that are really important to you." This, as we have discussed earlier, will evolve into a discussion of earnable privileges: access to the bicycle/car, talking to friends on the telephone, watching TV, having a radio/stereo in the bedroom, and so on. "Now, Mary, tell us what we expect of you and what the consequences are if you meet or fail to meet our expectations."

It is important that you as parents know that the child is absolutely certain of your expectations and the consequences of meeting or failing to meet those expectations. Require the child to repeat those back to you and to continue to repeat them back to you until you are completely satisfied the child knows exactly what you expect and what the consequences are if those expectations are or are not met. Don't simply ask the child if she understands what you are talking about. It is very likely the child will protest and even cast aspersions on what is happening: "This is the dumbest thing I ever heard of. This is so stupid. You are treating me like a baby. I can't stand it." And so on. This is very typical, and it is important that you do not respond in kind. Rather, you respond proactively and stay on course: "Mary, let me repeat what we expect of you and what you can expect of us if you improve your behavior. First, you must never hit your sister again no matter how mad you are or how much you believe your sister deserves to be hit. You must never hit your sister again. If you control yourself and do not hit your sister you will continue to enjoy privileges you really like, including the use of your bicycle/the car, talking to your friends on the telephone, watching television, having your radio/stereo in your room, and so on. Now, Mary, repeat our expectations back to us. Tell us what we expect of you and what privileges you can continue to enjoy if you meet our expectations." Once the child realizes that you are not going to be drawn off course by her getting you into her argument, and once she realizes that you are adamant and are going to stay the course, she, though grudgingly, will repeat back to you what you need to hear. Don't

> *When children misbehave, do not respond in kind.*

be upset if she is surly and out of sorts. How she feels about it at the moment is really inconsequential. The point is, you must make absolutely certain the child understands what your expectations are and what the consequences are of meeting or not meeting those expectations. The best way of doing that is to have the child repeat those expectations back to you.

Once you are satisfied the child understands precisely what your expectations are and what the consequences for compliance are, then address the other side of the coin: "Thank you, Mary, for that response. You are exactly correct. We are really happy to know that you understand so clearly and so well what we expect of you, and what you can expect of us if you control your behavior. However, if you should lose control of your behavior and decide to hit your sister, you will deny yourself these privileges. For example, if you hit your sister once, you will have denied yourself the privilege of using the telephone for 24 hours. If you hit your sister twice, you will have denied yourself the privilege of using the telephone for three days, and you will also have denied yourself the privilege of using your bicycle/the car for 24 hours. Now, Mary, tell us what you can expect; tell us what privileges you will deny yourself should you decide to hit your sister." Then wait for a response.

As the days pass and Mary controls her behavior and doesn't hit her sister, be sure to acknowledge this self control. On the other hand, let's suppose that Mary hits her sister anyway, and the loss of the privileges just don't seem to be having any effect and she keeps on hitting. As with the illustration of the medical doctor whose first prescription didn't work, it isn't unusual for behavioral prescriptions to not work the first time. Typically, the rule of thumb

| |
|---|
| *Give treatment time to work.* |

is that if the first prescription doesn't work, increase the dosage; that is, apply a stronger prescription. In the case of human behavior, that would mean taking an inventory of those things Mary values very much and making those things contingent upon behaving appropriately.

It is necessary to give the treatment time to work. So often parents throw in the towel too quickly. We live in a world where problems are portrayed as being solvable in half an hour. It can take

| |
|---|
| *Parents tend to give in before their kids give out.* |

a long time to develop a behavior, and if its a dysfunctional behavior, it can take a long time to fix it. We need to give our prescription time to work. Denying a child a privilege for a short period of time might be something the child can tolerate, so we assume too quickly it isn't having an effect; but if it's allowed to continue over a longer period of time, the child's tolerance will break down and he/she will likely begin to yield to the treatment. Parents tend to give in before the kids give out.

## FINDING EFFECTIVE REINFORCERS

Before treatment is prescribed and put into effect, it is extremely important that parents carefully observe their children to make certain they know what their children value most, and to make a list of those things. By listing those things children really enjoy, we get a pretty good idea of what is of most value to them. These things typically go unnoticed by parents. Recently, I was working with the parents of a teenage boy. The boy was doing things the parents found to be very objectionable; things that were, indeed, too severe to just be ignored.

We tried a treatment which deprived the boy of some privileges. After about a week it was apparent the treatment wasn't working. By the way, we can generally tell in four to five days if the treatment is working. If treatment hasn't taken effect by then, it is probably time to change the treatment. And this is what we did in this case.

After visiting on the matter, during which time the parents were racking their brains trying to figure out what the child really valued, the mother observed that the boy was very anxious to earn and save money. He was a hard-working boy who had accumulated quite a bit of savings. This turned out to be the key to effective treatment. The prescription went like this: Whenever the boy behaved in an inappropriate way, the parents gave him a ticket, very much like a traffic ticket.

Tickets came in different colors, each one having a different value. The parents sat down with the boy, once again went over their concerns and reassured him that the behavior in question had to stop. That was not negotiable. They then told him that should he behave appropriately, he would continue to be able to do jobs around the house and earn money that he could then add to his savings account. However, if he chose to misbehave, it would be costly to him. And they used the word "costly." They pointed out that depending on the severity of the problem, tickets of different values would be given. This was all carefully explained.

Of course the boy objected vehemently, but the parents acted like a broken record and calmly repeated their concerns, described the consequences, and waited until the boy repeated back to them what was expected of him and what he could expect when either behaving or misbehaving. The parents didn't lose their cool nor did they allow themselves to be taken off track by an unhappy boy. They also told the boy that if he went a week without misbehaving, and for every week of appropriate behavior thereafter, a portion of his fines would be turned back to him. It was sort of like the option given to motorists who get a moving violation. If they go to traffic school, a certain portion of their fine will be forgiven. So, in this instance, the pill the boy had to swallow had a sugar coating and the medication was much more tolerable. The treatment worked. Of course, while the boy was behaving appropriately the parents were taking many opportunities to say nice things to him and to thank him for behaving so well.

> *Do not confuse a child's response to treatment with the effectiveness of treatment. A child might cry while a wound is being bandaged, but that should not keep the wound from being bandaged.*

There are so many ways one can cleverly approach the formulation of a prescription for treating inappropriate behavior. One couldn't possibly cover all of the facets of this in this chapter or in this book. However, with care and time, an appropriate treatment almost always emerges.

After you have tried everything you know to do and the inappropriate behavior persists, you might have to turn to a more intensive type of care and treatment. Sometimes our physical condition can deteriorate to the point where we need to be hospitalized. At times such as these, specialists may be called in and it might be necessary to place rather remarkable limits on one's activities to increase the probability that treatment will be effective. It is similarly so in the treatment of human behavior. Sometimes, a behavior will be so severe that it is necessary

Weeks Public Library
36 Post Road
Greenland, NH 03840

------------------------------------------------

Receipt for Patron
  Patron Report Class: ILL

Current Status

Fines Owed
  No fines

Items Out
  28509 Olive Kitteridge
  (Strout, Elizabeth.)
  05/15/2012

  13449 The road from Coorain
  (Conway, Jill K.,)
  05/18/2012

  18479 The power of positive
parenting : a wonderful way to raise
children
  (Latham, Glenn I.)
  06/19/2012

Reserved Items
  No reserves

------------------------------------------------

05/15/2012                    10:55:07AM

to bring in specialized help and to even have the individual placed in some type of treatment center where more intense, controlled help can be given. In this day of drug and alcohol abuse, we see an ever increasing need for this kind of intensive care. Behavioral problems that are a result of severe mental disorder should be treated in a more controlled environment by highly trained professionals. Though it is only rarely that this is the case, it is generally not reasonable to suppose that these problems can be dealt with adequately at home and without intense professional care.

> *Sometimes a behavior can become so severe, specialized help is needed to treat it.*

Don't be too quick to assume that just because a son or a daughter behaves in a manner that is remarkably unacceptable, intense, highly controlled treatment is needed. Before seeking such treatment, remember: (a) give love, empathy, understanding, and compassion a chance; (b) turn your back on inconsequential inappropriate behaviors and turn your attention to appropriate behaviors; and (c) make desirable privileges contingent on appropriate behavior. Over the years, I have seen some very difficult behaviors change dramatically. Parents have come to me at wits end. There seemed to be no hope. They were ready to throw their kids away. They had lost any feeling for their children. They were feeling numb, defeated, and beyond hope. As one mother noted, "I took my son to church last Sunday and I gave him back to the Lord." Before giving your children away, and before concluding that they need hospitalization or institutionalization, try the other things first. Give it an honest effort. It's worth it and you will likely be surprised at how well it works.

> *Never throw your kids away!*

If all else fails, there is still no need for despair. Let's assume that every effort has been made to save a child from the social, personal, and even physical destruction of his own behavior. What do you do then? What would you do with a child who was so badly diseased that no medical treatment known would be able to restore his health, and it was only a matter of time before the child would die? Would you throw up your hands, say woe is me, and abandon the child? Would you expel the child from your home and rid your life of him? Certainly not! You would still do everything you could to make life as pleasant as possible for both the child and you. And so it is with children whose behavior seems to defy all efforts to make it better. You become proactive in its finest and noblest sense. You continue to let the child know that he has value and that you love him. You continue to look for opportunities to be kind, gracious, and reinforcing. You look

> *When children deserve our love the least, they need it the most.*

beyond, and simply ignore, those behaviors which are tearing the child's life to shreds, while making absolutely certain that you do not assume responsibility for the child's circumstances. That is so important.

Parents are so quick to assume responsibility for the misbehavior and the errors of their children. The first question parents ask me when agonizing over the misbehavior of a child is, "What did we do wrong?" In all probability they did nothing wrong, or certainly nothing so wrong as to account for the child's behavior. Just because the child has decided to jump off the deep end doesn't mean the parents should jump into a swamp of despair, guilt, and shame. In all of my years working with parents, I have yet to note a single instance where parental guilt, shame, or remorse has done any good at all to improve the behavior of children. Instead, by feeling hopeless, by giving up, by throwing their kids away, and by disowning their children, matters only get worse for both themselves and for their children. It never fails!

It has been observed that when children deserve our love the least, they need it the most. There is a lot of truth and a lot of wisdom in that. It is during these trying moments when parents must do everything they can to strengthen the bonds between them and their children, while at the same time letting children know that they (that is, the parents), though sorry for the behavior of their children, are not assuming responsibility for it. The children are old enough to know better and they know help is available, but if they choose to ignore it they will simply have to suffer the natural consequences. Parents will surely anguish, but they must not assume responsibility for their children's circumstances. The suffering is up to those who are misbehaving.

I have seen parental guilt, shame, and suffering destroy otherwise solid marriages. This is unnecessary. It is generally caused by parents being overwhelmed by their own sense of failure and inadequacy. They conclude that they are not capable of dealing with difficult problems in life. They see themselves as incapable and hopeless. These negative and destructive thoughts creep into their marriages, and having lost confidence in their ability to parent, they succumb to the notion that they can't even deal well with their marital problems. Before long otherwise minor, even inconsequential, annoyances in the marriage relationship become magnified and distorted and the marriage is dissolved.

The better way is to step back from all of it and accept the fact that in life, despite how well parents do at raising their children and how hard they try to provide them with a good environment, there are a lot of influences outside of the home that are incredibly powerful, influences which may be too great for the good influence of the home to withstand, and children fall to those outside influences. As painful as it is, we must be ready to accept this reality, but not allow it to overwhelm us as parents as it has overwhelmed the children. We need to be mature and step back and say to our children, "It is terribly unfortunate what you have decided to do with your life, but it is your decision and you'll have to live with the consequences. We are always here to be of whatever help we can, but we're not going to force you to behave otherwise. That's up to

> *Bonding is your best assurance that children will ultimately remain within the value system.*

you. We love you, we will always love you. We recognize our mistakes as parents and are sorry for them, but we are more sorry for you that you have decided to do with your life as you have done. If we can ever be of help, let us know." It is not altogether unlikely when telling a child this that the child will lash back with verbal assaults: "You don't love me! You never did love me. Furthermore, I hate your guts. I don't need your help and I never will need your help. And as for your sorrow at being crummy, shove it! No one knows better than me what rotten parents you are, so save your breath!" And the kid goes stomping out.

Don't be intimidated by this. It is altogether likely the child was lashing out at the kindness that was being extended and was simply unable to accept it. We see this regularly with misbehaving children. When parents extend to their misbehaving children an increased measure of love and compassion, and extend to them the hand of fellowship and help, children sometimes can't accept it. It's too much. It sears their conscience, and they stomp off in a rage. If they do that, parents can almost always be sure they have made a positive impact on the child, as strange as that may seem.

As we observe the course of human behavior over time, it is typical that if bonding takes place between parents and children, once the child leaves adolescence behind and maturity sets in, the individual begins to view life in a different perspective, and the effects of bonding are realized. If the child (now an adult) knows that parental love is waiting on the other side of the door that he slammed shut in a fit of rage, he is very likely to pass back through it in search of that which he turned his back on earlier. I call that the Prodigal Son syndrome. Always remember, today is not forever. (This is explained further in Chapter 6, and illustrated with Figure 6.1, page 136).

By managing our own behavior as individuals, the odds are in our favor that in the long run—and that long run might take 10 or 12 or 20 years into the future—the relationship between parents and the wayward child will be back intact and everyone will have won. A mother of an older, wayward son wrote me a letter that illustrates this. She wrote, in part, "You said that you felt things would change, but they would not change overnight and I would have to be patient. I have been working on the positive and trying to overlook the negative, and it is working."

All parents make mistakes, obviously, some worse than others. I've listened to many, many parents recall in anguish their abusive, alcoholic, sexually deviant, enraged, ugly behaviors toward their children, and then ask in despair, "Is there any hope for me as a parent? Is there any way I can set things right and undo the terrible wrongs I've committed as a parent?" This is a tough question with no easy answers. A good, three-step approach to set the healing process in motion is as follows:

1. *Openly admit, with sorrow but without excuse, your errors and wrongs.* Don't dwell on them nor try to "get to the bottom" of them. Make it brief: "I have made some terrible mistakes as a parent for which I am dreadfully sorry. I apologize. I apologize from the very bottom of my heart."

2. *Resolve to replace dysfunctional behavior with functional behaviors.* "I assure you that those wrongs are behind me. I will understand your wondering if I really will change. I can't expect you to simply wipe away my years of abuse as though they had never existed, though that is exactly what I intend to do."

3. *Get professional help.* As has been discussed repeatedly to this point, since past behavior is the best predictor of future behavior, without treatment, the probability is great that behavior will regress to baseline, i.e., back to the way it was before.

## CONTROL

Although a good deal is said about it throughout this book, I want to address again the concept of "Control." It should be crystal clear by now that I'm not advocating control in an authoritarian, negative, exploitive way. My good friends Drs. Bill Jensen, Howard Sloane, and Richard Young put it well in their excellent book *Applied Behavior Analysis in Education:*

> The concept of "control," as it is used in behavior analysis, is often misunderstood. When a behavior analyst says that something "controls" behavior, all that is meant is that it has some reliable effect upon an individual's behavior. For example, for many people, rain clouds control the behavior of carrying an umbrella. If there are clouds in the sky in the morning, this behavior is much more likely to occur than if

there are no clouds.

"Control," as we use it in the analysis and treatment of human behavior, assures the skillful application of precise and highly civilized methods which have one aim and one aim only: to improve the quality of life. If the word control seems harsh, I refer you to comments of Dr. Paul Chance, delivered recently at a national conference of behavior analysts:

> Behaviorists talk about control, others about influence. But they mean essentially the same thing, though influence is softer.

*"Control" is not necessarily a dirty word, though "management" is better.*

It is also useful to think of control as management. But whatever term is used, the end product is the same, a better quality of life. There must never be any question about that! Perhaps the meaning of these terms, as they relate to treating human behavior, will be clearer by relating them to kinds of behavior being treated. Table 4.2 helps illustrate that. I've classified behavior into four types: A, B, C, and D. A-type behaviors are behaviors we as parents have a clear responsibility to directly *control*. Options to that are not available to responsible people. If a toddler walks onto a busy street, it is incumbent upon the parent (caretaker) to physically retrieve the child from impending danger. In this instance, the child is in the parents' immediate sphere of influence and the object of direct, hands-on control. It would be the only responsible thing for the parent to do.

*Learn to think in terms of "contingency management."*

B-type behavior is *managed* by the indirect control of those things which, in turn, directly control behavior. For example, a parent might not be able to *force* a son or daughter to do something, such as a chore, homework, and the like. It's at this point, as the child begins to grow beyond the parent's immediate sphere of influence, that parents begin to feel a loss of control. It is at this point that parents must think in terms of managing those things that *will* directly control behavior. These are referred to throughout this book as privileges, such as access to the TV, telephone, car, and so on. Put another way, the privilege is *contingent* on the chore or homework being done; hence, we call this contingency management. We manage the contingencies and they manage (or control) the behavior for us. When parents become skillful contingency managers—which is addressed repeatedly in this book—their fears and anxieties about being "out of control" diminish rapidly.

## Table 4.2—Categories of Behavior

| Type | Description | Treatment |
|------|-------------|-----------|
| A | Behaviors that are under the direct and immediate sphere of parental influence, such as the behavior of infants and small children. | *Direct*, hands-on *control* of the behavior, such as physically lifting and relocating the child, changing diapers, feeding and bathing. |
| B | Behaviors that cannot be directly controlled by parents, such as homework, chores, swearing, truancy, smoking, but which are still, to some degree, within the sphere of parental influence. | *Management* of the contingencies that indirectly control the behaviors, such as access to the TV, telephone, car, money, etc. The effective management of B-type behaviors requires parents to have good intervention skills, as discussed throughout this book. |
| C | Behaviors that are beyond direct hands-on control or even direct control via the management of contingencies, such as open defiance of parental expectations, comes and goes as he/she pleases, refuses to be accountable, and so on. These behaviors are only marginally within the sphere of parental influences. | *Influence* via suggestions, modeling, and counseling. To make this possible, the parents must maintain control of the environment generally even though the child is only marginally influenced by that environment. These are children for whom the term "unconditional love" takes on *real* meaning. |
| D | Behaviors that are totally beyond the sphere of parental influence. These are what I choose to call Prodigal Son behaviors. | Parents have no treatment options. They are only *observers*. The focus now must be on parental self-control, including developing coping skills. Natural consequences (typically of a traumatic nature) are the best, perhaps only, hope for effecting change. If that occurs, and the parent-child bonds are strong and intact, the child will likely return to his/her parent's sphere of influence (B-type behavior) in which event treatment in the form of contingency management can be applied. (This is nicely illustrated in the *New Testament* account of the Prodigal Son.) |

C-type behavior is behavior that is beyond our ability to directly control or manage, but is still amenable to our *influence*. C-type behaviors are *almost* beyond our sphere of influence, but not completely. For example, we might not be able to make a child do what we want, nor have available to us any contingencies (privileges) that are powerful enough to control the behavior; however, there is still a bond of love and respect between us and the child which allows us, through suggestions, modeling, and counseling to influence the child's behavior for good from time to time.

D-type behavior is behavior that is totally beyond our sphere of influence, in which event we are simply *observers*, hopers, prayers. A son or daughter is out of the home, on his/her own, has abandoned the family value system, and is beyond reach. At this point, it is incumbent on parents to think in terms of their own self-control, and to hope that the natural consequences of their child's behavior will have the influence they, the parents, don't have, but that these consequences won't be so severe that the child doesn't survive to benefit from them. (For example, being killed while driving under the influence of alcohol.)

I emphasize self-control. If parents get so caught up in or become so distraught about their child's seemingly hopeless circumstances, it can color their entire perception of life and can—and often does—lead to broken marriages, shattered families, and worse! Though it is so familiar as to be almost trite, the advice to "accept with serenity things one cannot change" is altogether applicable. For parents to allow the self-destructive behaviors of a child to destroy them is reactive behavior of the worst kind. Recalling the observation of my wife, "First we must control our own behavior."

## NOW TO REVIEW

The keys to control are skills and confidence, both of which come with study, practice, and time. Practice, practice, practice. To help you practice well so that you acquire skill and confidence, I strongly suggest the following:

1. First, be constantly on the lookout for appropriate behavior and pay it off. That is the most powerful tool you have available to you to shape your children's behavior.

2. Ignore those behaviors which are benign, inconsequential, and trivial; those behaviors which will heal in time if left alone.

3. If a behavior must be attended to, attend to it calmly and with a plan, a prescription.

4. In instances where these other attempts have been exhausted, and you are still unable to effect an appropriate change in your children's behavior, you may need to seek professional help and to employ more powerful strategies.

5. Do not despair and consider everything lost if every effort to effect a change

fails. Today is not forever. Do all you can through kindness, patience, and long suffering to keep the bonds of love between you and your children intact. Do not throw your kids away.

*Research has shown that the most effective way to reduce problem behavior in children is to strengthen desirable behavior through positive reinforcement rather than trying to weaken undesirable behavior using aversive or negative processes.*
*S.W. Bijou*
*The International Encyclopedia of Education, 1988*

# FIVE
# A Word About Consequences

Consequences come in two forms: natural and social (or social-cultural). A natural consequence is one which is directly related to the behavior, such as getting burned while playing carelessly with matches. When these kinds of consequences are experienced, the parent should be helpful, compassionate and empathetic without displacing the blame. For example, rather than say, "Oh, these terrible matches. I don't know why they can't be made to be more safe," or "Your father should never have left them where you could get them," say, "I'm sorry you hurt yourself." The child should not be absolved of his own responsibility—regardless of the shortcomings or carelessness of others.

In this same vein, parents should not be harsh, scolding, and accusatory. The discomfort caused by the burn will bear all the

> *Let consequences do the talking for you.*

message that needs to be borne. Rather than say, "Now, you see what happens when you play with matches? You get burned! If I've told you once I've told you a thousand times, don't play with matches! I only hope you've finally learned your lesson!," say "I'm sorry you burned yourself. It must hurt a lot. Let me see what I can do to help." Doing this, you are seen as a compassionate person who is interested in the other's well being, despite the error of that person's ways. This is the kind of response that builds bonds, whereas the other type of response puts distance between people.

Social consequences are consequences that make sense, but which aren't necessarily directly linked to the behavior. For example, withholding a child's allowance would be a social consequence for failing to get his homework done, though there is no direct relationship between homework and an allowance. Loss of driving privileges because of mishandling the car seems natural, but it is really social since such behavior may never, in fact, result in an accident. In this event, employing a social consequence might result in a natural consequence never occurring; that is, the person learns, via social consequences, to behave so well that natural consequences are precluded: by becoming a more responsible driver, the person does not have accidents. Examples of social consequences are denial of TV or phone privileges for failure to clean one's room, withholding dessert because the main course of the meal was not eaten, and no use of a favorite toy for a week because it was carelessly left outside in the rain.

Social consequences are often used to teach lessons that would otherwise be learned only at great risk. For example, the best way for a child to learn not to play near the top of the stairs would be to let the child play near the stairs then fall down them. Unfortunately, he might not survive to benefit from the lesson taught by natural consequences. Social consequences, on the other hand, can be just as instructive and a lot safer! And, of course, all social consequences must be nonaversive. Applying consequences which involve inflicting pain, unless done therapeutically in highly controlled clinical settings, is barbaric at worst and silly at best! (For an explanation of the clinical use of consequences, see pages 199–200.)

When administering logical consequences, five important guidelines should be followed:

## 1. Consequences Must be Clearly Understood at the Outset by Parents and Children

This is important for two reasons. First, it is too easy for children to get away with things, the unfortunate natural consequence being that inappropriate behavior becomes strengthened, and in time becomes more and more resistant to treatment. For example, a child pleads innocence and escapes the consequences: "I didn't know I wasn't supposed to....!" After successfully using this ploy a few times, the child learns that it is a dandy way to stay free of consequences that are no more serious than parental dirty looks and sighs of disgust and resignation.

Second, in moments of anger and frustration, parents tend to impose unreasonable and unenforceable consequences. A child does something that is particularly annoying and the parents lose their cool, blow up, and pronounce loudly and bombastically, "You are grounded for 2 months! No use of the telephone, the car, the TV! You will come directly home from school, go directly to your room, and you can come out only to eat or when I say you can!!!! Now do you understand that young man? Well, tell me! Do you?!!!!"

Such a response, borne out of a poor understanding of consequences, is, of course, unreasonable and only leads to bigger problems when it comes time to reconcile, negotiate, back down, give up......As one teenager noted, "I'll get my jeep taken away for a week but I'll have it back within 6 hours. I'll walk around the house, slam the door occasionally, this, that...and after a while this just plays on them...and they let me out. In a way I wish it wasn't like that. I've never really been punished. I wish my parents had been tougher on me." (From a treatment point of view, the words "...precise and consistent with me" are more instructive than "...tougher on me.")

## 2. Consequences Must be Reasonable, and Enforceable

A wise father once observed, "The plaster should be no wider than the sore." Reasonable consequences neatly fit the offense. To achieve that they should all be carefully thought out *before* they are stated or applied, and even then it will be necessary to modify and refine them as they are being used. Fine tuning a basically sound consequence is much easier than completely overhauling or scrapping entirely a kneejerk consequence that never had any chance of working in the first place.

In the following example, I illustrate how consequences are selected, applied, and enforced, and describe the principles of behavior upon which the procedure is based. Pay particular attention to the principles since a sound understanding of them will make it possible for you to respond appropriately to any number of situations requiring the use of consequences.

> Setting: A 10-year-old boy has been leaving his bike lying in the
> driveway. His parents frequently have to stop their car, get out and
> move the bike, then get back in the car and drive into the garage. Not

only is this annoying, but a less careful or alert driver might hit or run over the bike. Obviously, here is a problem that needs to be solved using logical consequences before the natural consequences of a smashed bike result in even bigger problems: replacing or repairing a bike, and perhaps repairing damages to a car.

Giving the boy a piece of one's mind, a good scolding, a heavy dose of logic, a spanking, and the pronouncement that "If I ever see that bike lying in the driveway again, you won't see it for a month—if you ever see it again!" is obviously worse behavior than leaving the bike in the driveway.

The better way is to decide in advance *exactly* what the boy is expected to do with his bike. This might be as simple as having him put his bike on the lawn, against the house, beside the porch, or out of the way in the garage. This, then, becomes the expectation of the boy's behavior. Knowing in advance the expectations of his behavior is of primary importance.

Next, the parents must decide how to state their expectation to the boy so he fully understands it, *and can demonstrate that he understands it*! This is best accomplished in a simulation or role playing exercise. It might go like this:

Dad: "Son, I notice you really enjoy riding your bike. It's neat having a bike. I sure enjoyed mine when I was a boy. What do you like best about your bike?"

*Note*: Start on a positive note, and be brief. Stop after a few seconds and give the boy a chance to respond. For example, the 32 words I used above take between 11 to 12 seconds to say. When you ask a question, be sure it invites a substantive response. Don't invite a yes or no response. If the boy says, "Gee, Dad, I don't know," probe a little. Say something like, "Tell me one thing." The chances are 95 out of 100 that after you have probed only two times, the boy will come forth with a substantive response, as follows.

Son: Well, I like it because I like to run around on bikes with my friend, Joe."

Dad: "Ya, Good example. Biking around with your friends can be a lot of fun."

*Note*: Once an acceptable response is forthcoming, reinforce the response with an enthusiastic acknowledgment, and perhaps even a bit of embellishment: "Biking around with your friends can be a lot of fun."

Dad: "Son, I have one concern. You sometimes leave your bike lying in the driveway, and before I can drive into the garage, I have to move it out of the way. And besides, leaving your bike in the driveway could be dangerous. How can that be dangerous?"

*Note*: In expressing your concern, do two things: First, state your concern calmly and in only a few words. No lectures! Secondly, make *your* concern *his* concern by inviting him to tell you what he has to lose.

Son:     "I suppose my bike could get run over."

Dad:     "That's right, Son. And why would that be such a terrible thing?"

*Note*: Get the child to see what *he* has to lose. Help him see what *natural* consequences could do to him. Don't dwell on your annoyance, inconveniences, or the possible damages to your car. A 10-year-old (or a 19-year-old, for that matter!) could care less about those things. But the loss of *his* bike! Now *that* means something.

Son:     "Well, I wouldn't have a bike to ride."

Dad:     "And what's so bad about that?"

Son:     "Gee, Dad. I wouldn't be able to go with my friends."

*Note*: Probe these consequences just long enough for the boy to get the message. Don't *you* tell him the message. Let him tell you. He'll be a lot more impressed by what he tells you than by what you tell him. Remember: never tell a child something he already knows!

> *Never tell a child something he already knows.*

Dad:     "I can see your point. That *would* be terrible! And I would never want to see that happen to you, so here is what I expect you to do. When you get off your bike, put it someplace other than in the driveway. Where would be a good place to put it so that it would be out of the way and safe?"

*Note*: Again, say only a few words and ask questions that put the boy in the role of problem solver—with you. This gets you both on the same side of the issue.

Son:     "I could put it in the garage, over to the side."

Dad:     "Good idea, Son. You're a good thinker. That would be a great place to put it. Any other place that is as good as that?"

*Note:* A positive response such as this is very reinforcing in itself, but it also gives you an opportunity to describe a behavior you want your son to develop; that is, "You're a good thinker." Tell the boy he is what you want him to be. Find something you can build on. This is called selective or differential reinforcement, and you want to reinforce those behaviors that are like, are related to, or which approximate the behavior you want. In this instance, the boy thought of a good solution. Being a good thinker is a highly desirable behavior, so it would be very wise to say, "You're a good thinker" since that is such a good approximation of the mature behavior you want the boy to ultimately possess.

Asking a follow-up question is good for two reasons. First, it helps identify other options. This will increase the probability for success. Second, it provides another opportunity for the father to reinforce the son's behavior.

Son: "Well, I could put it on the lawn by the driveway."

Dad: "Great idea. You're really using your head, Son. What a guy!"

*Note*: "You're really using your head, Son," is simply another way of saying, "You're a good thinker." When using selective reinforcement, it's a good idea to vary the words that are used to describe the desired behavior. Along with the declarative "What a guy," it would also be appropriate to use a physical reinforcer such as a pat on the shoulder or a light slap on the back. Pairing reinforcers is a powerful way to make a point.

Dad: "And Son, by putting your bike in these safe, out-of-the-way places, your bike will not get damaged and it will always be available to you. If, however, you should get careless and leave your bike in the driveway, you will deny yourself the privilege of using your bike for 24 hours. (This is contingency management: bike riding privileges are contingent on proper bike care.) What will happen if you leave your bike in the driveway?"

*Note*: When the consequence for non-compliance is stated, be sure you use only a few words and keep your voice low and calm, almost matter-of-fact. Make sure that the denial of privileges is stated in such a way that the burden for that denial is squarely on the boy's shoulders: "…you will deny yourself the privilege of using your bike for 24 hours." You *don't* say, "I'll take the bike away from you for 24 hours." The "bad guy" isn't you. The behavior is the "bad guy." Let the behavior (*his* behavior) do the talking, not you! When stating the consequence, be sure the time variable is clear: "…for 24 hours."

Son: "You won't let me use my bike for a whole day!?"

Dad: "Close. Listen carefully, son. *You* will deny *yourself* the privilege of using your bike for 24 hours."

*Note*: The boy will almost always dump the responsibility back on the parent. Don't say, "No, no son. I'm not keeping the bike from you…" Simply restate the fact: "You will deny yourself…"

Dad: "Now, Son, let's go outside. I want you to show me what you are going to do with your bike when you are not riding it."

*Note*: This is role playing and simulation. It's a very powerful teaching tool, as well as providing a wonderful opportunity to reinforce more appropriate behavior. Typically in such a situation the child is so anxious to do it right that opportunities to reinforce "right" behavior abound.

Dad: (Once Outside). "Ok, Son, here's your bike. Ride it into the driveway, then show me where you are going to put it."

Son: (Jumps on the bike, rides it out to the street, then up the driveway. Gets off the bike and parks it in an appropriate place.)

"There, Dad. That's where it will be safe and out of the way."

Dad:  "Son, I couldn't have done it better myself!" (Give the boy a hug, a pat on the back, and each goes his separate way.)

This entire encounter will take no more than 10 minutes, which is as it should be. Brevity, specificity, calmness, positiveness. These are the keys.

In the example above, everything went very smoothly. The boy never resisted or argued. But, as all parents know, it doesn't always go that way. In fact, it seldom goes that way. Here is what you do when problems arise. As you read through these, you will notice that the same principles apply to problem situations as they do to situations that run smoothly.

Suppose that at the outset the boy becomes belligerent and doesn't want to talk about it. Here is how you would handle that.

Dad:  "Son, I have a concern. Sometimes you leave your bike lying in the driveway, and before I can drive into the garage, I have to move your bike out of the way. Besides that, leaving your bike in the driveway could be dangerous. How could it be dangerous?"

Son:  "This is dumb, Dad. I don't want to talk about it."

Or, he might say something like, "Dad, do we have to talk about this now? The guys are waiting for me. I gotta go now!"

Dad:  (In a calm, controlled voice, and without any facial expressions that suggest anger or annoyance, say): "Son, how could it be dangerous to leave your bike in the driveway?"

*Note*: This is called the broken record approach. You simply repeat your question. Do not—I repeat, DO NOT acknowledge the distractors. Don't say, "Now you listen to me young man. You *will* talk about it whether you like it or not! Now you pay attention and do what I tell you to do!," or "Your friends can wait. This is more important than play. This is serious business. Do you want your bike to get smashed or something?"

Avoid these *reactive* responses. They are counter-productive; that is, they only make things worse by giving lots of attention

| Ignore distractors. Stay on course. |
|---|

to the very behaviors you *don't* want. The basic principle of behavior that applies here is that behavior is strengthened by the attention it receives. If you pay attention to things children do that you don't like, these are the behaviors that will tend to increase.

Son:  "Dad! I'm not wasting my time on this junk!"

Dad:  "I can see you are anxious to do other things, but this is important. Now, tell me, why is it dangerous to leave your bike laying in the driveway?"

*Note*: It's okay to show some empathy and understanding: "I can see you're anxious to do other things..." But don't back down or become reactive.

Son:   "I'm not taking any more of this. I'm outta here!"

Dad:   "If you leave now, Son, without talking about this, your bicycle will be locked up until we have had our conversation."

*Note*: If you think it will come to this, be prepared in advance to follow through. Have the lock ready. Don't have to go looking for one.

Son:   "Hey, you can't do that! That's my bike!"

Dad:   "As I said before, you can choose to talk about this now, or you can choose to lose the privilege of riding your bike until you do. Which do you choose to do?"

*Note*: By no means should the father try to impose his will through direct, hands-on control. That kind of tough-guy stuff is coercive and can come to no good. The parameters for decision making have been set. The child can choose either option and it's okay with the father. The boy can stay and talk or leave, having lost his bike privileges. The father is not the bad guy.

If the boy chooses to talk, despite a sullen demeanor, just proceed as illustrated above, not saying a word about the sullenness. If the boy chooses to relinquish his bike privileges, that's okay, too. In time, the odds are extremely great he will soon be willing to talk in order to regain his bike privileges. Initially, he might go off in a huff, saying something like, "Who cares. It's a crummy bike anyway. If you were as good a parent as Billy's dad I'd have a decent bike." Expect this kind of junk behavior. Since the boy is desperate and not being fully civilized, he will likely resort to about anything to get his way or to defer blame. If nothing is said about this behavior, it will soon extinguish.

When the time comes, and it eventually will, that the boy can simply no longer tolerate the loss of his "wheels," proceed as illustrated in the first instance.

Another problem that might arise during the discussion when the boy is told what the consequence is ("You will deny yourself the privilege of riding your bike for 24 hours.") might go like this:

Son:   "What! You mean you'll take my bike away for 24 hours. That's not fair! Billy leaves his bike in their driveway all the time and no one says a thing. This isn't fair!!!!"

Dad:   "Let me repeat so you'll be sure to understand: When you leave your bike in the driveway, you will deny yourself the privilege of having your bike for 24 hours.

Tell me Son, what privilege will you deny yourself if you leave your bike in the driveway?"

*Note*: The father didn't get drawn into an argument over what is fair. Never! I repeat, never get sucked into a discussion about what's fair. That's a black hole from which nothing enlightening or satisfactory ever escapes. Furthermore, the father didn't get sucked into a discussion about what goes on at Billy's house. He simply repeated himself.

After doing this two (certainly, no more than three) times, if the boy continues to protest and refuses to cooperate, then use the strategy just discussed: "The privilege of using the bike is yours when you are ready to discuss the matter," and then be prepared to lock up the bike.

It is important to keep in mind that the kind of calm, objective responding illustrated here (and elsewhere) between a father and a son must be the same between a father and a daughter. We know for a fact that girls can typically get their way and out of trouble and responsibility much easier than boys. Crying, being coy, and making verbal promises that are honey-sweet are all well known devices daughters can use to get their way and to escape the unpleasant consequences of their behavior. Fathers, particularly, must guard against caving in to such wiles.

As noted earlier, woven into this illustration are principles and strategies that can be applied to any number of situations. Once parents are able to effectively employ these principles and strate-

> *As the environment improves, the behavior improves.*

gies, the environment becomes much more pleasant, and behavior falls into line. Remember, behavior is largely a product of its immediate environment. As the environment improves and appropriate behavior is elicited, acknowledged, and praised, appropriate behavior will soon improve. The momentum of the behavior has been established in the right direction.

It is absolutely essential that parents learn to skillfully use consequences to do the talking for them. As illustrated in Figure 5.1, as children grow older, it becomes more and more difficult for parents to *directly* control their children's behavior. At birth, direct parental control is absolutely necessary since an infant has yet to learn the meaning of cause and effect relationship. At 4 weeks old, one of my granddaughters, while flailing her arms around in random fashion, touched a hot curling iron and sustained a little burn. At that age, her subsequent behavior relative to where she put her arm was not controlled in the least by that painful experience. It was completely up to her parents to directly intervene to assure the child's safety. By late adolescence and into adulthood, direct parental control is absolutely impossible.

Since parents begin their child-rearing experiences being in direct control of their children's behavior—and getting exactly the results they want!—they tend to stick with this approach when interacting with their children no matter how old the children are, not realizing that the use of consequences is not only an effective way to manage behavior, it is the best way. In some instances, and at some point in the child's life, it is the *only* way.

## 3. Parents Should Think in Terms of Consequences, Not Punishment

As was discussed in Chapter 1, consequences can be either reinforcing *or* punishing, but since the word punishment carries with it such negative connotations, we prefer that it not be the focus of therapy or management. Also, as one researcher noted, "Because punishment is so efficient and simple, there is danger that it could become the first and even exclusive technique. That would indeed be tragic. For one thing, punishment is painful, and…we should have as little pain as possible."

Physically pain-free consequences are so very, very important. It is the natural human response to flee pain and to get away from things and people that inflict pain. Pain-free consequences in the form of loss of privileges are, in the long run, more efficient. Furthermore, rather than being divisive, they bond children to their parents.

The punitive, punishing approach to behavior management is destroying society! It is not only divisive, it is non-instructional. As noted by B. F. Skinner, "The trouble is that when we punish a person for behaving badly, we leave it up to him to discover how to behave well." Left to their own devices, people seldom learn to behave well. Charles P. Ewing, a forensic psychologist and attorney, writing in the April, 1991 issue of the *Monitor*, published by the American Psychological Association, reported that "Juvenile killers are not born but made." He noted that between 1984 and 1989 the number of youth arrested nationwide for murder had more than doubled, from 1,004 to 2,208, and is continually rising. Among other things, he targeted the punitive nature of the American mentality as a cause for this alarming social menace, a mentality that is evidenced in families, in the juvenile justice system, in schools, and in society generally. A colleague of mine recently observed, "We have a culture with a passion to punish." We are paying for that dearly, and it *must* be stopped!

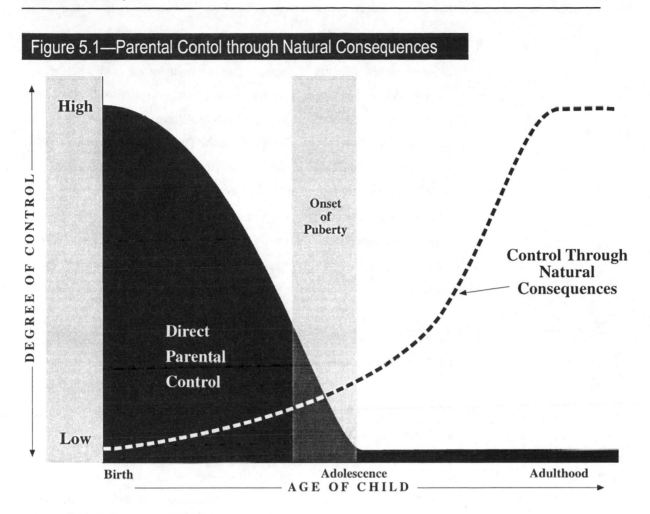

Figure 5.1—Parental Contol through Natural Consequences

## 4. Consequences Must be Applied With Precision, Accuracy, and Consistency

In the study of human behavior we observe a phenomenon known as "case hardened kids." These are children who develop an immunity, as it were, to consequences because those consequences are not applied appropriately. Consequences become somewhat like penicillin that is no longer effective because of being poorly applied. Be particularly careful to not take consequences away too soon. Wait until you are sure treatment has taken effect before you alter the "dosage" of consequences; before you relax them. If you are going to err, do so on the side of staying with the treatment (assuming it is potentially effective) too long rather than too little. When you have something that is working, don't alter it until a new, more appropriate, behavior is solidly in place.

> We have a culture with a passion to punish.

## 5. Consequences Must Not Be Punishing To Parents

As noted earlier, in a fit of anger, a parent might impose some outrageous consequences that becomes more aversive to the parent than it is to the child. For example, a parent might declare to a 16-year-old child, "You are grounded for a month, and that includes no use of the car!" But since the child has a valuable after-school job that is driving distance away, to enforce this dictum, the parent would have to leave work, pick the kid up at school, and drive him/her to work. Obviously, the parent is more inconvenienced than is the child.

To preclude this happening, as should be the case with all consequences, careful forethought should be given to the selection, administration, and management of consequences.

## NOW TO REVIEW

1. There are two kinds of consequences, natural and social.

2. Consequences must be clearly understood at the outset by parents and children.

3. Consequences must be reasonable, applicable, and enforceable.

4. Parents should think in terms of consequences, not punishment.

5. Consequences must be applied with precision, accuracy, and consistency.

*Research has shown that the most effective way to reduce problem behavior in children is to strengthen desirable behavior through positive reinforcement rather than trying to weaken undesirable behavior using aversive or negative processes.*
*S.W. Bijou*
*The International Encyclopedia of Education, 1988*

*Time heals all wounds.*

# SIX
# Using Time to Your Advantage

When used effectively, time is a powerful tool in shaping behavior. In this chapter, we look at using time to cool off, time to think things over, time to heal emotional wounds, and time to build self-esteem. Also discussed is behavior over time, as a function of age.

## Using Time to Cool Off

For as long as I can remember, the advice "count to ten" has been given as a way of putting distance between an *impulse* to do

> *When angry, counting to 10 is good advice.*

or say something stupid, and then *doing* or saying something stupid. And it's good advice. When dealing with feelings and behaviors, haste can make waste. When we are angry, frustrated, confused, at wits end, feeling hopeless and helpless, it is difficult to make good, sound, clear-headed decisions, a circumstance that applies not only to parents, but to children as well. Consequently, as parents we need to learn to use time to serve our needs, and we need to learn to use it to serve our children's needs as well. Consider the following example of a conflict that has arisen between a mother and her seventeen-year-old son over a privilege that he has not earned and is not getting. Even though the expectations and consequences were well understood beforehand by everyone, emotions soar:

Child:    "That's a stupid rule. I've always hated it. This miserable house is full of stupid rules! I hate them."

Mother:   "I'm really sorry you feel that way. Sometimes rules and laws can make you feel closed in."

Child:    "This place is like a prison. I am going to leave. You'll never see me again as long as you live!"

Mother:   "I can understand that you'd want to leave. As you get older and feel more independent, it's easy to see why you'd want to strike out on your own.

"Before you leave, though, I'd like to suggest that you go to your room and list the pros and cons that go along with being on your own. You know, in the pro section would be 'freedom to come and go as you please', and 'freedom to stay out as late as you want.' But in the con column would be things like 'having to get a full-time job to support yourself', 'cook your own food and do your own laundry', and things like that.

"As your parents we want you to be independent, but we don't want you to get hurt in trying to achieve it. Think it over for a day or two, study it out in your mind, then tell us what you've decided. In the meantime, if we can be of any help figuring the costs of things or whatever, just let us know."

Such a response helps to defuse an otherwise explosive situation, the family unit is still intact, and the burden of responsibility is placed squarely where it should be—on the shoulders of the child. This is an infinitely better approach than to respond in kind. For example:

Mother:   "I don't give a damn what you think about the rules around here. This is my house, and if you don't like it here, then just pack your bags and get the hell out!"

Such a response fractures the family unit, and to mend it will require a lot of pain and a lot of healing. And even when it is healed, ugly scars can remain. By maintaining your composure and using time as a tool, you demonstrate to the child that you are in control, and that the home is a stable, predictable, sturdy environment. Kids love that feeling, even though they may not let on that they do.

In the example just given, the child was in a rage and unable to deal with things rationally; hence, the need for time to cool things down. In the following example, the shoe is on the other foot: the parent is the one who is upset. Here's the situation: Mary, a 16-year-old, didn't get in until 3:00 a.m. Mother is waiting up and is furious. Mary enters the house, and mother is standing there fuming:

Mother: "Okay young lady. You'd better have a good explanation for this. A very good explanation for this!"

Mary: "Mom, don't be so upset. Nothing's the matter. We just lost track of the time."

The mother catches herself and realizes she is reacting badly. She uses a better way:

Mother: "Mary, as you can tell, I'm very upset. I apologize for that. I don't want to say anything in anger I'll be sorry for. Go to your room and get ready for bed, then let's get back together in 10 minutes to discuss this. I need to cool down, and we both need to get our wits about us.

"Oh, and by the way, Mary, I'm so happy that you're home safe and sound. More than being angry, I've been worried sick."

In such a situation, the mother has modeled excellent self-control, the mother's love and concern for the girl have come through as being more important than the girl's behavior, and the stage has been set for a constructive, positive mother-daughter talk, that might very well go like this:

Mother: "Mary, I'm so glad you're home safe and sound."

Mary: "I'm sorry I made you worry, Mom. I guess I knew you would be. I suppose this means no more dates this week."

Mother: "I'm sure you know the answer to that as well as I do. Losing privileges is a consequence of bad judgment."

(*Note*: The girl's judgment is bad. Not the girl.)

Avoid making decisions, issuing ultimatums, reprimanding, and laying down the law when you are angry. Use time to your advantage. We know that when time is used to separate anger from a response it can have a wonderful effect on the quality of that response. If a parent is angry, and reacts quickly when angry, that reaction is almost certain to be one the parent will regret, or will do more harm than good. But if time is allowed to pass, thus putting distance between the anger and the response, the anger will almost certainly give way to reason, and the chances for a constructive, positive relationship are much, much greater. In the situation that was just illustrated, the mother was wise to invite time to her rescue. It took the heat off, and allowed the mother to turn a situation that could have been destructive into one that was constructive. She also created a great teaching opportunity.

> *Avoid making decisions, issuing ultimatums, reprimanding, and laying down the law when you are angry.*

## Using Time to Think Things Over

Occasionally our children will come to us for advice or to share with us something about which they want our approval. Since youth are generally inexperienced, naive about many of the realities of life, and a bit impetuous, they tend to resist our advice (even when they ask for it), and their decisions often reflect only the rosiest of perspectives. To help them put things into proper perspective, time can be used to good advantage. Consider this situation: Bill comes home very excited about a conversation he's just had with a salesman at a nearby used car lot where he has been introduced to the car of his dreams. Bill is seventeen years old, works as a bag boy at the local supermarket, and will be a junior in high school next year. The discussion goes something like this:

Bill:   "Dad, I just came from the used car lot, and I have found the car of my dreams."

Dad:   "Tell me about it."

Bill:   "It's beautiful. What's more I drove it and it runs perfectly. It's what I've always wanted."

Dad:   "Sounds wonderful, Son. What's it selling for?"

Bill:   "It's not cheap, Dad. After all, this is one good car. It's perfect for me! They want $5,300 for it, and believe me, it's worth every penny of it."

Dad:   "If it's as good as you say it is, it probably is worth $5,300. What are the monthly payments, and how many years will it take to pay it off? You don't want a car that is worth less than you owe on it. Did they tell you what the interest rate would be on the loan?"

Bill:   "The payments are $157 a month. That's all I know about costs, and even though that's a lot, I'm sure I can pay it. The car is 3 years old and will be paid off in 3 years."

Dad:   "What about a down payment?"

Bill:   "I have $500 saved and that will do for a down payment."

Dad:   "Let's figure this out. You have a $157 monthly payment for 3 years. That comes to $5,652 + $500 down, for a total of $6,152. Have you gotten a Blue Book value on the car?"

Bill:   "The salesman told me it was Blue Book value."

Dad:   "Buying a car, Bill, is usually a person's first big purchase. Before you commit yourself to such a financial burden, there are some things you need to figure out. Remember, the monthly payments are only one cost. In addition, you have liability and collision insurance, gas and upkeep that will cost you about 20 cents a mile for a car that old, plus incidental expenses to personalize it. I'd suggest that you see Mrs. Jones at the credit union to check out the price and the terms. Visit Mr. Thomas at the garage about service and upkeep costs, and talk to Tom Atkinson about insurance costs. Also, go to the state license and tax offices and see about what it will cost each year to register the car and keep it licensed. Get all of these figures reduced to monthly costs so you'll know just what you'll be responsible for. After you're done—and by the way, Son, get these figures in writing— let's sit down again and look at this purchase after all things are considered. Also, estimate about how many miles you think you'll drive it each month. This will give you a lot of help in figuring costs."

Bill:       "Gee, Dad, I never realized there was so much to owning a car!"

Dad:       "The harsh realities of life. By the way, when can I see it?"

The time it takes to gather all of the necessary information—not to mention the things the boy will learn—will have a great effect on waking the boy up to reality.

If a parent tries to short circuit this process by putting the idea down on the spot, and questioning the boy's ability to afford the car before the facts are all known, it would likely make the boy more determined to buy the car, and to not seriously consider all of the realities. Statements like, "You're buying a $5,300 car! That's a joke, Bill! You're nothing but a bag boy at the grocery store. What makes you think you can afford a car? That's the dumbest thing I ever heard. Ride your bike. You can afford to ride a bike!" drive kids away from their parents. These kinds of responses do nothing but make a child feel inadequate, and deprives him of a great opportunity to learn about life and to practice good decision making.

But even with a careful analysis of the economic commitment one makes when considering the purchase of a car, the boy might still decide to buy, and be hurt in the process. That's not all bad. Consequences are powerful teachers, the results of which can be good in the long run. A few years ago, my youngest daughter invited me to go car shopping with her. She was excited and filled with anticipation as we visited several dealers and she test drove quite a number of cars. Finally, she made her selection. It couldn't have been a worse choice! After calmly prompting her to carefully weigh all of the important considerations, it was clear that her mind was set, and not wanting to put a guilt trip on her, or to make her feel that she had displeased her father, I smiled, gulped, and congratulated her on her very first major purchase. I can still recall how happy she was as she drove that brand new car off the lot and headed home to Logan. Three and half years, and several thousands of dollars of depreciation later, my now married daughter came to me distraught and in tears!

| Daughter: | "What am I going to do, Daddy? I owe $2500 more on the car than it's worth!" |
| Daddy: | "That's terrible. How can I be of help?" (She knew I'd not offer to pay it off nor did she expect me to.) |
| Daughter: | "I don't know, Daddy. But just tell me what to do. I'll do anything you say. When I bought it, I wouldn't listen to a thing you told me. (Actually, I told her very little!) But now I'll do whatever you tell me. Just tell me what to do. I'm not a mindless teenager anymore!" |

To make a long story short, she kept the car, paying it off one painful payment at a time, and in the process learning a great lesson about credit buying that will serve her well for years to come. Natural consequences taught her more than all of my wisdom and wonderful, sage advice could ever have taught, and my precious daughter made a giant leap into adulthood. (It was probably well worth the price she paid, come to think of it.)

## Using Time to Heal Emotional Wounds

Sometimes parents will say things to their children, and children will say things to their parents, they regret having said. Time can help heal the wounds inflicted by misused words. For example:

| Mother: | "Ted, there must be something the matter with you to get grades like this. All of your brothers and sisters do better than you do. Now quit acting like you're stupid, and bring those grades up—if you can!" |

> It's not necessary for the parent to always be right.

| Ted: | "I'm your kid, you know. If I'm stupid, where do you think I got it? You're no genius, you know!" |

If this kind of thing happens, put it behind you immediately, and let it die over time. Turn over a new leaf, acknowledge the error you made, then begin immediately to build the boy's self-esteem:

| Mother: | "Ted, I reacted badly to your report card. You needn't say anything in response to what I'm going to say. Just accept it as coming from my heart. I'm sorry. I'm really very, very sorry. You are an able young man and I love you." |

If Ted says something like, "That's okay, Mom. It's just one of those things." Respond appreciatively: "Thank's Ted. Things will be okay, I can assure you." Then let it go at that.

If, on the other hand, he responds in anger, don't depart from the spirit of what you said. Be compassionate and empathetic, but stay on course:

Ted: "Don't give me that bleeding heart crap! I'm stupid, you know it, and you love to rub it in."

Mother: "I'm not surprised you'd feel that way. After all, I did say some pretty mean things. I take responsibility for that. Whether you want to believe me or not is up to you. But I am sorry. That much I know."

> *Kids are tremendously resilient. Ah, that parents were, as well.*

By remaining calm, on course, and using time to your advantage, you will eventually make your case and wounds will be healed. Kids are tremendously resilient. They can bounce back from some pretty terrible assaults by parents. It's never too late to start the healing process, and there is generally plenty of time for the healing to take place.

## Using Time to Build Self-Esteem

Parents want their children to feel good about themselves; to see themselves as worthwhile and able. But self-esteem isn't built in a day. It takes time, time mixed with the right choice of words.

Children who have a low self-esteem not only feel worthless, they have difficulty accepting statements of support and confidence from others. Consider this situation:

Parent: "David, this report you wrote for English is really good! I had no idea you wrote so well and thought so deeply!"

David: "Aw, it's no good and you know it. You're always saying stuff like that just to make me feel good."

Typically a parent will respond with a statement to refute what the child has said. For example:

Parent: "No, David, I didn't say that just to make you feel good. You really do write well. I mean it! This is good work!"

Armed with the ammunition provided by such a response, David fires back, arguing in defense of his own short comings!

David: "Look, I'm stupid and you know it. It really makes me mad when you say things about me you know aren't true."

And the battle is on! Allowed to take its course, I've seen this kind of situation get worse and worse with every exchange until it ends up something like this:

Parent: "Okay, David, okay. So you're stupid and no good! Have it your way. I was only trying to help. I only wanted you to feel good about yourself, but if you can't accept that, then that's up to you. I don't care to discuss this any more. So much for my good intentions! How do you think this must make me feel as your parent!?"

> Self-esteem is the foundation on which one's life is built.

Parents often respond abruptly and defensively like this. They are so anxious to get the message across to their kids quickly, in hopes their kids' self-esteem will get better quickly. It's kind of a panic response intended to save a kid's life. It's a very natural way of responding. After all, if the child is in danger, one is inclined to act quickly.

A better way is to use time to your advantage. A damaged self-esteem isn't deadly. In time it can heal. But it takes time. Time is important for at least two reasons. First, there needs to be enough time to repeatedly get the message across to the child that he does have worth. Secondly, the child needs time to learn to accept the fact that he has worth. Self-esteem, or the lack of it, is a learned behavior. No one is born with it or without it, and learning a behavior takes time.

Let's revisit the situation with David and illustrate a better way. We'll start from the beginning:

Parent: "David, this report you wrote for English is really good! I had no idea you wrote so well and thought so deeply."

David: "Aw, it's no good and you know it. You're always saying stuff like that just to make me feel good."

Parent: "I'm sorry you feel that way, but I'm not a phony, and you do write well. You don't have to believe me if you don't want to, but I'd appreciate it if you did. After all, I wouldn't want you to think I'd lie just to make you feel good."

Now what can David say? With this response, David's ability to write is no longer a topic. The issues on the table now are the parent's genuineness and David's choice to believe the parent or not. Let's consider what David might say, and how the parent would respond so the channels of communication are kept open and, over time, the parents can continue to get this important message across.

David: "I didn't say you were a liar. I said you just say those things to make me feel good."

Parent: "But that's lying if I don't mean it, and I do mean it. And you wouldn't want me to be a liar. I love you, David. You're a neat guy. What do you say we have a game of ping-pong?"

A response like this completely defuses David's argument that he is no good, that

134

his parents are simply sheltering him from his own worthlessness. Furthermore, it provides an avenue for the boy and his parent to have a positive relationship, which will certainly open up other opportunities for the parent to build the boy's self-esteem:

Parent: "David, you play a mean game of ping-pong. You might have beaten me this time, but next time, watch out. I'll take you on again tomorrow night. Is it a date?!"

David: "You're on, Dad. You'd better be tough."

I've used the example of ping-pong. It could be checkers or chess, Trivial Pursuit, marbles, or any number of things. It makes no difference so long as the experience is a positive one, and the door is left open for a continuation of positive experiences. But be sure to pick activities in which the child is able to compete and even win. Don't invite the child to an activity that invites more failure into his life!

Let's suppose, however, that David's response is hostile, and argumentative.

David: "Aw, it's no good and you know it. Your always saying stuff like that just to make me feel good."

Parent: "But that's lying if I don't mean it, and I do mean it. And you wouldn't want me to be a liar. I love you, David. You're a neat guy."

David: "Don't give me that junk! Everyone knows I'm a failure and I can't stand it when people say stuff like that!"

Parent: (Completely changing the subject) "I heard that the high school baseball team has won five games in a row. Not bad!"

David: "What's that got to do with this conversation?"

Parent: "Nothing. I just don't want to argue. Let's play a game of ping-pong."

Either way, the parent did not allow the conversation to degenerate into an argument over the parent's motives, or into a fruitless attempt to convince the child he is able and does have worth. And best of all, the door to the future was left open, a future in which other opportunities could be created to build the boy's self-esteem.

Time is a powerful tool that parents can use to influence the way their children think, feel, and act. Learn to use that tool well, then use it to your and your children's advantage.

## Behavior Over Time As A Function of Age

Change can be a slow process, particularly where human behavior is concerned. And it gets slower the older the individual gets. With young children dramatic changes can be effected quite rapidly. The tantrums of a 2-year-old can be "fixed" in only a few days. Recently I worked with a young couple whose 3-year-old wouldn't stay in his crib at night. In 20 minutes we had that problem solved. A few weeks after our visit, I asked the mother how things were going. She said, "Oh, it's wonderful. Now when it's bedtime he comes to me and says 'It's time for me to go to bed, Mommy.'"

For older children, particularly adolescents who are under the reinforcement control of peer groups and other powerful influences outside the home, change for the better can come pretty slowly. Figure 6.1 illustrates this important reality. During childhood, it's fairly easy to keep children within the family value system. They are small enough that parents can pick them up and take them or put them where they are supposed to be. Parents are able to get their way by asserting themselves as adults.

> The family value system is the anchor of the family. No value system, no anchor.

However, as children enter adolescence, all of that begins to change as they become more and more vulnerable to out-of-home spheres of influence. Children can, and do, tell their parents to "bug off," and remind them that they (the children) can do what they want to do, "and you can't stop me!" And they are correct, we can't.

## Figure 6.1—Surviving Conflicts with the Family Value System

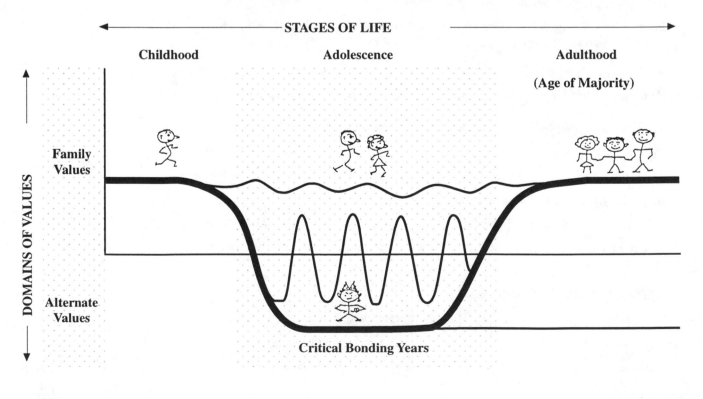

All children "play with fire" during adolescence. Even the best kids sneak outside the value system from time to time to taste forbidden fruits. One study by the juvenile justice system revealed that for every dalliance at which a kid is caught, at least 10 equally serious offenses have gone undetected. For the most part, children identify more with life in the value system than out of it; that is, they find it to be more reinforcing to be "in" instead of "out," so "in" is where they generally are. Some, however, given the reinforcers outside the value system, reject parental guidance and leadership; exploit the resources of home and family and make little to no contribution to either; groom, dress, and behave in a manner that brings embarrassment and shame to the family; avoid contact or association with family members except in pursuit of selfish interests (getting money, food, lodging, clothing, transportation, etc.); are generally unpleasant to be with, are sullen and surly and look and smell bad; and make light of things that are held dear within the value system such as religious teachings and family traditions.

When children have gotten to this degree of dissidence with the family value system, the probability of getting them back into the value system during adolescence approximates the probable survival rate of an ice cube in hell. So what do parents do? Since I've repeatedly extended the caution to parents to not throw their kids away, what are they to do under such desperate conditions as these?!? There is an answer, and it has two dimensions: bonding and consequences.

First, *bonding*. Though the kid might be out of control, that doesn't mean the parent(s) must be out of control. Though parents will likely be heartsick, they needn't react in kind. (See Figure 4.1, pg. 89.) Rather, they should go on with life, rise above the immaturity of the child's behavior, display strength and character, have the best relationship possible with one another and the other members of the family, and let the out-of-control child know that though he/she is out of control, the parents aren't. When the child comes home, greet him and interact with him on a mature, adult basis, without being victimized! An encounter might go like this:

> *Children can't force a parent to be out of control of his/her own behavior. That's something the parent chooses to do.*

Setting:   The boy has returned home after having been gone and unaccounted for several hours (even days!). He is disheveled, smells bad, is sullen— generally distasteful.

Dad:   (With a smile and a calm demeanor) "Hello, son. Glad you're home safe and sound. We've been worried about you."

*Note*: Unless you need information for problem solving, don't ask where he's been or what he's been doing. It will only encourage lying, evasion, and hostility, as discussed thoroughly in Chapter 8, Questioning Children About Their Behavior.

Son: (Less than enthusiastically) "Hi."

Dad: "If you're hungry, there's food in the fridge. Help yourself."

*Note*: Don't offer to fix a meal, unless it is mealtime and the entire family is eating, in which event let the boy know he's welcome to eat with the family.

Son: "Okay. Thanks."

*Note*: Under these conditions when the environment is being controlled in a positive, stable way, it is altogether reasonable the boy will say "thanks".

Dad: (Moving into a risk-free discussion) "I saw where your friend, Jason, joined the Army. I sure hope he likes it better than I did!"

Son: "Who cares. He was an idiot to join up. He only did it to get away from his old man."

*Note*: A more than a two-word response is very encouraging. But it's important to not get drawn into a values-laden discussion about "idiocy" and "old man."

Dad: "Well, I hope he has a good experience in the military. It is sure a lot different now than when I was in."

Son: "Ya."

*Note:* Oops. We are now back to monosyllabic responses. But don't despair. Progress is two steps forward and one step back.

Dad: (Changing subjects again) "Well, I'm gone. Gotta get the car serviced. You have a good day, Son. And, again, I'm glad you're home safe and sound," followed by a gentle touch on the shoulder or a pat on the back.

Son: "Ah, Dad. I need to talk to you a minute."

*Note*: Ah ha! The boy does have more than a monosyllabic vocabulary. But be careful. He probably isn't interested in just shooting the breeze.

Dad: "Sure. What's up."

Son: "Well, ah. I know I don't deserve it, but I need some spending money, bad. I'm flat broke. Could you loan me a few bucks."

*Note:* It is at a point like this where you have to be super cautious. The boy appears to have humbled himself ("I know I don't deserve it, but..."), and that can be very seductive. Do not interpret this as a sign of reconciliation or that his life is finally getting straightened out. In all probability, it is a simple con job. Adolescent behavior just doesn't change that fast. Kids who muck around outside the value system are usually thinking of no one but themselves. They tend to be basically exploitive. Hang on to your wallet.

Dad: "I'm sorry you're broke, Son. I know how distressful that can be. There are some things here at home that need to be done for which I'll be happy to pay you a fair wage, but I won't just give or loan you the money."

*Note:* At this point, the discussion could go one of at least three ways: (1) The boy could just get angry and bolt. If he does, just let him go. He'll be back, and when he is, he'll bring with him a new respect for his father; (2) He could argue; or (3) He could comply. Let's work through 2 and 3.

Scenario #2: The boy argues.

Son: "Dad, I don't have time to work for the money right now. I need the money right away. I'm only asking for a loan. I'll pay it back later, or I'll work it off later. It's no big deal, Dad. I'm only asking for five bucks!"

*Note:* Since past behavior is the best predictor of future behavior, and since, in the past, money given noncontingently (that is, having not been earned) has been money down a rat hole, there is absolutely no reason to believe things will be different now. Furthermore, the fact that the boy is only asking for $5.00 is immaterial. Whether it's $5.00 or $5,000 makes no difference. Noncontingent reinforcement of any kind or magnitude is destructive to one's well-being. So the answer is NO!, but said proactively, as follows.

Dad: "I know you're in a hurry, Son, and the quicker you get to work the quicker the $5.00 is yours. I can start you on the job right now, but I expect it to be done well. When do you want to start?"

Son: "Hey, man, what's going on here? Chill out, Dad. I'm not asking to break the bank. I'm not asking for any freebies. You'll get your lousy five bucks back. Come on, Dad. I got things to do!"

Dad: "The decision is really yours, Son. Maybe you ought to go to your room and cool down. Think it over. When you've decided to go to work, let me know. I'm ready when you are."

*Note:* Issues of amount, payback, time constraints—these are all beside the point from a behavioral perspective and should be ignored. The key is to make certain that reinforcers are not dispensed without a contingency being met.

Son: "To hell with you! I'm outta here! I don't know why I even bother to come home!" And out he goes, slamming the door behind him.

*Note:* Don't be intimidated in situations like these. If you were to bet money on the long-term outcome, the chances are great that you'd win money betting that by responding this way, the relationship between the boy and his dad would be strengthened and the boy would come to respect his father and use him as a role model later in life.

Before moving to Scenario #3, I need to remind you about the risks parents must take in the rearing of children. Parenting is a risk-laden activity, and those risks increase with age. To complicate matters, the probabilities for successful treatment decrease with age as risk goes up, as illustrated in Figure 6.2. Happily, that all tends to reverse itself as children move into adulthood. In these Scenarios, I've tried to capture the essence of what I've experienced over the years both as a parent and in my work with families. In all instances, I have always taken what I felt was the course of least risk, but realizing all the while, that risks were there. Virtually without exception, proceeding as I am illustrating here carries with it the *least* risk.

> *Parenting is an inherently risky business. The only way to avoid that risk is to not be a parent.*

No procedure or therapy is entirely risk-free. The medical treatment model gives us a good basis for comparison. Not long ago I had an appendicitis attack. For a nearly 61-year-old man, that was unusual and a bit more complicated. Before operating on me, the surgeon sat down on the side of my hospital bed and enumerated the risks of such a procedure for a man my age. He concluded by saying, "But, of course, the risk of doing nothing is the riskiest option of all." And so it is with behavior. In instances of behavioral problems, the risk of doing nothing at all can be the riskiest option of all. When the surgeon talked to me about the risk of treatment he and I both understood that commonly

**Figure 6.2—Course of Treatment Over Time— During Adolescence Things Are Really Upside Down!**

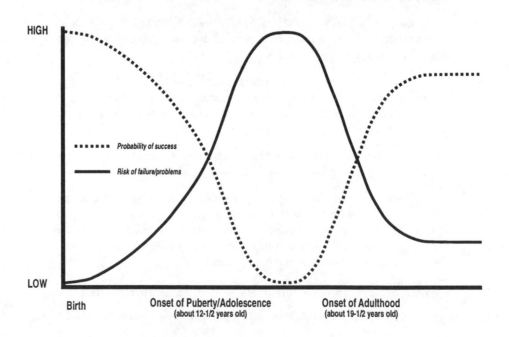

accepted surgical procedures would be applied. We weren't talking about witch doctoring! And so it is with behavioral treatment. Commonly accepted behavioral treatment procedures, based on science, are what is being applied here. These are not snake oil remedies. But even under the best conditions, whether it's a medical/surgical procedure or a behavioral one, we are not entirely free of risk.

Scenario #3: The boy complies and agrees to work.

Son:     "Okay, Dad. If that's the way it is. What do you want me to do?"

*Note*: If the boy is sullen or condescending or verbally "smart", cut through all the junk, put it completely on extinction, and get right on with the task—indeed, the *therapy*!

Dad:     "Great. I'm delighted to have you work for me. The fence along the back of the yard has begun to lean out. The shrubs are pushing it back. The section behind the pine tree is of particular concern. Let's go out and take a look at it so you'll know exactly what has to be done."

*Note*: On the way to the job, it would be a good idea to make physical and verbal contact: A hand on the shoulder, small talk about things going on in the neighborhood and family, and so on.

Dad:     "Here's the section that needs to be straightened up. You'll need to reset this post. To be sure everything is straight, you'll also need to string a guide-line from the two end posts. Now, do you have any questions?"

*Note*: The father's expectations are very clear. He didn't just say, "Go out and straighten out the fence."

Son:     "I think I understand, Dad."

Dad:     "Great. I expect it should take no more than a couple of hours. I'll pay you $5.00 an hour. Keep track of your time and let me know when your through. When the job's done, I'll pay you immediately. Fair enough?"

*Note*: Again, the specifics are all covered: estimated time, rate of pay, payment schedule, and the implied expectation that when "the job's done" it will have been done correctly and to standard.

Son:     "I'll let you know when it's done."

Dad:     "Super. You don't know how much I appreciate this. That fence has been working on my mind for weeks—to say nothing about your Mom! Thanks, Son. I love you tons and tons!"

*Note*: The boy has been cast into the role of a major problem solver, a contributor to the family, and he and his dad are honestly enjoying one another.

When the boy approaches his father to get paid, the father must inspect the work. This isn't just for purposes of accountability. It also provides the father an opportunity to acknowledge good performance, administer correctives should the job not be quite up to standard, and communicate to the boy the value of a job well done. After all, the boy is getting paid by the hour so more work means more money. (Of course, care must be taken to assure that the boy is not taking more time than is necessary just to increase the amount of pay. It is always important to estimate in advance how much time would be needed to get the job done correctly, and what would be a fair price to pay for the work.)

> *Trauma can be your parenting friend if you'll let its consequences do the talking for you.*

Little-by-little, over time, these kinds of relationships will build and bond, then, looking again at Figure 6.1, when the boy is leaving adolescence and about to enter adulthood, some interesting things happen, all of which work in the boy's and the family's interests, if bonding has taken place during the previous difficult years. For starters, the peer group begins to disintegrate. Its members marry, go away to school or work, join the military, and so on. Also, the reality of impending adulthood comes crashing down on the kid. Additional responsibilities mount. The need to be self-supporting has reared its sobering head. Combined, these introduce a measure of trauma into the now young man's life, and trauma always drives a person to seek relief. But where does one look for relief in an uncertain world? You guessed it, the predictable structure and security of a stable home and family. And if the child's home and family have been secure and stable while he has been away to the hinterlands of foolishness, home and family is where he will return, but now in an altogether different frame of mind. (Remember the Prodigal Son Syndrome? It is centuries old.) As noted by Laurens van der Post and Jane Taylor, in their book *Testament To The Bushmen:*

> "It remains an irrefutable social and individual premise, that no culture has ever been able to provide a better shipyard for building storm-proof vessels for the journey of man from the cradle to the grave than the individual nourished in a loving family."

Now another word about *consequences.* As you can imagine, among my favorite Bible stories is the story of the Prodigal Son, who when he "came to himself" said, "I will go to my father." And that tends to be the way it goes; not always, but usually. My experience over the years indicates at least 85% of those who leave the value system during adolescence return to the value system as adults. The probabilities of that happening even increase when the bonds between the family and the child are strong, when parents have been in control of *their* lives, even when the kids have been out of control of theirs.

Getting back to the parable of the Prodigal Son, there are two other notable lessons to be learned. The first lesson is that when the boy came home "the father fell on his neck and kissed him." The father made a loving, warm, embracing, physical contact with the boy and welcomed him home with rejoicing. He didn't say, "You dumb cluck! Look at you. What a mess. Dirty, broke, stinking (remember, he had been working and living with pigs!). I can't believe it! You make me sick. No skills, no nothing. How in the world can you expect to make a living? And look at the shame you've brought to the family! How am I to explain all that? Do you have any idea what a fix you've put me in!? I've told the neighbors and family you've been off on business. How am I going to explain this! Brother!"

No, he didn't do this kind of stupid thing. Behaving like that is little to no better than the way the boy behaved when he was living outside the value system. Rather, the father was positive and proactive. He didn't say a word about misbehavior but instead began immediately to build the boy up. That's the first lesson.

The second lesson to be learned from this parable is about consequences. When the brother who stayed home and tended to the family business began to complain about all the fuss being made over his prodigal brother, the father said, "All that I have is thine." Do you see the lesson in this? Though the father rejoiced at the return of the boy who was lost, he allowed the consequences of the boy's decision (that is, to take his portion of the inheritance and squander it) to remain with the boy. The father didn't go to his wiser son and say, "Let's rethink your brother's position with the company. Surely there's enough here for all of us to live comfortably. What do you say we carve out a portion for him." No, he let the consequences rest in place. No free lunch. No noncontingent reinforcers. No mercy being allowed to rob justice. What a powerful lesson in parenting!

When children leave the value system, they enter areas of high risk, and seldom return without having experienced some degree of loss. For some, this might be so severe that they suffer from it for the rest of their lives. Drug and alcohol abuse, disease, poverty are all losses from which it is difficult to recover. But those are the natural consequences of poor decisions and though we should love our children anyway—unconditionally— we must not deny them the lessons to be learned from the consequences of their own behaviors. Our support should *always* be there, but it should be there contingently.

Often, when I talk to parents of wayward children about being patient while at the same time being positive and proactive, they express a sense of despair. They don't want to wait that long. They want changes now! Well, it just doesn't happen that way. And besides, gradual change for the better is generally more lasting than is dramatic change, and much easier to maintain. Figure 6.3 illustrates this point. With dramatic change, the behavior tends to move rapidly away from the reinforcers that have maintained it. This puts a lot of stress on the system, as when one stretches an elastic band. The further it is stretched, the greater the resistance and the more powerful the force to get back to equilibrium. And so it is with human behavior, particularly the behavior of older children and adults. A too-rapid departure from baseline simply increases the forces of regression to baseline, forces that draw the behavior back to its reinforcers so fast, in fact, that conditions might ultimately be worse as a result of such a radical approach to treatment. Crash dieting is a perfect example. The great majority of people who go on crash diets not only gain back all they lost, but typically more. One study found that in a period of time roughly equal to twice as long as it took to lose the weight, the people gained back 105% of what was lost. For example, if a person lost 20 pounds in a month, within about two months, that person would have gained back 21 pounds.

Gradual improvement in one's behavior is far more lasting than is immediate, dramatic change for the better. Think in terms of little-by-little.

Gradual change, on the other hand, where reinforcers are kept close to the behavior, thus creating a new baseline of behavior (as illustrated in Figure 6.3), is much more likely to be lasting change.

In some instances, however, it has been found that dramatic change treatments, e.g. going "cold turkey," are the best, in the long run. Drug, alcohol, and tobacco addiction are examples of behaviors that are best treated through abstinence. And, of course, some socially deviant behaviors must also be treated with abrupt, dramatic-change methods. Child and spouse abuse, kleptomania, pyromania, homicide, and so on are not behaviors that can be allowed to decrease gradually. These are behaviors that almost always need professional help, and where precise and direct support systems are put in place to prevent regression to baseline.

**Figure 6.3—Dramatic vs. Gradual Change**

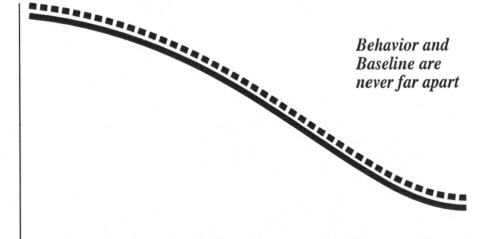

# DRAMATIC
## *vs.*
# GRADUAL CHANGE

*Baseline*

*(where all the reinforcers are)*

*Regression to Baseline*

**DRAMATIC CHANGE**

*Behavior and Baseline are never far apart*

**GRADUAL CHANGE**

## NOW TO REVIEW

Use time to your advantage to

1. cool off,

2. think things over,

3. heal emotional wounds, and

4. build self-esteem.

By using time wisely, even though our children might be engaging in terrible behaviors outside the value system, we can still bond with them. Bonding time, plus the lessons children learn from the natural consequences of their risk-laden behaviors, will combine to bring errant children back to the family, back to the value system. But this all takes time. Gradual change is typically better and more long-lasting than dramatic, metamorphic-like change.

> *Research has shown that the most effective way to reduce problem behavior in children is to strengthen desirable behavior through positive reinforcement rather than trying to weaken undesirable behavior using aversive or negative processes.*
> *S.W. Bijou*
> *The International Encyclopedia of Education, 1988*

# SEVEN
# Proactive Responding to Reactive Adolescent Behavior

In an effort to wrest control from their parents, adolescents frequently resort to reactive behaviors which can leave parents in a quandary as to how to respond. Reactive behaviors are defined here as selfish, argumentative, out-of-sorts things kids do to get their way. Typically, in such situations, the parents become as reactive as the children, and before long the situation degenerates into a shouting match and the drawing of battle lines, with any hope for reasonable problem solving being dashed completely.

In this chapter, I have recreated four typical reaction-prone situations, and have suggested ways of responding which are proactive; that is, the parents are in complete control of their own emotions, empathetic, understanding, are directing behavior towards the solution of the problem, and the reasonable consequences for behavior are appropriately articulated and applied.

Each of these examples follows a common format in which

> *Good parenting is first a matter of teaching, second a matter of modeling, and never a matter of reacting.*

    a.  the challenging, reactive behavior of the adolescent is stated,

    b.  a proactive response of the parent is given, and

    c.  possible outcomes and follow-up actions are proposed.

## Situation 1:

A 15 year old refuses to comply with a parent's directions, and is going to "do it" anyway.

    **a.  The Challenge.**

        "I'm going to do it and you can't stop me!"

    **b.  Proactive Response.**

        "You are right. I can't stop you. But before you do it, you might want to count the cost. What do you stand to lose or gain?" (Discuss here what the person has to gain or lose as a result of "doing it." You might even write them down in "pro" and "con" columns on a large piece of paper.)

        "Now, go to your room and think it over. Come back in half an hour and let's talk about it." (In situations like this, it's important to use time to your advantage. Time allows emotions to calm down and reason to influence decision making. It gives the individual time to think over the consequences in a more in-control setting.)

    **c.  Possible Results and Follow-Up Action.**

        (1)  He/she decides against "it," and drops the idea. You say, "Thanks, that's super. I'm proud of you."

        (2)  He/she decides to work for a compromise. Work it out, remembering to respect parental expectations that give direction to the behavior in the home.

        (3)  He/she decides to go with the original course of action to "do it." In such a situation, let the consequences fall where they may. Here again, it is important that the consequences, both positive and negative, be spelled out well in advance so the individual knows exactly what he/she is getting into. Before laying out the consequences, be sure to have thought them through carefully. Do not impose consequences that will not/can not be enforced. Be reasonable and rational! For example, to tell a child that he/she "will never be allowed home again as long as I live!" makes

no sense at all. Avoid this kind of extremism. (Read Chapter 5, "A Word about Consequences.")

## Situation 2:

A 16-year-old decides to leave home.

    **a.  The Challenge.**

    "I'm out of here" or "I'm going to get a place of my own. I can't stand living here in this rotten hole any longer!"

    **b.  Proactive Response.**

    "I'm sorry that living here causes you to be so upset."

    "But before you do that, let's talk over some of the details. If you're going to leave home and go on your own, there are some things you need to know to survive in the real world, and I don't want you to get hurt." (Spell them out: economics, logistics, etc. Write them down on a chalkboard or large piece of paper as is illustrated in point 3, below.)

    **c.  Possible Results and Follow-up Action.**

    (1)  Decides not to leave. You say, "I'm glad you decided to stay. I like having you at home (which might not be entirely true!). Let's sit down together and work things out so that living at home is more enjoyable."

    (2)  He/she decides to think things over and not make any rash decisions. This will likely have a moderating effect on behavior. Be sure you take every opportunity to acknowledge behaviors that are appropriate, and to have many, many positive and mature interactions. There will be times when you will be disappointed, want to scream, tear your hair, and even kick the kid out. Don't! Be proactive. Avoid traps like lecturing, moralizing, preaching, pleading, arguing, reasoning, or threatening. Endure and bond. In the long run, this will produce the better results.

        The "long run" might be a few years. That's okay. A *few* years of discomfort followed by a lifetime of success, happiness, and togetherness for all is many times better than rash and seemingly expedient reactions that find the child out of the home unable to deal successfully with the complexities of adulthood; a circumstance that results in long-term miseries and expenses for parents and children brought on by unemployment, problems with the law, poor health, unaffordable dependents, and the list goes on.

Remember this: The longer you keep an adolescent home (assuming you are maintaining a proactive, instructive, positive environment) the better able the child will be to succeed as an adult, and the more independence you'll ultimately enjoy!

(3) Decides to leave. Say, "I wish you well. Please keep in touch. We are concerned about how you are doing." Remind him/her that *leaving is done at one's own expense*. The natural consequences of behavior must not be mitigated by misplaced parental empathy or mercy. In this regard, it would be appropriate to visit with the child about the economic consequences of living on one's own, away from home. When doing this, use a large sheet of paper or chalk board on which to itemize those costs:

| | |
|---|---|
| Rent | $ _____ |
| Food | _____ |
| Car Payment | _____ |
| Car Maintenance | _____ |
| Gasoline | _____ |
| Clothing | _____ |
| Utilities | _____ |
| etc. | _____ |

When doing this, don't do it in a "See-what-you're-getting-into-kid" tone. Let it be a learning opportunity. Let it be a chance for you to help the child move successfully into adulthood.

## Situation 3:

A teenager is out of control.

### a. The Challenge.

The child launches into a terrible tirade: screams, hollers, is abusive, starts throwing things, hitting, and so on.

**b. Proactive Response.**

"In a voice that is calm but firm, and loud enough to be heard, raise your hand in a non threatening STOP position, look the child squarely in the eye, and say, "Stop that now! Look at me. Thank you for looking at me. Put your hands to your sides. Thank you for putting your hands down to your sides."

When control has been achieved, move directly into a teaching interaction procedure as found in Chapter 3, pages 67–68, as follows:

1.  "Son, I'm sorry you're upset.

2.  You said some profane and abusive things to your sister.

3.  Though you are angry, you must never say things like that. Rather, when you are angry and feel like saying such things, go to your room, cool down, and when you feel better, come see me.

4   When you control yourself and behave that way, you gain maturity and we are all a lot happier.

5.  Now, what do I expect you to do when you are inclined to get angry? Show me what you are going to do instead of being abusive.

6.  Right. Good job. You're going to go cool down first, then come to see me."

If you think the behavior will likely reoccur anyway, I would continue with a statement of consequences:

7.  "Son, when you control yourself as you have just demonstrated, you'll continue to enjoy the many privileges you have around here. What are some of those?" (Let the boy enumerate them, and write them down on a piece of paper.)

    "Super. Those are really neat things to be able to do.

    If you should lose control of your behavior and say things you shouldn't say, what privileges will you deny yourself?

    Correct, you'll deny yourself these things written here."

Of course, you must prepare in advance for such a moment as this by having the consequences of behavior clearly articulated. Make certain that *all* of the consequences of such behavior are clearly understood in advance, by everyone. For example, when you

> *Privileges are not given or taken, they are earned or not earned.*

make such a declarative statement as the one suggested above, and the word "consequences" is used, the child knows exactly what you have in mind. Thoughts of the loss of such valuable privileges as use of the car, use of the telephone, access to one's room and wardrobe, and so on will come to the child's mind. Hopefully, there will have been previous experiences which will have already taught the child that, indeed, behavior *does* carry with it some heavy consequences. If these conditions exist, then it will be the thought of the loss of these many desirable privileges which will have the greatest impact on the child's behavior.

c. **Possible Results and Follow-Up Actions.**

(1) He/she stops. You say, "Let's talk it over. I can see you are terribly upset. Go to your room (or some quiet, solitary place) and think this matter over. Let's get back together in half an hour or so and talk about it when we are both more calm and rational."

(2) He/she continues to scream and holler though not engaged in any destructive behavior. Simply walk away. Before doing so, say in a firm voice, "I refuse to be in your company when you behave this way. I'm leaving now. When you are calm and rational we can discuss this matter together. In the meantime, you have denied yourself many privileges." Do not allow yourself to vent your frustration on the child by going overboard and "throwing the book" at him, i.e., embellishing the consequences, or making up new ones even you can't follow-up on. For example, "You're grounded for a whole month!"

(3) He/she continues to rant and rave, but is also destructive. Use physical constraint *only* if in doing so you are not in danger, or if you need to protect yourself. If there is any chance the child can get the better of you, and perhaps injure you and/or damage property, do not use physical restraint. Rather, call someone to give you help—a family member, a neighbor/friend, the police. If you are in physical danger, leave the premises and go to a safe place to make your call.

If such a distasteful episode should occur, you must maintain your composure, but have the consequences of such behavior well in mind then allow those consequences to come into play to an extent consistent with the offense.

No system or set of responses will work if the scenario has not been well thought out and a proactive response anticipated well in advance. For this reason, I urge parents to put down in writing a description of the behaviors they anticipate will happen, script a proactive response, then practice that response with a spouse, another family member, or a trusted friend. Table 7.1 is an illustration of how this can be done. I emphasize practicing proactive responding. Without practice, there is little to no chance that one will be able to respond appropriately at a moment of crisis. Correct, proactive responding *must* be practiced well in advance of the onset of the anticipated problem behavior.

## Table 7.1—Anticipating Behaviors and Responding Proactively

| ANTICIPATED PROBLEM BEHAVIORS | MY PROACTIVE RESPONSE |
|---|---|
| 1. "Mom, I hate you! You're the worst mother in the world!" | 1. "I'm sorry you feel that way, dear." |
| 2. "No one likes me. I don't have *any* friends." | 2. "Golly, that's no fun. Would you like to talk about it?" |
| 3a. "Dad, how come I can't have nice things like the other kids at school?" | 3a. "It is easy to feel deprived, Honey. Do you have any suggestions about how to improve things?" |
| b. "Yeah! Just buy me more clothes!" | b. "That *would* be nice." |
| c. "Well! You asked for my suggestions! Is that all I get?!" | c. "Since I can't just buy you all the clothes you want, think of some things you can do, as well, to help improve things." |
| d. You can too buy me more clothes. "You just won't do it because you don't care how I look!" | d. "Can you think of some things *you* can do to help improve things?" |
| e. "Dad! I don't have any money. You *know* that!" | e. "Give this matter some thought, Honey, and I will too. Let's share our ideas tomorrow." |
| And so on... | |

## Situation 4:

A near-adult exerts his/her "maturity."

    **a.  The Challenge.**

        Your son/daughter says, "Next year I'll turn 18 and then you can't tell me what to do anymore. I'll do just as I please because I'll be an adult."

    **b.  Proactive Response.**

        Note: This response, though very direct, *must* be said in a calm voice without any hint that you are glad to see the day he/she leaves. Speak as one mature adult to another, with empathy and concern for his/her welfare. Practice before you say it!

        "That is true, you will be 18 and you will be considered an adult under the law; however, as long as you eat at my table and sleep in the bed that I freely provide, and use the facilities of this house, your agency is somewhat limited. All of the privileges I have mentioned, and many others, are yours so long as your behavior at home is consistent with our expectations. If you do not care to behave accordingly, then, since you are an adult under the law, you are free to leave and behave as you wish in whatever environment you care to create.

        "Remember, one's agency is not only a gift, it is a great responsibility. When the day comes that you are able to fully exercise that responsibility in your own home and at your own expense, then your agency is *all* yours. You'll then have the demands of society to answer to. In the meantime, we expect you to live in accordance with the values of the home which include being pleasant to live with and being a contributing member of the family. I'll be happy to visit with you about this if you have any questions. Think it over for awhile then let's get back together."

    **c.  Possible Results and Follow-up Actions.**

      (1)  He/she thinks it over and decides to talk to you about it. During this visit, make certain the child knows he/she is of worth to you, and you want home to be a happy place for everyone. Discuss your expectations. Where appropriate, negotiate without forfeiting control of the home environment. Since this situation addresses what *might* happen in the distant future, you have time to bond to the child by frequently and selectively reinforcing those

behaviors that are appropriate and that you appreciate, by ignoring those behaviors that are inappropriate but inconsequential, by teaching appropriate behavior, and by allowing natural or social consequences to do the talking for you in those instances where anything you might say would simply be rejected or be counterproductive.

(2) The child continues to be unpleasant and disagreeable.

Typically, this kind of behavior is best left alone—just ignore it. Later when the child is pleasant and agreeable, be sure to acknowledge that, as noted earlier. If the behavior becomes intolerable because of its effects on other children, then restate your expectations, outline the consequences, and let the consequences do the talking for you. Under these circumstances, the probability is remote that the behavior will persist for more than a day or two.

(3) The child's behavior improves and he/she is pleasant to be with.

Be sure to acknowledge this with frequent though very natural, positive reinforcement: a gentle word, a tender touch, a sincere hug, a genuine smile, a brief note. A few of these a day will do wonders.

The key to being successful in any of the above experiences and the situations they represent is that the behavioral guidelines of the home are well articulated, and the children know exactly what to expect in any given situation. They know exactly what to expect when they behave appropriately, and they know exactly what to expect when they behave inappropriately.

In the process of putting such a program in place, there will always be a need to "debug" the system. That is only natural. You will make mistakes along the way, but you will make fewer and fewer as time goes by and as you become more and more skillful.

Do not allow your children to intimidate you. Do not cave in to their anger and/or their wrath. Avoid ambivalence. That's like telling your kid, "No, you're not going to do that, and that's semifinal." Don't be like the dad who said to me, "But I *was* firm with

> *Management systems, like the environments in which they operate, are in constant need of tuning.*

him. For a minute there he really believed he wasn't going to get the car keys."

Now just a final word about procrastination behaviors. Children, and particularly adolescents, are masters at putting you off. They do this with verbal diversions which have a long history of knocking parents off balance. Here are a few of them, with some suggested responses:

1. *"Don't worry about it, I can take care of myself."* Nearly every "trouble" my kids ever got into was preceded with something like this. Don't be too easily comforted by such statements of assurance. Rather, say something like, "I appreciate your effort to assure me that everything is fine. Still, I'm not comforted." Then discuss the matter in light of the consequences of behaving appropriately or inappropriately.

2. *"Just Leave Me Alone!"*, or *"Get off my case/get off my back!"* "No, in this instance I will not leave you alone. I have an investment in this matter—a serious responsibility—and it is in my interest and yours that we get this matter resolved." Then proceed in an objective manner to discuss the problem and devise a solution.

3. *"I'm sorry."* Don't let mercy rob justice. Express appreciation for the remorse, but press for what you can expect in the future, and apply the consequences to what the child has done. You can bet your life the kid is sorry only because he/she got caught, and the humility is more likely related to getting caught than to remorse for behaving badly. It is the behavior that is in question, not the level of humility or remorse.

Also avoid the overuse of such terms as "I'm doing this for your own good," or "I'm doing this because I love you." Rather, say, "Despite the fact that I love you very much, I'm doing this because it's my responsibility to do it. It brings me no great pleasure, but it must be done."

## NOW TO REVIEW

1. Expect children to be reactive. They are not yet fully civilized nor adequately experienced.

2. Given your adulthood, years of experience, and the skills taught in this book, you should now be fully able to respond proactively to adolescent, childish reactive behavior. On the form below, fill in the "proactive" column for situations 3 and 4.

| Child's Reactive Behavior | A Negative, Reactive Response | A Positive, Proactive Response |
|---|---|---|
| 1. "I hate my sister. I wish she'd die!" | "Well, you're not the world's best kid, you know." | "I'm sorry you're upset. Sometimes people do things that annoy us." |
| 2. "So I hit him, so what? He was bugging me and he deserved it." | "Here, take this (smack!). How does that feel? How does it feel getting hit by someone bigger than you?!" | Use a basic teaching interaction procedure, (see Chapter 3, pgs. 67-68) |
| 3. Mother calls the kids to dinner but they don't come saying: "Wait 'till this TV show is over." | "You kids get up here right this instant or that TV goes off for a month. Is that clear?" | |
| 4. You know the truth, and this isn't it: "I was too in school today. Someone's been lying about me." | "Hey, you're the liar! I happen to know for a fact that you skipped school today. Now why? What did you do? Who were you with?" | |

*Research has shown that the most effective way to reduce problem behavior in children is to strengthen desirable behavior through positive reinforcement rather than trying to weaken undesirable behavior using aversive or negative processes.*
  *S.W. Bijou*
  *The International Encyclopedia of Education, 1988*

# EIGHT
# Questioning Children
# About Their Behavior

I am forever amazed at how much family discord and hostile parent-child interactions are caused by the improper use of questioning. When one carefully analyzes how questioning is used, it's no wonder problems arise. Consider this example:

Mary comes home from school an hour and a half late.

Parent:     "Where have you been, Mary? Out with that terrible bunch of kids again, I suppose. How long will it take before you learn what a bunch of losers those kids are!?"

Mary:      "Leave my friends alone. Who I run around with is none of your business. You've got some friends that make me as sick as mine do you."

Parent:     "Just leave my friends out of this. You might not like them, but at least they are responsible people. I don't need to be ashamed of being seen with them!"

Mary:      "Hah! I wouldn't be caught dead with that bunch of old fogies!"

Now, let's analyze this encounter. First of all, the parent answered his/her own question. This was immediately followed by another question which was not a question

| |
|---|
| *Parents almost never ask questions to get answers.* |

at all in the sense that an answer was expected. It was, rather, an assault on Mary's choice of friends. Mary's response, not an answer, as you would expect, wasn't even remotely related to either question. She had friends to protect, and that was certainly a lot more important than providing a hostile, accusing parent with information. It was down hill from there!

But let's suppose Mary did answer the question:

Mary: "I stayed after school to watch a soccer game. I wasn't even with my friends."

Parent: "Don't you lie to me, young lady. That crowd you run with is like glue to you. You don't go anywhere or do anything without them. What do you think I am, stupid?"

Let's analyze this encounter. The girl answered the question and it got her into more trouble than in the first instance because now she's a liar as well!

I could go on with any number of examples to make the point—which is, unless you *really* need information for problem solving (as I'll explain in a bit), don't question

| |
|---|
| *Ask a stupid question and you get a stupid answer.* |

children about their behavior. There are two main reasons for this. First, you don't want an answer—and even if you get one, it doesn't improve things; behavior doesn't get any better. Here's an example. One child hits another child:

Parent: "Billy, why did you hit your brother?! Haven't I told you a hundred times not to hit your brother? How many times am I going to have to tell you to quit hitting your brother?!"

Billy: "I hit my brother because he is very ugly and I was only trying to fix his face. Yes, in fact you've told me 112 times to quit hitting him. I'll quit hitting him when he quits being ugly."

Parent: "Okay. Thank you. I just wanted to know!"

Though this example uses an absurd response from the child, and a subsequently absurd response from the parent ("I just wanted to know"), these are no more absurd than the questions being asked. In the first place, the questions were not asked to get information from the child. They were simply words the parent used to blow off steam, a desperate attempt to get the child to "shape up"! Nothing the child would have said would have been acceptable. For example:

Billy: "He started it! Why do you always get after me when it's not my fault?! I hate that dumb brother of mine. I wish he'd die. The only thing he does is get me in trouble!"

This is a more likely answer. Not absurd at all. But does it set the stage for problem solving? No. What typically happens is that the discussion—by now an argument—is off on a tangent and things will only get worse:

Parent:     "You're always blaming your brother for everything! And besides he's smaller than you are. Furthermore, don't you ever—do you understand me young man?!—don't you EVER say those wicked things about your brother!"

I hope by now you can see what's happening. It's a lose-lose situation no matter how you cut it. If the child answers the question, absurdly or otherwise, he's in trouble *because the parent was never looking for an answer in the first place.* That's the first reason you never ask a child to explain his inappropriate behavior.

The second reason is that by asking questions about the behavior, the child is getting lots and lots of attention for that behavior and the probability is very high that the attention will strengthen the very behavior being questioned; hence, the probability increases that it will reoccur. The principle to be kept in mind is this: behavior is strengthened by attention, and behavior that is strengthened is behavior that will more probably reoccur. In the examples I've used, the parents have strengthened the very behaviors they want to get rid of.

Never question children about their behavior unless (a) you are seriously in need of information, and (b) that information will help in problem solving. Always remember these! When our three oldest children were very young, our oldest son, standing tip-toe on a stool and using a long stick, managed to open a medicine cabinet where he and his younger sister found a bottle of baby aspirin. Thinking it was candy, they ate heartily, the youngest sister eating the most. The questions we asked the kids were intended to get information to help us solve a problem: "How full was the bottle when you started eating the aspirin? How much did each of you eat? When did you start eating it?" The answers convinced us that the children should be taken to the hospital emergency room and have their stomachs pumped. Which we did. No scolding, berating, or angry outbursts. And by the way, the natural consequences of their behavior—that is, having their stomachs pumped—did the talking for us relative to the dangers of eating aspirin, or feeding out of the medicine cabinet. (Have you ever had your stomach pumped? UGH!)

Rather than asking children to explain their inappropriate behavior, be directive, calm, and simply state your expectations. Following are some examples of questions you should avoid, accompanied by a better, proactive, verbal response to behavior.

Avoid asking questions if you expect the answer to:

1. Be one you don't want to hear:

   "Are you going to school today?"

   Rather, assume that he/she is going to school and be directive:

   "It's time to get ready for school."

2. Alienate you from others:

   "Why don't you get your hair cut?"

   Rather, use contingencies to do your nagging:

   "You bet you can use the car Saturday, Son. Just as soon as you get your hair cut."

3. Provide no answer:

   "How many times have I told you to hang up your clothes?"

   Rather, either ignore it, and wait until it's done, then acknowledge it, or let contingencies do your nagging:

   "Your allowance is ready once your clothes are hung up/room cleaned."

4. Prompt the child to lie:

   "Did you steal that money from my dresser?"

   Rather, say nothing until you have proof, then administer the *pre-understood* consequences. In the meantime, keep your money as secure as possible.

5. Be obvious:

   "Have you been smoking again?"

   Rather, give empathy:

   "I'm really sorry you have chosen to smoke. When you decide to quit, I'll be happy to help in any way I can." In the meantime, the natural and logical consequences of smoking must/will be felt.

   Natural consequences: Coughing, bad smell, damage to the body.

   Social consequences: No car privileges, allowance, etc.

6. Arouse personal animosities:

   "Why do you associate with such crummy people?"

   Rather, keep your mouth shut unless and until you can say something good.

7. Lead to further conflict:

   "Aren't you just about the biggest mess imaginable?"

Rather, wait for a positive characteristic to surface, then "pay that off."

A final note about questioning. Do not ask a child a question if you already know the answer: Alice has failed to get her homework done because she dawdled her time away watching TV.

Parent:  "Alice, why haven't you gotten your homework done?"

In light of what you've read, why is this useless and how can it even make a bad situation worse? Here's a better way:

Parent:  "Alice, turn off the TV and complete your homework now."

If you wonder how to get a child to respond appropriately to your directions, read Chapter 5, "A Word About Consequences."

## NOW TO REVIEW

Never question children about their inappropriate behaviors unless you need information to aid in problem solving. When, out of anger and frustration, parents question their children, several negative results commonly occur, including:

1.  The asking of more useless questions. Since, at times like these, parents really don't expect an answer, if an answer is given it is rejected, only to be followed by another dumb question. Eventually emotions get out of control and things get progressively worse.

2.  The strengthening of inappropriate behavior. Since questioning children about their behavior is a form of parental attention, that attention tends to strengthen the very behavior that is a problem; hence, that behavior is more likely to reoccur.

3.  The encouragement to lie. It is not at all unusual for children (or adults) to lie when questioned about things that could reflect badly on them.

> *Research has shown that the most effective way to reduce problem behavior in children is to strengthen desirable behavior through positive reinforcement rather than trying to weaken undesirable behavior using aversive or negative processes.*
> *S.W. Bijou*
> *The International Encyclopedia of Education, 1988*

*"I hate this lousy house! By the way, what's for supper?"*
   *(You know who.)*

# NINE
# Dealing with Hate and Anger

Hate is a complex emotion which is not understood very well at all by children; consequently, when they say they hate someone it is more likely an expression of an emotion that is much less complicated than it appears, and certainly immature. In fact, somewhat less than civilized!

When a young child says, "I hate you!" what the child is really saying is "I'm really mad at you!" This is typically associated with a frowny face, tears/crying, an angry voice, physical expressions

> **When a child says, "I hate you," he is really saying, "I'm really mad at you!"**

such as stomping about, head bent forward, arms flailing in menacing ways, name calling, and perhaps throwing objects and even hitting. Small children are less able to hide, disguise, or delay their feelings; consequently, they all come pouring out impulsively, creating a great scene and filling the environment with a dramatic and colorful display of behaviors that invite all the attention they can get. It's as if the child is saying, "Just try ignoring *this* one." It's something of a tantrum: loud, intense, compelling, sometimes embarrassing, and generally difficult to ignore.

Older children (12 and above) also feel anger and frustration which they interpret as hatred, but in fact, are not really feelings of hatred in a literal sense. The older the child gets, the less inclined he/she is to be as theatrical in the expression of anger and frustration. Although there will typically be some outward signs of what's boiling inside (a menacing glance instead of a menacing gesture, a rolling of the eyes toward the ceiling, facial expressions which declare disgust, and subvocal or barely audible mutterings),

> *Nothing is more indicative of one's having lost control than is anger.*

older children are more inclined to take their hatred to their rooms (or some other place away from home and family) where they seethe, lick their wounds, rationalize, agonize, philosophize, make the best of it, turn their attention to other things, and on and on. Our youngest son told my wife and me that when he was a teenager and didn't get his way, he'd go to his bedroom, put our picture on his desk and swear at it using every profanity he knew. "I hated you so bad," he said. "But of course, I didn't *hate* you at all," he continued, "And all the time I was cussing at your picture, I knew you were right."

Nothing is more indicative of one's having lost control than is anger.

How children express their anger depends in large measure on how people have typically responded to that anger. This raises the important question: How should people respond to children when they express anger and hatred? Surely not *with* anger! That would be umpteen times more stupid and juvenile than the kid's anger! Nothing is more indicative of one's having lost control than is anger. It is perhaps the most immature of all inappropriate parental responses to the inappropriate, annoying, age-typical behavior of children. To be angry is to be out of control. Let's discuss mature, controlled ways of responding, beginning with the behavior of younger children.

As noted earlier, young children tend to be very outwardly expressive of their emotions—positive and negative. When angry, they let you know it in no uncertain terms. Though it is annoying, it isn't all bad. At least you know how they feel, and you have some well defined behaviors to work on. Generally, when a child engages in a tirade of emotion, parents are best advised to just ignore it, despite all its colorful splendor. It's likely nothing but a big play for attention, and is best left ignored.

Here is a wonderful example of what I mean. Several years ago I was in the home of friends who have five young children, at the time all pre-teens, the oldest being twelve and the youngest about a year and a half. It's an exemplary family. Outside the home, the children were the model of propriety and good behavior, so when I observed in the home what I am about to describe, I was taken aback—though ultimately very pleased. Here is what happened:

The father and I were standing in the living room talking. The 6-year-old daughter was seated on the couch reading a book. The 3-year-old son was standing in front of his sister playing with a toy. In walked the 1-year-old who made a beeline for his 3-year-old brother. He was after the toy in his brother's hand. Well, you can guess what happened. The 1-year-old grabbed the toy, and a scuffle began. In an instant, the 3-year-old boy had flung the 1-year-old to the floor, and his head hit with a resounding thud! Naturally, the 1-year-old let out a blood curdling scream. Not to be outdone, and as an expression of justification for his protection of rights and property, the 3-year-old, with the toy well secured in his arm, stormed out of the room, shouting behind him, "I hate Billy!"

The 1-year-old was hurting, I'm sure. His head hit the floor like a brick. It made me wince. The father, completely unruffled by it all, gently rubbed his hand over the 1-year-old's head as he clung to his father's leg, and said simply, "It will feel better soon." The daughter, on the couch, got angry that her dad was comforting the kid who started it all, threw her book at him, and said, "But he started it! I hate you Daddy!" as she stomped out of the room. All of which Daddy ignored, and through which Daddy remained completely unruffled and aloof. Within 1 minute and 39 seconds (as a student of behavior, I measure things like that) the 1-year-old had stopped crying and was playing with his brother who had returned to the room calm and unemotional, and the sister had retrieved her book and was reading it as though nothing had happened.

Let's analyze this situation. First off, it would be completely inappropriate to have characterized the expressions "I hate you" of the 3-year-old boy and the 6-year-old girl as literal feelings of hatred. They were expressions of anger - impulsive, brief, and generally shallow, immature expressions of anger. Second, the father gave absolutely no attention to any of the junk behaviors that were exhibited: shouting "I hate you," the book throwing, the sibling rivalry. None of that junk got one single word of attention from Daddy. It was as though it had never happened. Even when he comforted the wailing baby, he didn't acknowledge any of the wailing-related behaviors. He only said, "You'll feel better soon." Third, within a very brief period of time, less than two minutes, the incident had begun, run its entire course, and was followed by three happy siblings playing with one another as though nothing had happened. The reason, of course, being that Daddy had treated it all as though it was nothing. No attention was given to any of the inappropriate behaviors.

Now you might ask, "But wait a minute, wasn't comforting the crying boy a reinforcer for either crying, grabbing his brother's toy, or both?" That is a good and reasonable question. In this instance, it wasn't for at least two reasons:

First, the father gave no verbal attention to the child's crying or book grabbing. He simply said, "You'll feel better soon." The pain of being thrown to the floor and hitting his head with a THUD was punishment enough and Daddy couldn't have said a thing to heighten the reality of that. The kid was suffering from the consequences of his own behavior. Daddy left that alone. He simply comforted the child. He ignored the behavior.

Let me put it another way. Suppose that an adult, through carelessness and foolishness, sustained a serious injury, and was laying on the ground in a puddle of blood writhing in pain. You wouldn't ignore the plight of that person's body for fear of reinforcing his foolishness. You would give comfort and treatment to the person, but ignore the foolishness that had created the need for comfort. You'd say something like, "Help is coming," or "What can I do to make you more comfortable?" or "Just relax, everything will be fine," and similar soothing expressions. You wouldn't say, "That was a really stupid thing to do, you know? I mean, after all, look at what happened to you! Because of your stupidity you're likely to bleed to death! What a klutz you are!" By now, all of this is perfectly obvious to the victim. Natural consequences of his behavior have taught him about the foolishness of the behavior. It wouldn't do any good for you to harp on and on about it. In fact, such reactive statements can lessen the teaching effects of natural consequences by building up resentments about them!

Second, the response of the father put the environment back in order. In less than two minutes, the whole affair had run its entire course from beginning to end. Everyone was happy. The children were playing together compatibly and were appropriately engaged in other things. Remember, the only way you can tell how effective your responses to behavior are is by the effect those responses have on the behaviors that follow. If the environment is quickly brought back to order, if the people within that environment resume a "normal" character, and the incident passes as a flash in the pan, then it is highly probable that what was done was appropriate.

As parents, we must be extremely careful to not overreact to emotion-packed statements like "I hate you!"; "You make me sick!"; "I hate this terrible home!"; and so on. From the moment this kind of junk spews out of the mouths of our irate children, the tension in the environment is usually so elevated as to make it difficult for us as parents to be calm and objective about it all. Our first inclination of course is to respond in kind: "Well loving you isn't always the easiest thing to do"; or "If home is so bad, why don't you just leave?! Make my day!"; or "Just wait a minute, you insolent brat! You don't talk to your mother that way!" Such in-kind reactions are inappropriate, out of order, low on the scale of civility, and serve to only aggravate the situation. Not only are the children out of control, the parents are out of control. No one wins, everyone loses, and the environment of the home is left in shambles with all kinds of repair work to be done. Here is a better way:

> An ounce of don't say it is worth a pound of I didn't mean it.

Child:      "I hate you, Mother. You make me sick. I wish you'd die!"

Mother:     "I'm really sorry you feel that way, Dear. I can tell you're angry. Let's talk about it in a while when you're not so angry."

Child:      "Don't pull that active listening, empathy crap on me, Mom. That makes me sicker than you do!"

Mother:     "When you're angry, it's hard to hear anything that's acceptable. You'll feel better soon. Let's talk then."

And so on. You recognize this as active listening and empathy giving. It is an excellent way of defusing explosive and potentially explosive situations. Sure, the kid is probably going to stomp off mad as hops, and you're going to be left standing there agonizing over his anger, feeling guilty about what you did wrong to raise a child to feel such anger, hate, ingratitude, disrespect, and so on. Feeling that way is totally useless since it solves no problems, does nothing to improve what's happened, and provides no direction to securing the future. Take three or four deep breaths, say to *yourself*, "I'm really proud of you for keeping your cool. You did a masterful job! What a tiger you are! Boy, I like you!", then pat yourself on the shoulder, stroke your arm or shoulder affectionately a few times, put a smile on your face, and go about your business humming or singing or whistling.

Now let's consider the child. He is alone fuming. Wild thoughts are racing around in his head: "I'm going to run away!"; "I hate this hell hole!"; "I wish my lousy parents would just die!"; "I'll get even. Just wait and see. I *will* get even!" Huff, puff, pant, pant, snarl, snarl! Then the kid remembers, "Hey, I can't run away, I have a date tomorrow night, and I need the car. Boy, I better settle down or I'll never get to use the car." (15 minutes later.) The boy is now upstairs in the fridge. He is calm and collected. Mom walks in:

Mom:        "Time to fill up the empty leg, huh, Son?" And as she passes, she runs her hand warmly and affectionately across his shoulder.

Boy:        "Yeah." (He's starting out easy. He doesn't want to overdo it.)

Mom:  "Leave a little room for supper."

Boy:  "Okay. What's for supper?"

By now, the hostility of a short time ago is gone, the parents are in control of the atmosphere of the home, the boy has put his anger behind him, and he has reminded himself about a reality of adolescent life: "If I want the car, I'd better behave myself." And things are now stable.

As a parent, you might say to yourself, "But that's terrible. The only reason he's good is because he wants the car! That he told me he hates me means nothing. I, his mother, who walked through the valley of the shadow of death to bring him into the world, then nourished him, cared for him, loved him, and sacrificed for him. I mean nothing to him. These sacrifices mean nothing to him! The only good I am to him is to keep his stomach full, and to give him permission to use the car. What a terrible kid I've raised! Where did I go wrong!? How could this have happened to me?!"

The parent isn't terrible at all. What's terrible is adolescence! For kids this age, parents aren't there to be loved, they're there to be used, exploited. We are resources, not love objects. We must remember that love is a very mature sentiment. Some kids, as kids, never feel it as love. They are so absorbed with gratifying their own appetites—whatever those might be (acceptance into the peer group, making the ball team/pep club, etc.)— they typically give no thought to loving their parents. It seldom if never enters their head! "But what about my feelings?" you might ask. "Can't he see how he's hurting me? Doesn't he care that this is killing me?! That it's tearing me apart? That he's putting me through a meat grinder every day of my life!?! Can't he see that?" The answer to that is very likely "No," or at least, "Probably not." And so what? This too will pass. Just stop and think for a minute about your relationship to your parents when

> Adolescence: The age of raging hormonal imbalance.

you were a kid. Did you ever worry about how they felt about anything? Did you ever say to a teenage friend, "Out of respect for my parents' feelings I'm not going to ask for the car tonight. In fact, I'm going to be as selfless, loving, compassionate, considerate, gentle, and kind as I can possibly be. I'll do whatever I have to do to spare my parents despair or sadness or discomfort." If you want an example of weird, that's it! It's not only weird, it's not healthy. Studies have shown that kids who are docile, always neat, always do what they are told to do, don't talk back, are always well-behaved in school and get nothing but good grades, are basically charming and passive are most likely to grow up to be the least healthy adults.

Don't worry that your hurt is completely lost to a kid, eclipsed by his need for self-gratification. Don't agonize over this. It's just all part of the territory. It's the heat of the kitchen, and in a few years,

the probability is very good that same kid will become a loving, appreciative son who will say to you, "Boy, Mom. How did you stand it? You don't know how much I appreciate you. I really do love you. Please forgive me for being such a dink!" Then he'll hug you, and kiss away the hurt. And you'll go to your bedroom to cry again, but this time-out of joy and happiness.

A few years ago our oldest son, now a father, called his mother from California and said, "Mom, I just called to apologize for all the dumb things I did as a kid. I love you," then hung up. In this instance, when he said "I love you," he knew what he was saying!

While I was on my way to a nearby community to give a talk on parenting, my 18-year-old daughter was with me. I was giving her a ride to a friend's house on the way. She asked where I was going and what I was going to do. I told her I was going to give a talk to some parents about living with teenagers. Our conversation went like this:

Daughter:   "Oh, I'd like to hear that. I'd like to know how to live with teenagers."

Dad:   "What advice should I give to these parents?"

Daughter:   "Tell them to hang in there, Dad. Don't give up. Pretty soon everything will be all right and their kids will love them.

For a year or two, their kids will hate them, but then they will love their parents. I hated you and Mom for about a year and a half, but now I can't believe how much I love you."

Dad:   "What did we do to make you hate us?"

Daughter:   "By always saying 'no', and not letting us do the things we wanted to do—things our friends could do and were bugging us to do."

Dad:   "But if I hear you correctly, you're saying that it's important occasionally for parents to say 'no', and to exercise some control over their teenagers."

Daughter:   "Oh, yes! Otherwise we get spoiled rotten and our lives are miserable."

Do not be intimidated by verbal or gestural expressions of hatred. Do not be distraught or plunged into despair because you think you raised an ungrateful, selfish, mean, ugly kid! None of those descriptions of the child are any more accurate of his character than is "I hate you" an accurate expression of his feelings toward you. A 1982 study on the relationship between child temperament and parent-child relationship revealed that, "Child temperament was more strongly related to *parent* behaviors than to child behaviors. Children of parents who were negative, non-accepting, submissive, critical, disapproving, severe, and had low levels of interaction were more likely to have severe behavior problems." Parents, don't walk around the house with a long, expressionless face etched with grief, eyes and shoulders drooping, shaking your head back and forth in despair, hoping your kids will get the message to shape up. It won't work. It disgusts them! Be the model of happiness and with-it-ness. Smile, stand and walk erect, laugh and joke. In a word, be "up!"

> **Parents, be the model of with-it-ness.**

Do not react in kind to kids' ugliness. Rather, in complete control, and being calm as a summer's morn, respond with empathy. Defuse the situation. In this regard, just a word of caution since it is *so* important to be in control and to respond appropriately. If the environment at the moment is so highly charged with emotion that it would be extra difficult to come up with a controlled response, buy some time. Say these words, or words to this effect: "Excuse me for a few minutes while I collect my thoughts. My head is spinning and I don't feel like I can be as rational as I want to be. I'll be back in a few minutes." This will give both you and your child time to calm down, and it will give you time to collect your thoughts, review your notes, and so on.

Upon returning you are able to get off to a fresh start:

Parent: "Now then, even though you denied yourself the privilege of going to the movie by not getting your chore done, you want me to grant you that privilege."

Child: "Yeah! It's no big deal. Just this once. I'll never ask again! Promise! And next Saturday, I'll do my chore plus wash the windows. Isn't that fair?!"

Parent: "I'm sorry. I can tell how badly you want to go to that movie. I'm sure it would be fun. But I can't solve your problems. This is your problem. You created it, you own it, and now you must live with it."

Child: "What! You mean I can't go? You're not going to let me go!? This is unreal!"

Parent: "You're partly right. You can't go, but not because I won't let you. You can't go because to go is a privilege you didn't earn. I gave you the opportunity to earn it. You chose to do other things."

Child: (Stomping off in anger) "Boy, you're the meanest person I ever knew. I hate your guts!"

But this too will pass. A great lesson will have been taught. You will have kept the environment in control, and you will be emotionally intact. It's really the better way. One more experience in my family to illustrate this. I was visiting with one of my daughters about her growing-up years and our performance as parents. She said, "You and Mom really did a good job." (So far, so good.) "But one time I was really disappointed in you, Dad." (Oops. I braced for this one.) "One time I wanted to do something that I really had no right doing. It was against your expectations. You stood your ground, but I kept after you relentlessly. I begged, got angry, said mean things. I did everything I could think of to beat you on this one—all the while hoping you'd *not* give in. What I was doing was only what teenage kids do to their parents. It's a game, a contest. Well, you gave in, Dad. I was so disappointed in you. I thought I could trust you more than that, and that's stuck with me all these years." (Ouch!) In recalling this I'm reminded of a 1990 study done by the Girl Scouts of the United States that found that for 49% of the children surveyed, grades 4–12, an adult had been a major disappointment to them!

This is not to be interpreted to mean that parents must *always* get their way, and kids must always lose. The message here is that in situations where parental expectations are clear to everyone and obviously in the best interest of the child, when it is evident that what is happening is nothing more than a power struggle over a matter that shouldn't be an issue, the understood expectations of behavior should be protected. Angry and hateful outbursts to the contrary should not be recognized. There is a better way of dealing with hate and anger.

## NOW TO REVIEW

1. Children's expressions of hate and anger (and even love) do not carry the same meaning as do those expressions coming from adults. Remember , children are in the process of learning the meaning of things, including words.

2. Children who always get their way through such intimidation, or who are docile and never complain, are less likely to be behaviorally and emotionally healthy as adults.

3. A truly loving, accepting home is one where kids can express hate and anger without being hated and without evoking anger.

> *Research has shown that the most effective way to reduce problem behavior in children is to strengthen desirable behavior through positive reinforcement rather than trying to weaken undesirable behavior using aversive or negative processes.*
> S.W. Bijou
> *The International Encyclopedia of Education, 1988*

# TEN
# Building Self-Esteem

Among the many good things parents want for their children, a high regard for self is at or near the top. Parents frequently ask, "What can we do to make our children feel good about themselves?" Concerns are then expressed about children who mope around the house complaining about their inadequacies, being afraid to try new things, and despairing that they have no friends.

> Guard your children's self-esteem with the same zeal with which you would guard their very lives!

To some degree, this is to be expected. Occasionally we all feel unattractive and down on ourselves. But as parents, we need to be extra cautious that we don't inadvertently contribute to our children's sense of low self-esteem by giving it the wrong kind of attention, or by actually saying or doing things that would make a child wonder about his ability and worth.

Though it happened over 50 years ago, an experience during my impressionable days as a boy pressed an indelible image of self into my mind that I am sure will stay with me for as long as I live. In elementary school, my friend Billy and I sang together in school and community events. We both had clear, boy soprano voices which blended well. On some occasions, we sang solo. I enjoyed those opportunities to perform since they were among the few really reinforcing events in my life that bolstered my self-esteem.

During summer vacation between my 4th and 5th grades, my parents took my younger brother, Ed, and me on a vacation to California to visit friends and family. At the home of an aunt and uncle, my aunt asked me if I would sing a song. Though a bit embarrassed to sing for such a small group of family members, I was pleased at being asked and agreed to sing a song from a recent school program at which I had performed. When I finished my aunt was effusive with praise, and I was pleased, to say the least. At the height of my euphoria, my mother said, "Glenn tries hard, but Eddie has a much better voice." WHAM! That was the end of singing for me. Never again did I—even to this day—perform vocally. I was crushed! That light went out forever.

In recalling this, one must not assume that my mother was an insensitive, harsh, careless person. In fact, the very opposite was the case. In life, my mother was my hero. In death, she remains my hero. She was the anchor in my life, and is still a powerful force for stability to me. Perhaps in saying what she did, she was just hoping to share the spotlight with my brother. Who knows. But to a 10-year-old boy, it hurt!

Can you see, now, the point I am wanting to make? Be very, very careful what you say to children that reflect on them personally. Don't even joke about it. Words like, "You're so awkward," or "You'll never amount to anything," or "Won't you ever learn?" are terrible. We can all agree on that. But less obviously offensive words like "She does her best and we'll just have to be satisfied with that," or "Yes, I'm glad you got all passing grades, but I know you can do better," can be just as deflating. Here's a little exercise for you. Opposite each of the esteem-deflating statements, compose an esteem-building statement.

| ESTEEM-DEFLATING | ESTEEM-BUILDERS |
|---|---|
| You're so awkward. | |
| You'll never amount to anything. | |
| You did your best and we'll just have to be satisfied with that. | |
| I'm glad you got all passing grades, but I know you can do better. | |

Too often, we think of self-esteem only in terms of what it causes people to do, we see it only as a "causal variable." For example, "He does poorly in school *because* he has low self-esteem." But remember, self-esteem is shaped, day-by-day, word-by-word. It doesn't become a causal variable until it has been shaped into a causal variable. Never forget that!

> *Self-Esteem is more likely to be a caused behavior than a casual behavior.*

Self-esteem is more likely to be a caused behavior than a causal behavior.

Here are four things you can do to help build in your children a healthy self-esteem.

1.  Do and say things which let your children know that you feel good about *yourself*. Smile a lot, be happy, laugh; in a word, be of good cheer. At times this might be tough to do. You might have to work at it. You might have to put on a bit of an act and appear bigger than life. But that's okay so long as it is a sincere act. Lord Mountbatten put it well when he said, "If you want to be a leader…you can't go around like a shrinking violet hiding yourself: You've got to put on a bit of an act. It must be sincere, it's no good having a bogus act. You've got to play up any qualities you have and blow them up larger than life." This is good advice for parents since parents are in the most important leadership role of all.

2.  Say and do things to and with your children that show you highly regard them and their ability. In fact, go out of your way to look for opportunities to build your children's self-esteem through positive physical and verbal interactions, as noted frequently throughout this book. Put little reminders up around the house and in the car to prompt you to say esteem-building things to your children. Your prompts can be very subtle and have meaning only to you. For example, put a piece of furniture, a plant, a picture in an odd, out-of-the-way place. Every time you see it *out of place*, it will remind you to put *in place* a well chosen word of praise or loving attention. Don't worry that what you say may not seem to be appreciated. A cold, stormy look on the outside of a kid can hide a lot of warmth on the inside.

    Never! I repeat, never! put kids down, use sarcasm (cute or otherwise), or berate kids. A few years ago a high school boy came to me simply distraught. He told me about one of his teachers who was always calling him dog breath. "He doesn't need to say that. He thinks it's cute, and even though I just shrug it off with a smile, deep down inside it really hurts." I was in the company of a father

> *Aversives prompt children to avoid, even escape, their parents.*

and his teenage son while the father was telling about some work the boy had done around the house. The father said, "Well, he did a very good job, actually (with a tone in his voice that suggested he was quite amazed at that). Of course, he made a terrible mess. No, really, he didn't make much of a mess at all, only a little mess. You know, what you'd expect from a kid." The boy, a big, strapping, bright, fine-looking fellow, was standing a few feet back of his dad during all of this, and the more the father said, the lower the boy's countenance sunk until at last, with bowed head, sagging shoulders, and an expressionless face, the boy slowly turned and quietly walked away, barely able to lift his feet off the ground.

How much better it would have been had the father said, "Yes, he did a good job." Then, turning to the boy, say, "You're a good worker, Son. An able young man. Thanks a ton," while giving him a hug and a pat on the back. Figure 10.1 should be put up in your home as a constant reminder to *never* put a child down. One of the happiest parenting-related experiences of my life came to me during a conversation I was having with a fellow who knew one of my daughters. He told me that during a recent visit with her he had jokingly told her something I supposedly said about her that was uncomplimentary. "Instantly," he said, "she grew serious and replied, 'My dad didn't say that. My dad would never say anything like that about me.'" And she was absolutely correct. Louise and I never say anything about or to our children or grandchildren that is uncomplimentary. NEVER! Not even in jest. And I suggest to you to abide that same rule.

3.  When children say disparaging, uncomplimentary things about themselves, acknowledge those feelings with empathy and love, but press for a solution. Suppose a child says to you, "I can't do anything right. I'm just no good. I wish I'd die." Say, "I'm sorry you're feeling down, Son. To me you're priceless. I want to help. Let's talk about it." During these talks, respond with hope. If a child says he wants to die, it's because he's looking for reasons to live. If we react with despair, we simply reinforce the behavior we want to extinguish. Don't try to convince the child that he shouldn't, or really doesn't, feel that way, that he is just having a bad day. To the child these feelings may be as real as life, and if that's the way life really feels, it just might not be worth it to live. If children are hurting enough and desperately seeking relief, they will say some

pretty bizarre things to get attention. But be careful that you don't reinforce the very behavior you want to get rid of. Don't just talk about problems. Provide help. Regarding why we *shouldn't* try to talk a child out of negative feelings of self, consider the following. In this scenario, ask yourself the question, what is the child *really* doing?

## Figure 10.1—Creating A Positive Environment

# This is a put-down-free environment

# Put-downs

Child: "I don't know what's the matter with me. No one likes me. I lose friends as fast as I make them. I must be ugly as a post."

Parent: "Now, now. Don't be so hard on yourself. You're not ugly as a post. You're cute as a button, handsome as can be. For proof, just go look in the mirror."

Child:     "You know very well I'm ugly. You sure don't see the good looking kids at school without friends!"

What's happening in a situation like this? Despite what the parent says, the child is arguing *in defense, in support* of his/her own miseries! Think about that! The child becomes the advocate for what's the matter, and no one is advocating for the child—or at least not in a way the child will accept. The better way is to use empathy, understanding, and an offer to help:

Parent:     "I never realized you felt like this. It's obvious to me that you are really hurting. Let's talk about it and see if we can find solutions."

Avoid giving quick-fix adult advice. The wisdom of the ages—or the aged— typically doesn't cut it with kids. If you are unable to help the child, seek help from professional counselors, clergy, or knowledgeable family or friends.

4.  Put failure into perspective. Failure is a part of life, a natural obstacle on the road to success. Several months after he had had surgery on his leg, our oldest son entered a foot race as part of a scout activity. As you might guess, he didn't do very well competitively. In fact, he finished last—distant last. As he finally crossed the finish line, only his scout leader and I were there to greet him. We were as proud of him as though he had won by the margin by which he had lost. As I held him tight and told him how proud I was of him he said, "I did okay, Dad. I finished the race. I didn't quit." To which I replied, "And that's the mark of a *real* winner." A failure experience became a success experience.

In a great article written by the renowned family counselor and child psychologist John K. Rosemond, entitled "The Three R's of Self-Esteem," published in the January, 1993 issue of United Airlines *Hemisphere* magazine, he made this important point in an article entitled "Back to the Basics":

Assisting children toward the discovery of true self-esteem requires
that parents create family environments that communicate the Three
R's of respect, responsibility, and resourcefulness. In the family,
parents, not children, should command center stage. Children should

have a daily routine of chores for which they are not paid, they should do their own homework, find the majority of their own after-school recreation, and should not be allowed to waste great amounts of time in front of the television sets and video games. A child who is *respectful* of others will conduct himself with a sensitive regard for other human beings. A child who is *responsible* will do his best, regardless of the task or the situation. A child who is *resourceful* will try and try again until success is at hand. Out of these strengths gradually emerges a genuine sense of self-worth and self-respect.

Is that old-fashioned? Absolutely, as in tried-and-true.

No one thing is going to make a child feel that he/she is or isn't of worth. It's cumulative. Building a child's self esteem is not a difficult or a complicated matter. It's one little positive interaction built on another. It's the journey of a thousand smiles taken one smile at a time.

Though I can rightfully be criticized for not going more deeply into this topic, I have chosen the course I've taken because, in reality, no one chapter in any book is going to adequately address the many facets of the subject. I do, however, have three suggestions for

> *Self-management is the best management of all.*

parents as they work with children who are questioning their worth. They are self-management skills that children (older children particularly) can learn to use in their own defense, and to build their own self esteem. I say "in their own defense" because not infrequently children are verbally assaulted by other children, parents, teachers, and others in ways that could make anyone question his worth. (For additional reading on this aspect of building self-esteem, I refer you to an article written by Elin McCoy entitled "Bully-Proof your Child," published in the Nov. 1992 issue of *Reader's Digest*, pages 199–204.)

Here are a few strategies that have been shown to be effective. To work, children must be taught to use them, and they must be practiced. These are no panacea, but they certainly can be a big help, and can keep small problems from becoming large ones.

1. *Private speech*. As the term implies, private speech is a conscious talking to oneself; saying esteem-building things, particularly at times of risk. For example, a teacher says something harsh or negative to a child. Rather than allow himself to be put down by this type of thing, the child learns to say

something neutralizing or positive to himself. For example:

"My teacher put me down during class, but later in the hall she smiled at me and said hello. That really made me feel good and I appreciated it."

Note: This keeps such negative, self depreciating thoughts as "my teachers hate me" out of the child's head.

"Dad called me stupid because I made a mistake while mowing the lawn. I feel that I did a good job on the lawn. I wish Dad could learn to be more positive."

Note: Saying this, the boy is less likely to entertain thoughts of being stupid.

"My friend Don avoided me at school today. He even looked at me like there was something the matter. I hope I haven't offended him. I'm a good friend to a lot of kids at school."

Note: In other words, "maybe one person is down on me but that doesn't mean everyone is."

2. *Assessing cause and effect*. Assessing actual causes helps a person explain in a very specific way why something happened, and helps avoid the tendency to engage in over generalizations that can cast a negative light on oneself. For example:

| Rather Than This Being The Cause... | This is the Cause (*very specific*) |
| --- | --- |
| I failed the test because I am dumb. | I failed the test because I didn't study as I should have. |
| Billy didn't invite me to his birthday party because no one likes me. | I guess Billy is angry at me so he didn't invite me to his birthday party. |
| I didn't make the ball team because I am clumsy and a terrible ball player. | If I expect to make the ball team next year, I'm going to have to practice harder than ever. |

3. *Self-control with self-reinforcement.* This involves engaging in alternative behaviors in times of disappointment, times when a person would be likely to get down, depressed, and even feel unfairly put upon, then verbally reinforcing oneself for behaving well. For example:

| Situation | Self-Control/ Self-Reinforcement Response |
|---|---|
| Gets teased at school and made fun of. | Smiles, walks away and counts to 10. Find someone else to play with. Later says to self, "Good job. I knew you could do that. You have a lot on the ball. I'm really proud of you." |
| The school bully hits you for no reason and tries to pick a fight. | Say, "Oh, hi. How's it going? See ya. I gotta get to class." Say to yourself, "Boy you were really the tough guy in that situation. What a tiger!" |
| There is a strong temptation to eat something fattening. | Leave the area as quickly as possible, or put the "goodies" out of harms way—in the cupboard, locked up, or whatever. Say to yourself, "That was definitely the right thing for me to do. It might have tasted good, but I'll look and feel better." |

## NOW TO REVIEW

Building self-esteem is a life-time effort. It must start at home with parents saying and doing self-esteem building things to and with their children: setting reasonable standards for behavior and performance, appropriately acknowledging the accomplishment of those standards, establishing a healthy model of self-esteem (not arrogance!), and practicing good parenting skills.

1. The key to developing healthy self-esteem in children is for parents to be positive and proactive in their interactions with their children.

2. The self-management skills of private speech, assessing cause and effect, and self-control coupled with self-reinforcement provides children with tools they can use to protect themselves from the inevitable slings and arrows of the world that tend to put us down and get us down on ourselves.

> *Research has shown that the most effective way to reduce problem behavior in children is to strengthen desirable behavior through positive reinforcement rather than trying to weaken undesirable behavior using aversive or negative processes.*
> *S.W. Bijou*
> *The International Encyclopedia of Education, 1988*

*"There is really no such thing as crying babies. They are simply angels singing out of tune."*
    *Glenn Latham*

# ELEVEN
# A Word About Fussy Babies

Three things are sure: death, taxes, and fussy babies. With no other way to express themselves, babies *must* fuss to make their need for attention known. We can be thankful they know how to do that. Without that ability, it is doubtful many of us would have made it beyond infancy.

As with adults, however, babies often go beyond what is necessary to make their *need* for attention known. Before long, babies will fuss just to get the attention; no compelling needs exist. In fact, the attention parents give their babies to eliminate the fussing is usually the very thing that encourages the fussing. Fussing then becomes a conditioned response to parental attention.

In this chapter I discuss ways of decreasing fussy behavior in three situations: (a) general fussiness, (b) bedtime/naptime fussiness, and (c) the colicky baby. The methods I am suggesting are supported by research reported in the *Journal of Applied Behavior Analysis*, and *Behavior Research and Therapy*.

## General Fussiness

Parental attention is a powerful reason for babies to fuss. Being picked up, held close, patted, cooed to, walked about—these are all very pleasant sensations which, when given by parents and care givers as a response to fussiness, will certainly encourage

> Babies are never bad. Unhappy, perhaps, but never bad.

more of it. In fact, it isn't at all unusual for babies to learn to crave this warm and tender attention and will do about anything to get it. (Can you blame them!) In fact, they will cry their little lungs out in an attempt to get it, and once they get it they often keep crying to make sure they don't lose it. (They're not so dumb!) What we often observe, therefore, is babies who will fuss for no apparent reason, and continue to fuss even when every effort has been made to comfort them. This circumstance frequently wears on parents' (and care-givers') nerves. They become frustrated, angry, desperate, at wits end, then POW!—the child gets it!, when, in fact, the child was only doing what he had been taught would get him what he wanted: attention. Well, there is a better way of handling fussy babies.

To begin, when a baby fusses, don't think of it as a "bad baby." There is no such thing as a bad baby! *All* babies are good. *Never forget that*. Babies are as good when they

> Be precise. Be clinical. Don't be emotional.

fuss as when they don't fuss. *ALL BABIES ARE GOOD*. (Ah, that you and I could say that of ourselves!) They are good in the sense that they have inherent value, they do not purposely violate other's rights or violate standards of decency. I urge you to *never* refer to, or say to, a baby "Bad baby!" True, a baby will cry and fuss, but that's simply age-typical behavior. When a baby fusses, it is simply its way of saying, in very primitive language, "I *need* attention," or "I *want* attention."

Let's say he needs attention. This is fairly easily determined. Check his diaper, see if he's hungry, make sure he isn't too hot or too cold, check his clothing and bedding to see if his ability to move around is hampered, look for signs of illness—in other words, see if he *needs* comforting, then meet those needs. If every effort is made to make him comfortable—he's fed, changed, well, etc., but no amount of holding, cuddling, cooing and so on will console him, gently put him in his bed and let him do his fussing there. If he cries long and hard, don't worry about it, so long as his *NEEDS* have been met. I suggest you time how long he cries. If in the past, he has gotten lots of attention for crying, he might cry quite a long time before quitting. I've timed babies who have cried up to 32 minutes without stopping, and I am familiar with the work of others who have timed babies who have cried for 45 minutes! That's a long time to listen to a baby cry, so turn your attention to other things as much as possible. (By the way, this is called planned or purposeful ignoring.) Don't pace the floor wringing your hands and feeling terrible about being such an insensitive, neglectful parent. You are neither. You are helping the child out of some behavioral patterns that could make his life unhappy later on.

Eventually, the child will stop. Wait between 30 and 45 seconds. (Studies have shown this to be a reasonable range of time: 30 seconds for tiny babies on up to 45 seconds for older babies. But anywhere within this range is okay—even for tiny babies.) If the child has not cried or fussed during that time, quietly pick him up and tenderly hold and caress him, or just pat him a moment while he lays or plays quietly. If he fusses or cries at all before the 30–45 seconds are up, wait until he stops, then restart the timing. You must *not* pick him up or attend to him until he has been quiet for the required time (30–45 seconds). Heart rending cries of a tiny infant, or appeals to "Mommy, Mommy," "Daddy, Daddy" accompanied by pitiful sobs should not weaken you. Do *not* give in before the child gives out! After the child has been quiet for 30–45 seconds, as you pick him up, do not be effusive—gushing all over the child with affection and verbal outpourings. Be loving and tender and quite natural. If the baby starts fussing again, gently put him back in his bed, say no more than "It's okay. You'll feel better soon," then calmly leave the room, close the door quietly, and start the process all over. A graph of your timings will probably look something like this:

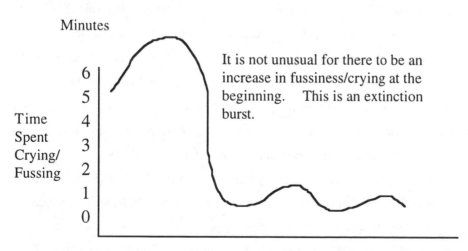

Minutes

Time Spent Crying/ Fussing

6
5
4
3
2
1
0

It is not unusual for there to be an increase in fussiness/crying at the beginning.    This is an extinction burst.

Time

At first, there will very likely be an increase in crying/fussiness, but the baby will gradually cry and fuss less and less once he has learned that when he is crying and fussing he is doing it alone, but when he is content, he has company—warm, snugly, gentle company. When the baby is content, have him in your company where he can see you and hear you and where you can occasionally give him a pat, a hug, a kiss, and a gentle, affectionate word. When doing this, follow these three simple guidelines:

1. *Be composed.* Give the attention in a very easy-going natural way. Use a calm voice and smile.

2. *Be timely.* The encounter shouldn't take more than a few seconds: 3–5 seconds. You don't want the encounter to turn the child's interests away from what he is doing. Rather, it should reinforce what he is doing: "You are having a lot of fun playing with your toys!"

3. *Be brief and descriptive.* Say only a few words, if you say anything at all, and use words that describe the behavior that is getting attention. As with the amount of time the encounter takes, too many words can be distracting. A gentle touch, accompanied by, "You are such a happy baby" or "You are playing so nicely with your toys" are altogether sufficient. In 12 words or less you can briefly describe what the baby is doing that has brought him your attention. Once that is said, move on to other things. (Again, an example of purposeful/planned ignoring.)

Having said this, I hasten to add that from time to time it is appropriate, in fact critical, that the baby be picked up for longer periods of time during which you would read to him, sing to him, play with him, rock him. Just enjoy him, and let him enjoy you. However, the baby should be picked up only when he is not crying, unless, of course, he *needs* attention. After 15 to 20 minutes, when you are ready to put the child down to continue his play, do so in a gentle, loving, matter-of-fact way then go on about your activities. If the child fusses for a bit after having been put down, and you are sure his needs are all met, ignore the fussing. If it continues for more than 20 to 30 seconds, and particularly if it becomes intense, gently pick the baby up, quickly check the diaper and look for other things that might be causing the distress. While doing this, *say nothing to the child*. Once assured that all is well, gently place the child in his bed, and if you want to say anything, say only "It's okay. You'll be happy soon," then leave the room. If the child goes to sleep, that's fine. Let him sleep. If he stops crying within 30 seconds, feel free to pick him up and let him play in your company, as I have already described.

To be sure these procedures are carried out properly, especially if parents are inclined to become angry and upset when the baby cries, I strongly suggest they be practiced using a doll. Have a spouse, an older child, a friend help simulate the behaviors of the baby. They can even be the ones who do the crying in behalf of the doll. I am not being facetious in suggesting this. Simulating a circumstance, then responding to it in a role-playing setting with feedback from an observer, is a powerful, efficient, and risk-free way to learn a new skill. Airplane pilots learn many—if not most—of their skills in simulators where they can make mistakes without sending themselves and a plane load of people to their untimely deaths. In learning circles, it is called "preventing the failure of the first attempt." Doctors learn this way to prevent them from killing their first patient. Engineers learn this way so their first bridge won't collapse under a load of traffic. And parents can learn this way just as well and for reasons that are altogether as important.

## Bedtime/Naptime Fussiness

Virtually all babies, at one time or another, experience problems of sleeplessness and fussiness during bedtime and naptime. Most of these problems are maintained, and even made worse, by too much attention being given to babies while they are fussing. This simple three-step process will do wonders in eliminating bedtime/naptime fussiness and sleeplessness:

1. *Establish a routine and stick to it.* Critical to this routine would be time and place for sleeping/napping. You should be as consistent as possible: put the baby in his bed at the set time(s) each day. Other routine activities could include story reading, singing, listening to records, and so on. These should be quiet, calming activities.

2. *Place the child in bed quietly, gently, and without fanfare.* If the child cries or clings or protests, in calm control, and saying nothing more than "Good night" or "Sleep tight," place the child in bed and leave the room *immediately.*

3. *Do not return to the room unless absolutely necessary.* Except for danger, illness, or distress from entanglement in bed clothes or not being dry or fed, stay out of the room. If it is absolutely necessary to check the child do so in silence (don't say a word!), do so in as little time as is absolutely necessary, and do so with a minimum of light.

If the child is ill, follow the doctor's orders, but apprise him/her of the procedures you are using to control unnecessary crying and fussiness at bedtime/naptime. Unless otherwise directed by the doctor, proceed with the program as I have described it.

I want to emphasize the importance of point three: Do not return to the room unless it is absolutely necessary. In the study of human behavior we have learned that when behavior is attended to at irregular times, it is strengthened; it is more likely to reoccur in similar situations, and is more resistant to change. For a crying and fussing baby, this means that if a parent or care giver keeps trying to comfort the baby by intermittently going into his room and patting, hugging, holding him, and so on, the result is much more likely to be counter-productive than helpful. The child will fuss more and longer, will be up more often in the night and will sleep less and less well. This "intermittent reinforcement" of an undesirable behavior serves only to make the behavior less desirable and much more difficult to change.

> Through simulation, we prevent the failure of the first attempt.

As I stressed earlier in the case of general fussiness, it is terribly important that during the waking hours, there must be frequent and pleasant interactions between the parent/care giver and the child.

## The Colicky Baby

Research indicates that between 10% and 40% of all babies experience colic. These data apply equally to male and female babies. Heretofore, the general consensus was unless a medical treatment was effective, the parents were "stuck" with a fussy baby until the baby outgrew it. Research recently reported in *Behavior Research and Therapy* has given new hope to parents of colicky babies. The findings, consistent with what I have already discussed here, have introduced a new variable, *tape recorded music*, as a form of treatment. Here's how it all fits together. While the baby is quiet, happy, and content, the parent should give it lots of attention, and play the music on a tape player. (Note: Giving attention intermittently for quiet, happy, and content behavior will have a powerfully reinforcing effect on the non-colicky behavior. You see, intermittent reinforcement works both ways: it will strengthen both appropriate *and* inappropriate behavior!) If the baby begins to cry, the music should be stopped and attention withdrawn. After 30–45 seconds of quiet behavior, the music and the attention resume. This simple strategy resulted in a 75% reduction of crying among colicky babies!

Akin to this is a similar device known as "Sleeptight." It simulates the vibration and sounds of an automobile traveling 55 miles an hour and attaches to the baby's crib. It is available from Sleeptight, Inc., 3613 Mueller Rd., St. Charles, Missouri.

Now, a couple of closing thoughts. Occasionally, indeed rarely, a child will have a physical problem that will account for inordinate amounts of crying, a problem that is not easily discernible. If after using these methods *precisely*, a child's inconsolable crying continues beyond a few days, you should probably have the baby examined by a physician. But don't be too quick to conclude that medical attention is needed. Give this program long enough to have an effect, usually within 3 or 4 days.

Also, it is important to keep in mind that since babies fuss when they need to be fed, they shouldn't be left unattended until they quit fussing before being fed. But once feeding is over and the parent has spent some time holding and tenderly interacting with the child, the baby should be put down to play, sleep, or whatever. If he cries or fusses, but you know his needs are met, leave him alone and he'll soon become content. Since children vary so in their feeding behavior, if it seems that your baby fusses too frequently for food, call your pediatrician for advice on how often to feed him, then proceed as I have described here.

Though I have focused attention on how to decrease fussy behavior and increase happy, contented behavior, the research upon which this approach is based has revealed other significant benefits for parents and care givers that are certainly as important as the benefits experienced by the babies. When parents (and care givers) use these procedures, there is a significant increase in parental sleep, improved parent-child relationships, decreased risk of child abuse and the "shaken baby" syndrome, and improvements in

> *I have never known a child to cry himself to death.*

children's waking/daytime behavior. While completing the final draft of this chapter, a tragedy occurred in my home town. A father, beside himself over what to do about a crying, inconsolable infant, in anger picked him up, shook him violently, and in a few moments, the child died. In a split second an out-of-control father put an end to his infant son's life. If you have any questions about how to handle a fussy baby, reread this chapter with great care. Don't allow ignorance to unleash savage rage on a helpless and perfectly innocent infant.

Figure 11.1 shows the results of an experience I had recently working with a 5-week old infant who had become conditioned to cry inconsolably because of being picked up instantly while crying and subsequently being held almost continuously. You'll notice that crying-to-be-held behavior steadily decreased, while being-content behavior steadily increased.

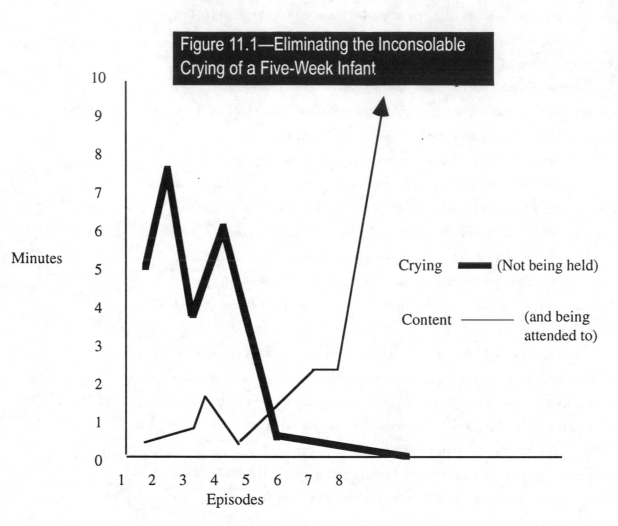

Figure 11.1—Eliminating the Inconsolable Crying of a Five-Week Infant

Following are 20 "Tips to Cope with Crying," published by the Child Abuse Prevention Council of Ogden, UT. I recommend them wholeheartedly as things parents can do to console a fussy baby. If, after a reasonable time (usually no more than a few minutes), the baby continues to cry and fuss, follow the program(s) detailed above, as we are reminded by item 20, below. If, after a few days of the treatment suggested here, the child continues to cry inconsolably, see your pediatrician.

## Tips to Cope with Crying

1. Walk or dance with the baby.

2. Rock the baby.

3. Bounce the baby gently in your arms or on a bed—a water bed is especially soothing.

4. Take the baby for a ride in the carriage.

5. Take the baby for a ride in the car.

6. Put the baby in a wind-up swing.

7. Turn up the music on the radio or stereo, run the vacuum or let the water run in the tub for a few minutes.

8. Offer the baby a "noisy" toy; shake it, rattle it.

9. Sing or talk in a quiet, sing-song way.

10. Put the baby in a soft front carrier, close to your body.

11. Lay the baby tummy down across your lap and gently rub or tap his or her back.

12. Lay the baby across a warm hot-water bottle on your lap or a bed.

13. Massage the baby's body and limbs gently; use a warmed lotion if the weather is cool.

14. Swaddle the baby tightly.

15. Feed and burp the baby one more time. Or offer a little warm water. In desperation, add a tiny bit of sugar to the water.

16. Offer a pacifier (the Nuk allows less air to pass in around the baby's mouth and so is better for a colicky baby) and hold it to the mouth if necessary.

17. Hold the baby close and breathe slowly and calmly; the baby may feel your calmness and become quiet.

18. Cross the baby's arms across the chest and hold him or her down on a bed with gentle, firm pressure.

19. Remove yourself and let someone else take over for a while. If a family member is not available, consider hiring a sitter for a short time.

20. If nothing works, put the baby in his or her bed, close the door and turn up the TV or radio. For your own peace of mind, it's okay to check the child but do so in a way that does not reinforce fussy behavior.

Though it has nothing to do with fussy babies, and since I don't address infant problems, specifically, elsewhere in the book, I do want to pass on a word about what research has to say about preventing Sudden Infant Death Syndrome (SIDS). A recent major study reported that remarkably fewer SIDS cases were reported when infants were laid on their side or back, rather than on their stomach. A research finding well worth putting into practice at home!

## NOW TO REVIEW

1. Through undo attention to crying and fussiness, babies can become conditioned to cry and fuss simply to get parental/care giver attention.

2. If a baby, whose needs have been met, continues to cry when left alone or will not be consoled, it might be a sign that medical attention is needed.

3. Babies will often increase the intensity of their crying and fussing in an attempt to get attention. This initial burst of displeasure is typically short-lived (a few to several minutes).

4. In the long run, babies are much, much more likely to be happy if undo attention is not paid to them when they cry and fuss.

5. Skilled parents produce happy babies. The primary responsibility for who is happy is—you guessed it!—that of the parents.

> *Research has shown that the most effective way to reduce problem behavior in children is to strengthen desirable behavior through positive reinforcement rather than trying to weaken undesirable behavior using aversive or negative processes.*
> *S.W. Bijou*
> *The International Encyclopedia of Education, 1988*

*"Children are not animals that need to be beaten into an acceptable form of behavior. Children are animals. But no animal deserves to be beaten under any circumstances."*
      *Sarah Forbes, Virginia Beach, VA.*

# TWELVE
# Regarding Spanking: Don't!

It doesn't take much time or space to say *all* that needs to be said about spanking! In a word, don't!

Spanking is intended to hurt a child, and by that hurt communicate some lesson or message. But it is a poor tool, a barbaric method, for teaching good behavior. I was delighted to learn that Representative Major Owens (D-NY) introduced legislation that would deny federal funding to schools that physically punish students. Noted Mr. Owens, "Of all public institutions in America, schools remain the only institutions in which battery and assault are legal, accepted forms of discipline," which he further characterized as a "barbaric practice." Mr. Irwen Hyman, Director of the Philadelphia-based National Center for the Study of Corporal Punishment and Alternatives in the Schools, reported that "There is no pedagogical, psychological, or moral reason to continue hitting and inflicting pain on children in the name of discipline." On the contrary. As reported by the National Education Association and the National Association of School Psychologists, research indicates that physical punishment modifies student behavior only in the short run, and often leads to psychological problems and academic failure. Such aversive approaches to managing student behavior also prompts students to avoid and escape school, which helps explain the nearly one million students who drop out of American schools annually. It also produces counter-control (or get-even) behavior. I recently read where a group of students, fed up with the coercive

> **Physical punishment modifies behavior only in the short run.**

policies of their high school, went on a rampage and slashed the tires on the cars of over 40 teachers. (Parents, at the time of this writing, only 22 states ban corporal punishment in their schools. If you live in a state where corporal punishment is allowed in schools, I urge you to use every reasonable, lawful means at your disposal to get it outlawed.)

Rather then correcting "bad" behavior, spanking teaches a child that when someone does something that is annoying or frustrating, or causes one to be angry, the way to handle that is to strike out physically, to hurt someone. This is a terrible message to deliver to a child, a message that TV, for example, gives our children dozens of times a day! Is it any wonder that we live in a world of violence?

While I was sitting in the boarding area of an airport waiting for a plane, across from me was a boy whom I estimated to be 5 years old, and his parents. He was sitting between his parents fidgeting about as 5-year-olds do, excited about riding in an airplane. Sharply and abruptly, his father angrily said, "Knock that off or I'm going to smack you!" The boy's sad eyes looked up to his father then he slid off his seat and climbed into the seat on the other side of his mother, took hold of her arm and drew himself close to her. He was seeking protection. It was a sad but dramatic illustration of the effects of coercion: the boy escaped and avoided the coercer, his father. Pitifully, the father probably thought he did exactly the correct thing since the kid immediately quit fidgeting and became very quiet, in fact docile.

I agree, spanking and other coercive methods might work for the moment. That is, the child might momentarily quit behaving badly. But think about it. The child is being good only to avoid being hurt. Being good is not necessarily desirable to the child. No attention whatsoever has been given to good behavior. As one parent put it so well:

> No child is ever 'asking for a whipping.' He or she is asking for attention, concern, involvement, love. Unfortunately, in many families, kids don't get that parental involvement until and unless they screw up. In other words, *from a child's viewpoint, negative attention*

*is better than no attention at all.* If more men *talked* with their sons and daughters, we'd have a better and safer society.

C.D. Grant, Cloverdale, California

Parents spank children to punish them only to find that they turn right around and behave the same way again and again. More spankings follow with the assumption being that once the necessary pain levels have been reached, the children will finally get the message and "shape up." Have the children been punished? No! Their behavior has been reinforced. This is evident because the behavior recurs. Remember the principle: the only way we can know whether what we do to a child is punishing or reinforcing is to observe what happens to the child's behavior in the future. If the behavior continues, or becomes more frequent or more intense, then our response—even a spanking—was reinforcing! If the behavior grows weaker, occurs less frequently, or stops entirely then we know our response was punishing. That's the only way we can know. We have to watch to see what happens to behavior in the future. (See pages 22–25.)

> *How much better it is if children learn that appropriate behavior brings pleasant consequences.*

Most of the spankings I observe, and am told about by parents, are really an expression of parental frustration and anger, not a method for teaching good behavior. Parents vent their frustrations and anger on the kid. The spanking has little or nothing to do with what's good for the child. One day dad comes home after having had a good day at work, the kid behaves badly and dad just lets it pass. The next day, dad comes home from a bad day at work, the kid does the very thing that was ignored the day before, but this time it set dad off and POW!, the kid gets a beating. What does the child learn? He has learned to avoid dad. He has learned that dad hurts. Then later in life when the boy is really hurting and craves comfort and understanding in an uncertain and insensitive world, guess who he *isn't* going to go to for help! You guessed it!

Pain is not a bonding agent. Rather pain teaches us to avoid the pain giver. The better way is to let social or natural consequences of behavior deliver the message. If the child misbehaves, he deprives himself of desirable privileges; he separates himself from pleasure, and has no one to blame but himself. But when pain is imposed on him, as with a spanking, it is easy for the child to resent the pain giver while justifying the bad behavior. Every lesson has been taught except the right one.

Parents, eliminate spanking as a teaching tool. It does teach, but it teaches the wrong thing! And those it teaches pass the lesson along to future generations, and coercion lives on. What a terrible legacy! Hitting, which spanking is, becomes a learned behavior. It becomes paired with anger and frustration. Before long, every bit of anger or frustration is accompanied by hitting and spanking. The child learns that the natural thing to do when he is angry or frustrated is to hit. Hitting leads to hurting, and hurting others leads to the degeneration of society in the form of assaults, abuse, riots, homicide, and war. It typically begins benignly by parents who really don't believe in spanking. A gentle slap on the hand or tap on the bottom. Then a little harder and a little more often as the child gets older. My oldest daughter, a school teacher, gave me a copy of a wonderful story, a child's account of spanking entitled "Momma Spanks Me." It's a story of inconsistencies seen through the eyes of a child:

> *Spanking is more an expression of parental frustration than it is a reasonable teaching method.*

> Why is doing a thing all right sometimes when doing the same thing you get spanked for other times? Spankings come and go so suddenly you can never be sure about anything.
>
> Daddy is big and he spanks me. Spankings hurt. Somebody is always licking somebody on our block but not any of the little kids ever like any of the big ones. Daddy says any fool can force his will on someone smaller.
>
> My parents don't believe in spanking. They do it because they are mad about something. What would they do if they *believed* in spanking?
>
> Author Unknown

Spanking does not teach a child how to behave. It only teaches a child how *not* to behave.

Anyone who raises a hand against another to hurt, harm, or inflict pain is to that degree a barbarian, one who has yet to learn the full meaning of civility.

The spanking behavior of parents is maintained by three things:

1. *Ignorance*. They don't know a better way.
2. *Immediacy of results*. The child immediately comes into line, thus convincing the parents that spanking works. The fact that the behavior for which the child was spanked continues, and even gets worse, almost never suggests to the parents that spanking is really not solving anything.

3.  *Conventional wisdom.* Since everyone does it, and since it's been a staple parenting strategy for thousands of years, it must be the right thing, or at least *a* right thing to do. How often I hear fathers say, "My dad beat the tar out of me everytime I misbehaved. If I even looked like I was going to do something bad—WHAP! He gave it to me good. It was the best thing my dad could have done for me. I thank him every day of my life for keeping me on the straight and narrow."

> *Anyone who raises a hand against another with the intent to hurt, do harm, or inflict pain is to that degree a barbarian, one who has yet to learn the full meaning of civility.*

I sincerely hope, by the time you've finished this book, you'll accept as fact that spanking, or any kind of hitting for the purpose of inflicting pain as a method of teaching, has its origins not in the science of behavior but in ignorance, half truths, and our barbaric past. Furthermore, I hope you'll abandon it *completely* and use scientifically sound teaching methods as the strategy of choice when your children need to be taught to behave well.

The enduring and venerable adage "Spare the rod and spoil the child" has inadvertently heaped mountains of misery on children in the guise of discipline masquerading as good parenting. It has its origin in a Biblical scripture found in Proverbs 13:24, "He that spareth the rod hateth his son; but he that loveth him chasteneth him betimes." Subsequent verses in Proverbs reinforce the notion that "beating" children is a reasonable way of correcting them (Chapter 23:14). It is not my intention to take on the book of Proverbs, nor to question the wisdom of Solomon, but a lot has been learned through science in the last 3,000 years about teaching children to behave well, and I'm sure if Solomon were alive today, and as wise as he was then, he'd counsel us to learn wiser and more fitting lessons from science. He would probably even quote his father, David, who said, "Thy rod and thy staff comfort me" (Psalms 23:4).

I heard a wonderful, modern-day adaptation of the word "rod." It was redefined as "the word of God"; hence, in this context, the scripture would read "Spare the word of God and spoil the child." I like that! In light of what contemporary research about high and low risk families has taught us, not only is that a fitting interpretation, it's good advice.

Now a note of caution. I'm sure you have heard it said that to every rule there is an exception. Though, in a literal sense, I don't regard what I'm about to say as an exception to the rule "don't spank your children," it might be unjustifiably used by some as an excuse to use pain as a teaching or management tool. Just remember, what I'm about to touch on is a caution, *not* an excuse. Here goes.

In some clinical settings, where it is used therapeutically, is highly controlled and supervised, and is very selectively administered by expertly trained professionals who document every imaginable facet of the procedure, pain-based therapies are altogether appropriate. In fact, in some instances, for example with self-mutilating subjects, it might very well be the *only* therapeutic procedure left. Such procedures, used under the controls described above at leading research institutions and treatment centers across America, have freed children of a life bound up in straight jackets, confined to padded enclosures, and manacled to a bed or a crib. In such instances, pain-based therapies have been found, after all else failed, to be the most humane treatment available. It is not unlike a surgeon who might have to inflict some pain and discomfort—such as rebreaking a bone then resetting it—in order to do what is ultimately in the best interest of the patient. As with a medical procedure that would be accompanied by pain, pain-based behavioral treatment is typically short-lived, professionally managed, and the client is ultimately better off because of it.

I am very aware that this is a highly emotionally charged issue. In fact, there are state legislatures that are considering legislation that would ban any and all behavioral therapies that involve pain-based methods. After 33 years working with behavior problems, and knowing well the range of treatment needs, I regard such bans as irresponsible. In the final analysis, in matters of extreme behaviors that have failed to respond to any other clinically-sound treatment, for the well-being of the involved individual, treatment must be a matter of science, not a matter of emotion or politics.

## NOW TO REVIEW

1. Behavior responds better to positive than to negative consequences; therefore, spanking a child is a super crummy consequence for an inappropriate behavior.

2. Spanking is more likely to be an out-of-control expression of parental frustration than it is a serious attempt to teach children to behave better.

3. Teaching children to behave well is initially more appropriate than hurting a child for behaving badly.

4. Inflicting pain—even the threat of inflicting pain—on children will prompt children to escape us, avoid us, and even get even with us.

5.  In highly selected instances, as part of a well controlled and managed form of professionally administered therapy, pain-based treatments may be appropriate.

> *Research has shown that the most effective way to reduce problem behavior in children is to strengthen desirable behavior through positive reinforcement rather than trying to weaken undesirable behavior using aversive or negative processes.*
> S.W. Bijou
> The International Encyclopedia of Education, 1988

# THIRTEEN
# Using Time-Out

"Time-out," a behavior management strategy known to nearly every parent, is one of the most misunderstood and badly used strategies for dealing with the inappropriate behavior of children. But when well understood, and well used, it is a wonderful tool for managing children's difficult behaviors.

First, we need to understand what time-out is. The term time-out is really an abbreviation for "time out from positive reinforcement." As is so often the case when we are dealing with the inappropriate behavior of children, we become punitive; i.e., we forget about trying to shape behavior through the use of positive, reinforcing consequences, and instead come crashing down on kids with all kinds of negative, punitive, aversive kinds of consequences. This is no more evident than in the general misuse of time-out.

> *"Time-out" really means time out from positive reinforcement.*

Whether I am observing parents or teachers, it is only rarely, so rarely in fact that I can't even think of an instance right now to the contrary, that time-out is used appropriately and in the appropriate context. What I typically observe is mountains of appropriate behavior going totally unrecognized, totally unacknowledged. Then a child misbehaves and WHAM, the kid gets thrown into time-out. And I mean that quite literally! The youngster is grabbed by the arm, marched across the room, shoved into time-out and told, "Now you better behave yourself or you're going to stay in there all day long!" And while the kid is being put in time-out, the parent or the teacher is scolding the youngster and flooding him with all manner of verbal reprimands: "I'm so sick and tired of you acting like this. You're driving me crazy!" "I don't know why we have to go through this a half a dozen times a day. Why can't you just behave like a normal kid!" And so on. When this happens, time-out is not an alternative to an environment where the child is being positively reinforced for appropriate behavior, since appropriate behavior is totally ignored. Remember, behavior responds better to positive than to negative consequences.

Time-out from positive reinforcement is intended to place the child in an environment where he is *not* getting any positive reinforcement. It should be so *un*reinforcing, in fact, that the child decides that it is better to behave appropriately and get positively reinforced than to behave inappropriately and be timed-out. But this is almost never the setting. The setting is typically one where good behavior is ignored and time-out is simply a way, or a place, for getting the kid out of someone's hair. Interestingly enough, being put into time-out can be a very positive reinforcer to a child. If the child is supposed to be completing a distasteful task and is put in time-out because he is dawdling away his time, he has beaten the system: while in time-out, there are no expectations of him. He won. Time-out can be reinforcing in other ways. While the child is being taken to time-out, given all of the ceremony surrounding it, it becomes an immensely reinforcing event by bringing to the child the attention of everyone in the classroom or every other person in the home. And to make matters worse, the time-out area is frequently an extremely reinforcing place to be in. Here's a classic example. Recently I was invited into an elementary school to observe a 9-year-old boy who had the entire school system beside

> Used badly, time-out can quickly become a reinforcer.

itself. (I am continually amazed, as I visit schools across the United States, how it is that a 7- 8- 9-year-old kid can bring an entire school to its knees! It continually amazes me that schools staffed by certified personnel with years and years of professional training, and degrees heaped upon degrees, find themselves prostrate before the behavior of a little kid!)

Without the boy knowing that I was observing him, I followed him around for the better part of the school day, making note both of his behavior and of the behavior of the teachers and the administrators of the school. I had been told in advance that when the boy got out of hand to the point where he was totally disrupting the classroom environment, he was "put in time-out." Sure enough, like a self-fulfilling prophecy, the child's behavior quickly became intolerably disruptive, and he was led off ceremoniously to time-out. Occasionally, the boy behaved appropriately in class for long periods of time, for which he was completely ignored. But he was a marked kid, and the instant he acted up, the system came down on him like a ton of bricks, and it wasn't long before he was happily on his way out to time-out. Now remember, for time-out to really be time-out, it has to be time-out from positive reinforcement. From what I'm about to describe, you tell me if this child was experiencing time-out *from* positive reinforcement.

Time-out was a seat behind a desk in the corner of the main office of the school. (See Figure 13.1.) Adjacent to this area was the principal's office and the assistant principal's office. Inside the main office were the mailboxes for the faculty and two other desks, each one occupied by a secretary. Also, the wall that separated the main office from the main hall of the school was all glass, so that anybody walking past the main office could see everyone in there and what was going on.

As the boy was brought into time-out, both secretaries in the front office made wise cracks about his being brought to time-out: "Oh, I see you're back again! Aren't you ever going to learn to behave and act your age?" Shortly after the boy was seated at the desk and told to "sit still and be quiet!" the principal came in, waved at the boy, smiled, and said, "Well, I see you haven't wasted any time," and then, chuckling to himself, went into his office. The assistant principal, who was less gentle than the principal (remember, assistant principals are typically the "heavies" that do the dirty work) made a point to go over to the kid and give him a good tongue lashing before disappearing back into his office.

Though things quieted down in the front office for a few minutes, the kid was being adequately entertained by those passing by the office waving to him through the windows. Students, teachers, and support staff were waving and making gestures to the boy as he sat at his desk reveling in the massive amount of attention he was receiving. Teachers going to their mailboxes spoke and waved to him.

Moments later, an irate teacher came storming into the office to express his displeasure over an administrative decision that had been made by the assistant principal. This displeasure was expressed to the secretary, who in turn called the assistant principal.

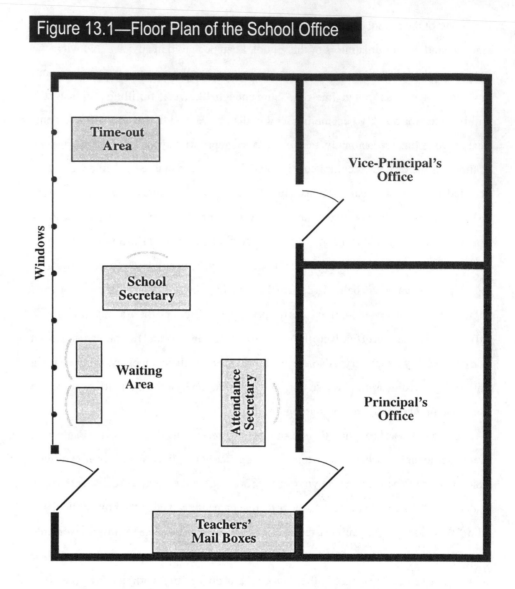

Figure 13.1—Floor Plan of the School Office

It was easy to tell that emotions were building to a fever pitch, and instantly the assistant principal emerged from his office to confront the irate teacher in very combative tones. They stood there toes to toes, nose to nose, arguing, even shouting at each other! This engrossing scene continued for several minutes and then the teacher stormed out of the office shouting behind him, "I refuse to work under these conditions. I am going home!", and out of the building he went in a huff. The assistant principal, obviously angry and frustrated, went stomping back into his office muttering something unintelligible under his breath. All the while, as you can imagine, this kid is having a wonderful time! Shortly thereafter, a bell rang signalling time for recess. Without

> *Time-out has no remedial value unless the child is away from a reinforcing environment.*

anyone saying a word, the boy got up and went outside to recess, after which he went to his next class.

Now, I will restate the question I asked earlier, "Was this time-out from positive reinforcement?" The answer is obvious! Absolutely not! On the contrary, the *classroom* was time-out from positive reinforcement. While in "time-out," the youngster was being heaped with reinforcement. While in the classroom, the child was receiving no reinforcement whatsoever. Granted, this is an extreme example (but not as extreme as one might think!), but it does illustrate the important point that time-out does not have any remedial properties unless it is, in fact, time-out from positive reinforcement. This all goes back to the critical point I hope is crystal clear by now: it is absolutely essential that while children are behaving appropriately, they are acknowledged for that behavior.

Here are several points and suggestions you will want to consider when implementing a time-out procedure. Let me remind you that when properly used, the time-out procedure is one of the most effective strategies we know for managing otherwise unmanageable behavior. When used effectively, it is a power-house strategy. Here are suggestions that will help you use this strategy effectively.

The first thing you **MUST** do is establish a reinforcing environment in the home. To do this, do the following:

a. Use the inappropriate behavior of the child as a cue to you to attend to the appropriate behavior of another child. If the child is acting out, and another is behaving well, give your attention to the one that is behaving well.

b. Make a note to "catch your children doing something right" several times each day. But remember, do this very naturally, using a variety of verbal and physical gestures. You needn't think that you have to acknowledge *every* right behavior. Intermittent reinforcement is the best kind of all. Intermittent reinforcement is reinforcement given at unexpected times.

c. To the extent possible (which is most of the time) ignore inconsequential, annoying behaviors. Just walk away from them!

d. Exercise complete self-control and be unemotionally directive when it is necessary to attend to inappropriate behavior. No shouting, screaming, ranting, raving, moralizing, preaching, and so on. Use as few words as possible to get your point across. Try to keep your message to 10 or 12 words: "No, Billy, You may not take the baby's toy."

e. Stop then redirect inappropriate behavior that can't be ignored. When appropriate, use the stop, redirect, reinforce strategy (pages 59-62) or the teaching interaction strategy described on pages 67-68.

If these conditions are in place, then you'll have a very reinforcing environment from which to take the child; in which case, time-out really is time-out, and not just isolation for the child or relief for the parent.

Second, make certain you have carefully rehearsed your actions when taking a child to, putting the child in, and removing the child from time-out. What we typically observe

> *Do not allow the use of time-out to degenerate into a punitive response.*

is an angry parent or an angry teacher who gruffly and abruptly hauls the kid off to time-out, all the while carrying on with a lot of verbal reprimanding and venting of frustration. In some respects, this is what one would expect. After all, time-out isn't used until the situation has become intolerable, so it is reasonable to expect that the parent or the teacher is at wit's end, patience has been tried to its limit, and this is simply the last straw. Despite the fact that this might be so, it is important that the parent or the teacher not stoop to the behavioral level of the child in an effort to deal with the child's behavior. (See Figure 4.1, pg. 89.) The better way is to rise—and remain—*above* all that, and proceed calmly and according to plan. When this is done, the time-out procedure can be employed quickly, efficiently, and with remarkable success.

Immediately, when the child exhibits a behavior which deserves time-out, gently take the child by the hand, or, if you have to, carry the child or partially support him by

> *Practice, practice, practice. Rehearse, rehearse, rehearse.*

holding him under the armpits, then lead the child directly to the time-out area. There is no jerking the child's arm or dragging him along the floor. Do nothing that would suggest that you are taking your frustrations out on the child. While taking the child to time-out, say very simply and calmly, "When you behave this way you may not be with us." That is all you need to say. For goodness sake, don't apologize or express personal anguish at having to do this. Words like, "I'm sorry I have to do this," or "Please don't make me take you to time-out," are *no good*! You might need to rehearse what you're going to say to be sure it is *all* you say. In a moment of anger and frustration, we are all inclined to say more than we should, and to say things we shouldn't say at all. That is why it is so very important to practice and rehearse this procedure to make certain the procedure itself does not become a reinforcing event for the child. We don't want the procedure to degenerate into an opportunity for the parent or teacher to simply work off his or her frustrations on the kid. To do that is to behave no better than the child. I am reminded of an instance when I was working with a mother of a 5-year-old child who had developed some severe tantruming, clinging, and crying behavior. Whenever the mother left the child's presence, or even appeared to be moving in the direction of leaving the child's presence, the child would rush frantically to his mother, grab her legs and launch into an intense display of emotion including pleading, crying, weeping, and wailing. It was a very dramatic scene that had completely gripped the mother and virtually rendered her a victim of the child's behavior.

> *You can put a distraught child in time-out with as much love and tenderness as you would put a sleeping child into its crib.*

I convinced the family to prepare a time-out area, and I carefully reviewed with the mother how time-out was to be used. A few days later she called and told me it wasn't working; that the child was still behaving as before. I then visited the mother at home where I was able to observe both her and the child's behavior. I was impressed with the amount of fuss on the part of the mother as she was putting the boy in time-out. As it turned out, the mother felt she was being somehow mean and unfair in putting the child in time-out, so prior to doing so she fussed over the child, gave him a great deal of compassionate attention, and let him know that this was more painful to her than it was to him. She would hold the child close in her arms, cuddle him, love him, stroke him, kiss him, and even shed a few tears over what she was about to do. She would tell him how sad she was and how much it hurt her to put him in time-out and how much better it would be if he would just learn to behave himself so she wouldn't have to do this terrible thing. Finally, after several minutes of this, she put the child in time-out and by now she was crying and he was crying. I rehearsed with the mother once again what time-out was supposed to accomplish, and then demonstrated for her the appropriate use of the time-out strategy. This consisted simply of holding the boy up by the armpits and, though his feet were dragging the floor and he was kicking and screaming all the way, taking the child directly downstairs, saying nothing more than, "When you behave this way, you may not be with us." I then put the child into the time-out area, closed and locked the door, and walked away. I waited to observe the mother doing this herself to make certain she was able to do it properly. Though there was still some anguish in her face, she learned quickly, and was soon able to carry it off without a hitch. As soon as the hoped-for results were realized, her anguish and concern left. It took only a few days to become a very routine procedure, and it quickly solved the problem.

My point is that talking about time-out and actually using it as a means for eliminating inappropriate behavior are two different things, and for most people, before it can be used effectively, it has to be practiced and rehearsed.

Thirdly, make certain that the time-out area is, indeed, time-out. The time-out area must be totally devoid of anything the child would find enjoyable or gratifying. There should be no toys to play with, nobody available to speak to, no music or pleasant sounds, nothing to eat, just a bare, stark area. It mustn't be dark, frightening, foreboding, cold or hot, dangerous, or cramped. It should just be a bare, stark room. Creating such an environment might require some creativity, some expense, and even some temporary inconvenience to the family.

The nature of the time-out area will depend, of course, to a large extent on the behavior of the child. For some children, a chair placed behind a simple cardboard partition over against the corner of a room is all that is needed. To another child, it might mean the construction of an area with a lock on the door. It might simply mean converting an existing area such as a bedroom or bathroom.

> *The time-out environment must be non-reinforcing, otherwise it's not time-out.*

I am reminded of one set of parents who used a child's bedroom for the time-out area, but made it absolutely stark and barren by removing all toys, books, pictures, and even the bedding off the bed. The only thing in the room was a bed without bedsheets or pillow. Another mother took a hula hoop and sewed a curtain to it that was about six feet long. She suspended this from the ceiling and put a sign on it that said "Think-it-over room." When children behaved in a way that lost them the privilege of playing as they pleased, she gently took them by the hand and said, "When you behave that way, you must spend some time thinking it over."

The point I want to make is that the time-out area needs to be appropriate for the child. If a child will sit in a time-out area that is as fragile and delicate as a curtained enclosure hung from a hula hoop, that would be sufficient. If, on the other hand, the child needs something that is more confining, then that should be devised. One of our daughters-in-law used the steps leading upstairs as a time-out area, and it *worked* perfectly well, because it was *used* perfectly well! Another used a small utility toilet off the kitchen.

It is typical for parents to resist the suggestion that a time-out area be developed even when one is needed. Excuses such as trouble, expense, and inconvenience are usually forthcoming. My response is that if that is the treatment that is necessary, then it is worth any time, expense, and inconvenience that a family can reasonably afford. It is a form of intensive care, and just as it is sometimes necessary to prescribe intensive care to make a person well physically, it is necessary to prescribe intensive care to make someone well behaviorally. I am reminded of an instance where on my suggestion, a family went to considerable expense to build a time-out room in the unfinished basement of their home. The cost of the lumber, a door, the electrical work, and the hardware, plus the time that it took to build it, added up to a considerable effort and expense. In less than a week the mother called. She was an interesting case of mixed emotions. She said, "That behavior has completely stopped. The time-out room has worked perfectly and has done the job. But it seems to us like

> *A good time-out area is a small price to pay for the good it can do.*

such a waste to have spent all that money and to go to all that effort to build a time-out room that we've only needed to use for a few days!" When she told me that, I thought of the fellow who bought traveler's insurance before boarding an airplane. When he got off the airplane, having safely arrived at his destination, he threw the insurance receipt in the garbage can and muttered, "Nuts! Another $2.50 wasted!" My response to the mother was that the money and time had apparently been well spent. Now, one might argue, they should have planned better and built that time-out room so that it fit in to the broader plans of refinishing their basement. That might be so, but that is still beside the point here. The point is, they did the right thing and accomplished the right ends, and it was all well worth the time, effort, and money that it took to do it.

I am convinced that with a little ingenuity and imagination, virtually every home can be arranged to provide an adequate time-out area. We must remember that if the procedure is used correctly, time-out may not be needed for more than a short period of time. Believe me, it is worth the time, effort, and expense.

Next, it is important that parents have clearly in mind those behaviors which are severe enough to require the use of time-out. One common error is using time-out for any and all inappropriate, annoying, or bothersome behaviors. As I mentioned earlier, the temptation is great to use this strategy in a punitive way rather than in a precise, therapeutic way. Before the time-out procedure is used, the parents must have a clear and precise understanding of which behaviors will justify the use of time-out. Furthermore, for children 2 to 3 years old and older, this should be told to them and its use demonstrated through role playing.

As a general rule, behaviors that are severe enough to require time-out are behaviors which cannot be ignored. These are behaviors which, if left unattended, either disrupt the environment to the point where others are unable to proceed normally and without interruption, or they are behaviors which interfere with the child's normal behavioral development. For example, let's suppose that some children are playing nicely together and one child becomes so disruptive that he interferes with the play of the other children to the point where they simply can't continue. In such an instance, the disruptive child has taken over the situation and, through inappropriate behavior, has become the object of everyone's attention. Other efforts to bring the child's behavior into line have failed.[1]

> **The child should know exactly which behaviors earn time-out.**

The child continues to be disruptive. In such an instance, the parent should gently but firmly and resolutely remove the child from the environment and place him in time-out saying no more than, "When you behave that way you may not be with us." The key to determining whether a behavior is so severe as to be timed-out is whether the child and his inappropriate behavior have taken over and have become the major objects of attention. This could include tantruming, whining, incessant crying, being overly demanding, being overly possessive, being physically and/or verbally abusive, and so on.

On the other hand, a child's behavior might interfere with normal behavioral development. For example, a child might call other children degrading, demeaning names, or be abusive in other ways. In such instances, the time-out procedure can be very successful.

Now a word about how long one should be left in time-out, and the conditions under which a child may leave time-out. Generally speaking, a child should remain in time-out for two to three minutes *after* he has quit making a fuss or a ruckus *while in* time-out. What this means is that a child might spend half an hour in time-out screaming, hollering, and carrying on, but not be allowed to leave until he has remained quiet for two or three minutes. Monitoring this can be a bit of a problem for parents, but it is worth the effort. Whatever you do, do not interrupt a child's crying, screaming and hollering to say something like, "When you decide to quiet down in there, then I will let you out!" This is a form of intermittent reinforcement that does nothing more than encourage the child to continue screaming, hollering, and carrying on. When you role play the time-out procedure with a child, let the child know that you will start timing him once he is quiet, and that if he is quiet for two or three minutes (as appropriate) then he may leave time-out. It is not at all unusual for a child to spend 30, 40, even 50 minutes or an hour in time-out. That's perfectly okay, so long as the conditions for leaving time-out have been met.

---

[1] For example, a simple verbal directive to stop, the use of the teaching interaction strategy, and the use of extinction.

If this is done consistently and accurately, after a relatively short while, perhaps a few days, the child will begin to realize that no amount of screaming, hollering, kicking the door, and carrying on will do any good, so he might as well behave himself and get out of there to more pleasant, reinforcing things.

> *Be certain that when the child is not in time-out, he/she gets lots of positive attention for good behavior.*

Let's suppose a child has been put in time-out and after having fussed for a few minutes, finally decides to quiet down. The required time passes without any commotion. You go to the door, open it, and the child immediately begins to cry, scream, and so on. Don't try to convince the child he shouldn't have done that. Simply say, "When you are ready to behave nicely, you may be with us." Then gently close the door and start the whole process over again. The point is, the child *earns* the right to leave time-out and come back into a reinforcing environment as soon as he is ready to behave appropriately. Since crying, screaming, and hollering are not appropriate behaviors, if those are the behaviors the child exhibits when he is invited to leave time-out then it is obvious that he is not ready to leave. It is obvious that he is still determined to get attention by behaving inappropriately. Since you are not going to allow him to do that, you really have no alternative but to close the door, and while doing so remind the child that when he is ready to behave appropriately he may leave time-out; then start the process all over again. This may take a while. Do not be discouraged. Remember, the behaviors for which children are put into time-out are severe behaviors and have developed over a long period of time. It is not reasonable to expect a child to abandon those behaviors all of a sudden. The child has learned as a result of a lot of experience that these behaviors have brought him an immense amount of attention. He is not going to give up those behaviors in a hurry.

I mentioned earlier that occasionally exceptions to rules pop up. Here is one as it relates to removing a child from time-out. Particularly for young children, two or three years old, being left in time-out at times when they are anxious about other things such as being left behind while the family is gone, or fearing that they might have to spend the night in time-out, it is advisable after a few minutes in time-out, to remove them even if they are still fussing. But if this is done, two conditions must be met by the child: one, the fussing must stop; and two, the behavior which resulted in his being put in time-out in the first place must cease. If both of these conditions are not met, the child must be returned immediately to time-out, as discussed earlier.

Now, let's consider the child who will take his medicine without making a fuss. He will sit on a chair in a corner, or in a think-it-over room, or on the stairs and be quiet and compliant and not do anything that requires a more secure setting. If this is the case, put the child on the chair and beside him place a kitchen timer set for three minutes, and say, "When the timer goes off, if you are ready to behave nicely, come see me." That's all you need to say. Here again, you will want to role play this in advance so the child knows exactly what to expect and what to do. When the timer goes off, and the child comes to you, do not say, "Okay, are you ready to behave yourself?" This is an inappropriate question. The fact that the child has come to you is evidence that he is ready to behave appropriately since you already said, "When the timer goes off, if you are ready to behave appropriately, come see me." The fact that the child is standing there before you is evidence that she/he has decided to behave appropriately. Rather, say to the child, "I am so happy that you have decided to play nicely. Thank you so much." Then give the child a hug and a pat and send him off to play. This is a self-management dimension of time-out and is very effective in teaching children the consequences of behavior, *and* self control.

I mentioned earlier that we typically require a child to remain in time-out for 2 or 3 minutes beyond the time he quits being disruptive while in time-out. Until age 3, use about half a minute of time-out for every year old the child is. Three minutes is used for children 4 years old and older. With children over 7 years old, the use of a time-out procedure as has been described here tends to lose its effectiveness, and the management of other consequences tends to be a more appropriate option; e.g., denial of privileges.

Time-out is a proven effective strategy for eliminating certain kinds of behaviors. There can be no question about that! But it is a procedure which should be used very carefully, and **ONLY** in those instances where other strategies don't work. Always use the easiest-to-use strategies first. If telling a child to stop behaving in a certain way is effective, then use that. If using the teaching interaction strategy is all that is needed, use that. If denying a child a privilege is effective, use that. If making a child sit alone on a stool in the corner works, then use that. Only in the most extreme instances should one architecturally rearrange a home to create a secure time-out procedure.

I have often been asked if it's okay to put the child in the bathroom. The answer is yes, assuming that the bathroom is a safe place and doesn't become a reinforcing environment in itself. As I mentioned earlier, it is not unusual for the time-out setting to be more reinforcing than not being in time-out. I have worked with parents who, because of space and living limitations were simply not able to create a totally sterile environment, so they put the child in a bedroom or a bathroom only to find that when it was time to allow the child out (that is when all of the conditions had been met), the child had made a mess of things. In each instance, the parents simply told the child, "You may leave time-out when the room is cleaned up and put back in order just the way you found it." They then closed the door and went about their business while the child cleaned up his own mess. This worked very effectively in every single instance.

Lastly, a child should never be *threatened* with being sent to time-out. A parent should never say, "If you behave like that one more time, I'm going to put you in time-out!" Threats are never appropriate! Typically a child learns that threats simply buy time during which he is able to continue his disruptive behavior and earn a lot of undeserved attention. My father wasn't what one would call a good disciplinarian. He was too harsh and inflicted much more pain than was necessary. I didn't appreciate that. But I do appreciate the fact that I knew **exactly** what was going to happen to me if I behaved in a certain way. There was no warning or no threatening. When I behaved in a particularly inappropriate way the consequences fell immediately, and believe me I learned in a hurry not to repeat certain behaviors. But we don't need to be harsh and abusive when we discipline our children. We need to be firm, precise, immediate, and well planned.

Though you should never threaten a child with time-out, there are soft warning signals that are appropriate. For example, simply stopping and redirecting a behavior can become a warning, particularly if the child learns that by ignoring this, he/she will be immediately placed in time-out.

## NOW TO REVIEW

1. Time-out means "time-out from positive reinforcement."

2. Time-out is an effective strategy only if the child is away from a reinforcing environment when in time-out.

3. The time-out area must be secure and totally unreinforcing. It must be a sterile, dull environment that does not offer the child the slightest opportunity to enjoy himself.

4. The time-out area must not be frightening, dangerous, or physically threatening. It should be of a reasonable temperature, well lighted, but dull.

5. When taking a child to and removing a child from time-out, use as few words as possible, and all physical interactions with the child must be as gentle as possible. This does not mean that the child is coddled. It is possible to be gentle

and at the same time firm.

6. A child must not be allowed to leave time-out until he has remained quiet for the required number of minutes, depending upon the age of the child (with the one exception as noted).

7. Both parents and children must have a clear understanding of which behaviors will be treated with time-out, and the time-out procedure should be rehearsed with children in advance so that they know exactly what to expect.

8. Never threaten a child with time-out. If a child exhibits a behavior that is so severe as to require time-out, the child should be removed immediately to time-out.

> *Research has shown that the most effective way to reduce problem behavior in children is to strengthen desirable behavior through positive reinforcement rather than trying to weaken undesirable behavior using aversive or negative processes.*
>
> *S.W. Bijou*
> *The International Encyclopedia of Education, 1988*

# FOURTEEN
# Eliminating Tantrums

Tantrums, though among the most obnoxious behaviors of young children, are generally quite easy to eliminate. It is very important for us to understand that tantrums are a behavior children *learn* as a result of the attention given to them when they don't get their way. It is a dramatic way of getting attention. When a child tantrums, he is, as it were, pulling out all the stops by screaming, crying, falling on the floor, kicking and flailing arms and legs, and is almost impossible, in the minds of most parents, to ignore. Parents typically regard a tantruming child as unmanageable. They feel like they are the victims of the child's behavior and will do almost anything to stop it.

Tantrums are nearly always caused by a child not getting what he wants. Anyone who has had a child who tantrums knows full well what I'm talking about. A child asks for something (regardless of whether it's at home, at church, in the grocery store, at grandpa's and grandma's, or wherever) and is refused. Over a period of time, he has learned that if he behaves in a dramatic way—typically by crying, screaming, and falling to the floor—he will get what he wants; and as long as tantrums get him what he wants they continue, usually getting worse and worse over time. When children tantrum, we must be careful that we don't think some type of sophisticated scheming is going on in the child's mind, that the child is saying, "Ah hah, now I know how to control my parents. All I have to do to get my way is to rant and rave and eventually they will cave in and I'll win!" The child has learned to tantrum through conditioning, not through logic or reason. It works like this. A child wants something: a candy bar at the grocery store, a cookie right before dinner, to go outside and play when the weather is bad, or whatever, and the request is denied. But from many experiences, the child has learned that by putting up a fuss, he gets his way. Consequences shape behavior!

Determined to not let the child get his way all the time, parents will often hold out only to find that the child becomes even more dramatic and less able to be ignored. Finally, the parents "can't take it any longer," so they give the child what he wants. This becomes a short-term solution to a problem that only gets worse. As

> **Children are taught to tantrum.**

time passes, the parents become more and more resolved that they are simply *not* going to let this kid get his way, so they hold out for longer and longer periods of time, then eventually cave in. This, of course, conditions the child to become even more dramatic, more bizarre, and more determined in his behavior. Rather than just crying and tugging at one's leg, the child throws himself on the floor, kicking, screaming, and flailing his arms! The parents can't take it any longer and they give in before the child gives out. Once again the child has successfully managed the environment to his own satisfaction. Since the parents find that short-term relief is better than no relief at all, they decide it is just better to give the kid his way and hope he will grow out of it. Both of these decisions are wrong. Giving the child his way is certainly not in his best interest, and he probably isn't going to gracefully grow out of it; rather, the behavior simply takes a different form and becomes even less manageable as the child grows older. (Adults have tantrums too. They are a bit more sophisticated, but they are tantrums nonetheless!)

As children enter school, tantrums interfere with learning and instruction. In a study reported in 1991, researchers at the State University of New York found that teachers, when attempting to instruct kicking, screaming, and biting children, attempted *far less* instruction with them than with "normal children." Also, teachers were less likely to invite children who tantrum to participate in instructional activities: calling on others to answer questions and participate in class discussion. In all, teachers spent 40% less time instructing problem children, and involved them 42% less in instructional activities, than they did non-disruptive children. Eliminating tantrums as quickly as possible is, from any perspective, in the child's best interest.

As I have already mentioned, tantrums, though very dramatic and bizarre and sometimes alarming, are typically quite easy to eliminate if they are treated early and dealt with consistently. In fact, if a parent is alert, the behavior never gets started in the first place. But if it does get started, if it does get established, it can still be eliminated quite easily. Let's look now at how you eliminate tantrum behavior in several likely settings, beginning with the home.

## Eliminating Tantrums at Home

The easiest place in which to deal with tantrum behavior is at home. In this regard, we need to look at the behavior from two points: 1) how to deal with pre-tantrum behavior (i.e., whining, begging, whimpering, etc.) and 2) how to deal with a full blown, well developed tantrum. Let's look first at how to handle pre-tantrum behavior.

1. *Pre-Tantrum Behavior.* Though whining, whimpering, begging, crying, and so on, are examples of what a child will do to get his way, they should never be reinforced. What I mean, simply, is that when a child whines, whimpers, cries and carries on to get his way, you must be absolutely certain not to pay that off by giving the child what he is whining, whimpering and crying for. Such behaviors should never, ever be reinforced. When a child whines, cries, and whimpers for something, say to the child in a calm, unemotional, fully controlled voice, and with complete composure, "You may not have that"; "Say that nicely"; or "Talk to me only with your best voice." If the child persists, call him by name, and say, "When you behave this way you may not be with me," and then firmly but gently lead the child to a time-out area, as described in Chapter 13, Using Time-Out. Don't do this in a jerking or angry manner. Be very calm. Of course, when the child is behaving appropriately, it is necessary to acknowledge that behavior in a very positive and reinforcing way. It must always be remembered that it is much better to acknowledge appropriate behavior, and to have appropriate behavior developed in the first place, than to have to remediate an out-of-control behavior.

2. *Established Tantrum Behavior.* The single greatest lesson the child who tantrums needs to learn is that mommy and daddy will not give in! He must learn that he can scream, holler, and carry on, but he is not going to get what he wants by doing so.

When a child uses a tantrum to get his way, the parent needs to *immediately* remove the child to a time-out area. This is done unemotionally, but with firmness, and without anger or apology of any kind. There must be no anger or frustration on the parent's face. The parent simply says, "When you behave this way, you may not be with us," and then remove the child to time-out. And this is done immediately, *every single time* a child *begins* to tantrum, and it is done essentially the same way each time so the child learns quickly exactly what to expect. This is called the "zero tolerance response." That means that a tantrum is *never* tolerated, even a little bit!

> **Parental warnings only encourage more tantrums.**

Before doing this, however, explain and role play the time-out procedure with the child so he knows exactly what to expect the *instant* he begins to tantrum. When time-out is used for the first time, the child will tantrum for what seems to be an eternity. (The old extinction burst bit!) That's all right, let him have at it. The key is that the parents go about their business as though the tantruming child didn't even exist. (This is called planned/purposeful ignoring.) It's possible that the child might carry on for an hour or more. He might stop for a few minutes to catch his breath and to regain some strength, then launch right back into it. The reason the child will persist this way is because he has been taught in the past that if he just keeps it up long enough, he'll eventually get his way. For the first few times, he will figure that it's only a matter of hanging in there longer. In fact, it is not unlikely for a child to become so exhausted while in time-out that he will fall asleep. And that's fine. Let him sleep—in time-out. Don't feel that you are being a terrible parent for allowing the child to tantrum for a long period of time. It might seem rather insensitive, and even heartless, but remember, the child has a lot of new learning to do, and this can be a long process. Whatever you do, *do not give in before the child gives out!* Remember, the behavior exists because it has been heavily reinforced in the past.

> **Do not give in before the child gives out.**

If the tantrums have not been severe, or of long duration, it might not be necessary to place the child in time-out. In fact, it might be sufficient to allow the child to carry on in your company, but to pay no attention to him while he's doing it. Just walk away. If he grabs onto your leg, free yourself with as little bother as possible and go on about your work. In fact, it's not a bad idea for you to leave the room and go where the child can't get to you, such as the bathroom or the bedroom. This is effective when, as I mentioned earlier, the tantrum isn't that disruptive, and when you are certain the child won't destroy anything when he is being ignored.

If there is any notion that being ignored will provoke the child to bite, destroy something, or hurt someone, then the child should be placed in time-out immediately. Breaking things and hurting people are behaviors that can be neither ignored or tolerated. The point is, you must put the child where he receives no reinforcement at all, and where he can do no harm to himself, to other people, or to other things. After the tantrum is over and the child has been quiet for about 2 minutes, go to him and say, "I'm glad you're feeling better," give him a hug and a kiss, then go about your business. If, at this moment, the child begins to tantrum again, gently place the child back in time-out and start the process all over again!

Here again, as I mentioned before, it is *absolutely necessary* that the child get lots and lots of positive attention when he is behaving appropriately, i.e., not tantruming.

## Eliminating Tantrums That Occur Outside of the Home

Children learn quickly to generalize their behavior. What brings attention in one place can frequently be counted on to bring attention in another. Tantrums, as dramatic as they are, are a number one attention getter in most any setting. A question parents often ask me is "How do I deal with the child who tantrums at church, at the supermarket, at the home of family and friends?" To begin, I advise them against taking a child to any of these places if it is likely he will throw a tantrum. Remember, it's a tough behavior to ignore, and if it is reinforced elsewhere, it will be just that much more difficult to get

> *Plan in advance for tantrums. Ask yourself, "What will I do if..."*

rid of at home—or anywhere. Rather, I would wait until his tantrums have been eliminated at home, and you have good assurance that he won't tantrum elsewhere. I realize when making this suggestion it could complicate one's life, and even be unfair to others. Nevertheless, if the strategies I have described earlier are used effectively, even if it takes a week or two to get rid of tantrums, it is well worth the sacrifice, inconvenience, and even lack of fairness it might cause, and it will certainly be in the best interest of the child.

Let's suppose, though, that the child does have a tantrum in another setting. For example, the child tantrums when he is dropped off at the baby sitter's or preschool. In a situation like this where parents don't have time to quiet the child, or to take the child back home to time-out, the single best thing to do is just ignore the tantrum, walk away and go on with your business. The sitter (or preschool people) should be instructed to pay no attention to the tantrum behavior, should leave the child alone (preferably off by himself), and should go on about their business until the tantrum ceases. If possible, in such a case, it would be well to establish a time-out area in that new setting. When the child has quit the tantrum, then he should be allowed to participate with the others as long as he behaves appropriately. Again, make certain that when he *is* behaving appropriately this behavior is acknowledged and is properly reinforced. He should be told things like, "You are having so much fun playing" or "You are so happy" or "I can tell you are enjoying yourself because you have such a big smile on your face."

*Remember the zero tolerance response.*

I have seen parents drop a child off at the baby sitter's or preschool and the child begins to tantrum. The parents go through an agonizing ritual of trying to calm him down. This wastes time, it reinforces the very behavior they want to get rid of, and generally starts the day on a sour note for everyone. In such instances, parents are better advised to just drop the child off and leave as quickly as possible. And as they turn to leave, they should do so cheerily, with a smile on their faces, and a lilting, "See you tonight, Honey. Have a happy day."

If a child tantrums at a supermarket, at church, or at the home of family or friends, *immediately* remove him to a quiet, solitary area and leave him alone. If he will not remain there alone, take him home and initiate the time-out procedure. I realize there are any number of reasons why this might not be possible: you're a long way from home, you don't have transportation available, and so on. But wherever you are, if it is *at all possible*, remove the child to a nonreinforcing setting as quickly as you can. Think this all through carefully in advance and know what your options are if a tantrum should happen away from home. Ask yourself, "What will I do if…?" Two good ways to prepare for such an eventuality is to (1) review and practice with the child expected behavior in advance, and (2) reinforce appropriate, nontantrum behaviors.

Reviewing and practicing expected behaviors should occur shortly before the child leaves the house. It would go like this, as the parent visits face-to-face with the child:

| | |
|---|---|
| Parent: | "Kay, we are about to go to the grocery store. When we get there I am going to put you in the seat of the shopping cart where you will sit all the time we are shopping." Where are you going to sit *all* the time we are shopping? |
| Child: | (about to whimper) "But I don't like to ride in the shopping cart." |
| Parent: | "Kay, in your best voice tell me where you are going to sit while we are at the store." |
| Child: | (Still whimpering.) |
| Parent: | "Kay, when you are ready to talk in your nicest voice, we will get ready to go shopping. For now, you must sit quietly in the chair for three minutes. (Put a kitchen timer by the chair.) When the buzzer goes off, if you are ready to talk to me in your happy voice, come see me." (The parent then leaves immediately.) |
| Child: | (Three minutes later.) "I'm ready to talk in my happy voice." |
| Parent: | "Wonderful! Now, while we are shopping, where are you going to sit?" |
| Child: | "In the shopping cart." |
| Parent: | "Right. Good answer. You are such a sweetie to listen so carefully." (A gentle hug and kiss.) |
| | While we are shopping, you will see many things you'll want to buy. You can buy one thing with this money. (Give the child a coin.) If you want something that costs more than this, will you be able to buy it?" |
| Child: | "No." |
| Parent: | "Why not?" |
| Child: | "I won't have enough money." |
| Parent: | "That's right. You won't have enough money. If that makes you sad and you feel like crying, what will you do instead of crying?" |
| Child: | "I just won't cry. I'll wait to find something else I can buy." |
| Parent: | "Exactly! Boy, it makes me happy when you have such good ideas. So while we are shopping, you will sit happily in the cart looking for something you can afford to buy. And when you do these things, it's going to be lots and lots of fun. |
| | "If you start to cry or make a fuss, you'll need to give me your money and we will come straight home to a baby sitter and I'll go back and do the shopping myself. What will happen if you decide to cry and fuss?" |
| Child: | "You'll take me to a baby sitter and I won't be able to buy anything." |
| Parent: | "Yeah. And that won't be any fun for you *or* me, because I like having you with me. So what are you going to do instead of crying or fussing?" |
| Child: | "I'm going to be happy and buy something with my money." |
| Parent: | "Right on! You are such a sweetie. I love you so." (Hug, kiss) |

This strategy, with appropriate tailoring, can be used in preparation for going to family visits, church, the park for a picnic, or whatever.

> Be constantly on the alert for opportunities to acknowledge appropriate behaviors.

If, at any time during such a dialogue, the child departs from your instructional intent, as I have noted repeatedly in this book, simply ignore all that and proceed with empathy, understanding, and the "broken record" approach. It works like a million dollars and is infinitely better than saying to a child, "Okay, we are going shopping and you'd better be good or I'm going to whip your butt! Now! Do you understand that!!?"

Reinforcing appropriate "intermediate" behaviors is a powerful way of stopping little inappropriate behaviors from accumulating to the point where there is a big blow up that degenerates into a tantrum, or any other negative behavioral episode. Blow ups, including tantrums, are typically the end result of a lot of smaller, "intermediate," behaviors that go untreated. A person doesn't die of lung cancer after smoking one cigarette. The lung cancer is the end result of smoking thousands of cigarettes. Though this is an extreme example, it helps make the point. If, as parents, we can effectively intervene at intermediate points, we can keep the end behavior from ever occurring. For example, suppose that when going anywhere of any distance in the car, the child ultimately ends up having a tantrum, usually after having been told "no" to several things the child did or wanted to do. A good way to keep the end behavior (tantruming) from occurring is to reinforce (using verbal praise, a smile, a touch, and so on) the child's appropriate intermediate behaviors:

"You are sitting so nicely. Thank you."
"Look at the animals in the field. See them eating?"
"I really like having you with me when I go places. You're my sweetie."
An occasional wink, smile, gentle tap on the knee.

Lots of these kinds of "intermediate" responses defuse what would otherwise be an emotional time-bomb just waiting to explode. We also refer to this as establishing behavioral momentum. You get the behavior going in the right direction in the first place, then keep it going in that direction.

As you consider these two strategies—review and practice expected behaviors, and reinforce appropriate intermediate behaviors—consider their worth in other settings as well. They can be applied very effectively in situations other than tantrum prevention, including playing nicely alone or with others, helping around the house, and getting homework done.

A strategy that has been reported by researchers in Canada to be effective for out-of-home tantrums involves the use of a hand-held tape recorder. Though most appropriate for older children, it is certainly worth considering by parents where public tantrums are particularly difficult to manage. The strategy is quite simple. The child is informed in advance that any tantrums out of the home will be recorded. (At this time, the tape recorder should be shown and its use demonstrated.) When the child tantrums in an out-of-home public setting, the parent simply turns on the recorder and records the event for later reference. Back home, in the presence of the parent(s) and the child, the tantrum is played back, and the consequences immediately applied—be it time-out, withdrawal of privileges, or whatever. Using this approach, the consequences of tantrums are linked immediately to the tantrum; there is no doubt in the child's mind what the relationship is between the behavior and the consequences. Just as reinforcers for appropriate behavior can be delayed, so can costly consequences for inappropriate behavior be delayed.

> *Believe it or not, most tantrums can be eliminated within 3 or 4 days.*

If this strategy is used, it is important that tape recordings also be made of the child's *appropriate* out-of-home behavior, and these played back as well, followed by pleasant, reinforcing consequences.

Although this might seem a bit cumbersome, it is a good strategy for older children who tantrum, and should be considered as a viable remedy for a tough-to-deal-with behavior.

Again think of this as intensive care. If a person is seriously ill it may be necessary to dramatically alter that person's environment long enough for him to get better. If a child has a difficult-to-manage behavior like tantrums, it might be necessary to establish an intensive care arrangement, realizing that such an arrangement, if well managed, will be needed for only a short time. I can assure you that if the tantrum behavior is handled well at home (i.e., is eliminated there) and the child learns that he can't go places if he tantrums, he will have learned a new behavior. Furthermore, if he is properly given attention for appropriate behavior when not tantruming, he will not feel the need to tantrum. It is worth the effort!

## NOW TO REVIEW

1. Tantruming behavior, though bizarre, dramatic, and outlandish, is simply a child's uncivilized way of getting what he wants, and can be remediated.

2. The instant a child begins to tantrum, attention must be turned away from him even to the point of walking away, or putting him into time-out. Use the zero tolerance model.

3. Regardless of how long the child continues to tantrum, he should be given no attention whatsoever. Furthermore, the child should be left alone for a few minutes after he has quit the tantrum before he is given any attention whatsoever.

4. When the child is not tantruming, appropriate behavior should be acknowledged and reinforced.

5. When it is necessary to attend to a tantrum, be unemotional, direct, and brief in your interaction. Say as few words as possible, have as little physical contact as possible, and don't mention the tantrum. Simply say, "When you behave this way you may not be with us," then take the child away from the company of others. If he has to be taken there kicking and screaming, so be it. Just handle it with as little show of emotion or concern as possible.

6. If there is a good chance the child will tantrum when he is away from home, either leave him home, or have a plan prepared in advance to deal with the tantrum in that new setting. For example, if you are going to visit friends or relatives, you might ask them in advance if there is a place where your child can be put for time-out in case he does have a tantrum. Whatever you do, prepare options in advance in the event they are needed.

What I have suggested here has been used successfully in many, many families. I know it works, but I also know that situations vary from family to family and child to child. But the basics are sound and apply to all families. All children need love, all children need positive attention for those things they do properly, and they all want and need their parents' support. I urge you to give them that support in a calm, controlled, precise, loving way.

*Research has shown that the most effective way to reduce problem behavior in children is to strengthen desirable behavior through positive reinforcement rather than trying to weaken undesirable behavior using aversive or negative processes.*
*S.W. Bijou*
*The International Encyclopedia of Education, 1988*

*A gossip is one who will never tell a lie if
the truth will do as much harm."
Anonymous*

# FIFTEEN
# Eliminating Tattling

When children tattle, they are really engaging in a childish form of gossip. I once heard a gossip defined as a person who never tells a lie if the truth will do as much harm. And that's what tattling is: truth designed to bring harm to someone. Tattlers almost always tell the truth, and are virtually always out to do harm.

A tattler is seldom, if ever, the source of useful information, information that can be used to prevent trouble or solve problems. Rather, a tattler is intent on *causing* problems and *making* trouble.

This being true, tattling is a behavior that should certainly not be given credibility. Here are some things you can do to discourage and even eliminate tattling.

*In earlier generations circumstances in the environment helped parents manage most behaviors. But not now! Parents must have parenting skills.*

First, if a child comes to you tattling on someone, say simply, calmly, but directly, something like this: "I don't like it when you talk like that. I expect you to never talk like that again. Billy, the next time you feel like saying things like that, what are you going to do?"

Then wait for an answer. The answer should be something like, "I'm not going to do it. I'm just not going to say anything."

If necessary, continue the questioning until you get the answer you want. When you do get the acceptable answer, say:

> "That's correct, Billy. Thank you. Good answer. That's exactly what
> I expect. You just aren't going to do it. You aren't going to say
> anything. I'm really proud of you for that!"

Your response should (a) show approval of the correct answer, (b) repeat what the child said which reflects your expectations, and (c) let the child know how you feel about him for his correct behavior. This procedure should be followed with every one of your children. By doing this as a group (in instances where there is more than one child) not only is it clear to each child what is expected, but it is clear to *all* the children what is expected of *everyone*. Once the expectations are clearly established, and you are certain that everyone understands them, it is time to discuss consequences. Say words to this effect:

> "I'm really pleased that you understand what I expect, and I am sure
> that you will try really hard to control yourself. However, if you make
> a mistake and say things like that, I will say to you, 'Do not tell me that.
> I do not want to hear it. Because you lost control of yourself, you have
> lost the privilege of riding your bike for one day.'"

Ask the children to repeat back to you what will happen if they lose control. Emphasize that it is *their* loss of control that deprives them of valuable privileges. During this role playing, get the bike and put a lock on it to show them you mean business; this is no idle threat! Once the point has been made dramatically and illustratively, say:

> "Now that you understand what to expect if you lose control, I am
> especially happy to tell you that if you control yourself the privilege
> of using your bike will be yours."

At that moment unlock the bike before the child's eyes and let him ride away. Call him back, give him a hug and say:

> "That's great. I love to see you having so much fun. Life is really great when we
> control ourselves."

As with behavior generally, children tend to behave appropriately when they understand what is expected of them and when they are aware of the consequences for appropriate and inappropriate behavior.

Tattling is an unacceptable, juvenile behavior that has no socially redeeming qualities to it, and should not be confused with "whistle-blowing." Unlike tattling which is invariably aimed at

simply getting someone in trouble, or diverting blame away from one's self, responsible whistle-blowing aims at correcting problems: malpractice, waste, potential harm to others, harassment, and so on. Whistle-blowing is intent on serving the common good and is a socially appropriate way of behaving—though, as we have observed time and again—a very risky way to behave.

For a child to complain to his mother, "Amy is in your jewelry box again!" the intent being to get Amy into trouble rather than to protect mother's jewelry, is a far cry from a responsible employee in business or industry making it known to the proper authorities that billions of taxpayer dollars are being wasted or that dangerous products are being put into the hands of consumers.

## NOW TO REVIEW

1.  Tattling is intended to do harm to someone. It is typically not a source of useful information.

2.  When children tattle, parents need to put that behavior on extinction, then teach and reinforce appropriate behavior.

3.  Tattling should not be confused with whistle-blowing, which is a socially approved way of behaving in behalf of the common good.

> *Research has shown that the most effective way to reduce problem behavior in children is to strengthen desirable behavior through positive reinforcement rather than trying to weaken undesirable behavior using aversive or negative processes.*
> *S.W. Bijou*
> *The International Encyclopedia of Education, 1988*

*"You can best reward a liar by believing nothing of what he says."*
*Aristippus*

# SIXTEEN
# Eliminating Lying and Stealing

When children lie or steal, it isn't because they are liars or thieves in the moral sense of the word. They aren't moral degenerates. In fact, to most children, especially young children, lying or stealing isn't a moral issue at all, it's a functional matter: they are doing it for a reason. To them, a practical reason. As parents, we might gasp in horror and shock that our children would say or take something knowing full well it was wrong! To the child, the moral reality of the matter might very well be absolutely irrelevant. If a child doesn't tell the truth or takes something that isn't his/hers, it is important to remember not to deal with it as a complex moral issue. To do that puts an unreasonable adult burden on an almost moral-free childish behavior.

> *For most children, lying or stealing are practical matters, not moral matters.*

Having said that, I realize that the older a child gets the more lying and stealing *become* moral issues, and the more complex they become. But whether you are dealing with a small child or an older adolescent child who lies/steals, some basic rules apply.

## 1. Never accuse a child.

The following illustrates what I mean:

Parent      "I know you took that money out of my purse. Now give it back to me right now!"

Child:      "I didn't either take your money!"

Parent:     "You did too take my money! And if you don't have it back to me in one hour, you're grounded for a month. And when your father gets home, he's going to give you a good spanking!"

Let's analyze this. Without solid evidence that the child had taken the money, an accusation was all the parent had to offer. True, the child may have had a history of taking things that didn't belong to him and denying it, but despite this, in this instance there was no clear, hard evidence that the accused did, indeed, take the money. Secondly, accusations never solve anything. The child didn't confess or express any remorse, and the money wasn't returned. So from a behavioral point of view, nothing good was accomplished. Third, the relationship between the child and parent was in disarray. The parent had not modeled a mature, proactive behavior, hostility prevailed, no groundwork had been laid to develop a trusting relationship, the relationship of one toward the other was adversarial, the parent was frustrated because he/she didn't have a clue about what to do about the situation, and the child "won" in the sense that the parent was worse off than he was: the parent was mad but the child had the money (assuming, of course, he took the money).

## 2. Never question the child

Never question the child about the behavior, whether you know the child is at fault or whether you aren't sure. For example:

Parent:     "Mary, why did you lie to me about your homework? You told me you did your homework, but I found out today you didn't do your homework. I just don't know what I'm going to do about your lying. Isn't this ever going to quit!"

Child:      "Well, I thought I was going to get it done in time to hand it in, but something came up and I wasn't able to."

Parent:     "Are we going to have to go through this again? We have been through this very same thing a dozen times. How long is it going to be before I can trust you to do what you say?"

Let's analyze this one. In the first place, the question never brought an acceptable answer. No information was forthcoming that would help solve the problem of uncompleted homework or the problem of lying. The child's response was defensive not informational. The stage was not

> *Remember, never question children about their inappropriate behavior.*

set for anything good to follow. Nothing was done that would either discourage lying or encourage getting the homework done. And lastly, as with the first example, the relationship between the parent and the child was strained. Nothing constructive nor potentially good came out of the encounter. The parent was still frustrated and angry, and the child had convinced himself once again that he was unfairly put upon.

Interestingly, teenagers often lie about their behavior because they have learned that their parents can't handle an honest answer, particularly in such sensitive areas as sex, drugs, and dating. If a child admits to being sexually active, homosexual, or experimenting with drugs, parents simply can't accept it. They hit the ceiling, blow their stacks, come unglued—they do just about everything except respond appropriately and therapeutically. So what's the safest route for the child to take? Correct! To lie. The practical value of this approach is far safer, from the child's perspective, than is being morally honest.

## 3. Do not overreact

When a child lies or steals, do not hit the ceiling, come unglued, become verbally explosive, hit the child and so on. For example:

Parent:  "**WHAT!** You skipped school today by telling your teacher you were sick!? You lied to your teacher! That's terrible! What do you want to do, grow up to be stupid *and* dishonest! (And on and on and on and on…!")

Let's analyze this. First, the child got an immense amount of parental attention for behaving inappropriately. As I point out repeatedly in this book, behaviors that get attention are behaviors that are strengthened. In this instance, a massive amount of reinforcement was given to the behavior the parent wanted eliminated. All of the emotion and explosiveness served the wrong end. Nothing therapeutic or remedial occurred. The parent just blew off steam without accomplishing anything of value.

In contrast to these things you shouldn't do, here are five things you should do:

1. Respond proactively.

2. Make known your expectations.

3. Implement consequences.

4. Acknowledge appropriate behavior.

5. Model appropriate behavior.

## 1. Respond proactively.

A proactive response is a controlled, mature, constructive, empathic, understanding, directive, therapeutic response. For example:

Parent: "Son, I was sorry to learn today that you had not been absolutely honest with your teacher."

Child: "I didn't say anything that wasn't true. My teacher is always saying things that aren't true. She is a bigger liar than I am!"

Parent: "I can tell you are upset, Son. I only want you to know that it disappoints me when you are not absolutely honest."

Let's analyze this. Nothing was said that would create an adversarial relationship between the parent and the child. No one has reason to get mad or to be defensive. The child learned of the parent's disappointment and that better behavior is expected in the future. The child also learned that more attention—hence, more value—was placed on honesty than on lying. The concern was definitely with the child and not with what the child did.

## 2. Make your expectations known

Rather than arguing with the child about what's right and what's wrong, or moralizing over what's right and what's wrong, simplify the matter by clearly stating what you expect of the child. For example:

Parent: "When you say things, Son, I expect them to be true. What do I mean when I say I expect them to be true?"

Child: "Well, you don't want me to lie."

Parent: "Correct, son, that is a very good answer. Give me an example of telling the truth."

Child: "When I tell you that I'm going to do something, I do what I tell you I'm going to do."

Parent: "Very good. Please give me a real example of that."

Child: "Oh, I can't think of anything."

Parent: "That's okay. Help me with this example. Suppose you tell me you are going to do your homework as soon as you get home from school. What can I expect if you tell me that?"

Child: "That I'm going to do my homework."

Parent: "That's right. You tell me you are going to do your homework and then you do your homework. That is an example of being honest, and that's what I expect of you. I expect you to be an honest boy. I love you, Son."

Let's analyze this one. The child has learned, in an atmosphere that is completely under the gentle, mature, control of an adult, what is expected of him. An appropriate adult behavior has been modeled. (What a great teaching tool for when that child becomes a father!) The father's point has been driven home gently in a role-playing situation which removes any doubt from the child's mind about what is expected of him. He has been involved as a member of the problem-solving team. And lastly, all during the encounter, everything was positive. The father used lots of praise statements. Rather than using the word lying, the father used the word honesty and focused on the positive aspects of the lesson. The ground work was laid for a solid and constructive parent-child relationship.

## 3. Implement Consequences

In instances where children continue behaving inappropriately, it may be necessary to implement consequences. Although I'm going to use an example here about how to use consequences, I refer you to the Chapter 5 for a more detailed treatment of this matter.

> **When treating lying and stealing, focus on honesty.**

Consequences, when reasonable and well implemented, deliver the message better than tens of thousands of words. They put the responsibility for the child's behavior squarely where it ought to be: on the child. For example:

Parent: "It is very important for you to be trustworthy, and when you are, you will be able to do and have things you really like. What are some of those things? What things do you really like to play with, or what do you really like to do?"

Child: "I like to play my Nintendo game."

Parent: "Anything else?"

Child: "Well, I like riding my bike."

Parent: "You've named some really fun things. And when you are trustworthy, you'll enjoy these privileges as you want to.

"If, however, you take things that don't belong to you/say things that aren't true, you'll deny yourself these fun things. What do I mean when I say you'll deny yourself these fun things?"

| | |
|---|---|
| Child: | "I guess I won't be able to play my Nintendo or ride my bike." |
| Parent: | "That's correct. I'm glad you understand this so well. You have really listened carefully. That's good. Thanks.<br><br>Specifically, if you lose control, you'll deny yourself these privileges for 24 hours. How long is 24 hours?" |
| Child: | "That's a whole day." |
| Parent: | "Right. And that would be no fun. I'm glad you know what we expect and that you understand what will happen when you control yourself or don't control yourself. Which is better, to be in control or to not be in control of yourself?" |
| Child: | "To be in control." |
| Parent: | "Right! Good answer." |

Then let the consequences do the talking for you.

I realize that some behaviors cannot be monitored, such as sexual activity. In such cases, parents have to allow natural consequences to deliver the message for them. They have to regard these as Type C or D behaviors (see pages 111–113) and hope they can influence their children's choices through themselves remaining in control, by providing a mature model for how to behave, and by just hoping that in time their children will "come to their senses." It's tough, but that's the way it is!

## 4. Acknowledge appropriate behavior

Whenever the child responds appropriately, warmly acknowledge this. Don't assume that being "good" is its own reward. To the child, being good may not be a rewarding or reinforcing experience. Sometimes, for example, being good means facing the music, and that can even be unpleasant. So when a child behaves appropriately, that should be acknowledged in a very positive reinforcing way. For example:

| | |
|---|---|
| Parent: | "Son, you've really been in control. That's super." or "Son, you told the truth even when it was kind of hard to do it. I compliment you for this." (It might still be necessary for consequences to be applied, but under these conditions, it is done in a positive, constructive atmosphere.) |

If a child has a history of "stealing," keep things secure so they aren't easily taken. Remain calm when theft occurs. Calmly, deliberately, and clearly proceed as suggested and illustrated here. Once the child realizes that favorable, controlled parental attention and positive consequences come with being honest/trustworthy, that's the behavior that will most likely be forthcoming.

## 5. Model appropriate behavior

Keep in mind the adage, "I'd rather see a sermon anytime than hear one." Parents who fudge on their taxes, fib, tell half truths and "white lies" (whatever those are), and stretch the truth are modeling the very behaviors they deplore in their children—especially when those very behaviors are used by children on their parents! A study by a professor at the Rush Medical School in Chicago revealed that the average adult tells 13 lies a week, and that the older teenagers get, the *less* they feel lying is wrong. These are behaviors that are *learned*. We as parents must be sure that we never teach that behavior through our example, nor encourage it through our interactions with our children.

## 6. Teach appropriate behavior

Again, use lying and stealing as opportunities to teach children what is meant by property rights, what is meant by "yours and mine," and why it is in one's best interest to be trustworthy. Approaching such delicate matters as lying and stealing as a prompt to teach is far and away better than are flimsy excuses to verbally or physically beat on a kid. Rather than teaching a child to behave well only to escape the negative consequences for behaving badly, teach the child that there are positive consequences for behaving well.

## NOW TO REVIEW

1. Never accuse a child of lying or stealing.
2. Never question a child about lying or stealing.
3. Do not overreact to lying or stealing.

Rather:

1. Respond proactively.
2. Make your expectations known.
3. Implement consequences.
4. Acknowledge appropriate behavior.
5. Model appropriate behavior.
6. Teach appropriate behavior.

*Research has shown that the most effective way to reduce problem behavior in children is to strengthen desirable behavior through positive reinforcement rather than trying to weaken undesirable behavior using aversive or negative processes.*
*S.W. Bijou*
*The International Encyclopedia of Education, 1988*

# SEVENTEEN
# Eliminating Thumb Sucking

Chronic thumbsucking beyond age 3 should be eliminated if for no reason other than its harmful effects on dental development, including such problems as open bite, over jet, and cross-bite dental malocclusions. Research has demonstrated conclusively that chronic thumbsucking can be eliminated during both a child's waking and sleeping hours.

Suggested here are proven methods for eliminating chronic thumbsucking during daytime and nighttime hours. Note that I am addressing *chronic* thumbsucking. Nearly all children suck their thumbs to one extent or another. Children, from the moment of birth and before, learn that sucking is a very reinforcing thing to do. In fact, at the outset, their very lives depend on it! Consequently, parents shouldn't be alarmed if babies and little children suck their fists, fingers, and thumbs occasionally. By the same token, when they do suck their thumbs, particularly beyond age 1, parents shouldn't do things that call attention to that behavior. Avoid saying things like:

"Mary, you are sucking your thumb again! Don't do that. Do you want
to ruin your teeth?" or angrily,

THE POWER OF POSITIVE PARENTING

"Billy! Stop that! Quit acting like a baby. Do you want me to put you back in diapers and feed you from a bottle? That's exactly what I'm going to do if you don't quit that baby behavior!"

Though the intent behind such statements is in the child's best interest, they only make matters worse. In the first place, the child is being asked questions for which no answer is expected. As I emphasized in Chapter 8, Questioning Children About Their Behavior, never ask a child a question about his inappropriate behavior unless you need information to aid problem solving. (If you haven't read Chapter 8 yet, or have forgotten its key points, I suggest you read it—or read it again—soon.) Also, belittling or threatening a child is hurtful at best, and potentially damaging. Lastly, telling a child to stop a behavior that has a long history of reinforcement, then expecting the child to stop, is an absolute waste of breath and a prelude to dashed—albeit desperate—hopes. It does nothing more than build in the parents and the child an image of a disobedient, weak child who never minds and can't control himself. What a terrible foundation upon which to build self-esteem and a parent-child relationship!

## Daytime Thumbsucking

> **Most thumbsucking should simply be ignored.**

Daytime thumbsucking should simply be ignored. For emphasis, I'll say that again: Daytime thumbsucking should simply (and completely!) be ignored, put on extinction, while appropriate, non-thumbsucking behaviors should be selectively reinforced. Consider these scenarios as examples of how a parent should respond to a child who occasionally sucks his thumb:

| | |
|---|---|
| Scenario 1: | The parent and the child are in the same room together. The child begins sucking his thumb. |
| Response: Withdraw positive reinforcement: | The parent immediately, though calmly and without the slightest trace of frustration or despair on his face or in his demeanor, terminates any interaction with the child, and leaves the room. |
| Selective reinforcement: | Once out of the child's view the parent watches to see when the child removes his thumb from his mouth. After the child has kept his thumb out of his mouth for |

approximately 30 to 45 seconds, the parent returns to the room, pats the child, says "You are playing so happily," smiles, then goes on with whatever he/she was doing before the child began sucking his thumb.

| | |
|---|---|
| Scenario 2: | The parent and the child are sitting together. The parent is reading the child a story. The child begins sucking his thumb. |
| Response: Withdraw positive reinforcement: | The parent immediately quits reading and either sits there unresponsively or leaves the room. Remember, when this is done, nothing should be said or done that suggests rejection, disgust, or anger toward the child. |
| Selective reinforcement: | The parent waits until the child has taken his thumb out of his mouth and kept it out for 30 to 45 seconds, at which time he/she continues to read. |
| Scenario 3: | The parent(s) and the child are traveling together in the car. The child begins to suck his thumb. |
| Response: Withdraw positive reinforcement: | The parent(s) simply terminates/refrains from interacting with the child until he has kept his thumb out of his mouth for 30–45 seconds. |
| Selective reinforcement: | The parent(s) immediately, though naturally, begins interacting positively with the child when he quits sucking his thumb. |
| Note: | When parent-child interactions resume, do not say, "I'm glad you quit sucking your thumb," or words to this effect. Ignore thumbsucking completely! Don't attend to it, don't mention it, don't have a thing to do with it. Remember, behavior is strengthened by the attention given to it. |

As with all efforts to improve children's behavior, parents must be as alert for opportunities to interact positively with their children when their behavior is laudable as when their behavior is in need of improvement. The strategies that have been described above are effective with chronic as well as occasional day-time thumbsucking. If used consistently and precisely, such simple means have been known to be altogether sufficient for eliminating casual or chronic daytime thumbsucking.

Let's now look at some ways of treating chronic bedtime thumbsucking; chronic meaning that the child engages in it for long and extended periods of time, with potentially harmful results being the consequence.

## Chronic Bedtime (Nocturnal) Thumbsucking

Chronic bedtime thumbsuckers will have their thumbs in their mouths almost the instant their heads hit the pillow—or before—and the reinforcing effects to the child of such gratifying self-stimulation is immense. It is for this reason, if for no other, that eliminating bedtime thumbsucking requires very imaginative treatment. Fortunately, behavioral scientists have been equal to the task. I suggest the following:

More difficult behaviors, like bedtime thumbsucking, should be measured before any remedial procedure is put in place. This is to (a) provide evidence that the behavior really is as serious as parents portray it to be, (b) provide a measure against which to compare the success of treatment, and (c) produce a visual record that can be used to both motivate and reinforce the desired behavior. It is not at all unusual for parents to tell me in desperation, "That kid of mine is always…(whatever)!", but when we actually measure what the child does, we typically find that "always" really means a few times or a few minutes of occasionally behaving "that way." I was recently reminded of this while working with a young couple whose four-year-old son "never quits bugging us unless he gets what he wants!" We were in their living room, and the boy came in demanding immediate attention. Using words the parents understood, but which were unfamiliar to the child, I told the parents to completely ignore the child and continue talking with me and each other. I cautioned them to not even look at the child, nor lower their chins as though they were *about* to look at the child. They were skeptical; certain the boy would "come unglued" and create a terrible scene. I assured them that neither would be the case, and estimated that within a minute and a half to a minute and three fourths, the child would turn his attention to other things and eventually leave the room. They looked at me and at each other with a wry smile, but were willing to humor me, certain that I was in for the surprise of my life. I began my stop watch, remaining aloof of the boy's attention-getting attempts. A few times I had to prompt the parents to remain aloof. They gritted their teeth and held their breath. (Altering the parents' behavior was more difficult than changing the behavior of the child.) The boy went through his predictable routine, but this time he received no attention from anyone. He persisted as we expected he would, and became quite creative (a type of extinction burst) but all to no avail. One minute and thirty-six seconds later, with something of a perplexed look on his face, he walked out of the room in search of greener pastures. "Always" and "forever" took on a new meaning in this new environment. (Remember, behavior is a product of its immediate environment. Change the environment and the behavior changes accordingly.)

I hope my point is well enough made: get some data on the behavior before you begin treatment. It's easy to do. Don't be frightened by the task of gathering data, particularly in this instance. It's very simple, as you will see. For 4 or 5 nights before trying to eliminate the thumbsucking, go into the child's bedroom every 15 minutes after he has fallen asleep to see if he is sucking his thumb. If he is, record that as a time interval of thumbsucking. I even suggest that you color the intervals, red for thumbsucking and green for not. Record eight consecutive intervals each night (2 hours). Your chart might look like this:

| | 8 | Red | Red | Red | Red | Green |
|---|---|---|---|---|---|---|
| | 7 | Red | Red | Red | Red | Red |
| | 6 | Red | Red | Red | Green | Red |
| **Time Intervals** | 5 | Red | Green | Red | Red | Red |
| | 4 | Green | Red | Red | Green | Red |
| | 3 | Red | Red | Red | Red | Red |
| | 2 | Red | Red | Red | Red | Green |
| | 1 | Red | Green | Red | Red | Red |
| | **Days** | 1 | 2 | 3 | 4 | 5 |

With 5 days of recording, you have both the frequency of thumbsucking, and when it occurs. Once you have the data recorded and graphed, you are ready to begin your treatment.

Begin treatment by showing the graph to the child and say: "(name), we are going to help you quit sucking your thumb at night."

> *Shaping behavior is facilitated with data. If at all possible, work from a data base.*

"For the past 5 nights we have been quietly going into your bedroom when you were asleep to see if you were sucking your thumb. As you can see by this record, you suck your thumb a lot at night. The red squares mean you were sucking your thumb, and the green squares mean you were not. We want you to have all green squares."

This might evoke some discussion, but don't prolong it. If the child protests and says, "I do not suck my thumb that much! You are just making that up!" don't argue with him; rather, say, "I can understand that this would be a surprise to you. That's a lot of time sucking your thumb, especially if it means that it is happening all night—or even most of the night. Here is what we are going to do to help you."

Or, he might say something self-depreciating like, "Oh, I'm such a baby. I hate myself." If he says things like this, neither agree nor disagree. Do not try to convince him otherwise. Be directive and on task. Simply say, "Here is what we are going to do to help you quit sucking your thumb." Then explain and demonstrate the strategy, as described below.

> *Empathy and understanding. Remember empathy and understanding.*

In scientific terms, the strategy described below is called a "response prevention strategy using restraints." (This research was conducted by a team of Canadian scientists under the direction of Dr. Ahmos Rolider, University of Toronto.) What that means, simply, is that the child is restrained *from* sucking his thumb so he won't be reinforced *for* sucking his thumb. Thumb sucking is a self-reinforcing behavior; it is self stimulating. This strategy makes it impossible for the child to stimulate himself through thumbsucking. The strategy has the following five phases.

## Phase 1: Boxing Glove Restraint

At bedtime, place a boxing glove on the hand of the thumb that is being sucked. If the child exchanges hands in the night and sucks both thumbs, put boxing gloves on both hands. Tell the child he is to keep the glove(s) on all night long for at least a week to help him stop sucking his thumb(s). Tell him that every day you will show him the graph you are keeping as a record of his performance.

Tell the child that he will receive something really good if he keeps the glove(s) on all night and doesn't suck his thumb(s). What this "really good" thing is should be agreed upon in advance. It could be tokens the child earns to be traded later for something he wants, like a video movie, a toy, some special activity with Mom or Dad, an immediate prize like a piece of candy, the privilege of playing with a toy for the entire day, the privilege of watching TV, and so on. Find what it is the child *really* wants, then make having that contingent upon his going all night long wearing the glove(s) and not sucking his thumb(s). Also, tell the child what he can expect if he takes the glove(s) off and sucks his thumb(s). For example, maybe he denies himself the privilege of watching TV after 5:00 o'clock that night, or he will lose the privilege of riding his trike/scooter/bike for 24 hours, and so on.

If the child cries and complains in the night about having to wear the constraint, just let him cry and complain. Don't go into the bedroom to comfort him. The discomfort is all part of the treatment.

In the morning, show him the graph of your observations from the night before. If the child made it through the night with success, enthusiastically say something like, "Super good job! You left the glove(s) on all night and didn't suck your thumb(s). That's wonderful!" Then give the child the agreed-upon prize. If he was not successful, say nothing and withhold all reinforcers. When you do this, don't be moody or show disgust or displeasure, or put the child down. Complete your graph, and have it handy that night to show the child when he goes to bed. The graph becomes both an incentive and a reinforcer, so keep it up to date every day.

After the child has had 7 to 8 successive successful nights, move to Phase 2.

## Phase 2: Absorbent Cotton Restraint

Tell the child that since he has been doing *so* well for the last 7 to 8 days, he won't have to wear the boxing glove(s). Rather, he will wear cotton over his thumb(s), held in place by adhesive tape. It will be very evident if the child sucks the cotton. If he does so two nights running, in addition to the denial of privileges, go back to Phase 1, using the boxing gloves. But don't threaten the child with this. It's okay to tell him in advance in a matter-of-fact way that this will happen, but don't say something like, "You'd better not suck on this cotton or it's back to wearing boxing gloves for you! Do you understand that!" Let the consequence deliver the message. If the child does go back to wearing the boxing glove(s), return to the use of the cotton restraint after 5 successive days of continuous success with the glove(s).

Use the cotton restraint until the child has had 11 days (nights) of continuous success. Again, keep the daily record and follow each success with enthusiastic verbal praise and the agreed-upon reinforcer. Eleven days might seem like a long time, but stick with it. For more difficult behaviors such as self-stimulating or self-reinforcing behaviors, "over learning" is often the best way to go.

### Phase 3: Finger Tip Bandage Restraint

After 11 continuous successful nights using the absorbent cotton restraint, replace this with a bandage over the end of the thumb(s). Use a bandage that is 2" long and 1 3/4" wide. Secure it on the thumb(s) with adhesive tape so it won't come off easily. Continue with this phase, as described for the other two phases for 11 consecutive days of success. In the event of 2 consecutive days of failure, go back to 5 days using the cotton restraint. After 11 consecutive days of success using the bandages, proceed to Phase 4.

### Phase 4: No Restraint

During this condition, fingertip dressings are no longer used and no restraint of any kind is to be placed on the thumb(s) or hand(s). However, *any* failure is met with the loss of privileges/reinforcers, and if failure is experienced two days in a row, go back to Phase 3, the bandage restraint. After a week of continuous success at this phase, move to Phase 5.

### Phase 5: Follow-up

Continue to check the child 3 nights a week: every other night or 3 randomly selected nights. Success is to be reinforced with the agreed upon privileges/prizes. Any thumbsucking is met with a loss of privileges. If at any time 2 consecutive nights of thumbsucking are observed, go back to Phase 3. Continue this follow-up phase for 3 months.

This five-phase strategy has been shown to be 100% effective when used properly. It is permissible to modify it if you have good reasons to believe the child is making rapid progress. The number of days per phase can be reduced. An entire phase can be skipped. But don't make these adjustments unless you are *absolutely certain* the behavior is changing for the better. Let the behavior tell you, as shown by the data, how much to modify the program, not the child. If the child says, "Honest, I won't suck my thumb tonight. Please! Don't make me wear that dumb boxing glove!" Say, "I can understand why you wouldn't want to wear it. Neither would I. As soon as you have learned to go all night without sucking your thumb, you won't have to wear it." Then proceed with the program.

Don't get excited or angry at a child's resistance to the program. If you calmly and systematically proceed, you will calmly and systematically succeed.

## NOW TO REVIEW

1. Daytime thumbsucking can be eliminated with the systematic application of

    a.  withdrawing positive reinforcement, and

    b.  selective reinforcement of appropriate behavior.

2. Chronic bedtime (nocturnal) thumbsucking can be eliminated using a five-phase process called "response prevention strategy using constraints," as follows:

    Phase 1:    Boxing glove restraint.

    Phase 2:    Absorbent cotton restraint.

    Phase 3:    Finger tip bandage restraint.

    Phase 4:    No restraint.

    Phase 5:    Follow-up.

> *Research has shown that the most effective way to reduce problem behavior in children is to strengthen desirable behavior through positive reinforcement rather than trying to weaken undesirable behavior using aversive or negative processes.*
> S.W. Bijou
> *The International Encyclopedia of Education, 1988*

# EIGHTEEN
# Toilet Training

Several years ago I supervised a program at a pediatric hospital for children who were developmentally delayed, and in some instances seriously retarded and emotionally disturbed. A member of my staff was a brilliant young behaviorist who specialized in toilet training children. He became absolutely gleeful when a child came into our program who was enuretic or encropetic (lacking in bladder or bowel control). He was often heard to say, "I like nothing more than to get my hands into a dirty diaper." His enthusiasm for dirty diapers was certainly not shared by the parents of children with whom he worked. In fact, he is the only person I ever met who was enthusiastic about a dirty diaper.

> *Becoming toilet trained: The first big milestone to becoming grown-up.*

In the developmental process, there are few milestones achieved by children that parents accept with more joy and enthusiasm than that of becoming toilet trained. In this chapter, I discuss some important facts about the development of children relative to achieving bladder and bowel control. I also describe several approaches to teaching children to control bladder and bowel movements. I emphasize "teaching" since 90% of bladder and bowel control is a matter of learning, as I will explain later.

Typically, once a child has reached about two and a half years old and has not learned bladder and bowel control, parents become concerned. This concern for the normal growth and development of the child is aggravated by the ever increasing burden of work that must be assumed by the parent. After all, as children increase in age and size, so does the volume of waste material being eliminated from those growing bodies. All things considered, it is certainly understandable that parents would want their children to become toilet trained as quickly as possible.

Although some children will learn to control their bladder and bowel very early in life—in some instances before the age of a year and a half—about 80–85% of children acquire this skill by the age of 5. Boys generally take a little longer, on the average, to learn complete bladder and bowel control, and are twice as likely as girls to wet the bed at night. So far as the child is concerned, parents shouldn't become concerned about bladder and bowel control until after the child has approached his or her third year and is still not toilet trained.

| |
|---|
| **Persistent bladder control problems should be addressed by a physician.** |

As I noted earlier, bladder and bowel control are learned behaviors; still, there are some precautionary measures parents should take if children find it inordinately difficult to learn this skill.

The single best precaution is to have the child examined by a physician to see if there is something physiologically or chemically the matter. Occasionally, children will have smaller than normal bladders. A study done by a team of Danish researchers concluded that chronic bed wetters don't produce enough of the hormone that regulates urine production while they sleep, a condition that can often be treated with the drug imipramine hydrochloride (Tofranil). Also, the drug desmopression (Stimate) which decreases bladder fullness, is frequently prescribed. But as is the case with virtually *any* behavior problem that is treated with drugs (for example, attention deficient disorder), behavioral therapy should also be a major component of treatment, if not the treatment of choice.

Regarding the treatment of bedwetting (nocturnal enuresis), this was recently borne out by research conducted at Boystown, under the direction of Patrick Friman, Mary Louise Kerwin, and Mary Osborne. They found that medication is effective in only about half the cases, and that for well over half the children, bedwetting reoccurred as before once drug treatment stopped. They concluded that behaviorally-based strategies (as described in this chapter), including urine alarm systems, pelvic muscle exercises, "dry bed training", and simple incentive/reinforcement techniques are ultimately the best since they *teach* children bladder control. (I am indebted to Dr. Joseph Wyatt, Editor of *Behavior Analysis Digest*, for bringing this study to my attention.)

Since infections and diseases of the urinary tract can also aggravate bed wetting, it's always a good idea, if a child is having an inordinately difficult time learning bladder and bowel control, for the child to be examined by a qualified physician.

Assuming that nothing is amiss physiologically or from a medical point of view, there are some very effective methods that have been well documented in research for teaching children to control their bladder and their bowels. In this chapter, I speak only about bladder control. Bowel control problems tend to be so rare in comparison to bladder control problems that I've chosen to focus on bladder control. If you have a problem with a child who is encropetic (lacks bowel control), your pediatrician, family physician, or a urologist will very likely have information that will be helpful.

As I have noted elsewhere in this book, when selecting methods for improving a child's behavior, we are well advised to begin with those methods that are the easiest to put into place and to manage. I will follow that same approach in treating bladder control.

Typically, parents don't become concerned about the behavior of their children until something is the matter. Our tendency as parents, unfortunately, is to leave well enough alone and hope nothing goes wrong. The toilet training of children provides an excellent opportunity for me to illustrate and emphasize the importance of not waiting until something goes wrong before something is done. My recommendation, therefore, is that parents take a proactive, before-the-fact, approach to teaching children to control their bladder (and their bowel, for that matter).

## Treatment #1: Initial Daytime Bladder Control

To begin, when the child has reached about a year and a half (unless he/she has exhibited an interest earlier in remaining dry or using the potty), the parents should look for opportunities during the day to find the child dry and to comment on that by saying something like, "Good for you, you're doing a really good job staying dry." You might also say, "When you need to wet, tell me and we will go to the potty." If, through observations of the child's wetting behavior, you can predict fairly accurately when the child is likely to wet his diapers, before "it" happens take the child to the potty and say, "Thank you for sitting on your potty chair." You might even give the child a small edible, like a piece of animal cracker, to emphasize your appreciation and as a reinforcer for sitting on the potty. While the child is sitting on the potty, the parent should then say something like, "Try hard to wet in the potty." To help facilitate wetting, it is frequently useful to turn the faucet on or even place the child's hand in warm water.

If the child urinates while on the potty, be sure to acknowledge this enthusiastically by smiling, opening your eyes wide with excitement, and saying something like, "That's wonderful! You wet in the potty. What a big-boy thing to do!" You might even give the child another small piece of animal cracker. I hasten to note that edibles should be used very, very sparingly. Small pieces of animal cracker (no more than about a quarter of an inch square), a fourth of a jelly bean, and so on are sufficient. In fact, if you can get by without using edibles at all, so much the better since the use of edibles has to be faded out as quickly as possible.

If after sitting on the potty chair for 2 or 3 minutes the child still hasn't voided, even after encouragement, take the child off the potty chair, put his diaper and clothes back on, and say, "When you need to wet, come get me and we will come to the potty chair

*Never—I repeat NEVER—scold a child for soiling his/her clothing.*

together." If you have found edibles to be effective, put one in a tightly sealed jar and set it by the potty, and say, "When you wet in the potty chair, you may have this." Then send the child on his way to play. If the child asks for the edible right then (which he will very likely do), say, "When you wet in the potty chair you may have this cookie (or a piece of candy, or whatever)." Later, if the child comes to you dry and wants to use the potty chair, receive this warmly and enthusiastically, and, as the child is sitting on the potty chair urinating, enthusiastically show your delight. You might even call attention to the sound the urine makes as it hits the potty chair. Being reinforced for making that sound happen will increase the probability that the child will want to make it happen again in the near future.

If, however, the child continues to play and eventually wets his diaper, whether you discover the diaper is wet or the child comes to you complaining that the diaper is wet, *do not say a word*. I repeat, *do NOT say a word*. Don't scold the child for wetting his diapers. Don't ask the child why he didn't come to you when he needed to wet. Don't even look at the child as though you are angry or upset. In fact don't even make eye-to-eye contact. Simply change the diaper without saying a word as though you were preoccupied with many other important things. Don't tickle the child's tummy, don't hold the child close in a warm embrace, don't kiss the child, just change the diaper with efficiency and without emotion. When the diaper is changed and the child is ready to go back to his play, say, "When you feel like wetting, tell me so we can go to the potty chair together." Again, you will want to check the child occasionally to try and find him dry so you can take him to the potty chair, and to practice what it is you want him to do. It's during those times, when the child is either actually urinating or at least sitting on the potty chair that he should get a lot of enthusiastic, positive parental attention and praise. Any other time, the child should be responded to caringly, but not with enthusiasm, exuberance, or affection. Using this simple teaching strategy, all (and by that I mean every one) of the parents I have worked with have successfully taught their children bladder control. With some children, the skill was learned rapidly, sometimes within a day or so. Others took longer, even up to a week or two. But in *every* instance, this simple pro-active approach proved to be effective. Nothing more involved or complicated was necessary.

## Treatment #2: Daytime Bladder Control for Older Children

When teaching bladder control to older children, follow exactly the same procedures outlined above except for one added step: role playing. With older children (i.e., children who are two and a half to three years old and older), I have parents role play their expectations with their children. It goes like this:

Parent:     "Billy, when you need to wet, I want you to come and tell me. What do I want you to do when you need to wet?"

*Note*: Wait a moment for the child to answer. If he doesn't answer, simply restate what you expect him to do.

Billy:     "You want me to come and get you."

Parent:     "That's right, Billy. Thank you for that good answer. I want you to come and tell me. I want you to come and tell me *before* you wet. When do I want you to come tell me, Billy?"

Billy:     "Before I wet my pants."

Parent:     "That's right, Billy! I want you to come tell me before you wet your pants. Let's pretend, Billy, that you have not wet your pants and you need to go to the toilet. Show me right now what you are going to do. Tell me what you are going to say to me."

Billy:     "I'm going to tell you that I need to go to the toilet."

Parent:     "Thank you, Billy. I appreciate your listening so carefully. Now go into the living room and let's pretend that you need to go to the toilet. I want you to show me what you are going to do and tell me what you are going to say."

Note: The parent then sends Billy into the living room. The parent might even prompt the child about what to do next by saying, "Okay, Billy, show me what you are going to do and say."

Billy: (Comes to the mother) "I need to go to the toilet."

Parent: (Checks his diaper/pants to be sure he is dry) "Great job, Billy, you are dry and you came and told me that you need to go to the toilet. That's wonderful. Now, let's walk together into the toilet and I will show you what I expect you to do next."

*Note*: It is important for the parent to check the boy to make sure he is dry. This emphasizes an important precondition, and it also gives the parent a chance to praise the boy for being dry.

The parent and child then go together into the lavatory.

Parent: "When we get to the toilet, Billy, I want you to sit on the toilet/potty chair[1] until you are finished wetting. What do I expect you to do, Billy, after we get into the lavatory?"

Billy: "I'm supposed to sit on the toilet/potty chair."

Parent: "That's right, Billy. Thank you for listening so carefully. I want you to sit on the toilet/potty chair. How long do I want you to sit on the potty chair?"

Billy: "Until I am through wetting."

Note: It is important that the boy say back to the parent all the conditions that are to be met.

Parent: "That's exactly what I expect of you, Billy. Now, show me what you are going to do after we have gotten to the toilet."

*Note*: At this point, let Billy show you how well he understands your expectations. If he has any trouble along the way, simply restate your expectations and have those repeated back to you. Once he demonstrates to you exactly what you expect, acknowledge that enthusiastically by saying something like, "That is exactly correct, Billy. You have listened so well and you were able to do exactly what I want you to do. That is so wonderful." Then give the boy a hug, a kiss, a back rub, or whatever it is the child enjoys in terms of verbal and physical contact.

Once you are completely satisfied that the child understands perfectly what it is you expect, move on to the statement of consequences, which in this case, will only be of a positive nature.

Parent: "Billy, come and tell me when you need to wet and then wet in the potty chair, I'm going to put a smiley face on this chart." (Figure 18.1)

---

[1]Use whatever term you usually use to describe the toilet.

254

## Figure 18.1—Toilet Training Record

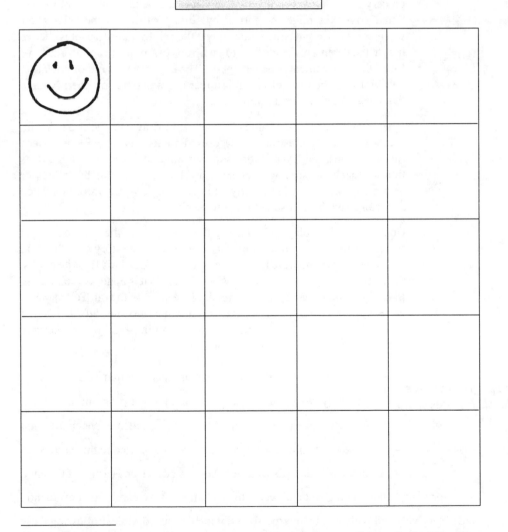

---

[2]A clever technique suggested by Friman and his associates at Boystown is dot-to-dot pictures of things the child wants (a book, toy, or whatever). With each dry night, the child is allowed to advance to one more dot. Once the picture is completed, the child is given (has earned!) the item drawn in the picture.

*Note*: Show the child a chart which will be fixed to the wall near the potty chair. To heighten the effect of the chart, I have parents take a picture of their child sitting on the potty chair smiling, and affix it to the top of the chart.

To illustrate the chart's use, say, "Billy, sit on the potty chair the way you showed me."

When the child does, draw a smiley face on the chart, and say, "You see, Billy, when you sit on the potty chair I will draw a smiley face. When you wet in the potty I will draw two smiley faces. When you have six smiley faces, then we will read a story from your favorite book." I have used a story only as an example. If something else is more desirable to the child, use it. It might be the privilege of playing with a favorite toy that is available only upon urinating in the potty chair. It might be going to the grocery store during family shopping. It could be any number of things. Some privileges might be earned by simply sitting on the potty chair whereas others might be available only if the child actually urinates. I leave it up to the parents to decide how to set up this part of the program and have found their judgement to be very good. The key is that an important target behavior must be met before a reinforcer is granted. Remember: No free lunch. No noncontingent reinforcers.

I mentioned earlier that a smiley face would be drawn on the chart. Again, that was only for illustration purposes. Parents have used smiley-face rubber stamps, smiley-face pressure sensitive stickers, and sometimes things other than smiley faces such as stars, pictures of butterflies or animals, or whatever. Frequently, children find it very reinforcing when *they* can draw or affix something on the chart.

Continue the role playing by having the child get off the potty chair, get redressed, then, using the example of reading a favorite story, take the child into the living room, have him pick a story from one of his favorite books, then sit down together and read the book. When that is done, say something like, "Billy, that was so much fun reading the story with you. Tell me what I can expect you to do so that we can have another fun time together reading a story." Then wait for a correct response, prompting the child as necessary until the correct response is forthcoming.

> Most toilet training programs produce the desired results within a week or two when used as prescribed.

As soon as the child has demonstrated that he understands perfectly what your expectations are, put the program into effect. Recalling Treatment #1, above, it's a good idea to check the child once in a while to see if he is dry and acknowledge that enthusiastically as I described earlier. Also, as I described earlier, if the child is wet or complains of being wet and wants to be changed, take care of that efficiently and objectively and with as little interpersonal interaction as possible. Following these procedures, the probability is very good that you will have the success you want within a week or so.

## Treatment #3: Nighttime Bladder Control

Bladder control during the day is almost always achieved ahead of bladder control at night. With most children, once they have learned to control their bladder during the day, it is only a short while before they learn to control their bladder at night, especially when they receive a lot of verbal praise as they begin waking up dry. However, it is not unusual for nighttime bladder control to be a persisting problem. In fact, up to 2% of the adult population has nighttime bladder control problems! One study found that 3% of United States servicemen still wet their beds.

If your child continues to have a problem with nighttime bladder control, I suggest the following treatment developed by a group of Israeli scientists lead by Dr. Ahmos Rolider of the University of Haifa in Haifa, Israel. This treatment requires a heavy commitment on the part of parents, but its effectiveness is well worth the effort parents put into it.

The treatment begins with giving the child as much of his or her favorite beverage as the child can drink. This is done during the afternoon, and is done for two reasons. First, it helps to enlarge the bladder. Occasionally, children have difficulty with nighttime bladder control because their bladders are smaller than ordinary and are unable to hold much liquid. Filling the bladder to capacity helps stretch it to its desired size. The second reason for filling the bladder is to increase the child's ability to restrain the flow of liquid using what is called a "strain and hold procedure." This involves having the child lay on his bed in a darkened room, concentrating on full-bladder sensations produced

> *Filling the bladder causes it to stretch, and helps the child learn bladder control.*

by straining and holding back the flow of urine, and then hurrying to the toilet to urinate.

Most parents I work with who are having problems teaching their children bladder control skills typically tell me they keep liquids away from their children as much as possible. Conventional wisdom would suggest this to be an appropriate thing to do if the child has a problem wetting the bed at night. However, research in the area of bladder control has taught us that, contrary to conventional wisdom, children who are having bladder control problems should consume a lot of liquid and then learn to hold it, thus, increasing the size of the bladder and learning bladder control skills.

The strain and hold procedure should be practiced for 15 minutes during which time the child is given as much of his or her favorite beverage as he can drink. Practicing the strain and hold procedure should be done several times (six to eight times during the afternoon). Appropriate practice can be reinforced using a wall chart (much like the one shown in Figure 18.1) posted conspicuously in the child's room on which is recorded the trial successes using smiley faces or whatever other symbol would communicate success to the child.

An hour before bedtime, the parents should practice with the child what is called a "cleanliness and positive practice procedure." The cleanliness procedure involves practicing with the child what would be done to clean up after an accident, including remaking the bed with clean linen and blankets, etc. The positive practice procedure involves having the child lie in bed while counting to fifty then getting up, going to the toilet and attempting to urinate. Remember, the child has been drinking *lots* of liquids.

At bedtime the child describes the cleanliness and positive practice procedures and is asked to feel the sheets and describe how good they feel being dry. Before actually going to bed to sleep, the child should try to urinate—*following* a strain and hold procedure.

Once the child is asleep, the parents should allow him to sleep to within 5 or 6 hours of his usual time of awakening in the morning. For example, if the child usually wakes around seven o'clock, he would be awakened by the parents at about two o'clock in the morning. The key is to wake the child shortly before he/she would otherwise urinate. Research has demonstrated that children who have bed wetting problems can usually control their bladder for about 5 hours. Since most children go to bed about nine o'clock, 5 hours of sleep would take the child to two a.m. which is about 5 hours before the child would ordinarily be getting up. Since all children's sleeping habits are different, parents must take individual sleeping habits into consideration when preparing this treatment.

Upon waking the child, it is very important that he is fully awake before proceeding with treatment. This can be accomplished by asking the child several questions, for example, what day of the week is it, what his/her name is, how old he/she is, names of brothers and sisters, and so on. Once fully awake, the child is required to urinate as much as he can in the toilet. If the child is dry for *6 consecutive mornings*, the time for waking should be set back for 1 hour. In other words, rather than waking the child at two o'clock he should be awakened at one o'clock in the morning. This procedure should be continued until the child is sleeping at least 8 full hours (after having been awakened and taken to the toilet) and waking up dry in the morning.

If, when awakened, the child has already wet the bed, the child should clean himself with as little help from the parent as possible, including changing any bedding as necessary. While this is being done, the parent must say nothing about the child having wet the bed. Once everything is all cleaned up and it is time for the child to go back to bed, the parents should have the child feel the bed and make comments about how nice it is to be able to sleep in a clean, dry bed, then have the child go to sleep. Adjustments should be made in what time the child is awakened to assure the child is dry. It is very important that the treatment go forward in an atmosphere of success. The child should be given lots of verbal praise for succeeding, and if necessary, to earn points that can later be used to acquire desirable things.

## Treatment #4: Dry Bed Training

This treatment was first described by a team of three researchers (Azrin, N.H., Sneed, T.J., and Foxx, R.M., in 1974) and is known as "dry bed training" (DBT). This procedure employees a urine alarm device that is activated the instant moisture makes contact with the urine alarm pad. The pad is placed in the child's diaper/training pants so that it is immediately in contact with the urine. I've had parents use such a device with many children and have enjoyed 100% success with it.[3] These devices have taken several creative forms. My friend and colleague at Utah State University, Dr. Carl Cheney, developed his "electric potty chair." It could be programmed so that when urine flowed into it, music would play, bells would sound, the TV would go on, and/or any number of other delightful things would happen.

Before using such a system, it should be explained and demonstrated to the child. The following description of how the treatment is applied draws heavily from the work of Eugene Walker, Mary Kenning, and Jan Faust-Campanile of the University of Oklahoma Health Sciences Center, published in *Childhood Disorders*, edited by E. Marsh and R. Barkley, Guilford Press, New York, 1989. The treatment is described as follows:

> On the first night of the intensive training portion of the program, parents and child review all aspects of the procedure. About an hour before bedtime, the child is given a glass of his or her favorite drink, and the urine alarm is placed in the child's diaper/training pants. The child then performs 20 trials of positive practice (a form of the strain

---

[3]Such a system, marketed under the name Wet-Stop, can be purchased from Palco Laboratories, 8030 Soquel Ave., Santa Cruz, CA 95062. The system comes with complete directions and, at the time of this writing, sells for under $40.00.

and hold procedure). This entails the child's lying on the bed, counting to 50 (less for younger children), going to the bathroom, attempting to urinate, and returning to bed. The child is also encouraged to note the dry bed and feel how comfortable it is. Just before retiring, the child consumes more fluids and repeats the training instructions to the parents.

Every hour during the night, the parents gently awaken the child and prompt him or her to go to the bathroom. At the bathroom door, the child is asked whether he or she can retain urine for another hour. If so, the child is praised for his or her control and returned to bed without voiding. If not, the child urinates in the toilet, is praised for the correct toileting, and returns to bed. In the bedroom, parents call the child's attention to the dry sheets and praise him for a dry bed. The child is given more fluids to drink and then goes back to sleep for another hour.

If a wetting accident occurs, parents shut off the alarm, wake the child, express mild displeasure, and rush the child to the bathroom to complete urination. The child then performs cleanliness training by changing pajamas, removing wet sheets, cleaning the mattress, getting clean sheets, remaking the bed, and appropriately disposing of the soiled linens. The child then performs 20 trials of positive practice as described above.

Following the evening of intensive training, the posttraining phase begins. In this second phase, the urine alarm is again utilized, but encouraging fluid intake is discontinued. If the child has a dry night, he or she is praised throughout the next day for this success. Significant others are encouraged to praise the child as well (e.g., grandparents, a favorite aunt or uncle, etc.). If an accident occurs during the night, 20 positive practice trials are performed prior to bedtime the next night. Just before the parents retire (11:00 p.m. to 12:00 midnight), they awaken the child and encourage him/her to urinate. After each dry night, the child is awakened a half hour earlier on the following evening. When the waking time follows bedtime by no more than an hour, it is discontinued. This phase ends when the child achieves dryness for seven consecutive nights.

In the final phase of training, the urine alarm and periodic awakening are discontinued. The child's bed should be inspected each morning by the parents. If a wetting accident has occurred during the night, the child is to change and remake the bed immediately. That evening, 20 trials of positive practice are performed. If two accidents occur in the same week, the second phase of training should be reinstituted until seven consecutive dry nights are again achieved.

It is worth noting that a general toilet training program based on DBT procedures has been described in nontechnical language in a book written by N. Azrin & R. Foxx, *Toilet Training in Less Than A Day*, Pocket Books, 1976. The use of this book should not be expected to replace contact with a clinician, as research has shown that parents are better able to manage this program if they are receiving professional supervision.

## Treatment #5: Urine Retention and Sphincter Control Exercises

Children who have bed wetting problems are frequently aided by exercises that teach them to control the flow of urine and to control the opening and closing of the sphincter of the bladder, which in turn controls the flow of urine. Again, I defer to the writings of Walker, Kenning, and Faust-Campanile as cited in the discussion of Treatment #4 above:

> Urine retention and sphincter control exercises were developed to assist children in gaining control over the urination reflex as well as increasing functional bladder capacity, which, as noted earlier, is deficient in many enuretic children. In the retention control procedure, children are instructed to go to the bathroom when they feel the urge to urinate, but are told to refrain from urinating for as long as possible. Initially, most children can inhibit the urgency for only a few seconds. However, with practice they can eventually refrain for several minutes or hours. Fluid intake may be increased to provide additional training opportunities as well as overlearning. During their 15 to 20-day training period, each child is expected to increase the time of urine retention 2–3 minutes daily. He or she is rewarded for increases in retention time, urination in the toilet, and dry nights.

Sphincter control training has also been used in combination with retention control training. To accomplish this, the child is instructed to practice starting and stopping the stream of urine when voiding. Rewards may be offered to encourage the process.

When using these methods, care should be taken not to force the intake of excessive amounts of fluid or to require the child to retain urine for unusually long periods of time. A cup or two of fluid per hour with retention encouraged for up to 1–2 hours is well within safe limits. However, if the child shows signs of distress, these requirements should be lowered.

This method is a less intensive alternative that can be used with young children, especially those who exhibit excessive frequency and urgency in urination or who are known to have low functional bladder capacity. This method may also be employed with adolescents since they are generally resistant to methods requiring extensive supervision or control by parents.

The treatments described here will solve nearly any bladder control problem. If additional helps are needed with your child, I urge you to purchase the book written by Azrin and Foxx, *Toilet Training In Less Than A Day*. Also, there are two documents available at a nominal cost from the Division of Outreach and Development, Center for Persons with Disabilities, Utah State University, Logan, Utah 84322-6845. The one document is entitled *Toilet Training: Short Term* and the other is entitled *Toilet Training: Long Term*. These are both excellent guides to teaching children bladder control skills and are very inexpensive.

## NOW TO REVIEW

When toilet training children:

1. be certain there are no medical problems complicating a child's bladder or bowel control,

2. begin initial bladder control using the basic behavioral strategies of extinction and selective reinforcement of appropriate behaviors,

3. teach enuretic children "strain and hold" procedures,

4. for more difficult causes, employ the "dry bed training" using a urine alarm device, and

5. particularly for older children, teach urine retention and sphincter control exercises.

> *Research has shown that the most effective way to reduce problem behavior in children is to strengthen desirable behavior through positive reinforcement rather than trying to weaken undesirable behavior using aversive or negative processes.*
> S.W. Bijou
> *The International Encyclopedia of Education, 1988*

*"If a child was meant to obey, then who invented the term 'in a minute I will.'"*
   *Art Reid*

# NINETEEN
# Refusing to Do As Told

The refusal of children to do what they are told is another of the most common complaints I hear from parents. The complaint usually goes something like this: "This kid doesn't do a thing I say, and it's driving me crazy! I've tried everything, and nothing works." Though parents typically feel helpless to get their children to do as they are told, the problem is usually quite easy to solve when we keep two important points in mind.

First, we must remember that children don't see the world the same way we do as parents. The things that concern us are seldom of much concern to them. They don't see the urgency in things as we do. We must remember that all situations are not equally demanding. For example, in the morning when children are getting ready for school and the school bus is going to be there in a few minutes, there is little room for wasting time. On the other hand, if it's Saturday morning and a child is supposed to clean his bedroom, it may not make any difference whether the job is done by nine o'clock or ten o'clock or even by noon. One of the keys to getting children to do as they are told is to be sure they know exactly what is expected of them, including when the task is to be done and

> **Children don't see the world as adults do.**

how well it is to be done. If a child is doing his homework, there may be no option to high quality performance; that is, the entire assignment has to be done, and its quality must be checked by the parents before the assignment is considered completed. On the other hand, cleaning one's bedroom might be acceptable if the bed is made, the clothes are hung up, and a general sense of order has been established. That sense of order, of course, would vary depending upon the judgement of the parents. Be careful to not impose strict, unrealistically adult standards on children's performance.

In any case, the time frame and standard of quality need to be reasonable with the needs and maturity of the child in mind. Here again, let's not impose unrealistic conditions on children for our own convenience. Our role as parents is to raise children so *their* general well being is of first importance, not ours as parents. When parents tell me their children are "Driving me crazy!" it is altogether likely that the parents' behavior is having the same effect on their kids. But it doesn't have to be one way or the other. Neither has to drive the other crazy. Parents and children *can* happily coexist.

> *Parents and children can happily co-exist*

Now let's look at how we can communicate our expectations to our children. We can never expect children to do as they are told unless they know exactly what is expected of them.

Children generally understand that compliance is necessary. It is a simple matter of fact that in life there are times when we have to do what we are told and that our performance must meet certain standards of quality. That applies to behavior at home as well as behavior in school and society, among friends, and so on. The second point is that the consequences for complying or not complying will be immediate. Administering these consequences, both positive and negative, must be given immediately, fairly, and in a manner that is consistent with the behavior.

Let's assume that a child has a chore that is to be done routinely each night after school. Typically, however, the child comes home and dawdles around doing nothing about the chores. Also, typically, the parent begins badgering the child to get the chore done:

> "Mary, get with it! I've told you a dozen times to get that chore done.
> I don't know why we have to go through this every single day! Now,
> when are you going to get busy?!"

The child says something like,

> "I'll get it done just as soon as this television show is over. I'll get it
> done! Don't worry about it!"

Of course, this is nothing but a delay tactic that is generally followed by the parent badgering the kid even more. Then if the child does eventually get the chore done, and it is done to the parent's standard, either nothing is said or the parent says something like,

> "Well, it's about time you got it done. I hope we don't have to go
> through this again tomorrow!"

It's easy to understand what is happening and why the youngster isn't doing the chore: if she doesn't get it done, she gets an immense amount of attention; if she does get it done, she's ignored; or scolded for yet-to-be-committed offenses. In either event, doing what she is supposed to do isn't a very pleasant experience. And if a child does it, but not to standard, then the situation becomes even more negative with a parent saying something like:

> "You call that done? I could have done better with my eyes closed!
> Now get back there and do it right! Right now!"

A better approach is to make certain the child knows exactly what is expected in terms of when it is to be done and how well it is to be done. The child also needs to understand the consequences that follow compliance or noncompliances. For example, consider this:

Setting:     The mother is telling the girl what is expected.

Parent:      "Mary, tonight you are to come directly home from school, getting home no later than three o'clock. When are you supposed to get home, Mary?"

*Note*: Wait for an answer, if possible using the "broken record" approach: that is, be empathetic and understanding, but repeat your expectation.

Mary:        "I'm supposed to be home by three o'clock."

Parent:      "That's right, Mary. Good answer. Thank you for listening carefully. When you get home, the first thing you are to do are these two chores listed on this sheet of paper. (Have the child look at the paper as you read.) First, I want you to go through the house and empty all of the wastebaskets into this plastic bag and put the bag in the garbage can. Second, I want you to complete your homework and finish it no later than 4:30. As you finish these tasks, check them off, and then when you're all done, come and see me. Now, Mary, tell me what you are supposed to do when you get home from school tonight."

Then have the girl repeat back to you what you expect of her, clarifying any items that may not be clearly understood. Since behavior is set into motion by something (some kind of a cue or prompt), put the note and the plastic garbage bag where the girl is certain to see them when she gets home. With this you might attach a note that says something like,

> "I'm glad you're home safe and sound and hope you had a good day
> in school. I appreciate your getting your chore and homework done as
> we discussed this morning."

If you are home, and see the girl performing appropriately, give her a pat or hug, and use words that express your appreciation and approval:

> "You're a busy gal, Honey. I really appreciate your being such a help."

When she completes the tasks as expected and comes to you with the completed list, make certain to acknowledge her success in some reinforcing way. It may be just sitting down with the girl and talking about her day at school. At the very least, the child should be pleasantly and sincerely thanked.

If both parents work and are not home when the girl gets home or when she completes the task, make certain her work is acknowledged just as soon as you get home. If possible it would be great to have the girl call you at work and share her success.

Let's assume the parent is home when the child arrives but she does not get immediately to work, even though she knows exactly what is expected of her and has seen the note and the other cues that have been provided. *Don't say word one to the child!* Do not track her down and try to force her to get busy. Rather, just leave the tasks undone, and let the consequences do the talking for you. The world will not come to the end if in that particular instance the garbage doesn't get taken out or the homework doesn't get done. On the other hand, if the garbage is going to be picked up the next morning and it needs to be taken out that night, go ahead and do it yourself. Say nothing. But when the child wants to watch television, or do other highly desirable things, those privileges are not available; they have not been earned as a result of a failure to comply. Of course, these consequences have all been made known to the child well in advance. (See Chapter 5, A Word About Consequences.) For example, during the time the instructions were given that morning, the parent might say,

| Let consequences do the talking for you. |

268

"And Mary, when your chores and homework are all done you may
watch television. However, if they are not done, you will not have
earned that privilege. What can you expect if you do or don't do your
chore?"

If you are home and have observed that your expectations have not been met, but
the child starts watching TV, you should simply and unemotionally turn off the TV and
say something like this,

"Once you have completed your chores and your homework you may
watch television. Until then, you may not because you have not earned
that privilege."

It is altogether likely that the child will argue with you and try to take you off track.
She will very likely call you "unreasonable," or use words like that. She might even
attack the necessity of doing the chore or homework calling it a "stupid" thing that
doesn't make any sense at all. She might even attack your judgement and perhaps even
attack your attitude toward her by saying something like,

"You don't trust me. You don't ever believe that I'll get my work
done. You just lead me around by the nose and don't give me any trust
at all," and so on.

If this is the case, do not, and I repeat *DO NOT*, get drawn into that argument. Do
not come to your defense with words like,

"Oh, Mary, I do too trust you. How can you say a thing like that? You
know very well that we trust you!"

Also, avoid saying,

"It is not stupid. After all, I'm just doing it for your own good. What
do you want to do? Do you want to grow up and be an irresponsible
girl who hasn't learned to read or write or to make a contribution to
her home. Everybody in this home has to assume some responsibility
and since you live here you have to assume your share of that
responsibility!"

This puts you squarely where the kid wants you, gives her a ton of attention for
behaving inappropriately, and all the while nothing is getting done. So just avoid saying

things like that. It is junk language. It gets you nowhere and it invariably makes things worse. Rather respond like this:

> "I can tell you're upset Mary. I'm sorry you didn't get your work done as you were told. Hopefully, tomorrow you will get your chores/ homework done so you can enjoy these privileges."

Then leave it at that. If the child objects, remind her that you're not going to discuss the matter any further, then turn your attention to other things (ignore with a purpose, a plan).

Let's assume now that the child has yet to get her work done but still has an hour before time is up. It is altogether possible that sufficient time does remain for her to get her work done and to get it done in a quality way. If so, and she does get done, and to standard, give her your positive attention. However, if enough time doesn't remain to get the work done, and the child gets it only partially done, or done but not well enough, then *all* the consequences must apply. The child must learn that shoddy and half-finished work are not acceptable. It is possible after the child has made a last ditch attempt to get the job done but has failed and is denied the desired privileges, she will moan, groan, and cry about how unreasonable you are, how you don't love her, and what a rotten place home is. She might pull out all of the stops! Actually, that's a good sign! It tells you you really have a grip on those things that are important to her. If she doesn't complain, doesn't protest, doesn't get the work done, and doesn't seem to care about being denied television or whatever, it could very well be a message to you that you are not using the best consequences, that you might have to dig deeper in search of things that are highly valued by her that you manage and which in turn will manage her behavior. If the child does complain and protest, use the approach that was discussed earlier where you show a great deal of empathy and understanding, but you stand your ground. Hopefully tomorrow will be a better day.

Here's an experience I had recently with a mother of an 11-year-old boy. The complaint was that the boy would simply not do a single thing he was told to do. "It's driving me crazy," the mother told me. "I simply do not know what is going to become of this boy if he doesn't learn some responsibility. I've tried everything and nothing works!" As we discussed what "everything" was, it fell generally into the area of badgering, coercion, persuading, begging, reasoning, and all of the other ineffective things parents do to get their kids to do as told. I asked the mother to list things of value to the child that were under her control, things that the boy simply *craved*.

To begin with, she couldn't think of anything. Television was no big deal. Riding his bicycle was fun but he could do without that. Using the telephone was not important at all. She had taken away his radio, and that didn't seem to make any difference. And on and on. Finally, she remembered how the boy insisted that he have his Teddy Bear with him when he went to bed at night, and without it he didn't sleep well at all. Nights were miserable to him without his Teddy Bear. In the same breath, however, she reminded me that she just couldn't possibly keep that Teddy Bear from the boy. It was just too important to him! I agreed but reminded her that *she* wasn't going to keep the Teddy Bear from the boy; rather, *he* was going to keep the Teddy Bear from *himself* through failure to do as told. This new twist caught the mother's attention and we finally hit upon the following idea.

I had the mother prepare five strips of paper, each one containing her own signature. (This was to prevent counterfeiting.) The mother then explained to the boy that whenever he did what he was told to do he would get a slip of paper to put in a jar that was located on the kitchen counter. Once all five slips had been put into the jar, the boy would have earned the right to take his Teddy Bear to bed with him. To emphasize and clarify this, they role played the situation to show the child exactly how the system worked and what the positive and negative consequences were. Not only did this work, but when it came bed time, if the child didn't have five slips of paper in the jar because the parents hadn't assigned him enough things to do, he came to the mother begging for something to do. This one simple strategy was all that it took. The problem of noncompliance ended. After a few weeks, the use of the slips of paper in a jar was replaced by thanks and hugs. Doing as he was told became its own reinforcer.

## NOW TO REVIEW

Typically, solutions to problems that appear to be insurmountable are simple, easy to administer, and extremely effective. The key is to make certain the child knows precisely what is expected, the time frame within which expectations are to be met, the level of quality, and the consequences for compliances and noncompliance. Remember, let the consequences do the talking for you.

1. Be absolutely precise in what is expected of the child, including the time by which the task is to be completed, and the quality at which it is to be done. Use cues as reminders of your expectations. Role play your expectations.

2.  Be certain the consequences for obeying and not obeying are completely understood, then let those consequences do your talking. Role play the consequences.

3.  Don't allow children to pull you into arguments over the logic or sense of what you expect them to do. Simply restate your expectations and leave it at that. With empathy and understanding, use the broken record strategy.

4.  Remain calm and in complete control when children have not completed their tasks. Your mood will have an immense impact on the child's behavior. Your being calm will instill in the child a sense of security, a sense of strength, a sense of stability. You will soon become an object of the child's admiration. Kids love it when their parents are composed and in control.

    I remember a time when one of my daughters when asked by a boy, "Is your father big?" she answered, "Well, he doesn't look big, but he is." That's the kind of image children will have of their parents when the parents behave big, when their behavior is bigger than that of the children.

5.  Always be on the lookout for opportunities to let your children know how much you appreciate what they do, and how able and valued they are!!!!!

> *Research has shown that the most effective way to reduce problem behavior in children is to strengthen desirable behavior through positive reinforcement rather than trying to weaken undesirable behavior using aversive or negative processes.*
> *S.W. Bijou*
> *The International Encyclopedia of Education, 1988*

# TWENTY
# Sibling Rivalry

Sibling rivalry, though one of the classic age-typical behaviors of children, drives parents up the wall. Between the friction it causes and the upsetting effect it has on the family, it persists as a major concern of parents. When we study sibling rivalry we observe a couple of things that are important for parents to keep in mind. These help us put sibling rivalry into perspective.

First, it is characteristic of virtually all children. Pleasant, obedient kids fight with their brothers and sisters just as do unpleasant, disobedient kids. It's as much a part of growing up in a family setting as getting taller, having acne, and being worried about being accepted by the peer group. It is one way by which kids learn how to survive in society. It helps teach them what they can and cannot get away with. Remember, children are

*Sibling rivalry is a part of growing up, and is not all bad.*

in the process of becoming civilized. As children, they are generally—yes, even basically—selfish. They tend to be insensitive to the feelings of others. Name calling, fighting, insulting gestures—you name it—are all part of the syndrome. But like tantruming, we parents tend to give these kinds of behaviors far, far too much attention.

Secondly, running through our minds while our children are fighting with one another are visions of kids who, as adults, will behave toward others in society as they behave toward their siblings. These visions of despair are for the most part unwarranted. As parents we look back on our own lives and recall rivalry between us and our brothers and sisters and laugh about it. It's part of the bonding process. It's one of those things we must learn to endure.

There are some things we as parents can do to keep sibling rivalry within a tolerable range. Notice, I said "within a tolerable range." You are not going to completely eliminate rivalry among siblings unless you completely eliminate the siblings. In this chapter I discuss five rules of parenting related to sibling rivalry (rules that apply to many other settings as well, as has been discussed repeatedly throughout this book). I urge you to learn these rules and to skillfully use them. If you do, you will have a powerful and positive effect on the quality of life in your home. Now the five rules:

## Rule 1: Ignore Inconsequential Behavior (You've heard this before, right!)

The first and most effective skill for dealing with sibling rivalry is to simply ignore it. If kids are arguing and scrapping with one another, turn away from them and even leave the room. If other children, on the other hand, are behaving nicely, turn your attention to them and say something positive like, "It really pleases me to see you children enjoying yourselves so much." Then attend to that behavior a few seconds to further demonstrate your approval. Avoid with all your might the temptation to dash right in there, lower the boom, and put things in order, to "stop that nonsense!" This is ineffective, and in the long term even makes things worse. If it is simply common, garden variety, everyday bickering and arguing, just leave it alone. If there are others who are behaving well, direct your attention to them.

Upon advising a mother to just ignore her boys' fighting (which I learned was inconsequential), she replied, "If I just ignore my boys when they fight, someone will get killed." I asked, "Are you there to stop all their fights?" She responded, "Well, I don't

*Media violences, etc. (and you know what I mean by etc.!) is far, far more damaging to children than is sibling rivalry.*

suppose so." I then asked, "To date how many of your sons have been killed at the hands of each other?" She got the point. In fact, in studying her sons' fighting behavior, we found that the more she got involved in stopping them, the harder they fought, each one determined to get in the last lick. Unwittingly, she was either an audience, a participant, or both. When she got out of the way, things really calmed down. They become tolerable.

I understand perfectly, with society being in the mess it's in, that parents would feel anxious about the behavior of their children. The violence on television, on the streets, and in the schools is so overwhelming that it's no wonder parents want to eliminate anything in the home that even remotely resembles violence. But we must be careful to not overreact and feel compelled to turn our children into quiet, demure, compliant, obedient little robots. Imagine how weird it would be if, as your children returned home from school, they greeted one another with saccharin sweetness:

A 14-year-old to his 12-year-old sister:

Billy:    "Margo, how nice to see you. How was school today? Do you have any homework? I would be more than happy to help in any way I can."

Margo:    "Billy, thank you for asking how my day was, and for the offer to help. It *was* a demanding day and I surely have my hands full with homework. Happily, though, I understand the material."

Billy:    "It's comforting to me to know that you understand your assignments. Since I can't be of help there, perhaps I can buy you a little time by doing your dishes for you."

Margo:    "Billy, you are the sweetest brother in the world. I love you so much. Here, let me give you a hug and a kiss in appreciation for your thoughtfulness.

Now, if your kids talked to one another like that, you *would* have reason to be concerned!

Sibling rivalry is not violence. It's jousting. It's a way kids find out about other human beings and what the limits of tolerance are. If, on the other hand, the rivalry becomes cruel and abusive, that is, when name calling becomes very personal, when children's characters are being maligned, and when the verbal attacks become vicious, they can no longer be ignored. For example, for a brother to call another brother a scumball is one thing, but for him to deride his brother for getting a failing grade in a class at school, and then in that context call him stupid, a "retard," or some other demeaning name is a sign that the

> *Sibling rivalry is not violence. It is jousting.*

conversation has degenerated to the point where it is no longer simple sibling rivalry, it has become an offense to one's character and image of self. At this point it has exceeded the limits of tolerance. Though one is well advised to just walk away from relatively inconsequential sibling rivalry, parents should not allow mean, vicious personal attacks to go unattended. When attending to this type of rivalry, this basic rule should apply. Here is where we introduce rule number two.

## Rule 2: Remain Calm and Composed But Direct When You Must Intervene

Parents should remain calm and fully composed. Voices should not be raised. It is at this point the parents should show complete self-control, and demonstrate proactively that they know exactly what to do, that they have the necessary skills to bring order into the home. When attending to rivalry, always remember to begin with what is easiest to do. For example, simply saying to the child, "No, you may not say those things to your brother!" might be sufficient. On the other hand, if the offense is serious enough, or is repeated, it might be necessary to also remind the child that because of such inappropriate behavior, he has denied himself desirable privileges. Consider this scenario:

> A boy has leveled a personal and cutting remark at his sister. She is obviously hurt, has taken it seriously, and understandably so! The mother intervenes and in a stern though firm and controlled voice calls the boy by name while looking him in the eye and says, "George, no! You must never say those kinds of things to your sister or anyone. I will not remind you of that again. Should it happen again, there will be serious consequences. I do not care to discuss this matter further!"

The boy will very likely come back with something like, "Well, she started it!" Do not allow yourself to become a referee or judge of who is right or who is wrong or who is to blame. The point is that no matter who started it, and no matter who's fault it is, that kind of name calling is not allowed. Also, do not accept second-hand information as being true or false. Simply accept it as information. It may very well be true that the boy was provoked by his sister; however, no provocation justifies a cruel response. Do not allow yourself to be drawn into an argument or discussion over what is fair. In this instance, what's fair is beside the point. The point is, regardless of anything else, that language is not allowed in the home. Period!

*Don't allow yourself to become a referee or a judge of who is right, wrong, or to blame.*

Let's further suppose the mother observed the whole affair first hand, and sure enough, the daughter did do something inappropriate which provoked the attack by the boy. Should this be the case, the mother would say, calling the children by name, "George, Diane, stop right now. No more of that. I will not remind you again. If you persist, you will experience serious consequences." Do not use language such as, "Either you stop right now or you're in deep trouble!" The word "either" suggests you are giving them a choice. You are not giving them a choice. In these instances they have no choice. There are no alternatives to stopping. However, if they choose to ignore you and persist, then let the consequences fall. Therapeutically, these kinds of encounters are typically well taken care of using the intervention strategies detailed in Chapter 3, Applying Behavioral Principles in the Home and Family.

## Rule 3: Teach Appropriate Social Skills

Sibling rivalry is an uncivilized way of expressing one's self, uncivilized meaning uneducated, unrefined, and without proper social skills. When children are engaged in rivalry, it tells the parents, "This is the time to teach my children proper social skills." It isn't the time to wallow in despair and disgust, nor to retaliate with outlandish forms of punishment and discipline. That is reactive. Rather, it is a time to teach. So far as I know, there is no better approach to teaching children social skills than to use the University of Kansas Achievement Place model called the "Teaching Interaction Strategy," also known as the "Corrective Teaching Procedure," discussed in Chapter 3, pgs. 67–69. The use of this strategy is also nicely illustrated and dramatized on videotapes produced by Boys Town.[1]

Remember, stopping inappropriate behavior is not enough. If behavior is only stopped, it will surely reoccur again and again, usually getting worse along the way. *Teaching* appropriate behavior then reinforcing that appropriate behavior (as is discussed below in skill #5) is the only way of making sure that inappropriate behavior is gone forever. (Remember: stop, redirect, reinforce.)

## Rule 4: Apply Consequences

As I've emphasized before, consequence must be well understood in advance. There should be no question in the children's minds that you mean business, and that the consequences that fall are substantial and immediate.

Let's assume that one or both of the children persist in behaving badly. If the children are young and can be physically separated, do that, requiring that they go to their

---

[1]These are reasonably priced and available by writing Boys Town, Public Service Division, Boys Town, NE 68010.

rooms or in some way be separated. While doing that, you must remember that there's a price one pays for persisting in intolerable sibling rivalry. That price would involve being denied something that is very important such as the privilege of riding the bicycle, going to a friend's house, watching television, going to a Saturday movie, using the car, or whatever.

If the children are older and can not be physically separated, remind them again, very directly, that persisting in the behavior carries with it serious consequences. For most children, this would be sufficient. You will be surprised at just how effective such consequences are when the children know in advance what they are, and when they are delivered appropriately.

> **Attempts to physically restrain older children can backfire.**

With older children, attempts to physically restrain them are typically counterproductive. If they won't respond to being told, nor to the loss of valuable and desirable privileges, trying to physically force your point could be disastrous. If this is the case, it is better to just leave the situation, to drop it. Advise others to do the same, then let the consequences fall as predetermined. If the two insist on staying there and fighting it out, let them fight it out, but not in your presence. If the one who is being abused is willing to put up with that abuse, that's his or her decision. The point is, they are not going to do it in your presence. It becomes their issue, not yours. Don't stay there and fight it out with them or be their audience. This simply makes things worse. Later, when the kids want valuable privileges, they are simply not available. For example, let's suppose that during the rivalry the son was advised that serious consequences would follow, including the loss of using the car. Later on, after the whole affair is over, when everyone is cooled down, the boy comes to you for the keys to the car, or permission to use the car. It's then that you say, "I'm sorry you chose to disobey me earlier. As we discussed then, when you behave that way, you deny yourself your driving privileges for 24 hours. Assuming that in the meantime you control your behavior, the car will be available to you in 24 hours," or words and conditions to that effect.

The point is, you are never going to be successful trying to resolve an issue where anger is out of control. You are best advised to just walk away and let the consequences do your talking. You will never shout your way to a solution in these situations. You will only make things worse. *Remember, if what you are inclined to say or do is not likely to make things better, don't say it and don't do it!*

Never remind the children they shouldn't "do that," nor ask them why they are doing it. Never say, "I have told you kids a hundred times that you're not supposed to argue and fight like that! You're driving me crazy! Now stop it, and stop it right now!" or "Why are you kids fighting again? How many times am I going to have to go over this with you?! Haven't I told you time and time again that you are not supposed to fight like that?! If you don't stop it right now I am going to ground you for life!" The problems associated with this approach are numerous. The children don't need to be reminded of your expectations, or what behavior is desired. They know that as well as you do. They know they are

> *If what you are inclined to say or do is not likely to make things better, don't say it and don't do it.*

behaving badly. All of this verbal garbage does nothing but give attention to the very behavior you want to get rid of. It only makes matters worse. Just bite your lip, say not one word more than you have to say to put things in order, and let the consequences do your talking.

## Rule 5: Acknowledging Appropriate Behavior

While your children are behaving nicely toward one another, pay attention to them by saying things like, "It sure makes me happy to see you kids having so much fun together." Keep it short, keep it simple, and keep it coming. The pay-off is simply overwhelming. The single best way to bring sibling rivalry into tolerable limits is to pay attention to children when they are not engaged in sibling rivalry, when they are behaving appropriately towards one another. When they are not engaged in sibling rivalry, a mood is created in the home that should be there all the time, a mood that tells the children this is how we get our parent's attention. We know that most children value their parents' attention above almost anything else; therefore, maintain in the home a high general level of reinforcement.

In ending this chapter, I remind you again that sibling rivalry is a normal part of growing up. How you as a parent deal with it is the real key to success and to family harmony. In that regard, and in addition to what I've already suggested to deal effectively with sibling rivalry, I pass on to you the advice of Dr. John Rosemond, a prominent family therapist. He and his wife instructed their children that they could argue and bicker but they had to follow three rules. These are really quite wonderful and I enthusiastically commend them to you:

1. There will be no hurting, meaning no hitting, punching, kicking, throwing things at each other, and so on.

2. Their conflicts must not disturb the parents. ("In other words, keep it down.")

3. No tattling is allowed. The parents did not want to hear their complaints about each other.

## NOW TO REVIEW

The following five rules of parenting will serve parents well in dealing with sibling rivalry:

1. *Ignore Inconsequential Behavior.*

   Most sibling rivalry is age-typical behavior, most of which can and should be ignored. If left alone, it will likely just go away in time. It's something we all grew out of—or at least most of us!

2. *Remain Calm and Composed but Direct When You Must Intervene.*

   Sibling rivalry must be attended to only when it becomes cruel, abusive, and threatening to a child's normal, healthy development.

3. *Teach Appropriate Social Skills.*

   When attending to sibling rivalry, be certain that you maintain complete self-control, and that you use consequences that are important to the children to help bring behavior under control. It is up to you to manage those consequences and let them do the talking for you.

4. *Apply Consequences.*

   If what you are inclined to say and do is not likely to make things better, don't say it and don't do it. If you feel uncertain about what to do, if you feel unable to deal with the situation calmly and reasonably, if your ability to be in control is compromised, then just walk away. We know that when people are extremely angry, emotionally upset, drunk, stoned, or so on, it is very unlikely that a parent will be able to have a positive effect on things. It is better to wait for things to cool down and to let consequences do the talking.

5. *Acknowledge Appropriate Behavior.*

   Be constantly on the lookout for opportunities to have positive interactions with your children when they are behaving together nicely. If you have a tendency to allow these opportunities to get away from you, you might want to keep a record or put little prompts up around the house to remind you to say nice things to your children. These help us measure and pace our behavior. When our children were young and at home and we noticed an increase in sibling rivalry, I'd take data for a few days, sometimes up to a week, and keep track of how often it occurred, between whom, and under what conditions. Invariably, we would be able to see the relationships between the behavior and events in the environment that would explain what was going on. These data also gave us direction to what needed to be done to make things better. A copy of such a record is found as Table 20.1, below.

## Table 20.1—A Daily Record of Behavior

| Day | Behavior | Frequency | Comment |
|---|---|---|---|
| Tuesday | Kids argued over the TV: which shows to watch, whose turn it was to pick, keeping quiet, etc. | 3 | I told them to quiet down or I'd turn the TV off. I was tired and behaved worse than the kids. |
| Wednesday | There was a big fuss over the use of the car. | 1 | I argued with Philip and this incited other arguments over unrelated issues. Junk behavior breeds junk behavior. |
| Thursday | TV Problems again. Homework disputes. | 2 4 | Got after the kids for no good reason. |
| Friday | Big argument over when the kids should be home; when the car should be in the garage. | 3 | |
| Saturday | On the kids to get their chores done. | 6 | This has been a terrible week. We have been super negative as parents. I can recall almost no reinforcement of appropriate behavior. Shape up, Mom and Dad. |
| **Total 19 Negative Parent–Child interactions** | | | |

My wife and I discussed this record, and beginning the next day, we began making a conscious effort to praise the children when they were happy, playing nicely together, helping out around the house, and so on. We also consciously ignored inconsequential rivalries, and applied consequences as our spokesperson. Though I didn't keep a record of behavior for the following week, conditions in the home improved dramatically. In fact, as a result of this experience I devised a TV control program that had a marvelous effect on lowering the frequency of TV viewing and related sibling rivalry, and increasing the frequency of book reading. The program is described in Chapter 22, Managing TV Viewing.

> *Research has shown that the most effective way to reduce problem behavior in children is to strengthen desirable behavior through positive reinforcement rather than trying to weaken undesirable behavior using aversive or negative processes.*
> *S.W. Bijou*
> *The International Encyclopedia of Education, 1988*

# TWENTY-ONE
# Living with Teenagers:
# A Better Way

For centuries theologians have argued over Isaac's age when Abraham took him to the mount to be sacrificed. The only thing they can agree on is that he wasn't a teenager. Otherwise it would have been no sacrifice.

Without question, the most stressful years for parents are when their children are between 13 and 20. Those years have been referred to as the age of raging hormonal imbalance. For what it is worth, they generally aren't any easier on kids than they are on their

> *"God doesn't punish teenagers for their sins. He just gives them teenagers."*

parents. We must keep in mind that we were once adolescents and were probably of as much concern to our parents as our kids are to us. My mother-in-law once told me, "God doesn't punish teenagers for their sins. He just gives them teenagers." Goethe said,

> "Tell me how bear you so comfortably the arrogant conduct of youth?
> Had I too not behaved unbearably, they would be unbearable in truth."

Unlike Goethe, we parents are quick to forget our "conduct of youth," and what we don't forget, we trivialize by saying things like, "Oh that was just kid stuff. No big deal."

Of course, it was that "no big deal" stuff that drove our parents crazy and it's the very same thing that's driving us crazy today! Like their parents before them (meaning us), youth remember selectively, and rationalize conveniently.

As I look back over my life, and consider which years I would want to live over, the adolescent years would not be among them. The immense and sometimes ruthless peer pressure, the expectations to behave like an adult but still be treated like a child, and personal uncertainties about my ability all combined to make adolescence an extremely difficult time. I often think of the song Maurice Chevalier sang in the movie "Gigi": "I'm Glad I'm Not Young Anymore."

Though the behavior of teenagers can be maddening, it is still up to us as parents to do all we can to make life as pleasant as possible both for them and for us.

As I work with parents who are having problems with their teenagers, their concerns and frustrations tend to fall mainly into two areas: a) being out of control, and b) being intimidated. Let's look at some specific things parents can do to be in control, and what they can do to avoid being intimidated. I also discuss some questions, and types of questions, parents should not ask; questions which simply cause trouble and solve nothing. In all, in this chapter I discuss *being in control*, *being unintimidated*, *asking questions* and *talking with teenagers*.

## Being in Control

With young children, control tends to be quite easy. If a child doesn't do what he is told to do, he is simply made to do it. If a child is leaving the house and the parent calls him back but is ignored, the parent simply goes after the child, picks him up and brings him back. Control tends to be fairly easy. But as the child grows older and bigger, parents can't do that anymore. (See Figure 5.1, page 125). They can't just pick the child up and bring him back. With adolescents, control is best achieved when the parents manage those things the children want. They make wanted things available on the basis of appropriate behavior. In this way, the things the children want do the controlling for you. For example, the use of the car can be one of those things that is extremely valuable as a management tool. Having the child's room cleaned might be quite valuable to the parent but of no value to the child, therefore the child resists cleaning his room.[1] Rather than badgering the child to clean his room, the parent simply says, "When your room is clean you can take the car." It's the availability of the car that controls the behavior, not you. It does the nagging for you.

It is important for parents to understand how their use of control *must* change as their children grow older. Chapter 4, On Being In Control, and Chapter 5, A Word About Consequences, speak to that dynamic and demanding relationship.

As my children reached driving age, I realized I had an immensely powerful tool with which to maintain control, and I used that tool liberally. The car was available under a few prescribed conditions which included (a) the car be driven in accordance with the law, (b) the kids put gas in the tank, (c) no classes were skipped at school, and (d) on school nights they had to have the car back by ten o'clock, and by twelve o'clock on Friday and Saturday nights. The positive consequences for meeting these

> *"Things" can often do a better job of managing behavior than parents can, if parents do a good job managing those "things."*

conditions were that the kids were able to use the car fairly liberally. The negative consequences varied depending upon the offense. If they got a moving violation, they lost the privilege of driving the car for a month. If they skipped a class at school, they lost the privilege of using the car for a week. If they failed to get in at night on time, they lost the privilege of using the car for one week, and so on. (These, of course, were all spelled out in advance.)

There were other conditions which, from time to time, were also placed on the privilege of using the car, for example, getting the lawn mowed, getting their room cleaned, or getting their chores done. In a very calm, though businesslike and direct and pleasant way, we would tell the children that as soon as they got the task done, and done appropriately, the car was theirs. Of course, they would sometimes moan, groan, and carry on. They would assure us that if we would let them take the car they would get their jobs done just as soon as they got home. They reminded us with great passion that their friends were waiting for them and if they didn't leave soon they would be holding everybody up. They were the pivotal characters in this whole thing and they had to leave immediately! I never ceased to be amazed at the number of compelling reasons the kids were able to create to justify their immediate need for the car. Though we were not always

---

[1]A messy, unkept room can, in fact, be a status symbol. As one of our children once told me, "I wouldn't dare bring one of my friends into my room if it was clean. He'd think I was weird, or something!"
I am particularly fond of the poem by Oneita B. Sumsion in her book *Moments in Motherhood:*

The Night of the Prom

| | |
|---|---|
| She was a picture of beauty, | She's sure to steal glances from suitors |
| Not one single hair out of place. | As she promenades down the floor |
| Her dress was pressed to perfection, | But, oh, what a sight in her bedroom |
| She epitomized loveliness, grace. | She left as she walked out the door! |

as precise and consistent as we should have been, typically we were able to calmly respond like a broken record (with compassion, however), by saying something like,

"I can tell that you are really anxious to go. The sooner you get your work done the sooner you get the car and are out of here."

**Set conditions with care, and then sparingly.**

Of course there was a lot of stomping around, and a lot of silly behavior, and perhaps even some verbally inappropriate behavior. You just ignore all that junk and go on about your business and let the consequences—that you manage—manage their behavior. If they want to carry on and waste time, that's their business. You go on about yours and let them decide for themselves what they want to do with their time. The important thing is that you control those privileges that are so valuable and so important to them. It's also important that you are reasonable. Don't set mountains of conditions on top of every single behavior. I've worked with parents who wanted to set huge conditions on even the minutest details of grooming and dressing, of movies and records, and so on. This is counterproductive. It simply puts distance between parents and your children. Parents have got to use judgement and restraint and give their kids a chance to express themselves, even though at times those expressions might not be all that desirable.

I suggest that parents be careful about asserting themselves in too many areas, preferably, no more than four or five, which might include the use of the car, the completion of reasonable chores and duties around the house, being generally pleasant to live with, being home at a reasonable hour at night, and the completion and submission of school work assignments, including regular attendance at school. Once the children learn that reasonable and responsible behavior in these areas brings a lot of positive attention as well as a flow of desirable privileges, they will tend to behave appropriately in other areas as well. The major role of the parent is to manage this consistently and evenly. By that I mean that if the child behaves such that he loses his driving privilege for a week, the parent, in a fit of anger, doesn't come unglued, change the rules on the spur of the moment, and threaten to deny the kid the use of the car for a month. On the other hand, if the child has deprived himself the privilege of the car for a week because he skipped school, the parent must not cave in two days later and let the child take the car as though nothing unacceptable had happened.

**Respect the conditions you set.**

Suppose the child has lost his driving privileges and a few days later comes to Mom with a tender, repentant, humble, heartfelt plea for the use of the car. (Of course, the request is linked to a life-or-death situation!) The mother must respond calmly and according to plan:

> "Gee, Son, I can tell you are really going through a lot of misery over
>
> the loss of your driving privileges. I am terribly sorry about that. I
>
> know how anxious you are to be able to start driving the car again and
>
> I'm happy that privilege is going to be yours again in a few days."

Then let it go at that. True, the kid might stomp off angry, mouthing off, slamming doors, hitting the wall, pounding his feet, and so on. You may have already experienced these kinds of behaviors and know exactly what I mean. But you are not intimidated by that. The kid has gotten the message and you are in control! And that is *so* wonderful! I recently worked with a couple who were having a great deal of trouble with their 17-year-old son. And it was no wonder! We developed plans and set conditions, but almost immediately the parents caved in. Before you knew it the kid was running around town on his motorcycle, spending money at will, and coming and going as though nothing at all was the matter. The parents felt they were completely out of control, and they were! They refused to exercise control; consequently, the boy got everything he wanted. In fact, it had gotten to the point where the parents simply gave him what he wanted just to get him out of their hair. Nobody wins in this kind of situation. The parents have earned no respect from the boy and things are only going to get progressively worse. And why? Because behavior is strengthened when what follows it pays it off. The boy's obnoxious and intimidating behaviors were consistently being paid off; therefore, those are the behaviors that continued.

## Being Unintimidated

Teenagers can be menacing if they want to be. They will sometimes resort to almost primitive kinds of behavior to get their way. (This is understandable since they are still in the process of becoming civilized.) Menacing gestures, abusive language, throwing things, stomping their feet as they roar out the door (slamming it behind them), threatening facial gestures, and so on. They resort to these kinds of things because they are afraid they are not going to get their way—even though, in their hearts, they know they *shouldn't* get their way, knowing full well that what they are doing is childish, foolish, and irresponsible. That's the curious thing about it. They are old enough to know better, but too immature to do otherwise. So they *expect* their parents to do the controlling for them! Many teenage boys and girls have told me how disappointed they are in their parents when they cave in to adolescent outrage. As I noted earlier, one of my daughters

> Children appreciate parents who are in control of their own behavior.

maintains a vivid recollection of an experience from several years ago when she was a teenager and how disappointed she was in me when I wimped out and let her have her way when she knew she shouldn't have gotten it. All the while as she was carrying on, she was hoping I would say "No." When I gave in and let her have her way, she was so disappointed in me. Children appreciate it when *we* as parents are in control. When we resist their attempts to intimidate us, we earn their respect.

Let's look at some specific instances where a son or daughter might try to intimidate a parent, and how those situations can be handled.

One of the most common ploys children use to get their way—once their parents can no longer physically constrain them—is to say something like,

"I'm going to do it and you can't stop me!"

Rather than try to show them you *can* physically stop them (for this could very well result in disaster!), remain calm, look the youngster right in the eye, all the while maintaining a pleasant and controlled expression and say,

"You're right. I can't stop you. But before you do it, you might want to count the cost. What do you stand to lose by doing it?"

*Note*: Do not invite a discussion unless you are absolutely certain it will proceed reasonably and calmly. Do not get into a discussion that is likely to turn into an argument or a shouting match. This will accomplish nothing. Rather, simply say,

"Go to your room and think it over. Come back in a half hour or so after you've had a chance to think it over and let's talk about it then."

It is a good idea, whenever possible, to *use time to your advantage* (see Chapter 6). By putting time between an emotionally charged situation and a decision, it is more likely that the decision will be reasonable. Doing this will typically result in one of three actions. First, the child might very well decide against doing whatever he or she was about to do. If this happens, simply drop the matter there and say,

"Thanks. That's super. I'm proud of you for such mature behavior."

288

Then give the child a hug, or in some other way warmly express your appreciation. On the other hand, the child might return to work out a compromise. This is fine, assuming that everyone's emotions are in control and a reasonable compromise can be struck. For example, let's say the argument is over how late the youngster can stay out at night. A reasonable compromise might be made to adjust the time by half an hour or so.

> Never try to teach or reason when emotions are out of control. Leave the conflict alone to cool down.

But remember, you will never be successful in achieving a reasonable compromise when emotions are highly charged and when there is a lot of anger. You are simply better off dropping it and waiting until everyone's emotions are under control. You might even say, "I can't discuss this now. There is too much anger. Let's get back together in an hour," or something to that effect.

There is the possibility that the child will simply disregard any suggestion on your part and go stomping off and do whatever he was going to do anyway. If this occurs, make sure that the child experiences the consequences which have been earned.

Another form of intimidation frequently used by teenagers is the threat of leaving home.

> "I'm going to get a place of my own. I can't stand living in this dump
> any longer!"

Again, don't allow yourself to get into a dither or an argument over whether that's a good idea or a bad idea, or whether or not the kid can make it on his own. Rather, suggest something like this,

> "Well, okay, but before you do, let's talk about some important things
> about living away from home. If you're going to strike out on your
> own, there are some things you need to know. We don't want you to
> get hurt."

This puts the problem right back in the kid's lap, while showing that you are concerned about his welfare. However, despite your well chosen words and empathy, he might not be in the mood to accept them; he might respond angrily by saying something like,

> "You don't care what happens to me. If you cared about me, you
> wouldn't make my life so miserable!"

To which you would say, simply,

"I'm sorry you feel that way."

Then leave it at that. If the child insists that he is leaving, be prepared to talk very calmly as one adult to the other about what it costs to live away from home. You might show him some of the bills you have to pay every month. I'm reminded of the time our oldest daughter decided she wanted to live in her own apartment. She was tired of being the oldest in a family of six kids. She was working at a drive-in and earning a salary that she thought she could certainly afford to live on. We sat down together one evening with paper and pencil and a stack of bills and counted the costs of living away from home. After an hour of this very adult exchange, she kind of smiled, looked at me and said, "I guess home isn't so bad after all." And that was the end of that. This gave me an opportunity to say, "I'm glad you decided to stay. We like having you around," and the whole matter ended on a high note.

On the other hand, the child might want to think it over for a couple of days. This is fine. A couple of days of rational thinking about such an idea will almost certainly kill it, particularly if the child is given some information about the cost of living away from home.

If the child decides to leave, let him leave. But remember, he leaves at his expense! When he leaves, he must understand that he is making this decision at his own expense. This is not your decision and therefore you have no responsibility to support it. I realize there are some risks involved here. We're talking about a risky time of life, but the odds are that if the child leaves home at his own expense, he will be back within a couple of weeks, and in a mood to work things out. If the child leaves home, be emotionally upbeat.

> If a child decides to leave home it must be done at his/her own expense.

Smile, give him a hug, say goodbye, tell him to drop by or call, and let you know how things are going, since you are concerned about him. Ask him to leave you a telephone number so you can stay in touch. Treat the situation the same way you would treat any of your children who are leaving home to establish their own place in the world. Be upbeat, happy, and hopeful. This could be the child's first great opportunity to learn about independence. I realize we are living in a more dangerous time, one where drugs, sexual promiscuity, and sexually transmitted diseases are rampant. It is only natural for parents to worry that their children might fall victim to these things. But trying to force them to stay home is by no means a sure defense against the slings and arrows of a troubled world.

Let's look now at some of the realities of living away from home. There is more to leaving home than just having enough money to support oneself. There is the loss of family companionship and the loss of familiar surroundings. There is the loss of the conveniences of living at home: a refrigerator and cupboards full of food, clothes washed and ironed and neatly put away in dressers and closets, the availability of a radio, a television, a stereo. All of these things are missed, and typically they are missed quickly.

Another thing that parents have working for them in getting their children back home is the unfamiliarity and lack of certainty about their away-from-home environment.

People in that new environment are not as predictable as members of the family. Moods are not the same. The kids are less comfortable expressing their moods in that new environment. At home they can explode and be out of sorts and still be loved. But as a guest in someone else's home or living with roommates, they can't get away with that kind of junk. They feel less at ease to go to the refrigerator or into the cupboards for food, or to arbitrarily change the channel on the television, or put a tape in the stereo. A kid isn't in a new environment very long before he realizes just how much he walked away from.

> *Running away and bolting are two different things. Kids who run away are lost. Kids who bolt are only getting away.*

What parents typically experience is that the youngster will leave home (I prefer to call this *bolting* rather than running away) and be gone for a few days and not a word is heard. Of course, parents are anxious during these few days and envision all sorts of terrible things happening. Those visions are usually exaggerated. In a few days, the child will very likely call home. The call will generally be a pleasant one where the kid asks how things are going, how the dog is doing, what's new around the house, and so on. When this happens, be very pleasant and upbeat. Visit on the telephone pretty much as you would visit with another son or daughter who was "legitimately" on his/her own. Be sure to end the telephone conversation with a note of appreciation for the call and an invitation to drop by and *visit* any time. Don't invite the child to move back home!

Shortly after this telephone conversation, the child will very likely drop by the house and survey the kingdom that he abandoned a few days earlier, a survey which will typically increase the desire to be back home. This sort of posturing will continue for a little while, often resulting in hints on the kid's part that he'd like to come back home. As a parent, you would want to assure the child that that would be fine. But don't fall all over yourself with enthusiasm. Keep it all very even and calm. (Such a circumstance does not meet the conditions of the Prodigal Son Syndrome!)

When the child is back home, a good opportunity has been provided to sit down and discuss the problems that led to the departure in the first place. Negotiations are easier. It also gives you a chance to reiterate the value system of the home and the conditions that must be met by those who live under your roof. With teenagers, particularly older teenagers, negotiations are fine so long as they don't destroy the value system of the home nor undermine the parent's position of leadership and control.

The longer you can keep your children at home during these adolescent years the better! Do not throw your kids away! Do not encourage them to leave. It's for this reason that I have spent so much time talking about kids leaving home. In the long run, everyone

> *The longer you can keep kids at home during adolescence, the better. Do not throw your kids away!*

is much better off if you are willing to put up with some of the stress, strain, and junk behavior that go with kids' growing up. Those additional years at home will give you time to bond to your children and give the kids time to learn necessary survival skills. Either way, whether they stay or leave, there is going to be some pain and discomfort, maybe even misery and agony. But generally in the long run, everyone is better off if the family can be kept together while kids are in their adolescent years.

In my years of working with families whose teenagers have threatened to run away or leave home, and who have left home, in every instance where the parents took a reasonable, in-control position, their kids were back home within a couple of weeks, things at home became better because of it, and in the end things worked out pretty well. But in those situations where kids are kicked out of their homes, or leave home unprepared to support themselves adequately, the lives of everyone—parents and children—are miserable. There is a price to be paid in child rearing. We either pay it for a little while up front, or for a long while after adolescence.

I am absolutely convinced, all things considered, that up to young adulthood, the vast majority of children would rather live at home than away from home. Sure, there will be bad days when they'll want to be gone, and you'd like to have them gone! But those days pass quickly. One of the tenderest moments of my wife's and my parenting years came when our oldest daughter was 7 years old. It was a summer Saturday and Louise and I were working in the yard. Karen wanted something she couldn't have, and went off in a huff. After about an hour, we realized we hadn't seen her for a while, so I went in the house to see what she was up to. There was no Karen, but on the kitchen counter was this note:

*Dear Mommy and Daddy.*

*I have ran away. I am at Vickie's. Call me when you feel to cry.*

*Karen*

Another form of intimidation that an angry teenager might turn to is the threat of physical violence. The child threatens to hit others in the family with the intent of hurting them, or threatens to damage property. Of course, this simply can not be tolerated! This is a risky situation and one which might be so complex as to not be easily resolved, but if it does occur, and there is a threat that the child really will be violent, let the child know that if he elects to behave in a violent way, you will need to call the police and you will press charges. Assault and battery is no more excusable at home than it is on the streets. If a child can't be physically restrained and carries out his threats to hurt someone through physical assault, and particularly if there is some notion that the behavior might recur, then as parents you should call the police to intervene. Children should know that that is no idle threat!

If you have to defend yourself physically, do so short of striking back. Don't get into a physical exchange of blows. This does nothing but encourage the child to lash out even more viciously and with more determination. If possible, leave the house and make your way to a safer environment. Let the child know that you are *not* going to respond in kind. *He* might be out of control and behaving in a very stupid way, but *you* are in control and behaving rationally. That is the message you need to deliver. The other message you need to deliver is that violent, irrational, stupid behavior carries with it severe consequences.

I'm reminded of a situation where a family feared that a 17-year-old son would sometime soon become violent and could be dangerous. We role played how they would respond if that occurred. Shortly after, the parents' worst fears were realized one night when the boy came home angry and was about to take it out on his parents. The father gently raised his hand as a signal to the boy to stop, as we had role played, and said in an authoritative, bold, though controlled voice (no shouting!):

> *Assault and battery are no more excusable at home than it is on the streets.*

> "Stop! It's obvious you are very upset. Before you hit anyone you need to know what we are going to do. We will call the police and we will press charges! You will spend time in the juvenile detention center, and you will suffer the full consequences of the law. Furthermore, you will lose every privilege this home has to offer, including

the use of the car, telephone privileges, and so on! Now, before you

hit anyone or do anything for which you'll be sorry, go to your room

and think it over. We will be here to talk things over when you return."

The parents then stood there calmly looking the boy straight in the eye. Silence fell over the room. The boy realized that he was not intimidating his parents in the least. They had a plan to deal with his inappropriate behavior. They were in control. He had no plan for dealing with the consequences of his behavior. He was out of control. Everyone just stood there looking at each other. The parents were firm and composed. The boy was angry and trembling. After what seemed to be a long time—but in reality was only a few seconds—it became obvious to the parents that the boy had run out of steam, and was not going to follow through with his threats. The father lowered his hand, and in gentle tones said,

"I'm sorry you've had a bad day, Son. I'm sorry you're upset. Go to

your room now and regain your composure. Then let's talk about it in

the morning."

He then walked over to his son, put his arms around him, gave him a hug, a kiss on the cheek, and told him that he loved him. The mother did the same. The boy went to his room and that was the end of any subsequent threats of physical violence.

The key to dealing with intimidation is to predict the kind of intimidation your teenager might use on you, prepare a response, and practice that response. Remember, your response must find you in complete control, must demonstrate to the child that you are not about to be intimidated, and should the child behave inappropriately, the consequences will fall squarely on the child.

Remember also, don't try to get to the root of the child's problem, hostilities, and anxieties until after the child is calm and in control. The time to talk about the problems that give rise to intimidating behaviors is not at the time those behaviors are being exhibited. The time to talk about those anxieties and frustrations is when the child is able to talk about them rationally and calmly.

## Asking Questions

Let's talk again, briefly for emphasis, about asking questions of teenagers. It is not at all unusual for parents to ask teenagers questions which simply set the parents up for trouble. As children grow older, it is interesting to observe the changes that take place in how parents talk to them. Verbal interactions between parents and their teenage children tend to become basically functional. Rather than just "shooting the breeze" with their children, their verbal interactions are almost always related to getting incriminating information about what kids are up to: "Where have you been?"; "Where are you going?"; "Why did you do that?";

> Ask questions only when you need information for problem solving.

and so on. My advice to parents is that though it may be necessary from time-to-time to ask these kinds of questions if information is needed for problem solving, parents should more often spend a great deal of time just chatting with their kids. This provides a wonderful opportunity for children and their parents to keep getting acquainted. It's wonderful for bonding! I recently attended the funeral of a very dear friend of mine. His oldest son, who was out of the country and unable to return for the funeral, wrote a touching letter to his father in which he spoke of the many wonderful times they spent "just talking about things."

When asking questions of teenagers, be careful to not ask questions that make things worse. For example, consider the question, "How many times have I told you to hang up your clothes?" This question only makes things worse because even if it can be answered, nothing has gotten better. The youngster can reply, "You're going to have to tell me 20 more times." The kid has answered the question, but the clothes are still not hung up. Furthermore, things are even worse because the parents are angrier. The kid is seen as a smart-mouth brat! Rather than asking a question, make a statement of your expectations and then let the consequences get the job done for you. For example, rather than asking the question "How many times have I told you to hang up your clothes?" wait until the child does hang up his clothes and then acknowledge that; or, if the clothes aren't hung up, say something like, "Your allowance is ready once your clothes are hung up." Let the consequences do the nagging for you. (For a thorough discussion of questioning, read Chapter 8, Questioning Children about Their Behavior.)

The questions we ask our teenage children can go a long way toward improving or destroying our relationship with them. Think about the questions you ask your children and analyze the consequences of those questions. As I work with parents and children I am alarmed at the tendency of parents to ask questions simply as a way of needling and digging at their children, questions that fall into the category, "Have you quit beating your wife?" Don't ask questions that lead to further conflict or that open the door for disharmony between you and your children. Ask clean questions, questions that get at *needed information for problem solving*, not that deliver an angry message. It is not unusual for parents to ask questions that are not at all intended to get answers or information for problem solving. Rather, they are simply clumsy things parents use to say something that's eating away at them, to blow off steam!

Constantly look for opportunities to say nice things to your kids. Substitute questions with statements of your expectations, and leave the consequences to carry your message and to do your nagging for you.

## Talking to Teenagers

A lot has been said, and will yet be said, in this book about how to talk to your children. As it relates specifically to teenagers, I want here to call your attention to a couple of particular points. First, as children enter adolescence they more and more find themselves in situations where they must make decisions on their own behalf. This is generally unfamiliar territory to them and they both need and want direction. Secondly, confounding their problems is their equally compelling need to become independent. For parents, it can be a real challenge to maintain balance on the fine line that separates their need to help children make good decisions and their need to help them achieve independence. Of course, since children will never become truly independent until they learn to make good decisions, the parental role in this delicate situation is compelling. As parents, my wife and I can recall many, many instances when our teen-aged children came to us in a quandary about what to do (they still do, for that matter, though they are all on their own!). Though in need of information and direction, they were also needing to hang on to, and even nourish, their so-called independence—as faint and fragile as it might have been.

Typically, in such situations, it's best to avoid telling children what they should do; rather , create a "for your consideration" setting as follows:

| Rather than saying | Say |
|---|---|
| "You should ." | "You might want to think about…" |
| "This is the way to do it." | "Consider this." |
| "You can't possibly be serious." | "That's an interesting way to think about that." |
| | "Have you thought about…?" |
| "Do it that way and you'll be sorry." | "Give it a try." |
| "Take my word for it, there's only one way to go." | "All things considered, if it was my decision, I'd…" |

I suspect you get the drift of what I'm proposing. An open-door policy to talking provides us with unlimited opportunities to have a maturing influence on our teenagers. That puts us both on the same side of the issue, the problem solving side. It's a great way to model maturity, the importance of which is nicely addressed by Roger and Carol McIntire in their excellent book *Teenagers and Parents:*

> The effects of modeling should not be underestimated. The conversation of the moment may mislead parents to think they have no influence through modeling. But most school teachers will tell you that they are amazed at the similarities between the students and their respective parents. Parents are the constant models for their sons and daughters. If we want them to respect us, speaking and acting in ways that show consideration for their needs and capabilities will produce respect in return.

Parents often ask me what the warning signals are they should look for that would tell them their teenagers are in harm's way. On page 298 I've classified behaviors into three areas: threatening, unreasonably annoying/distracting, and normal garden variety weed behaviors. You might find this useful.

## Now to Review

1. Being in control means that *you* must first be in control of yourself, and then in control of those things your children want and value. You must learn to be calm, even when tempers are flaring. You must have a plan by which the privileges you control do the controlling for you. Remember, with older children you can no longer directly control their behavior.

2. When teenagers say or do intimidating things, remain composed, be empathetic and understanding, remain firm and composed, have a well thought-out and rehearsed plan and, stand your ground. Do not try to physically control the behavior of a teenager unless you know for certain that it will not get out of hand. If a child does get physical to the point where it is harmful to you or others, call for help and let the child know you will press charges.

3. Use time to help cool things down. Put time between an emotional situation and a response. That helps cool things down so that a reasonable solution can be reached. Never try to work through a problem when emotions are high.

4. Avoid asking questions that are either going to create problems between you and your children or are simply a means of blowing off steam. Questions should only be asked to get information that is needed for problem solving. They should not be loaded down with a lot of useless emotional baggage.

5. Take an open-door policy to talking with your teens. The key to good talking is good listening. And telling is almost always counterproductive, or useless at best. There is probably nothing that is so immediately doomed for failure than is an attempt to "talk some sense into that kid's head."

> *Research has shown that the most effective way to reduce problem behavior in children is to strengthen desirable behavior through positive reinforcement rather than trying to weaken undesirable behavior using aversive or negative processes.*
> *S.W. Bijou*
> *The International Encyclopedia of Education, 1988.*

## Classification of Behavior

| Behaviors that threaten the teen's life | Behaviors that are unreasonably annoying or distracting | Behaviors that are just normal garden variety "weed" behavior |
| --- | --- | --- |
| Drugs (including tobacco) | Loud Music | Messy Room |
| Alcohol | Swearing | Dishes in the Sink |
| Gang Membership | Non-Compliance | Using up the Gas |
| Lazy/Slovenly | Mouthing Off/Talking Back | Sibling Rivalry |
| Chronic Truancy | Outbursts of Temper | "Disinterest" in Family |
| Sexually Active | Out Late | Poor Eating Habits |
| Pornography | Bizarre Dress/Grooming | Dislikes School |
| | Insensitivity to Feelings, Nature, the Environment | |
| | Cruelty to Animals | |
| | Vandalism | |

# TWENTY-TWO
# Managing Television Viewing

Television watching is one of the most powerful reinforcing events in the contemporary American home. Nothing needs less elaboration than that fact. A recent PTA report revealed that more children felt they would miss TV if it were taken away than they would miss their fathers!

From the studies I read and have done, it is difficult, if not impossible, to reach any conclusion but that TV viewing in families has gotten completely out of hand. Its causal relationship to poor health, obesity, violence, low-school performance, hyperactivity, and warped values, to name a few, has been solidly established. As one family therapist noted, "the thing kids learn from TV is how to stare." If TV viewing is going to be controlled and put into proper perspective in children's lives, it will have to be done at home. To

> *"The thing kids learn from TV is how to stare."*

expect the TV industry to clean up its act is idiocy of the first order. No one in that industry is going to walk away from the reinforcers dished out in such abundance no matter how much damage is being done to children. Several years ago the president of NBC, in response to the company's TV "sleaze," said, "It's not important whether I was proud of [it]. It was popular entertainment." "Popular," of course, translates into money, and *that is* the bottom line! A prominent movie and TV personality recently defended "sex, violence, and obscenity" as "stage conditions [that] have been a part of drama all the way back to Shakespeare." This is the kind of sick apologizing that continues to plunge the entertainment industry deeper and deeper into a sewer of filth and wretchedness, and further away from anything that even remotely resembles professional standards. If these so-called "stage conditions" are destroying society's sense of decency, then it's time to change the stage conditions. I seriously doubt that Shakespeare would condone much that goes on in the name of entertainment today. To expect the government to clean up TV is tantamount to expecting the government to clean up the government. The courts have already demonstrated their indifference. So, Mom and Dad America, it's up to you!

When our children were young (long before TV programming was as awful and disgusting as it is today!), my wife and I became concerned about the time our children spent watching TV, and I wondered what we could do to put TV viewing into proper perspective. We knew it wasn't reasonable to completely disallow TV viewing, but we knew something had to be done to keep it from squeezing out many other important things in their lives, including getting homework done, reading books, doing chores, and being physically active. We were also concerned about the amount of sibling rivalry that occurred in front of the TV where there were never-ending squabbles and arguments over who got to choose, who was in the way, who was talking too loud, and on and on.

We decided to put into place what is called a "token economy" system to control TV viewing. First we collected some data on the kids' behavior before the plan was implemented. We wanted to see what effect, if any, it was having not only on TV viewing, but on other things as well. For one week, we collected data on the amount of time the kids spent watching TV, doing homework, reading books, and playing away from the TV with one another and/or their friends. We also collected data on the frequency of sibling rivalry, and made note of the GPAs of those of our children who were in school.

With data in hand, we explained the program to our children during a Monday night family meeting. It went like this.

1. Each child was given 10 "tokens." These were 1" square pieces of poster board which my wife and I initialed (to prevent counterfeiting!).

2.  Each token was worth 1/2 hour of TV viewing. Some programs, which my wife and I regarded as too violent or otherwise distasteful, cost two tokens to view for 1/2 hour. (The children could still watch them, but they paid for it, and they paid dearly!)

3.  No matter how many children were watching the same show, each one "paid" for the privilege of watching.

4.  Each Monday night, as a family, we would review the TV program for the following week to pick out which programs the family wanted to watch. The children took turns choosing. One program a week was a family freebie, usually a Disney program.

5.  All unused tokens were redeemed by my wife and me at the end of the week for 10¢ each. (We also eliminated allowances!) (Today the redemption value would be considerably higher, I suspect. Parents who recently put this program into effect in their home told me they redeemed unused tokens for 50¢ each, and have had wonderful success. "A small price to pay," they told me.)

6.  Additional tokens could be earned for grade-level book reading. These tokens if unused could also be redeemed at the end of the week for 10¢ each.

7.  Sibling rivalry while watching TV resulted in a loss of the TV viewing privilege for all six children for the remainder of the day. Tokens that had been spent for the show being watched at the time of the rivalry were forfeited (that is, they were "spent," no matter how much of the show remained to be seen).

At the time we put this program into effect, we had six children at home ranging in ages from 5 to 15. The program applied equally to all the children, and though it required fine tuning and modification along the way to assure its equitibility and effectiveness, it remained in place, as described, for about 3 years.

Regrettably, I no longer have the data and the graphs we kept which showed the program's effect, but it was startling and long lasting. TV viewing steadily decreased until the kids lost interest in it entirely. After only a few weeks, we would go for days without the TV even being turned on. Before long, other events in their lives became more reinforcing than TV, and the number of books being read skyrocketed. Our oldest son read everything Tolkien wrote. Homework increased and grades went up. Sibling rivalry was reduced to a trickle. We credit that program for all but eliminating sibling rivalry as a problem in our home. In every respect, the program was a resounding success.

I've been asked why we quit it. We quit it because we no longer needed it. After 3 years, I took a position with another university and after the move, everyone just decided to eliminate the program. It had served its purpose.

People have asked about TV watching by our children at the homes of their friends. Sure they watched TV at their friends' homes. But it was no big deal. Since our children had to be home by certain times in the afternoon and evening (depending on age), there wasn't that much time to watch TV elsewhere. Furthermore, we didn't even try to control TV viewing in those settings since doing so would have been next to impossible. We concerned ourselves first and foremost with the management of that environment over which we had immediate control, that is, within the walls of our own home, and in this case, that was sufficient.

I've also been asked what conditions need to exist for such a program to work. That is a very good question. The program I have described won't work in all homes. For the program to work, it must be managed. Management, not magic, is the key. Since my wife did not work outside the home, she was always there to oversee things and to give the kids lots of positive strokes for doing things other than watching TV. TV watching was absolutely its only reward, but when the kids weren't watching TV, they got lots of hugs and kisses and positive parental attention.

Access to a TV has to be limited. During our child-rearing years, we had only one TV in the house, and it was situated where it could be managed. Today, nearly 50% of all U.S. school children have a TV in their bedroom! If you have multiple TV sets scattered throughout the house, you can forget about managing their use, unless you have master switches at your control. By the way, if a child has a TV in his/her room, I'd strongly suggest that its use be made contingent on good school performance and the reading of good books!

> **Access to TV has to be limited. That is a must!**

To make such a program work, the manager (usually the parents) have got to be consistent, and abide the program to a T. If you ever allow yourself to get into a "But you let *him* do it without paying a token! This isn't fair!" situation, your credibility is badly damaged and your effectiveness as a manager is compromised. There should be *no* freebies unless they are enjoyed simultaneously by the whole family on a prearranged basis. Such freebies should be few at most. Kids will gang up on parents and if the parents aren't alert and committed, they'll be down for the count and wonder what hit 'em.

Being committed doesn't mean parents have to be mean, negative, and ugly. No! Not at all. Quite on the contrary. They can be—yes, they *should* be—sweet, kind, understanding, and empathetic, and all of the rest of those wonderful things. The following dialogue illustrates how:

Child: Mom, I'm all out of tokens and it's only Wednesday. Please, Mom, let me watch the Disney channel for just an hour. It's a wonderful family show. It's even educational! It will make me a better person. Isn't that what you want, Mom, for me to be a better person? This show will improve my life!

Mom: I'm really glad you want to watch such good TV shows. Bless your heart for using such good judgement. What a sweetie you are. I love you so much. I really wish you *could* watch that show, and I'm sorry you've spent your tokens on other, less desirable, shows. I can understand that you'd feel bad. I would too.

Child: (Anguished) But Mom. What's it going to hurt if I watch this show without tokens, just this once? I'm the only one home. No one will know but you and me, and I sure won't tell! Whadaya say, Mom. Be a sport. Just this once?

Mom: (Smiling) Spending our resources unwisely can surely create problems for us later. Right now, I'm certain you know that better than I do. What can you do in the future to make sure something like this doesn't happen again?

Child: (Desperate) Mom, I know I messed up. I don't need to be reminded of that! It isn't a lesson in life I want right now. I only want permission to watch one TV show, and an especially good one at that! Even you've agreed to that! Please, Mom. The show is about to begin!

Mom: (Resolved) I don't take any particular delight in this, Honey, but you know the position I have to take on this as well as I do. We discussed this thoroughly as a family and agreed as a group what the conditions are for watching TV. I have no intention of arbitrarily violating these conditions.

Child: (Frustrated and stomping off in a huff) Lousy, stupid family rules. I hate 'em. I'm no baby. Why do I have to be treated like a baby!

Mom: (Smiling)

Sure the kid's going to be angry. Having not gotten his way, it's only to be expected. But his anger isn't half as intense nor a fraction as long-lasting as is his respect and admiration of his mother for her leadership, loyalty, control, and calm. Fifteen minutes later he'll be back in his mother's company, and then it's her opportunity to strike up a chit-chat conversation by which she further demonstrates her love and composure. No lingering hard feelings or sense of frustration on her part. She is cool!

Mom: (Cheery) I saw Mrs. Jones downtown today. She told me Jeff is recuperating wonderfully well from his football accident and should be back to school soon—though he'll still be on crutches.

*Note*: It's a good idea to strike up a conversation about something that has a sentimental or compassionate character to it. These are more difficult to take offense at.

Child:       (Subdued) Oh. Glad he's better.

Mom:       (Matter-of-fact) I'm sure he'll be glad to get back to his friends. I'm surely proud of you for having visited him while he's been down. You're a good friend. (As she gives her son a hug and pat on the back and a kiss on the cheek)

Child:       (Warming up) Thanks, Mom. Lots of kids visited Jeff. He has tons of friends.

Mom:       When you see him, give him my regards. He's a nice boy—like you.

Child:       (Smiling)

Not getting what one wants, whether it's the unearned right to watch TV or anything else, can be turned into a wonderfully positive encounter when done skillfully. And that's what this book is dedicated to!

Though the program described here won't work for all families in all situations, by applying the principles described and discussed in this book, TV viewing can be managed if parents are willing to create an environment in their home that is reasonable.

> *Be creative. Devise a TV management program then tell me about it. I love to share ideas that work!*

Take a shot at creating your own program, then write me a letter and tell me about it and how it worked. A family in California implemented our token economy system, with a few modifications to make it fit the family, one of which was an "honor system" since both parents worked. In a letter the father wrote me several months after implementing the program he said, "It is wonderful!" He reported that among his five children TV viewing had decreased from as high as 25 hours per week to about 8 hours a week. And, he added, "The children are happy, too." Parents come up with some of the most wonderful ideas and management programs, and I am eager to share them with other parents. I can be reached by writing to me at Utah State University, Logan, UT 84321-9620. In this regard, one of the best articles I've ever read on TV viewing for children appeared in the October 1991 issue of *Reader's Digest*, pages 157–162, written by Edwin and Sally Kiester, titled "Make TV Help Your Kids." I recommend it to you.

Obviously, TV isn't all bad. Educational television for use in schools; *Sesame Street* and other such commercial programs for children; programs of an educational/informational nature such as *National Geographic, Wild Kingdom*; and wholesome entertainment such as is typically found on the Disney Channel can and do make a valuable contribution to children's education and awareness of the world around them.

But even in these best-case scenarios, control needs to be exercised. Just the very act of passively sitting for long periods of time watching TV has been shown by solid research to be detrimen-

tal to children (and to adults, for that matter!) Hyperactivity, for example, has been shown to be linked to excessive, undisciplined TV viewing. At a time when so many children are labeled as ADD/ADHD (Attention Deficit Disorder/Attention Deficit Hyperactivity Disorder), getting a child away from the TV and engaged in wholesome physical and intellectual activities is sure a lot better than putting him on Ritalin! Not that ADD/ADHD behavior is caused only by excessive, undisciplined TV viewing. But much of it is (in my experiences working with families, it's a lot), and to the extent that a cause and effect relationship exists between ADD/ADHD and TV, getting the kid away from the TV is certainly among the best treatments.

## NOW TO REVIEW

1. When devising a TV management program, create an environment in which there are highly positive consequences for *not* watching TV. Simply telling children "No TV!" is not adequate. There has to be a highly desirable, incompatible behavior to take the place of TV viewing.

2. Put into place a system that is manageable. Make it as simple to manage as possible. Like a machine, the fewer number of moving parts, the less likely the system will break down.

3. Be precise, consistent, and disciplined when managing the system. Children will bug their parents to death to get them to weaken. Don't weaken. Be compassionate, empathetic, understanding, calm, and firm! Otherwise, you're dead in the water!

4. When children aren't watching TV, be sure to have lots and lots of positive verbal and physical interactions with them.

> *Research has shown that the most effective way to reduce problem behavior in children is to strengthen desirable behavior through positive reinforcement rather than trying to weaken undesirable behavior using aversive or negative processes.*
> S.W. Bijou
> The International Encyclopedia of Education, 1988

# TWENTY-THREE
# Helping Children Achieve in School

Parents have reason to be concerned about the school success of their children. Recent studies have shown that two out of every five children graduating from high school are functionally illiterate, meaning they don't have the skills needed to apply for, or successfully perform, a job in the open market that requires reading, writing, and computational skills. A more recent report published by the Secretary of Labor's Commission on Achieving Necessary Skills reported, "Good jobs will increasingly depend on people who can put knowledge to work. What we found disturbing was that more than half our young people leave school without the knowledge or foundation required to find and hold a good job. These young people will pay a very high price. They face the bleak prospects of dead-end work interrupted only by periods of unemployment."

Too often, parents oversimplify what it takes for their students to succeed in school. Almost without exception, parents will tell me that if their children will just get their homework done, turn in their assignments, attend class regularly, participate in class discussions, and have a good attitude about school they will succeed. I suppose it is true

> *Children, as children, rarely appreciate the value of a good education.*

that if all students did all of those things there would be a remarkable increase in the level of student achievement, high school graduation, functional literacy, and all of the other wonderful things we want for our children as a result of schooling. The problem with this lament is that it places the entire responsibility for school success on the child.

Children, as children, rarely appreciate the value of a good education; they rarely see the relationship between getting homework done, going to class, and having a good attitude about school with success and happiness as adults. For children, the moment is the matter of greatest importance; not being able to comfortably feed and clothe a family 10 or 15 or 20 years down the road. I believe it is quite safe to say that when you and I were young, how responsible we would ultimately be as providers and how happy we would someday be as members of the work force were just about the farthest things from our minds. While we were sitting in class dreaming about the fun things we were going to do after school and on the weekend, and doing our best to tune out the teacher who was doing his/her best to compete with our dreams, our some-day responsibilities as adults were of no (i.e., zero!) concern to us.

When I was a boy, unfortunately, I never enjoyed but one relationship with a teacher who, from what I can remember, was at all interested in me as an individual. In fact, I had a lot of super crummy experiences as a student in public schools. I came from a very poor home, and the educational system I went through expected, therefore, that I could not succeed in school. Unhappily, I never found myself in a school situation like that of the kindergarten child who, after 2 days in school, was asked "What did you learn in school?" Her answer: "I have learned that I am very, very smart!" On any number of occasions I was reminded of just the opposite by school teachers and administrators. Happily, my parents never told me that. I knew they expected me to succeed in school, get my homework done, attend class regularly, and at least meet all of the minimum requirements for advancement and graduation. Nothing was ever said about liking it. Nothing was ever said about how important it was to get a good education so that I would make a good living and be a good provider. My parents never argued with me when I complained about a crummy school teacher. They never tried to convince me that if I would apply myself more my classes wouldn't be so boring. I was simply expected to go to school whether I liked it or not, so I went.

I went to school and did what I was supposed to do for two reasons. First, my parents expected that of me, and secondly, I wanted to avoid the unpleasant consequences of not attending, or succeeding in, school. (We had a very active and unpleasant truant officer who tracked down non-attenders. Being caught was a very unpleasant experience.) Also, in order to maintain my eligibility to be a member of my high school golf team, I had to get at least a C grade in all of my classes. These are the reasons—the *only* reasons—I attended school and ultimately graduated from high school.

I hope by now you are getting my point: I went to school and I succeeded in school for reasons other than why it is important to go to school and succeed in school, but now as an adult, husband, father, provider, and member of the work force whose success is in large measure due to the functional tool skills I acquired in school, I'm glad I succeeded in school—though I hated it for 12 years. Granted, it's wonderful if parents and educators can do things to make schooling exciting and to make learning fun and meaningful. It's a wonderful thing if students have a good attitude about school, get involved in lots of school activities, and build happy memories of their years of public education that will enrich their lives. I certainly wish I could look back over my public school

> *A successful life is filled with doing things that are not pleasant to do. That's just the way it is, folks.*

years and recall such wonderful experiences. Despite my unhappy memories of it, and how I felt about it at the time, I got through, not on the strength of compelling intrinsic motivators but via the force of propelling extrinsic motivators. Be careful to not let yourself get carried away with the charming though vacuous notion that to *really* succeed in school, children need to be intrinsically motivated to learn: to love learning, to be thrilled by knowledge. Baloney! By any measure, external motivation is a far more powerful force in the achievement of success—in any endeavor—than is internal motivation (whatever that is!). External motivation is what *really* gets things done in society. Were it not for external motivation few people would get to work on time, if at all. Very little of what keeps the wheels of industry and society moving would exist if only intrinsic motivators were operating.

Relative to school success, no external motivator is more powerful than well placed verbal praise by teachers and parents, yet so little of that *ever* finds its way into the eager ears of learners. Dr. John Goodlad, an eminent American educator, in his seminal work *A Place Called School*, reported that, on average, only 2% of class time in the elementary grades is devoted to reinforcing students for performing well, and only 1% at the high school level; this, despite research which shows that to optimize learning, students should be reinforced once every 15 seconds; that's more than 1000 times in a typical school day! This is altogether consistent with my research which has revealed that, particularly in grades 4 and above, well over 90% of the appropriate and laudable things students do are totally ignored, while they are several times more likely to be attended to negatively when behaving inappropriately than to be attended to positively when they are behaving appropriately. Under such conditions, how in the world can we expect students to be intrinsically motivated to learn and to love learning when extrinsic negatives and coercers are on the rampage, day in and day out, year in and year out!

Now, lest I be labeled completely anti-intrinsic, I'm going to take a moment and discuss intrinsic motivation, show it the respect it deserves, and define its rightful role in shaping human behavior. First, intrinsic motivators and reinforcers don't come into play until the act itself, that is, the behavior, becomes its own reinforcer. It isn't until the act

> *Intrinsic motivation never occurs until the act itself becomes its own reinforcer.*

of reading becomes so enjoyable that it motivates a person to pick up a book and start reading, then reinforces the person to keep reading, that intrinsic motivation and reinforcement have become functional. It's at that point that it is no longer necessary to use extrinsics, including incentives.

When I began my daily exercise program I used several extrinsic motivators to get me going and extrinsic reinforcers to keep me going, such as points I'd earn that could then be exchanged for money to buy a new golf club. Without them, I'm sure I would never have gotten that bed off my back at 5:30 or 6:00 in the morning—particularly on winter mornings when it was pitch dark and many degrees below zero. In time, though, the act of running became its own reinforcer, and now I run because I love it! If I am going to be traveling, I plan ahead to be sure there is a time and a place to run my 4 to 5 miles. The act itself is now all that is needed. Sufficient intrinsic motivation is now provided by the act of running.

Second, though many things we do have matured to the point where intrinsics are fully operational, there will always be a need, in one setting or another, for extrinsics. Always! Don't become so idealistic that you begin thinking, "She/he ought to love school just for the joy of learning." When something is *being* learned by a child— especially the basic tool skills (the three Rs)—it is almost never an intrinsically reinforcing experience. Extrinsic motivators and reinforcers are generally the only things that get and keep behavior going long enough for that act—the behavior—itself to become reinforcing. They are simply the best means for achieving the most desirable ends. So don't discount their importance.

The most important variable in school success is parental involvement in the education of their children. Given all of this, what must be done to create an environment in which students succeed sufficiently in school to acquire the necessary academic tool skills that will in turn facilitate their success as adults in the home, the family, the community, and the work place? Contrary to what we are forever hearing in the media, it isn't money. There is very little reported in the scientific literature of education that shows a positive and direct correlation between how much money is spent on education and how well students learn. A recent report issued by the National Education Association showed that Utah had the lowest annual spending per pupil in America and New York had the highest, yet Utah has the highest or near highest (depending upon which study one quotes) overall literacy rate in America, far ahead of New York. Nor is the number of school days in the school year or the number of schooling hours in the school day the key to student's academic success. Though students in Japan (the country that is always thrown in our face as the educational model for our country—which is an insanely foolish comparison), spend 243 days a year in school, compared to the 180 day school years in America, it is not in the public schools where Japanese students acquire the tool skills necessary to ultimately compete and succeed in that society. It is a mountain of other sociological variables, including attendance at the private "juku schools," otherwise known as "cram schools," where they spend evenings, weekends, and holidays getting prepared for the national examinations, the results of which largely determine how well students will succeed as adults in society. (In the Japanese system of education, extrinsic motivators are virtually everything, and intrinsic motivators are virtually nonexistent!)

> *Do not discount the value of extrinsic motivators and reinforcers.*

Dr. James Coleman, a noted sociologist at the University of Chicago, reported in 1966, as a result of a mammoth in-depth study on what it is that accounts for school success, that school success is highly correlated with none of these peripheral things. As Dr. Coleman and others since have found time and time and time again, the most important variable for school success is *parental involvement in the education of their children*. As noted by Dr. Benjamin Bloom, Professor Emeritus of the University of Chicago, and an eminent educator and educational researcher, "A home has the greatest influence on the language development of the child, his general ability to learn, and his motivation to learn well in school." In saying this, I don't want to create

> *Schools today are basically coercive, punitive environments from which children hope to escape as quickly as possible.*

the impression that schools are of no value whatsoever. It isn't a question of value or no value, it is a question of how much value. In this regard, the role of parents has a value greater, generally speaking, than that of the schools. Of course, when the best of what parents have to offer is combined with the best that schools have to offer, then success is all but assured. As noted further by Dr. Bloom, "It is clear that when the home and the school have congruent learning emphases, the child has little difficulty in school learning. But when the home and the school have divergent approaches to life and to learning, the child is likely to be penalized severely by the school—especially when school attendance is required for 10 or more years."

In this chapter I do not deal with what schools should do to increase their effectiveness in behalf of children, though there is much to be done there, not the least of which is to make schools more positive places to be! At the moment, schools are inordinately coercive, punitive environments children want to escape, particularly at the upper grade levels. That is a matter of considerable discussion in society generally which I prefer not to treat here other than to say that education has the right goal, that is, to get students to love school. Unfortunately the goals say nothing about the methods necessary to achieve them, even though we know exactly what these methods are and how to employ them.

In this chapter, I pinpoint what the research in education and learning has taught about the role of parents and home in the education of their children. What this research has taught us is not at all difficult to understand. Putting these findings to work, however, demands a high level of rigor, management, consistency, and endurance on the part of parents, but it is altogether worth it considering the consequences to children of their succeeding or failing in school.

The research on the topic of school success is broad and deep. In this chapter, I highlight six things parents should do at home to enhance their children's success in school. They are:

1. Talking with children, and the proper use of language.
2. Encouragement to learn.
3. Reading daily to and with children.
4. Sharing of parental aspirations for their children.
5. Providing direct help with studies.
6. Organizing time and space for study and homework.

## 1. Talking With Children, and the Proper Use of Language

In this regard, parents are encouraged to speak intelligently and intelligibly, and to speak in complete sentences, using correct English ("He doesn't" rather than "He don't"; "She doesn't have any" rather than "She don't got none"; "They aren't" rather than "They ain't"; "They were" rather than "They was"). Parents should talk to their children daily about matters of substance such as current events, great ideas, and the accomplishments of great people.

It is also important that parents speak to their children in the conventional language of the dominant culture. In America, that's English. Despite the many controversies that rage across America about the importance of preserving cultural and ethnic diversity, in these United States, if people hope to succeed in school, in society, and in the work place, they must be able to communicate fluently in English. In saying this, I am not speaking against cultural or ethnic diversity nor the languages and dialects they represent. I think it is wonderful to be fluent in as many languages and in as many dialects as possible. How much richer all of our lives would be if we could communicate fluently with people

> *To succeed in society, one must be fluent in the language of that society.*

of other countries and dialects. In my work I travel broadly and whenever I am in a country where a language other than English is spoken, I'm reminded of how much richer my life would be on these visits if I could speak directly with the people rather than always having to rely on a translator. But as we look across the United States and identify those areas of the country where students tend to have the greatest problems succeeding and staying in school, and prospering in society at large, we find that to a remarkable extent those are areas of the country where languages and dialects other than English are spoken in preference to English.

I'm not going to take time in this chapter to address the several dimensions of this issue and the controversies that surround it. Rather, for emphasis, I'm going to restate the original point: If you want to enhance the probability of your children succeeding in school and society, you should spend a lot of time talking intelligently to them, preferably using good English.

## 2. Encouragement to Learn

Despite the fact (and it is a fact) that there is a good deal about getting educated that isn't pleasant at the time learning is taking place, children should be encouraged to learn and encouraged to respect the learning environment. As I mentioned earlier, I can't look back on my 12 years of public schooling with much delight or pleasure, but despite that, and despite the fact that I came from a very, very humble home in the poorest part of town, I never ever heard my parents speak critically about my teachers, my schools, or my schooling. If I complained, which I seldom did because I knew it wasn't going to get me anywhere, my mother would respond very simply: "Just do your best, Glenn. Now get your homework done." I don't recall my mother or my father spending 30 seconds during the 12 years I was in public school ever telling me how important education was. And I'm glad they didn't because I'm sure it would have been a monumental waste of time. What they did do, however, was tell me about the lives of individuals they knew and I knew which exemplified the value of applying oneself to getting an education. I can remember my mother telling me about our family doctor, Dr. Hunt. Dr. Hunt was a wonderful, wonderful man who was immensely gracious, generous, and charitable to our family, a man who made endless concessions to assure that we got proper medical treatment even when the dollars weren't there to pay for it. He accepted vegetables from our garden. He traded labor with my father who was a house painter. And most of the time, I suspect, he just smiled, wished us well and didn't bother to send a bill. I was very fond of Dr. Hunt, and as mother and I would walk home from his office, she would tell me stories about how Dr. Hunt had worked his way through school and had become a great success in life in the service of others despite the odds against him. He, too, had been born into, and grew up in, poverty but despite all of that he worked hard, studied hard, and made a success of himself.

I doubt that while telling me these things mother thought for an instant that she was encouraging me to learn, but the net effect of it was that I was being encouraged to learn. I was able to identify with Dr. Hunt's humble beginnings, and it occurred to me that if Dr. Hunt could do it I could do it despite being poor and not really liking school. All of the negatives were really beside the point. I suspect that the best encouragement to learn is not found in verbal admonitions nor lofty logic. Rather, I suspect that encouragement to learn is better found in acquainting our children with people of high character and admirable bearing who achieved what they did by applying themselves to scholarship.

Parents, introduce your children to great people, living and dead.

I can remember the encouragement to study and to learn I received by reading the biographies of Booker T. Washington, Albert Einstein, Madame Curie, and other outstanding people. Despite the fact that Booker T. Washington had been a slave, came from abject poverty, and endured almost unbelievable privations to get an education, he achieved monumental success and his name is etched in history as one of the great educators of all time and of all people. Despite being classified as a misfit and one for whom education would never play a role of any value, Albert Einstein will be forever remembered as the greatest physicist who ever lived. And despite the almost primitive circumstances under which Madame Curie conducted her seminal research on the properties of radium, conditions which ultimately cost her life, she will forever be remembered as one of the great scientists of all time.

Telling children to do well in school and verbally pouring over them floods and floods of logic about how wonderful, useful, and beneficial it is to get a good education will probably dampen the desire to learn more than irrigate that desire. Surround your children with literature, regale them with stories of good people and events, take them to exciting places like children's museums, and rent videos of exciting people doing exciting and wonderful things. Do things with your children that are aimed at piquing their curiosity about the world around them, inspiring them to better things, motivating them to pattern their lives after the lives of great people. Visits to museums, attendance at cultural events, and trips to the library are just a few virtually cost-free experiences that can enrich children's lives and point them in the right direction.

Help them find heroes who are honest-to-goodness heroes. I was thrilled recently to hear a news broadcast reporting the effect that a Supreme Court Justice had on the life of a 12-year-old black student in the South. The boy lived with his mother in a seemingly hopeless situation, but because of a special interest shown to him by a great man whom the boy had never met, his education took on new meaning. He said, "I was getting C's, but now I get B's and A's." Isn't that a wonderful thing! To see a boy's life awakened by the interest of a great man, a great model, a hero! I see very few people running up and down the playing fields or courts of the athletic world today who qualify as the heroes I have in mind. I don't see many of the youth idols in the entertainment world who qualify. I'm sure you know what I mean so I won't labor the point. Unless we as parents do something to elevate the quality of our children's aspirations, they will almost surely sink to aspire to the lowest common denominators, many of whom are daily in headlines of the sporting and entertainment news as drug abusers, sexual deviants, and rebels without a cause, many of whom are at cross-purposes with the law. If there *are* any personalities in those worlds who are noteworthy and bear adulation, seize upon them as means of encouraging your children to learn. In a word, enrich your children's environment and let the environment encourage them to learn.

### 3. Reading Daily to and with Children

It has been proved beyond any doubt that only 15 to 20 minutes a day spent reading to children will have a remarkably profound and positive effect on how well children succeed in school. One researcher concluded, "There is no doubt in the research that the best way to encourage children to read and to help them become good readers, is to read with children everyday for at least fifteen to twenty minutes...It will make a tremendous difference in the child's later reading success." And remember, of all the basic tool skills, reading is paramount. Children watch between 3 and 5 hours of TV a day. Substituting 20 minutes of that with reading is not asking too much.

> Read to your children 15 to 20 minutes each day.

In addition to the beneficial effects on the child's reading ability, the togetherness between child and parent in such a warm, happy, conflict-free relationship does wonders for bonding children to their parents. It's not expensive, it's not time consuming, it's not exhausting. It's a win-win situation no matter how it's sliced!

### 4. Sharing of Parental Aspirations for Their Children

Children need to know that their parents expect them to succeed. These expectations don't have to be stated in long, pompous, eloquent dissertations about why you expect them to succeed at school. That sort of grandstanding would never have impressed you as a child and there is very little reason to suspect that it will impress your children. And for goodness sake, when stating your aspirations of your children, don't couch those aspirations in self-serving language. For example, avoid saying things like, "I want you to do well in school so that you can be a credit to the family name," or "Academic achievement is a great tradition in our family, and we expect you to keep that tradition alive," or "It's embarrassing for me to go to parent-teacher conference and have to endure the agony of your poor grades as I visit with each of your teachers." This kind of stuff generally turns kids off like a light, and if the kid is angry with you about something, it just might provide him/her with the idea that, "Ah hah, now I know how to really get even with you!" (Kids often think that way, you know. It's called countercoercion, or getting even.)

Rather, declare your aspirations in language that strokes the child. For example, "I want you to do well in school because I want you to be happy and someday have the things you want and need to be happy." For children, material things have more meaning than do high sounding ideals and long range goals. Reference to material gains can be used as motivators to learn. Several years ago when our children were all at home my wife and I were anxious to impress upon them the relationship between learning and economic success so we spent an evening as a family in an activity that proved to be exciting and which had long range effects. Rather than telling our children about the economic value of an education, we illustrated it in a role-playing situation that went like this.

We first had the children think ahead in their lives to a time when they would be on their own as parents of their own families. We asked each of them to describe what they would like their circumstances to be: What kind of a car would you like to drive? What kind of a home would you like to live in? What kind of clothes would you like to wear? and so on. We wrote their responses down on large sheets of paper using a wide felt tip marker, one sheet for each of our six children. As you might imagine, they described circumstances fairly similar to the circumstances in which they lived, since as their parents, we had provided them with the only model they really knew. We then asked them to estimate how much money they would have to earn to enjoy the kind of lifestyle they had described. Again, we wrote their estimates on their respective sheets of paper.

When teaching your children, use concrete examples, not abstract rhetoric.

Earlier that day, I had gone to the bank and borrowed (I wish I could say I withdrew!) an amount of money equal to what it cost us per month to support our family and our lifestyle. I got the money in several different denominations all the way from hundred dollar bills down to pennies. I put the money in a paper sack and shook it up so that bills and coins were all mixed together. The children didn't know that the paper sack beside me contained all of this cash. (No play money! At times like this, you must go with the real thing!) Also earlier in the day, my wife had accumulated all the monthly bills. She also prorated, on a monthly basis, other costs such as insurance payments, projected medical costs, projected clothing costs, and so on. These were put in individual envelopes and put in a separate sack.

After we had completed our estimates, I passed the sack of money from child to child. Each one was invited to reach in and pull out a handful of money. You can imagine the excitement that filled the room as the children filled their laps with fists full of *real* money. They were euphoric! When the bag was empty, my wife then passed around the sack with all of the bills in it and each child took a hand full of bills. Then I followed behind with an empty sack into which they put back the money it took to pay the bills. Of course, you can imagine what happened. Euphoria gave way to the hard realities of life. Ultimately, every dime that was in their laps was now back in the sack. By now, we had their undivided attention and proceeded with a discussion of how much money I earned and how much education and training I had gotten (endured!) that put me in a position to be able to earn that money. We then shared with them some U.S. Department of Commerce figures about what kinds of incomes people can expect to earn based on varying levels of education. Then we asked the children, "What must you do in terms of education if you hope to achieve your aspirations in life?" (Notice, we talked about *their* aspirations not our aspirations, though our aspirations were, in fact, their aspirations.) Needless to say, each of the children had gotten the point and each of them responded reasonably and maturely. That lesson had a profound effect on our children, one they speak of even to this day. Each has achieved or exceeded that point in life they had envisioned that evening as a family at home.

I don't want to imply that this was the only thing we did to share our aspirations with our children, but it does illustrate the kinds of things we did to help our children identify with our aspirations. We translated our aspirations into language and experiences with which they could identify; thus, our aspirations became their aspirations and from that point on, our job was to help them achieve *their* aspirations.

## 5. Providing Direct Help With Studies

Although I have many years of education beyond public schooling (in fact, about as many years in college as was spent in public schools), I was always taken aback by the number of questions my children used to ask about their homework that I couldn't answer! It made me wonder how I ever earned a high school diploma to say nothing about the college degrees I subsequently earned. I suspect it is because parents so often find

> *Make your aspirations their aspirations, but for their good.*

themselves in this predicament that caused Dr. Benjamin Bloom to observe, "The home has least influence on specific skills taught primarily in the schools." In other words, the most important role of parents relative to the school success of their children is *not* the teaching of specific subject matter skills. What, then, is the responsibility of parents relative to "providing direct help with studies?" Certainly, in most homes, parents *can* help their children achieve mastery with the basic tools of learning, particularly math facts related to adding, subtracting, multiplying, and dividing; helping children appropriately practice their spelling words; helping them learn their lists of basic sight vocabulary words; helping them interpret current events; and so on.

Studies have shown that if parents will spend as little as 30 minutes a day with a child in drill and practice exercises alone, academic achievement increases dramatically and significantly. Using flash cards, word lists, work sheets, timed take-home tests, etc., parents don't have to know the answers themselves to be able to help their children learn what they need to return to school prepared to succeed in their next day's work. Learning is achieved an hour at a time and a day at a time. Children who return to school having fully learned the assignments for the day are armed not only with knowledge but with

> *30 minutes a day in drill and practice will have a profound effect on student's academic achievement.*

confidence that they are prepared for what lies ahead. It's a great self-esteem builder. When I was a classroom teacher I could spot almost immediately those students who were ready for the day's work. They came into the classroom with a spring in their step, there was a sparkle of anticipation in their eyes, and they typically said such things as, "I know my spelling words, Mr. Latham. I studied them with my mom last night until I got them all correct."

Where parents *can* help they *should* help, but in instances where they are unable to provide the help their students need in terms of content, they should find someone who can help: a knowledgeable friend, a tutor, a fellow student, or a teaching aide of some sort. It is not at all unreasonable to go to these lengths to help students master a subject. In classrooms across America it is typical to find 30 to 40 students—and even more— in a classroom with one teacher. Studies have indicated that in a six hour school day the total amount of time a student receives one-on-one instruction from teachers is about one minute and 30 seconds. That's the way it's going to continue to be so long as the American public school system is structured the way it is. That is certainly the way it's going to continue to be into the foreseeable future, not getting better but very likely getting worse.

Rather than wringing our hands in despair and cursing that dark and dismal future, it is up to us to assume important responsibilities relative to our children's school success. One of those responsibilities is for us as parents to provide direct help with studies, or to find someone or something else that can do that in cases where we cannot. Nothing is going to be gained by sloughing off that responsibility with the excuse, "That's what we have schools for. That's why I pay taxes!" True, we do pay for schools, and we pay for them dearly with hard-earned dollars, but all of that is beside the point if your child isn't learning! Whether you paid your fair share of taxes or not, if the child hasn't learned and you as a parent are in a position to help the child learn, you have not done your share. That is realized only when you have put forth *every* effort at your disposal to assure your child's academic success. It's more important than watching prime time television (or television at anytime, for that matter!), going out on the town, visiting with friends and neighbors, attending a sports event, or about anything else.

The grim reality is before us and is well documented, as I noted at the outset of this chapter when I quoted the Secretary of Labor's Commission on Achieving Necessary Skills. For emphasis, I repeat that here: "What we found was disturbing: more than half our young people leave our schools without the knowledge or foundation required to find and hold a good job. These young people will pay a very high price. They face the bleak prospects of dead-end work interrupted only by periods of unemployment."

> **You must do what it takes to assure your children's academic success.**

## 6. Organizing Time and Space for Study and Homework

It is a rare student who is sufficiently self-motivated to go directly home from school to a predetermined place in the house and complete his/her homework. Getting homework done is almost always a function of direct and consistent parental influence and supervision. The research is crystal clear on that point.

When we talk about organizing time and space for study and homework we don't need to think in terms of an elaborate setting or arrangement. A kitchen table is a very good study area. It's worth noting that the kitchen is one of the most reinforcing areas in the house since it is in the kitchen that people enjoy so much pleasure and satisfaction in the form of primary reinforcers: Food! The kitchen table is a very good study area. It's better if the television isn't on or radios aren't blasting away with their cacophony of beats and screams, bangs and twangs; but if they are, you'll gain more headway with your kids by having them turn them down rather than turning them off. Somehow or other kids have evolved (or maybe devolved is a better word) to the point were they can maintain their thought processes despite noxious noises masquerading as music. Of course, if your children are agreeable to turning this stuff off so much the better. If they're not, rather than fighting, compromise; turn it down to a reasonable volume.

> **As hard as it is to believe, kids do seem to be able to learn even when the radio/ TV/Stereo is blaring away. Amazing!**

In addition to workspace, it is important that a study schedule be established. Usually, an hour to an hour and a half each evening set aside for homework will be enough to keep a student on top of his or her studies. Obviously, establishing a schedule must take into consideration other things going on in a child's life: piano practice, a part-time job, extracurricular activities at school, and so on. But for the most part, the lives of our children are predictable enough that a reasonable amount of time can be set aside each day devoted entirely to homework. Many parents come to me in a quandary over how they can get their children to do their homework. Here is a strategy I have found to be very effective, and which I have parents of students of all ages using. It consists of a six-part program as follows.

- *A task area.* I have found it useful to designate the homework area as a "task area." Children understand that a task is something that has to be done, and designating the area as a task area helps characterize homework as something that has to be done. In fact, I've even had parents make up a sign that says, for example, "Mary's Task Area" and that sign is hung on the wall or put in a conspicuous place when it is time for Mary to do her homework. Attached to the sign might even be a picture of Mary busily doing her homework.

- *A homework schedule.* This is a schedule, outlined on paper, which specifies the time of each day during which homework is to be done. In some cases, it can't always be done at the same time every day or for the same length of time, so variation is noted on the schedule.

- *Timer.* This can be a kitchen timer or clock on the wall that keeps track of the amount of time the child spends on task. If the child has to leave the task area to go to the toilet or answer the telephone or whatever, the clock is unplugged then reengaged, or the timer is reset to accurately account for the amount of time spent on task. The parent should similarly note when the child begins the homework so that adequate accountability is enforced.

- *Outline/checklist of homework studies.* Before the child begins the homework, he/she shares with the parent what it is that must be done. In some cases, this outline/checklist can involve written teacher-input as the child goes from class to class during the day. This is typically a good thing to do in instances where children are not completely honest or forthcoming with their parents about what they are supposed to do or what they are to have ready for the next day.

- *Sign-off sheet.* This is a sheet on which both the child and the parent sign-off that the work has been completed and completed to standard. When the child finishes the homework, he/she signs the sheet as completed and takes it to the parent for review and sign-off. If something more needs to be done than what the child had in mind or had completed, the parent specifies this, and the child continues with the work until parental expectations are met, at which point the parent signs-off that the work is done, and the child can enjoy the pleasant consequences of achievement and success. Figure 23.1 is an example of what a sign-off sheet might look like.

- *Consequences.* If the child completes the work and meets all of the expectations, he/she will have earned valuable privileges, as has been stated so frequently in this book. If the child has not met expectations then he/she has deprived himself/herself of these privileges. In addition to the immediate consequences that can be earned (for example the use of the bike or of the car), students can also earn additional points toward the "purchase" of some highly desirable future event such as parental help in purchasing an item of clothing, a toy, a computer or whatever. Be careful that these delayed reinforcers are not too long in coming; otherwise, the child loses interest and the strategy ceases to be effective. In addition to the earning of privileges and even material things, be certain the child receives a lot of verbal praise and recognition for remaining on task in the task area, completing the work assigned, and acquiring the skills.

To help formalize both expectations and consequences, some children respond very well to "behavioral contracting." This is a take-off on legal contracting in which expectations in the form of goals are written down, consequences in the form of privileges are specified, and responsibilities are clearly stated. Figure 23.2 is an example of a behavioral contract. Though this contract is used for homework, the form can be used for any number of behaviors. But don't go overboard with contracts. Never have more than one or two in operation at any one time. Also, remember that a contract can be amended, but *all* amendments *must* be discussed and agreed upon by all parties. Amendments should be made only when it is absolutely necessary.

For a final word about homework and consequences, I turn to the advice of Dr. Howard Sloane as found in his excellent *The Good Kid Book*:

> Whether or not the child does his or her homework is "optional." The
> parents should never reprimand, cajole, urge, threaten, or do anything
> else of this nature to get the student to work.

You should be very matter-of-fact or businesslike about homework. It may take a while before you note any effects. The attitude must be "Here are the consequences—

## Figure 23.1—Homework Record

_____'s Homework Record

| Date | Beginning Time | Ending Time | Student's Signature | Parent's Signature | Acknowl-edgment/ Comments |
|---|---|---|---|---|---|
|  |  |  |  |  |  |
|  |  |  |  |  |  |
|  |  |  |  |  |  |
|  |  |  |  |  |  |
|  |  |  |  |  |  |
|  |  |  |  |  |  |
|  |  |  |  |  |  |
|  |  |  |  |  |  |
|  |  |  |  |  |  |
|  |  |  |  |  |  |

take it or leave it." Other than setting up the program, you leave all responsibility to the child.

Avoid any argument over the program with the child. If he or she does not like the rules or regulations set up, just say that this is the way it is, take it or leave it. If the child continues to argue, tell him or her you have things to do and *leave*. Do this consistently.

I've had so much success with parents using this simple six-step strategy that I recommend it to you without hesitation. I realize when saying this that some adjustments might need to be made given individual circumstances, but for the most part it's a strategy that can be adapted to any home setting. I recently used it with a Navajo family. The 5th grade son simply had no use for school or school work. But once the program was put into effect and the boy began enjoying the many benefits of compliance, as well as earning extra points for additional reading, he was hounding his mother for "more homework!"

> *After-the-fact, delayed, re-inforcers are powerful as well.*

Frequently, parents ask me how this strategy can be used in homes where both parents are working and aren't home when the children get home. The system is still applicable. Rather than parent involvement occurring before the fact, it occurs after the fact. For example, the outline/checklist of studies is reviewed after the parent gets home, even after the work is done. The child must still initial the sign-off sheet when tasks are completed, which is then checked by the parents. Consequences remain pretty much the same, with "costs" being levied as children avail themselves of privileges they have not earned.

For example, if the work wasn't done as the child indicated by signing-off, and he went ahead and rode his bicycle, he would not only deny himself the privilege of riding his bicycle for the remainder of the day but would also forfeit the right to watch television for the rest of the day. Under these circumstances, assuming the program is managed appropriately, the child quickly learns what the consequences will be for an appropriate or an inappropriate response.

Table 23.1 is a home learning questionnaire prepared by Dr. Bloom. It contains 12 questions to help parents determine whether they are providing an environment that will lead to academic success for their children. I encourage you to give careful thought to each of those 12 questions and then do everything you can to ultimately be able to score a +2 on every one of the 12 questions.

Shortly after taking office as the Secretary of Education in the George Bush administration, LeMar Alexander made the following three suggestions that bear

## Figure 23.2—Behavioral Contract

Student: Pamela Stout

Dates of this contract: Oct. 1 to Oct. 31

**GOALS**

Long-term:          Pamela will successfully complete 8th grade

Short term:         Pamela will complete and turn in on time all assignments for all

her classes, and maintain at least a C+ average in all her classes

**RESPONSIBILITIES**

*Who does what by when and how well*

1.  All assignments will be turned in at the beginning of each class period.

2.  The teachers will grade the assignments and give them back to Pam with other instructions as necessary.

3.  As necessary, Pam will rework the assignments until a letter grade of at least C+ is earned.

**PRIVILEGES**

*What will happen*

1.  Pam will earn 5 bonus points for each assignment turned in, which points can be used to purchase baby-sitting privileges.

2.  All assignments that earn a C+ grade will also earn 5 additional bonus points, B grades will earn 10 bonus points, and A grades will earn 15 bonus points.

3.  Bonus points will be earned: assignments that are graded B (2 points) and A (3 points).

**BONUS:** Bonus points can be used to purchase baby sitting privileges: 50 points for each baby sitting job.

**PENALTY:** None

How will this contract be monitored?_____

What records must be kept? *A daily record of assignments, their grades, and bonus points earned.*

Signed _____     Date: _____ _____

                                                    Student

Date: _____ _____

          Parent(s)

Adapted from Sulzer-Azaroff and Mayer Behavioral Analysis for Lasting Change, Holt Rinehart and Winston. At the end of this chapter is a blank copy of this form for your use.

reprinting here. As you read these, you will see they relate closely to what is covered in this chapter. Consider them with care and act upon them.

1. *Start with your own children.* Have you spent 15 minutes in a conversation with your child today (the national average)? Read to this child? Discussed right and wrong and religion? Played together? Gone somewhere together? Listened? Hugged? Checked on homework? School attendance? Monitored (and limited) TV watching?

2. *Find out how children—especially yours—are growing up today.* Go sit in the back of a classroom, quietly, for three hours (ask permission first, of course). Visit the juvenile judge, the hospital neonatal care center, the police station. Watch six hours of cable television in one day, including MTV. Visit your child's teachers, and then compare notes.

3. *Ask your school principal these questions:* Is this school drug-free? Violence-free? What are your goals? Your academic standards? Do you have a report card that measures how well my child is learning English, math, science, history, geography? How are the social needs of the children met so they do not become a barrier to improving academic achievement?

In this chapter, I have described several things parents can do to create in their homes an environment that will facilitate their children's success in school. In a word, parents *must* be actively involved. As was noted in a report issued in 1992 by the Sylvan Learning Centers and the National Association of Secondary School Principals, "Parents, you cannot drag your children off to kindergarten and expect to pick them up 13 years later ready for careers, for college and for the rest of their lives."

> *"Parents, you can't drag your kids off to kindergarten and expect to pick them up 13 years later ready for careers, college and for the rest of their lives.*

Though there are endless numbers of things parents can do to promote their children's success in school, the list of "Twenty-five Ways to Help Your Child Succeed in School" is as good as anything I've seen. I include it here for your consideration as Table 23.2.

In concluding this chapter, I return again to a statement by Benjamin Bloom which I believe is of utmost importance and deserves a second mention:

"It is clear when the home and the school have congruent learning emphasis, the child has little difficulty in his later school

years. When the home and the school have divergent approaches to
life and to learning the child is likely to be penalized by the school
especially when school attendance is required for ten or more years."

My hope of you as a parent is that you will work diligently to improve the learning
environment in your home and at school.

## NOW TO REVIEW

For children to succeed in school, parents and educators must work together. At
home, there are at least six things parents should be particularly attentive of:

1.  Talking with children, and use language properly.
2.  Encouraging children to learn.
3.  Reading daily to their children.
4.  Sharing with children their parental aspirations.
5.  Providing direct help with studies.
6.  Organizing time and space for study and homework.

> *Research has shown that the most*
> *effective way to reduce problem be-*
> *havior in children is to strengthen*
> *desirable behavior through positive*
> *reinforcement then trying to weaken*
> *undesirable behavior using aversive*
> *or negative processes.*
> *S.W. Bijou*
> *The International Encyclopedia*
> *of Education, 1988*

## Table 23.1—Does Your Home Encourage Learning?

These 12 questions can help parent's determine whether they are providing an environment that will lead to good school learning for their child.

Score two points for each statement that is "almost always true" of your home; score one point if it's "sometimes true"; score zero if it's "rarely or never true."

|  | Almost Always True (+2) | Sometimes True (+1) | Rarely or Never True (0) |
|---|---|---|---|
| 1. Everyone in my family has a household responsibility, at least one chore that must be done one time. | _____ | _____ | _____ |
| 2. We have regular times for members of the family to eat, sleep, play, work, and study. | _____ | _____ | _____ |
| 3. School work and reading come before play, TV, and other work. | _____ | _____ | _____ |
| 4. I praise my child for good schoolwork, sometimes in front of other people. | _____ | _____ | _____ |
| 5. My child has a quiet place to study, a desk or table at which to work, and books, including a dictionary or other reference material. | _____ | _____ | _____ |
| 6. Members of my family talk about hobbies, games, news, the books we're reading, and movies and TV programs we've seen. | _____ | _____ | _____ |
| 7. The family visits museums, libraries, zoos, historical sites, and other places of interest. | _____ | _____ | _____ |
| 8. I encourage good speech habits, helping my child to use the correct words and phrases and to learn new ones. | _____ | _____ | _____ |
| 9. At dinner, or some other daily occasion, our family talks about the day's events, with a chance for everyone to speak and be listened to. | _____ | _____ | _____ |
| 10. I know my child's current teacher, what my child is doing in school, and which learning materials are being used. | _____ | _____ | _____ |
| 11. I expect quality work and good grades. I know my child's strengths and weaknesses and give encouragement and special help when they're needed. | _____ | _____ | _____ |
| 12. I talk to my child about the future, about planning for high school and college, and about aiming for a high level of education. | _____ | _____ | _____ |
| **TOTAL** | _____ | _____ | _____ |

If you scored ten or more, your home ranks in the top one-fourth in terms of the support and encouragement you give your child for school learning. If you scored six or lower, your home is in the bottom one-fourth. If you scored somewhere in between, you're average in the support you give your child for school learning.

## Table 23.2—25 Ways to Help Your Child Succeed in School

✓ Talk to your child from the day of birth. Early language experience builds the foundation of reading success.

✓ Read aloud to your child.

✓ Young children learn best through direct experience with their environment. Allow exploration. Set aside a part of the house just for this.

✓ Write down what your child says and read it back. Your child will soon discover that reading is a logical extension of speech.

✓ Encourage your child to keep a journal.

✓ Go for a walk in the woods with your child and collect pine cones. Have your child arrange these from largest to smallest.

✓ With your child, make cookies or jello or other foods in which steps must be followed. Read the directions step by step and have the child carry them out. This provides practice in listening and following oral directions.

✓ Encourage your child to write a family newspaper.

✓ For the beginning reader, label objects around the house.

✓ Encourage your child to interview family members and write their biographies.

✓ Ask your child to count items for you— the cans on a shelf, apples in a bag, etc.

✓ Read along with your child aloud to provide a model for expression and fluency.

✓ Write some messages that require written answers.

✓ Provide a book shelf for your child's bedroom.

✓ Take your child to the library.

✓ Conduct an oral scavenger hunt. Ask your child to find all the objects in the kitchen that begin with a specific sound—F—fork, fan, fish, food, for example.

✓ Ask your child to locate an item in a cupboard by saying it is next to, in front of, over or behind another item.

✓ Have your child write words that are interesting or meaningful on an index card. File in a special word file box. Your child can use these words to write stories, etc.

✓ Lay different shaped crackers in a row to create a pattern. Have your child try to reproduce the pattern.

✓ Do not expect your young child to spend long periods of time at homework. Change the activity often.

✓ Let your child measure ingredients when you cook or bake.

✓ Ask more "why" questions of your child instead of questions that require a simple yes or no. This stimulates critical thinking.

✓ Prepare a shopping list with your child. Read it together while shopping.

✓ Have your child make a scrapbook with a beginning letter sound on every page. Provide old magazines for your child to cut out pictures to fit the beginning letter sounds.

✓ Establish a message center on a bulletin board. Leave messages for your child often.

329

Student: _____

Dates of this contract: _____

## GOALS

Long-term: _____

Short term: _____

| **RESPONSIBILITIES** | **PRIVILEGES** |
| --- | --- |
| *Who does what by when and how well* | *What will happen* |

1. _____     1. _____

   _____        _____

   _____        _____

2. _____     2. _____

   _____        _____

   _____        _____

3. _____     3. _____

   _____        _____

   _____        _____

**BONUS:** _____

**PENALTY:** _____

How will this contract be monitored? _____

What records must be kept? _____

Signed _____     Date: _____

                                    Student

Date: _____ _____

             Parent(s)

Adapted from Sulzer-Azaroff and Mayer Behavioral Analysis for Lasting Change, Holt Rinehart and Winston. At the end of this chapter is a blank copy of this form for your use.

*"There is hope in the knowledge that despite the suffering it causes, drug dependence is usually not a death sentence or even a life sentence."*
    *Harvard Medical School*
    *Mental Health Newsletter*

# TWENTY-FOUR
# Dealing with Substance Abuse

"All of the United States Surgeon General's warnings and anti-smoking messages aren't enough to deter teens from lighting up." So begins a report by the Centers for Disease Control study of 11,831 students in grades 9–12 throughout the 50 states, Washington, D.C., Puerto Rico, and the Virgin Islands, a study that showed that more than one-third of students within this age range smoke tobacco. Similar results are reported relative to school-aged children's use of alcohol and drugs (although, happily, there appears to be a decline in the use of cocaine).

As unfortunate as it is, children (like adults) are going to do stupid things. Children from wonderful homes who have loving, caring, and concerned parents are going to do stupid things just as children who come from less caring and less wonderful homes (though better homes and better families produce fewer problems). Again, it is largely a matter of probabilities, where the probabilities of children abusing drugs goes up as the home environment becomes less functional (high risk), and goes down as the home environment becomes more functional (low risk). (See Chapter 1 for a review of the variables that relate to risk.)

> The family organization, like any organization, needs a leader.

Though many families today are headed by a single parent, there is research which indicates that families can still be "low risk" if that parent takes an authoritative role (as contrasted with authoritarian) as the leader in the home. The point is, children need a leader who behaves like a leader and inspires a sense of confidence and respect. Some studies have indicated that the adult hero or heroine in a child's life isn't always a parent. An aunt or an uncle, a grandparent, or even a close family friend who is stable, dependable, approachable, safe, caring, and wise has been shown to effectively lead youth out of harm's way who would otherwise be at high risk of failing life's tests including the ability to resist the pressures to experiment with and abuse drugs. The research is clear: The family organization, like any organization, needs a leader. A leader is someone people follow. A person with a title is not necessarily a leader.

In families, the best leaders are those who are skillful at shaping an environment where it is more reinforcing to be *with* the family than to be without it. Behavior follows its consequences. If those consequences are more positive, inviting, and pleasant within the family, that's the environment children will most likely cherish above other environments. But when the reinforcers outside the home and family become more desirable than those inside the home and family, and when punishers inside the home and family are greater than those on the outside, children will leave home and family. It is predictable. It is lawful, in a behavioral sense. At length, the reinforcers for misbehavior become so potent (as is the case with substance abuse), that knowledge of, and even damaging and painful experience with, drugs is not sufficient to deter the children from behaving in ways that "earn" those destructive reinforcers. When this happens, they are "hooked." Remember, behavior is shaped by consequences available within one's immediate environment. Our responsibility as parents is to do *all* we can to create in our homes an environment that comes forth with an abundance of positive consequences for appropriate behavior rather than punishers for inappropriate behavior. It is a matter of people interacting well with people. (Children are people!)

Teenagers typically see themselves as invincible.

In drug abuse matters, drugs are generally less important than are people. When people who use alcohol, tobacco, and drugs advise children not to abuse substances that are harmful to the body, the appeal falls with a thud on uninspired ears. When adults who have not bonded well with children and whose behaviors are coercive, aversive, negative, and unpleasant speak to children about the good life free from addiction to drugs, the message tends to ring hollow, even repulsive, rather than inviting. In fact, it is not unusual in such instances for the message to invite a child to do the very thing the words speak against. Being scolded, accused, and verbally harassed for even experimenting with such things is known to heighten a child's inclination to use them.

Typically, since they see themselves as invincible, teenagers are unimpressed with the signs that are posted all around them warning them of the dangers—even mortal dangers—of using alcohol, tobacco, and drugs. Certainly, being without these things, and therefore without their friends, is regarded as a much greater threat to their well-being than being with these things and therefore with their friends.

So what do we do as parents to keep our children away from drugs, and what do we do when they get involved with them? The answer to the first part of that question should be obvious by now: we do our very, very best to create a low-risk family environment. We laugh a lot as parents; we show our children by what we do and say that we enjoy life and we enjoy people; we model a life free from indulgence in alcohol, tobacco, and drugs; we build our children's self-esteem through frequent and repeated references to their strengths, their successes, their great value to us as human beings and as members of the family; we appropriately and affectionately touch them, hug them, kiss them, and tell them we love them; we surround ourselves and them with good literature, good music, and good influences that show how much we value things that promote healthy minds, healthy bodies, and healthy value systems; we are quick to acknowledge appropriate behaviors and to skillfully treat inappropriate behavior; we spend more time than money on them; we are firm and resolved yet gentle and composed when order must be maintained; we teach our children our expectations of them without trying to force or coerce them into achieving our expectations; and we portray to them an image which is sometimes bigger than life, an image they will look up to and respect and emulate. As I noted earlier in this book, one of the great tributes ever given to me by my children was when one of my daughters, in response to a friends question, "Is your Dad big?", answered, "Well, he doesn't look big but he is."

Certainly, to keep our children safe from the ravages of drugs, alcohol, and tobacco, we need to teach them the skills they will need when they are put in those difficult social circumstances where substance abuse is so inviting. You'll notice I said, "We must teach them the skills they will need." Teaching them only *about* the dangers of drugs and the horrors they will experience in life once they are hooked on drugs is simply not enough. Reason, logic, good sense, conventional wisdom, and all of those wonderful things aren't worth a tinker's damn if a child isn't able to translate them into avoidance skills. If the only thing we needed to *be* happy was to know *how* to be happy, there would be a lot more happiness in this world. The tragic fact of the matter is we all *know* more about being happy than we *do* about being happy; therefore, knowing is in itself not enough! Knowing is important, it just isn't enough. Research done at Utah State University, under the direction of Dr. Dan Morgan has identified nine "basic resistance *skills*" that have been shown to be effective in keeping children from succumbing to peer pressure to indulge in drugs.[1] They are:

1. **Resist with a Reason**
   - "I don't want to do that."
   - "My parents would kill me."
   - "I don't like the taste."
   - "I don't like the smell."
   - "I have a lot to do today."

2. **Say "No thanks"**
   - "No thanks."
   - "No thank you."
   - "No way."
   - Shake head no.

3. **Use Humor**
   - "I can't afford to kill any brain cells."
   - "I'm in surgery today."
   - "I have an appointment with the President today."
   - "My doctor won't let me."
   - "Santa Claus is watching."

4. **Change the Subject**
   - "Why don't we go to a movie tonight?"
   - "I'm going to the mall. Want to come with me?"
   - "Did you see the game last night?"
   - "No, let's have something else to drink."

5. **Leave the Situation**
   - "No" (and walk away).

6. **Avoid the Situation**
   - Walks into the picture, notices the "inviter," and walks away.

7. **Ignore**
   - Ignores the question altogether.

8. **Be a Broken Record**
   - "No thanks."
   - "No thanks."
   - "No thanks."

9. **Putting Them Off for Now/Stalling for Time**
   - "No...not now."
   - "Naw...maybe later."

---

[1]These training materials are available from Family Development Resources, Inc., 3160 Pinebrook Road, Park City, UT 84060; or by calling 1-800-688-5822. Ask for the RESIST materials.

I urge you to teach these skills to your children through role playing. Actually simulate a situation typical of what your child might experience and have the child say the words he or she should

> *Teach children through role playing and simulation. That's concrete.*

say, as suggested above. I remember several years ago when our children were at home, my wife and I had a family meeting with our children to discuss, and to role play with them, what they would do if they were confronted with the temptation to use drugs. During the role playing with our oldest son, I bore down on him as though I was one of his peers tempting him to use drugs. In each instance, he said, "No," or "I don't want to," and so on. Finally, I said to him sneeringly, "What are you, a chicken?" There was a brief pause, then he responded, "Cock-a-doodle-doo." Of course, the family cracked up at this absolutely marvelous response. A little humor, evoked by role-playing, taught a great lesson.

It goes without saying that even our best efforts, even our best role-playing activities, may not be enough. After all, by the time children are old enough to become members of peer groups where alcohol, tobacco, and drugs are being used, they are generally spending a good deal of their time outside of the direct sphere of influence of their parents. It isn't at all unusual for influences outside the parents' sphere of influence to be greater than those within. In those instances, children become very, very vulnerable and it is not at all unlikely for them to stumble and even fall. Some of them fall extremely hard, as noted in the November, 1989 issue of the *Harvard Medical School Mental Health Newsletter*,

> Most people who are dependent on drugs use more than one. The vast majority of them smoke tobacco. Most heroin addicts have been, are, or will be alcoholics, and most people that start to smoke marijuana do not stop drinking alcohol.

That's a frightening scenario. The article goes on to point out that,

> Most alcohol and drug dependence resolves itself without treatment, sometimes after many years of remissions and relapses. Dependence usually begins in the teens; and dependence that develops in youth often ends in middle age, as social responsibilities change and the full weight of chronic physical and psychological effects begin to be felt. Recovery becomes more difficult the longer the problem persists, but it is never impossible. At least half of alcoholics eventually

recover…heroine addicts break the habit after an average of 10 years. There is hope in the knowledge that despite the suffering it causes, drug dependence is usually not a death sentence or even a life sentence.

Although there is hope for those who become addicted, that hope is but a faint silver lining around a massive, dark, and threatening cloud of despair, unhappiness, and misery that can affect many lives for many years. This brings us, then, to the last part of the question, "What do we do when our children become involved with alcohol, tobacco, and drugs?"

> *"Despite the suffering it causes, drug dependence is not a death sentence or even a life sentence."*

There isn't any absolutely satisfactory answer to that question. For starters, however, I refer again to the *Harvard Medical School Mental Health Newsletter* I just cited. It emphasizes that for purposes of treatment, "The drug is often less important than the person." Then it continues with the statement of an important principle, the principle of substitute activities:

> The best treatment aims at the social causes of substance dependency, and is provided in non-professional settings where hope is restored by an emphasis on spiritual renewal and moral regeneration; where there is relief from loneliness, and where self esteem is enhanced by giving the abuser an opportunity to help others. These can eliminate the social roots of youthful frustration, rage, and alienation.

> *Service to others is a good therapy for substance abuse.*

I want particularly to emphasize the value of service to others as therapy. I'm reminded of a great story—a story with a marvelous message—that came out of the Second World War. As Hitler's armies invaded France, the peoples of Southern France who escaped into Spain had to cross the Pyrenees Mountains. The story is told that in one instance, a group of refugees was about to give up and either perish in the mountains or succumb to captivity because it was so difficult crossing the mountains. Rather than allowing them to give up, their leader called on the more able-bodied to help the less able-bodied and in this spirit of helping, the entire group made it across the mountains safely into Spain.

I am quick to acknowledge that not everyone who is having drug-related problems is going to be willing to do things to serve and help others. And by all means, I'm not suggesting that this strategy would very likely help hardened drug addicts on the streets of inner cities whose lives are almost totally absorbed with getting another "fix." But I am suggesting that service to others is a viable strategy for individuals who are wanting help, are amenable to treatment, and who want to break out of the self-imposed prison of drug abuse into which they have become incarcerated. Under proper supervision and with the right direction, such individuals have been able to free themselves from the bondage of drug abuse by giving service to the handicapped in Special Olympic activities, by being involved in community cleanup activities, by spending quality time with the elderly in nursing homes and day care programs, by serving as aides and tutors in public school programs, and by engaging in any number of other community service activities. It is a matter of common knowledge that service to others can be very therapeutic to the service provider. For the drug abuser, it is a viable alternate reinforcer that can bring the individual more satisfaction—and an even greater high—than is realized from "shooting drugs." It is certainly worth parents' efforts to involve their drug-abusing children in activities which provide services to others.

The Harvard study cited above spoke of the restoration of hope by "an emphasis on spiritual renewal and moral regeneration." I am continually amazed at what the research has taught us about the importance of spiritual and moral values in the establishment and maintenance of personal happiness and well-being. I'm not going to review that literature here, but it is sufficient

> **Emphasize the need for "spiritual renewal and moral regeneration."**

to say that in families where religious values are taught and practiced, and where families actively participate in the activities and offerings of the church of their choice, social and personal problems, including substance abuse, are remarkably less probable. One of the 12 steps to recovery of Alcoholics Anonymous—the most successful program in history in the fight against alcoholism—specifies the need for the recovering alcoholic to accept into his or her life a "higher spiritual value." When I was in the armed services, and topics of a religious or spiritual nature were discussed, it was frequently noted that "There are no atheists in the fox hole," the point being that when conditions get life-threateningly bad, nothing provides more hope than the promise of help from a higher source.

And so it is with individuals who are captive to the addictive effects of alcohol, tobacco, and drugs. Recently, an individual very dear to me who had suffered with alcoholism for nearly 20 years—and in the process lost his family and his health—told me, "The thought overwhelmed me like a flood that I could not beat this alone so I dropped to my knees and pleaded with my God for help! When I got up off my knees, I knew I could beat it, and I am beating it. Not only have I not had a drink for three months, I don't even have a taste nor a desire for drink. Furthermore, I'm avoiding those places where I would be tempted and inclined to drink." These are not the kinds of cause and effect relationships that can be explained by science, but we know they exist and I urge parents to consider them as they work with their children to keep them away from drugs in the first place or to break the grip of substance abuse in their lives.

Lastly, as pointed out in Chapter 25, When All Else Fails, maintain the bonds of love and affection with your children even when they are struggling—and perhaps losing the battle—with drugs. Never cast them out of your lives! I repeat, NEVER CAST THEM OUT OF YOUR LIVES. Keep talking to them. We know that in homes where parents and their children are able to talk with one another with ease and with mutual respect, problems with drugs decrease remarkably.

> There is a vast difference between experimenting with drugs and abusing drugs.

If you find that a child has used drugs or is experimenting with them, don't come unglued. There is a vast difference between experimenting with drugs and abusing drugs. Nearly all children (including many of us when we were kids!) "try drugs." If you find that your child is using drugs (including alcohol and tobacco), use that as an opportunity to get close to the child, to bond, and to demonstrate in your home and family what great leadership is. Suppose it has been known that your child has been experimenting with controlled substances. Your encounter with the child might go like this:

## Encounter 1: The child is not happy and wants help.

Parent:   "I understand you've been experimenting with drugs (or alcohol or tobacco). I can imagine that the pressures you experience to do that sort of thing must be pretty great. How do you feel about all of that? How do you cope?"

Child:   "I don't feel good about it, and I'm not coping very well. But I don't know what to do. It is really hard to say no when your friends are doing it and putting pressure on you to do it, too."

Parent:   "I suppose one thing you could do would be to change your circle of friends, but that would probably be pretty tough."

Child:   "I've thought of that. I don't know if I could do it or not."

*Note:* Don't try to convince your child that his/her friends are no good and should be dumped. That has to be the kid's choice, and pressure exerted by parents would just produce counter-coercive resistance and the kid would be more determined to remain a part of that peer group. Rather, try to teach the child how to survive with his/her peers and to gradually make the change to a better group. And don't forget, members of that peer group might regard *your* kid as one of the problems. It can all be pretty relative.

338

Parent: "I can understand that. I have friends who aren't the best influence in the world, still there are things about them I enjoy—at least in small doses. Do you have friends that are less inclined to want to fool around with drugs (or what ever) who feel like you do?"

Child: "Oh yeah."

Parent: "Do you ever talk to them about what you can do to change things?"

*Note:* Use words like "change things" rather than "stop what you're doing." It's less assertive and leaves more room for the child to do some of his/her own problem solving.

Child: "Sometimes, but neither one of us knows what to do. We aren't much help to each other."

Parent: "If you'd be interested, there is some interesting stuff out about what's called "Training in Life Skills." It teaches people specific things they can do and say in tough social situations, how to handle stress, and have self control. If you and your friend(s) would like to learn about it, let me know. I'm sure I could arrange for someone to visit with you about it. It's really good stuff."

Child: "Sounds good."

Parent: "Think it over. Talk to your friend(s) and if you'd like to know more, let me know."

*Note:* Invite your child *and* his/her friend(s). There is strength in numbers, and they will be able to help and reinforce one another when they are back among their friends.

Child: "I will. Thanks."

Parent: "In the meantime, I just want you to know that I love you and am terribly, terribly concerned for your well-being. Take care of yourself. Be wise. You know, it's possible to be a friend and still make wise decisions. Let me help when I can. I love you."

Child: "Thanks. I love you, too."

And leave it there. The child has had a great bonding experience, has been reassured of the parent's love, an unconditional love, and has been given something to think about and to possibly act upon. Everything was positive. The child hasn't been made to feel inadequate, the child's friends have not been put down, nor has the child been told what to do—"in no uncertain terms!" The child has known all along that things weren't right. Telling the child he/she was in trouble would have been like telling an inmate in Sing Sing that he was in prison. No one knows that better than the kid. Never tell someone something he already knows!

### Encounter 2: The child is apathetic, even resistant.

Parent: "I understand you've been experimenting with drugs (or whatever). I can imagine that the pressures you experience to do that sort of thing must be pretty great. How do you feel about all of that? How do you cope?"

Child: "It's no big deal. We just mess around with it. No one's hooked. It's just the in thing to do. I'm not worried. Don't worry about it."

Parent: "I appreciate the reassurance that we have nothing to worry about; but, of course, we do. Why would we be concerned?"

Child: "Parents are always worrying about something. I don't know why. Nothing that bad's going on. It's no big deal."

Parent: "You're right. We do worry. Can you imagine why?"

Note: The parent remained on course. Without being confrontive, the parent came right back to the question at hand: "Why are we concerned?"

Child: "I guess it's because you think I'm going to screw up my life. Become a junk head. Get busted. Land up in the gutter or the slammer or the morgue. No way! I'm okay. I'm just having a little fun with my friends!"

Parent: "You surely have a good idea of where our concerns lie. You're right on target there!"

At this point the discussion could move in any one of several directions. The parent might continue to pursue concerns about the inherent dangers of "playing with fire." Should that course be taken, care must be exercised that emotions are kept under control, that a lot of advice isn't given, and the discussion doesn't go on so long that the child gets turned off.

The direction of the discussion could change to focus on things the child could do and skills that could be learned when, in time, the child decides he/she needs help and wants to change.

> Don't be afraid to discuss with all the children a sibling's problems with drugs.

The discussion could center on parental expectations and the natural and logical consequences of high-risk life styles. Should this be the direction the discussion goes, care should be taken to avoid ultimatums, coercion, guilt trips, or anything else that would drive the child further away from the family and the family values.

Remember, you want to keep the child at home and as much a part of the family unit as possible, even though his/her presence might, at times, be distasteful. In this regard, talking to the other children about the errant child's behavior is a good thing. When doing this, be careful that attention is drawn to the character of the behavior, not the character of the child. Love and concern for the child must stand above all else! The behavior is what's not good. Be sure the other children in the family feel free to talk about the problem without it turning into a lecture of "And for heaven's sake don't *you* do those stupid things!"

Whatever direction the discussion goes, be certain you as a parent never allow yourself to be drawn off course onto dead-end paths that get no one anywhere. The discussion in Encounter 2 (above) might end with the parent saying simply, "Well, it's obvious we see this matter from much different perspectives. My appeal to you is to be very careful. We both know there are dangers inherent in these things. As your parent, I just don't want you to be hurt. You mean the world to me, so, please, be careful. I love you." And let it go at that. The child will get the message, and at the moment, that just might be the best you can hope for. The chances are good that opportunities will be available later to continue the discussion more productively. In the meantime, remember, today is not forever. Leave the door open for more talking.

Parents frequently ask me how to protect their other children from the destructive influences of a sibling who is behaving badly. In such instances, parents should be concerned. Judith Brook, author of an article entitled "Sibling Influence on Adolescent Drug Use: Older Brothers on Younger Brothers," published in a 1991 edition of the *Journal of the American Academy of Child and Adolescent Psychiatry*, reported that older brothers had a profound effect on a younger brother's risk of using drugs. This is particularly significant in instances where everyone is living in the same house and the parents want to keep it that way, hoping the good influence of the family will have a greater impact than will the possibly bad influence of the errant one. In addressing this quandary, these three scenarios come to mind:

## Scenario #1:

The parents state their expectations to a misbehaving though willing-to-cooperate child.

Parents:  "We are concerned that the other children might be wrongly influenced by the things you're doing. We need your help to make sure that doesn't happen. Will you cooperate with us?"

Child:  "Sure. That's cool."

Parents:  "First, though you have chosen to use tobacco/drugs/alcohol, you must never bring these things home, nor show them to your brothers and sisters. Can we count on you to comply with that expectation?"

*Note*: Get verbal agreement of each point along the way.

Child: "Yeah. Well, but what if I don't have any place to put them? What am I supposed to do, hide 'em in the shrubs?"

Parents: "When we say you are not to bring them home, we mean you are not to bring them onto our property *or* into the house. We don't have any suggestions for how you'll manage that. We only want to be sure that they are never a part of our home environment. Furthermore, if we ever find any of these things on or in our property, they will be destroyed—no questions asked."

*Note:* The child must understand that you, as parents, will not facilitate in the least any use of controlled substances. If you use any of these things and are challenged on that basis, I'm not sure what you would say to justify your position while at the same time strengthening your case relative to the child's behavior.

Child: "Does that mean you're going to search me and my room everyday?"

Parents: "Not regularly or without cause. However, if we have reason to suspect these substances are in the house, and are potentially dangerous to the children, we will look for them and destroy anything we find. Why do we take this position?"

Child: "'Cause you don't want them to get started on the stuff. But if they do, don't blame me. I'm not the only one in their lives who use this stuff, you know. You can pick this stuff up anywhere. That's how I got started."

Parents: "We are sure that is sadly true. Furthermore, if we find drugs at home, we will call the police. Breaking the law at home is no more justified than breaking the law away from home. We will not allow ourselves to be made accessories to a crime. Why would we take such a strong position?"

Child: "Hey, I know what you're driving at. Don't worry. I'll keep the place clean."

Parents: "Good. We're glad you understand and are going to cooperate. One other thing. When talking to your brothers and sisters, never say anything to glorify the use of this stuff or to make them curious about it. Suppose one of the kids asks you about it. What do you say?"

Child: "I'll just tell them to forget it. To bug off."

Parents: What would you say to discourage them from trying this stuff?"

Child: "I'd tell 'em it's a loser; to stay away from it or they could turn out like me."

Parents: "We appreciate your help. Furthermore, we want you to be an active, participating member of the family. We want nothing to do with this stuff, but lots to do with you."

*Note:* Don't get sucked into a discussion about whether or not the child is a loser. Just be sure the child knows he/she is valued and is regarded as a viable member of the family.

I realize that a discussion would not likely go just as I have portrayed it. The points to remember are (a) stay with your expectations, (b) be clear about consequences, and (c) assure the child of your unconditional love. That's really the best you can do. If you try to force your position, the child can simply tell you to hang it in your ear and be gone. You will have simply driven a wedge into the very space where you need to build bridges and bonds. Either way, it's risky, but building bridges and bonds between you and your children is a lot less risky than driving wedges between you!

## Scenario 2:

The parents state their expectations to a misbehaving though less-than-willing-to-cooperate child.

Parents: "We are concerned that the other children might be wrongly influenced by the things you're doing. We need your help to make sure that doesn't happen. Will you cooperate with us?"

Child: "Hey, I got nothing to hide. This is me. I have nothing to apologize for, or explain, to anybody. I'm not hurting anyone—not even myself, despite what you think! I'm not the terrible person you think I am."

*Note:* Again, stick only with your expectations. This is no time to get into a life-style or character analysis.

Parents: "Will you cooperate with us in our efforts to make sure the children are not exposed in our home to alcohol/tobacco/drugs?"

Child: "Whaddaya mean, not exposed!"

Parents: "We mean a couple of things. First, you must never bring any of this stuff onto our property or into the house, and secondly, you must never invite the children to use it or to become curious about using it. Do you have any questions at all about what we expect?"

Child: "Hey, you can't tell me what to do with my stuff. If I keep it to myself you got no reason to worry. I'm not going to bother the kids. I want nothing to do with 'em anyway. The less I see of them the better."

Parents: "We are pleased to know that you have no intentions to introduce the children to it. Thanks for that assurance. As far as what you do with the stuff, you need to know that if we ever find any of it at home, it will be destroyed immediately, no questions asked."

Child: "Hey! Look! If I'm going to be searched every time I come home, or you're going to search my room when I'm not here, I just won't come home."

Parents: "We have no plans to search you or your room unless we have reason to believe you are breaking the law and we could be accessories to the fact. We will not shield you from the law, nor facilitate your breaking it. Why would we take that position?"

Child: "I know what you're saying. Okay. I'll stay clean at home."

Parents: "Super. We appreciate that. Also, we really want you to be with us and to participate in family activities. We love you tons and tons and enjoy having you around."

*Note*: Relative to both scenarios, the likelihood is great that the child will still bring "stuff" into the house. If it's kept out of sight of the children, don't go after it. If, however, it is carelessly or flagrantly displayed, destroy it—no questions asked. If illegal drugs are involved, you would be well advised to have the police (preferably in street clothes) search the premises. The child needs to know in advance that this is a distinct possibility. Home should be a refuge *from* social ills, not a safe harbor for social ills. When children learn that, they will soon come to value it, respect it, and hold it sacred.

## Scenario 3:

The parents visit with the "other" children about the behavior of a misbehaving sibling.

Parents: "We want to visit with you tonight about Pat. We have some serious concerns. April, why do you suppose we are concerned?"

*Note:* Get the others into the conversation as quickly as possible.

April: "I guess it's because he/she is doing things that are wrong."

Parents: "Yes. Unhappily for all of us, Pat has decided to do some things that can be very destructive to a person. Things that can ruin a person's life. When we say 'ruin a person's life,' what does that mean, Joseph?"

Joseph: "Well, I guess it means it can hurt them in some way. Maybe even kill them."

Parents: "Exactly. And because of that, we are very concerned about Pat. We would never want something like that to happen to any of our children. Not Pat, not you, not anyone."

Greg: "Ah, it isn't that bad. You're making it sound a lot worse than it is. Pat's just messing around. It's not this big a deal."

Parents: "I hope you're right, Greg. At the moment, that's our biggest hope. But what Pat is doing is very, very risky. What do I mean, Greg, when I say 'very, very risky,' and why would that concern us?"

Greg: "It means that Pat is taking some big chances with his/her life and could get hurt. And you don't want that to happen. But I still think you're blowing this out of proportion."

*Note:* Notice how the parent is not arguing with Greg about the seriousness of the situation. That's a beside-the-point matter and should be ignored. Stay with the central issues.

Parents: "Thanks for hitting the nail on the head regarding our concerns. Pat is taking big chances and certainly could get hurt.

"Nevertheless, despite the fact that she/he is behaving badly in that regard, we love Pat as much as we love any of you, and all of us must be kind, say nice things, be complimentary whenever we can, be playful and fun, and do nothing that would suggest we are angry or disappointed. Will you do that? Mary, what is something you can do when Pat comes home that will show you love him/her?"

Mary: "I can give him/her a big hug and a kiss and say I love you."

Parents: "That would be wonderful. I'll look forward to seeing you do that."

Greg: "That's all well and good, but what bugs me is when Pat gets away with stuff we can't do. I have to be in by 10:00 on school nights and Pat comes home whenever she/he darn well pleases. That's just not fair!"

Parents: "You've raised a very important point, Greg. It surely doesn't seem fair. But she/he pays a dear price for the privilege of coming and going as she/he wants. What is that price, Greg?"

Greg: "Well, she/he never has use of the car, for one thing. Nor does she/he get an allowance. I guess that's it."

Parents: "That's part of the price she/he pays, certainly. Would it be worth it to you, Greg, or any of you children, to pay such a price to behave that way? What about you, April? Would you be willing to give up all telephone privileges, your allowance, and the purchase of any new clothes, to name a few, for the privilege of coming home late at night?"

April: "No way!"

Parents: "What about you, Joseph? What privileges would you be willing to give up just so you could come home after hours?"

Joseph: "I suppose you're talking about my Nintendo, my bike, my allowance— that kind of stuff. I'd rather come home on time."

Parents: "I think you guys have gotten the point. Pat isn't *getting* anything for free. She/he is giving up a lot of things that none of you want to give up. Pat is paying a very big price to behave the way she/he is behaving."

"Greg, a moment ago you raised the issue of fairness. This really isn't a fairness issue. It's a matter of how much one is willing to give up to behave in a certain way. When you get to be Pat's age, you will be able to do things you want to do, despite how we or anyone else feels about it. We hope you will make wise decisions, decisions that won't cost you. What do we mean when we say 'decisions that won't cost you?'"

Greg: "Oh, I suppose you mean giving up things like the use of the car, and stuff like that."

Parents: "That could be part of the cost. What else? What if the decision is to break the law? What can that cost you?"

Greg: "If it's bad enough, it could cost me money, or even my freedom."

Parents: "Precisely. And what a terrible price that would be to pay."

"April, what would the cost be to you if you resisted the temptation to take drugs? If you said 'NO,' and just walked away?"

April:       "Oh, it might cost me a friend. Then again, maybe it wouldn't. Maybe there wouldn't be any cost at all, only benefits."

Parents:     "What do you mean, no cost at all, only benefits?"

April:       "Well, a *real* friend would never offer me drugs, and by staying clean, I have good health."

             *Note:* The parents steered the discussion away from negatives and toward positives. They got the children thinking about how much better off they are by behaving well than how bad off they are by behaving badly.

Remember, behavior is shaped better by positive than by negative consequences.

A recent study demonstrated that in homes where children and their parents are able to just talk with one another, the probability of children experimenting with drugs in the first place is half that of homes where parents and their children have problems talking with one another.

Also, maintain appropriate physical contact with your children who are struggling with drugs, alcohol, and tobacco. As I have noted elsewhere in this book, research has shown conclusively a positive relationship between appropriate physical contact between parents and their children, and the physical and emotional well-being of children. Studies done years ago identified a syndrome called "Narasmus," a disease among infants resulting in a "wasting-away" and even death as a result of being deprived of human touch. Hugs, pats on the back, back rubs, wrestling, an affectionate elbow in the ribs and tap to the shoulder—all of these are appropriate ways of maintaining important and necessary physical contact with children. These are doubly important with children who are struggling with substance abuse problems.

Research by Drs. Richard West and Richard Young and their associates at Utah State University has identified critical risk factors that have been associated with increased probability of eventual substance use and abuse. The risk factors are: (1) Absent or poorly developed social interaction skills; (2) Inadequate academic and academic-related skills; (3) Problems in family interactions and relationships; (4) Inadequate motivation and self management skills; (5) Pro-drug and insufficient drug knowledge and education; and (6) Drug use by peer group members. By looking at those six "critical risk factors," it is altogether evident that parents have a great responsibility to create in their homes an environment where children will learn the necessary skills needed to remain drug free as well as where children will acquire a relationship with their parents that will help decrease the probability that they will have problems with drugs.

In closing this chapter, it is appropriate once again to reflect upon "probabilities." When raising our children and shaping their lives, we can only hope to create an environment in our homes, including a relationship with our children, that will increase the probabilities that their behavior will develop in the right direction; and should they stumble and even fall along the way, they will have the necessary skills to pick themselves

> *When parents and children talk a lot with one another, drug problems tend to be less.*

up, set themselves aright, and move ahead in the direction of being healthy, productive, contributing members of society. Occasionally, even with our best efforts, this grand, hoped-for scenario may not be realized. But by doing the things suggested, illustrated, outlined, and demonstrated in this book, the chances of achieving this "grand and hoped-for scenario" are remarkably improved, even with children who abuse tobacco, alcohol, and drugs.

## NOW TO REVIEW

1.  The number one best way to prevent substance abuse problems is to create an environment in the home and the family that makes being free of dependency more reinforcing than being dependent.

2.  If children do experiment with substance abuse, parents are advised to not "come unglued." They should, rather, treat it with empathy and understanding, reaffirm their expectations, allow consequences to deliver the message, and strengthen the bonds between them and their children.

3.  Children who are substance abusers should be encouraged to remain at home as long as possible, and while living at home, be encouraged to participate in family activities, but to not encourage siblings to tamper with, or be curious about, the use of drugs/alcohol/tobacco.

4.  Siblings who do not abuse substances should be taught to show love and concern for any member of the family who does engage in substance abuse, but should also be taught how to avoid invitations to be users of drugs/alcohol/tobacco.

> *Research has shown that the most effective way to reduce problem behavior in children is to strengthen desirable behavior through positive reinforcement rather than trying to weaken undesirable behavior using aversive or negative processes.*
> S.W. Bijou
> The International Encyclopedia of Education, 1988

*If at first you don't succeed, fail, fail again.*

# TWENTY-FIVE
# When All Else Fails

The great majority of parents work extremely hard raising their children to be happy, responsible, productive adults who are a complement to family and society. These parents certainly want the best for their children. Despite how hard we try and despite our good intentions, it is not unusual for a child to rebel against the family value system and behave in ways that bring considerable pain and heartache to parents. Parents of such children frequently ask me, "What did we do wrong?" or "What should we have done differently?" In trying to answer such questions, parents will grasp at almost anything. It's as though knowing what they did wrong will solve the mystery and bring some comfort. They assume, of course, that they *did* do something dreadfully wrong and *are* to blame.

> **All parents make mistakes, but that is not necessarily reason for guilt.**

It is true, as parents we all make mistakes. Sometimes pretty serious mistakes. But as I work with wayward sons and daughters, they tell me almost to a person that their decisions to behave badly (and virtually all of them acknowledge that they are behaving badly) were their own; their parents are not to blame. Waywardness is a category of behavior that is very, very complex, too complex to be addressed here. Though it is reasonable that parents would feel bad, and though they probably did make some mistakes, they must not assume that they are *necessarily* altogether to blame for their children's waywardness. Even if parents are in some degree "to blame," looking back to discover and assess blame is of no value unless something can be learned which parents can use to interact better with their wayward children in the future. In other words, don't look for answers to questions unless those answers will provide information that will facilitate problem solving.

In this chapter are five suggestions for working with a wayward child. It is doubtful that by even following all of these suggestions one can expect any rapid changes to take place in a wayward child's behavior. Only rarely, and in unusual circumstances, does behavior change dramatically and stay changed, as was discussed earlier on pages 143–145. Great trauma and unmistakable threats to life can, but don't always, produce dramatic and lasting changes in a person's behavior. Many years ago my Uncle Harley was dying of lung cancer in a Los Angeles hospital. His brother-in-law, Uncle Adolph, went to the hospital to visit him to see if he could bring comfort and solace at this tragic moment in Harley's life. As Uncle Adolph entered the hospital room he was jolted by the pungent odor of disease, then shocked at the sight of the emaciated body of a man who only a short time earlier had been robust and the picture of health. Standing at Harley's bedside, holding his fleshless hand, Adolf greeted him with forced good cheer. But there was no response. Too weak even to smile, the only show of emotion that signaled Harley's awareness of his visitor were tears welling up in the corners of his eyes. At that moment of undeniable truth, the doctor walked in and said, simply, "Lung cancer caused by smoking." Immediately, Adolf, a life-long smoker, took his smokes from his shirt pocket and threw them in a waste basket. To this day, over 30 years later, Adolf has not put into his mouth tobacco of any kind. A moment of trauma had a remarkable effect on reversing the course of a life-long behavior. As parents, of course, we can't, nor should we try, to create these traumatic experiences as a way of teaching life's lessons to wayward children. These kinds of experiences are the best teachers when they occur naturally and unexpectedly in the course of one's life. Alcoholics have told me that nothing a loved one or a family member could have said would have altered their

*Some behaviors will change only in the face of natural, traumatic consequences.*

drinking habits. Those who have succeeded in kicking the alcohol habit did it only after they came to the undeniable realization that if they didn't change their behavior they would die or suffer some personally anguishing fate. As one reformed alcoholic told me, "I had to hit bottom so hard and then bounce a couple of times before I realized I simply had to change." Consequences delivered the message so powerfully that it couldn't be ignored, and the course of his behavior changed. Unfortunately, as parents we are sometimes left with no alternative but to wait and hope that wayward children will learn from the consequences of their own behavior, and that they will survive to benefit from those consequences.

The following suggestions do not involve trauma, nor are they expected to produce remarkable changes in a hurry. Rather, they are ways of building a relationship which, over time, has a high probability for bringing a child back into the value system. On page 136, Figure 6.1 illustrates the point I want to make. During childhood it is relatively easy to keep a child within the value system. During the childhood years, up to about age 12 or 13, parents can generally exercise sufficient direct and consequential control over their children to keep them in the value system. During these early childhood years, children tend to mind their parents. It seems to them to be the thing to do. But as they enter adolescence and come under the reinforcement control of influences outside the home (usually the peer group) that are more powerful than direct parental control, the tendency for them to leave the value system increases. As discussed in Chapter 6, during these adolescent years (from about 12 through 19) some children will leave the value system entirely, preferring the reinforcers that are made available to them by their peer groups to the reinforcers available to them at home.

> **Learn to endure waywardness well!**

How rapidly they come back to the family and back to the family value system is in large measure a function of the quality of their relationship with the family during the time they were "wayward." This is nicely borne out in Emmy Werner's fascinating study published in the April 1989 issue of *Scientific American* under the title "Children of the Garden Island." She reported:

> Among the critical turning points in the lives of troubled youths were entry into military service, marriage, parenthood, and active partici-pation in a church group. In adulthood, as in their youth, most of these individuals relied on informal rather than formal sources of support: kith and kin rather than mental-health professionals and social-service agencies.

Here are the suggestions I encourage you to seriously consider if you have a wayward child.

## 1. Accept the Child As Is and Go On with Life

First, accept the child and his/her waywardness as a matter of fact and prepare yourself to endure that reality. In fact, prepare yourself to endure it well. By that I mean that though the child is wayward and out of control, it doesn't mean you have to be wayward and out of control as well. Go on with your life, smile and laugh a lot, and take hope in the fact that in all probability, things will be better in a few years. I know, that isn't what parents want to hear. They want something that is going to fix this kid up by tomorrow evening at the latest. Well, it isn't going to happen, but this doesn't mean that things are hopeless or that all is lost forever. Just remember, most children who go off the deep end as adolescents eventually resurface as responsible adults. Once the reinforcers of adolescent waywardness have all been spent, reason and maturity begin to have a chance, the family value system begins to make sense, and a new adult emerges.

> *Most children who go off the deep end as adolescents eventually resurface as responsible adults.*

## 2. While Children Are Astray, Parents Must Double Their Efforts to Secure and Strengthen the Bonds of Love and Concern Between Them and Their Children

There is a saying that goes, "Kids who deserve love the least need it the most." I encourage parents to rise above their disappointments, to quit lecturing the better life to their children, to stop grieving, and to start giving. Hug them, hug them every day. Tell them you love them everyday. Smile at them and laugh with them even though you might be weeping or are furiously angry inside. As I noted earlier, if necessary, put on a bit of an act. It must be a sincere act, however. But the more you act the way you should, the more genuine that act becomes until it is no longer an act. Behave towards them as though you couldn't possibly love them more. You will *feel* better and they will *get* better. I have never met a kid who didn't want his parents' genuine love. He or she might disappoint you. After all, kids are kids. But don't you disappoint them. After all, you are the adult, the person you want your child to become, so set a good model. This is called unconditional love. You love them anyway.

## 3. Never Shield Children from the Responsibility and Consequences of Their Behavior

Consequences are the greatest teachers in our lives. If we protect our children against the consequences of their behavior we distort reality and interfere with healthy growth and development. When children do things that cause them problems, avoid saying things like, "Oh, it really isn't your fault," or "They shouldn't have made such a fuss over such a little thing," or "I know you didn't really mean to do it so everything is okay." I remember as a boy hurting myself doing something I was told never to do. When I went to my mother for comfort, she simply acknowledged that it must have been painful, and then said, "That's the kind of thing that happens when we aren't careful." She didn't scold me for being careless nor place the blame for my suffering on something else. It was one of the greatest lessons I ever learned in my life.

I've lost count of the number of parents I've worked with who insist on protecting their children from experiencing the consequences of their behavior. I recall one family whose son decided, prematurely, to strike out on his own. He had taken up some bad habits which were diametrically opposed to the family value system and this caused considerable friction between him and his parents, so he moved out. He took a job at a local supermarket as a checkstand grocery bagger. Every few days, his father would go shopping at that store, and he always checked out at the checkstand where his son was working. As he paid for his groceries, and still had his wallet in his hand, he would ask his son how he was doing. Invariably the boy would put on his saddest face and tell his father how hard it was to make ends meet on the meager wages of a checkstand bagger. Without fail his father (who was a wealthy business man) would hand the boy several dollars as a token of his concern and love for the boy. It was, without doubt, the absolutely worst thing the father could have done. The boy never did learn to deal with the consequences of his own behavior. To this day, as a man in his late 30s, he is still irresponsible and no closer to the family nor to the family value system than he was as a boy.

## 4. Support the Institutions of Society That Disperse Consequences

If a child gets a speeding ticket, don't blame the police. If a child gets caught shoplifting, don't blame company security. If a child is caught in possession of alcohol, tobacco, or drugs and is required to go to juvenile court, don't blame the juvenile justice system or the courts. It is true, from time to time the police are wrong, the company security forces are wrong and the juvenile justice system is wrong, but they are less likely to be wrong than is the child less likely to be guilty. I'm aware of one study that documented that for every offense for which children are brought to justice, they commit ten equally serious offenses for which they are never caught.

> **Getting caught is probably the best thing that can happen to children who engage in unlawful behavior.**

Getting caught is probably the best thing that can happen to children who are engaged in unlawful behavior. And when caught, parents should certainly support the institutions that are there to protect us all against the abuses of others even if those others are our own children. Although I am personally disturbed by much of the undue coerciveness of our justice system, I believe for the most part our police are conscientious, want to do what is best for the individual, are genuinely concerned about the welfare of individuals even when those individuals are behaving badly, and are doing the best they can under difficult circumstances. If they are right and the kid is wrong then the kid should understand that parental support is on the side of right and that being on the side of right is in the best interest of the child. One of our daughters was caught shoplifting at one of the local department stores and had to go to juvenile court. I can remember how personally painful it was watching her account for her misdeeds before that judge. We hated being in that courtroom. We didn't deserve to be there. We had done nothing wrong! But despite the discomfort and the unfairness of it all to us as parents, we couldn't allow our own discomfort to deprive our daughter of the lesson she had to learn as a consequence of her own behavior. Happily, the consequences were sufficiently devastating to her that she learned the lesson well and it put an end to that behavior. Several years later I was approached by a gentleman I didn't recognize. He introduced himself as the department store security officer who had apprehended our daughter. He asked how she was doing and expressed genuine concern for her well being. I told him that she was doing just great, that she had learned a great lesson, and as a family we appreciated what he had done in her behalf. Then he said something that I thought was quite remarkable: "If more parents would allow those opportunities to be learning experiences rather than an invitation to become defensive, *more* kids would turn out just great."

## 5. Use Empathy and Understanding

As wayward children experience the consequences of their own behavior, parents must not be hard, judgmental, or insensitive. Rather, we should be empathetic and understanding though unyielding in terms of justice. Indeed, mercy must not rob justice, but it is important to respond to the unpleasant consequences our wayward children experience as a result of their behavior by saying things like, "I'm sure you must be hurting. I am really sorry it has come to this. Despite all that is unfortunate about this, please rest assured that we love you. You are not abandoned." These are bond-building responses, and the stronger the bonds the more likely the child will return to the value system as an adult. Whatever you do don't say some stupid thing like, "Well, I tried to warn you. But no, you wouldn't listen! Now look at the mess you're in. To say nothing about what you've done to the whole family!"

I reiterate, today is not forever. Children who are wayward as youth are far more likely than not to grow up to be responsible, contributing, productive, happy adults who love their parents, love their siblings, and become loving parents. The probability of that happening increases dramatically when we as parents respond to that waywardness appropriately, when we respond in ways that

> **Mercy must not rob justice.**

strengthen the bonds between us and them. As I have repeatedly cautioned in this book, don't throw your wayward children away. Don't kick them out of the house. If at all possible, keep them home within the positive and reinforcing sphere of your influence. Though it might take a few years, even several years, for the child to get his act together, the wait is well worth it.

## Now to Review

1. Accept the child as is. Practice unconditional love.

2. While the child is astray, double your efforts to secure and strengthen the bonds of love and concern between you and the child.

3. Never shield a child from the responsibility and consequences of his/her behavior.

4. Support the institutions of society that dispense consequences.

5. Use empathy and understanding, but don't allow mercy to rob justice.

> *Research has shown that the most effective way to reduce problem behavior in children is to strengthen desirable behavior through positive reinforcement rather than trying to weaken undesirable behavior using aversive or negative processes.*
> *S.W. Bijou*
> *The International Encyclopedia of Education, 1988*

*How do I love thee? Let me count the ways.*
     *Robert Browning*

# TWENTY-SIX
# For Husbands and Wives/
# Moms and Dads

From time-to-time throughout this book, I've emphasized the need for parents to have a good relationship with one another since that has such a powerful influence on children. At this point, I am taking the opportunity to stress that. Whether parents are married and living together, or separated or divorced—in any event—children *will* be affected by their behavior. Regardless of the nature of the relationship, if parents behave themselves well, their children will tend to behave well. If the parents squabble and carry on badly, their children tend to do poorly. And in instances where children get caught in the crossfire between warring parents over visitation rights, financial support, and divorce court-appointed custody issues—well, that tends to be devastating to kids for a thousand reasons. When adults, in this case parents, behave worse than kids and the kids are trying to figure out what adulthood is all about—with badly behaving parents as their models—the consequences are predictably grim for the kids.

> **Divorce is not a skill-building activity.**

Parents, do your level best to love each other. If you need professional help to learn how to do that, get it. It's a lot less expensive than divorce lawyers. Learn the skills you need to be successful in marriage. In this day and age, successful marriages are almost certainly dependent on good marital skills. If a couple get a divorce because they lack the skills to make that marriage work, it is highly unlikely they will have the skills they need to make another marriage work. Divorce is not a skill-building activity. In fact, if couples in marital trouble would work as hard at marriage as they do at divorce, few marriages would fail.

I recall a talk show I recently listened to. The fellow being interviewed had been married seven or eight times (I don't recall exactly). The interviewer asked him, "What have you learned from being married so many times?" The man's answer was classic: "I should have made the first one work."

We have some really dumb notions about what a good marriage is, and almost no models of good marriage. The great love stories, whether in the classics or in fairy tales,

> *The key to a happy marriage is unselfish service to one's spouse.*

never portray love *in* marriage. Such stories all end at or before marriage. Think about it. Romeo and Juliet, Snow White, Camelot, Beauty and the Beast, the Little Mermaid—the story ends, the curtain comes down *at* marriage, not *in* marriage. As some astute observer noted, "All marriages are happy. It's living together afterwards that causes trouble." Chaucer, in fact, ridiculed "courtly love" (love before marriage) and said it should end with marriage.

So how is marriage portrayed? Badly, I fear. I'm reminded of the woman who said, "I never married because I don't need a man. I have a dog that barks at me all morning, a parrot that swears at me all afternoon, and a cat who always comes home late at night."

I heard a cute story that was reported to me as true. A young man and his fiance were attending a reception in honor of her great-grandparent's 75th wedding anniversary. Wanting to get his own marriage off on the right foot, the groom-to-be sought the advice of the great-grandfather. He asked, "Sir, what advice do you have for me as I am about to marry your great-granddaughter?" The old man motioned the boy to lean down. Whispering into the boy's ear, he said, "Don't do it!"

Though I doubt the validity of this next anecdote, in this context, it's worth telling. Another couple who had been married 75 years went to a divorce lawyer to dissolve their marriage. The lawyer plead with them to stay together, then asked, "Why get a divorce now after all these years of marriage?" The wife, in her creaky old voice, answered, "We wanted to wait until the children were all dead."

In sharp contrast to this is a remarkable event with which I am personally familiar. An elderly couple had two of their sons and their families over for Sunday dinner. As the father and his sons left the dinner table and were walking into the living room, the father fell to the floor with a massive heart attack. The commotion brought the others into the living room. The one son, a medical doctor, immediately tried to resuscitate his father, but with no success. Still kneeling at his father's side, the son looked up at his grief-stricken mother and said, "I'm sorry, Mother, Daddy's dead." She responded, "I cannot live without him," and fell dead at his side.

What's the difference between the two extremes portrayed here? Why, on the one hand, is marriage so badly represented, while on the other hand it is such a compelling relationship that one would willfully die for it? Certainly a thorough answer to that question is far beyond the scope of this book. But as simple as it might sound, as I study marital relationships and why some fail and some succeed, why some chug along, spitting and sputtering year after year, and why others liltingly sail and soar on one refreshing breeze after another, I have to conclude that at the heart of either is the matter of putting the needs of others before one's own needs. Marriages that succeed and sail find husbands and wives putting their spouse's needs first. They serve the other with all their hearts. They treat one another like kings and queens. Marriages that fail, or that limp along sick and wounded, are those where spouses regard *their* happiness as a function of how well the other behaves, and if he/she "would just shape up, everything would be wonderful." Well, folks, I hate to tell you this, but it just doesn't work that way.

Furthermore, the move to putting the other first almost always has to start with one *or* the other. Rarely do both husband and wife make the switch at the same time. One leads and the other eventually follows—in most instances. But it takes a while: days, weeks, sometimes months or more. Obviously, in some instances, particularly where abuse (of whatever type), neglect, and severe psychological/behavioral problems persist, the relationship may not only be intolerable, it might be potentially dangerous and must be dissolved.

But for the most part, in the great majority of instances, the problem marriages I work with boil down to "my happiness depends on your shaping up, so shape up or else." Unfortunately, "or else," sometimes gets translated by unstable minds to mean, "If I have to, I'll beat it into you." That notion has a long history in our system of things. I suspect you've heard the term "rule of thumb." Do you know its origin? It was a part of English common law, and later early American law, which allowed a husband to beat his wife with a rod no larger than the base of his thumb.

> *Most of the marriage problems I work with boil down to "my happiness depends on your shaping up, so shape up or else!"*

Between the dark side of its historical past, its trashy characterization in movies and on TV, and people's natural tendency to put themselves ahead of all else, is it any wonder that marriages drop like flies. And when they do, particularly where dependent children are involved, kids suffer.

My good friend, Dr. Glen Jenson of the College of Family Life, Utah State University, wrote a wonderful article entitled "Why and How to Treat Your Mate Like a Dog." He pointed out that a good way to improve your marriage would be to treat your mate the way a dog owner's manual recommends you treat your dog:

1. Reward your mate even for simple things.

2. Greet your mate at the end of the day with the same enthusiasm and affection you do your dog.

3. Don't punish your mate because the "pups" misbehave.

4. Allow your mate to choose his or her friends. You don't go around choosing your dog's friends.

5. Don't try to change your mate. The dog owner's manual would encourage you to give your dog the freedom to be the kind of dog he/she is. If he's a cocker spaniel you don't try to make him a pointer. The same goes for your mate.

6. Don't get angry at your mate for being tired. If your dog is too tired to play, you don't get mad at him.

"If you were to treat your mate like you should treat your dog," concludes Dr. Jensen, "your mate would probably receive better treatment than a good share of mates do." In the early 1980s, a researcher at the University of Maryland found that 44%—nearly half!—of the people surveyed said that of all family members, their pet got the most recognition in the form of touch, look, word, smile, gesture or any act that said, "I know you're there." Only 18% answered, "the children." In a similar study by some University of Pennsylvania researcher, 80% of their respondents said they talk to their pets as people, and 28% confided in them about events of the day.

Perhaps if you're having trouble with your marriage, you ought to get hold of a pet owner's manual and study up.

As I work with couples having marital problems, in the vast majority of cases—not all but certainly most—the origins of the problems are trivial. Some little annoyance is nourished by selfishness and self pity until it grows and grows and grows into a huge wedge that divides and ultimately destroys the marriage. I recall the couple that were on the verge of divorce. They could scarcely talk to one another. They had lost affection for one another. Their children were suffering. Laughter, happiness, fun and good times had fled the home. After considerable analysis it was found that the origin of this awful circumstance was the husband's annoying habit of squeezing tooth paste from the center of the tube rather than from the end of the tube. It had become a "thing" with them. The wife angrily insisted, and he childishly resisted. Before long, the poison spread throughout the entire body of their relationship, and even began to infect (in fact!) the other family members.

One of my favorite stories (which I understand is true) is about a fellow who, one late evening, had a flat tire on a lonely country road. He was annoyed to find that the jack had been taken from the car, so he headed off to a distant farmhouse for help. "I hope the farmer isn't angry," he said to himself, "for being bothered." The further he walked, the more concerned he got about how the farmer would respond to his request for help. "Hey, wait a minute," he said to himself, "I can't help it. I don't mean to bother him. It isn't like I asked for this trouble!"

As day gave way to night, the downstairs lights in the farmhouse went out and the upstairs lights went on. "Oh, my goodness," the fellow said, "I've got to hurry. The farmer is going to bed. If I have to wake him, he'll *really* be angry!" So he hurried on.

> Most marriages die from self-inflicted injuries.

Moments later the light from only one room was left shining. By now the fellow was sure the farmer would be really upset at being disturbed. "After all," he said to himself, "farmers need to go to bed early and get a good night's sleep for the long day ahead. But I can't help the fix I'm in. If he gets mad at me—well, that's just too bad. I need help and he's the only one for miles around who can give it to me." And he hurried on getting more and more annoyed at himself, his circumstances, and, yes, the farmer.

Finally, the last light went off. Everything was dark. "Oh, brother, am I in for it now. This guy is going to be so mad at me. But that's just too bad. I have no other option. He's just going to have to be mad!"

At last, the fellow got to the farmhouse. By now his anger had gotten the best of him. He took a small stone and threw it against the farmer's bedroom window. Moments later, the farmer appeared at the window and, in a pleasant voice, called down, "Hello, how can I help you?" To which the enraged traveler, with clinched fist, barked back, "You can keep your damn jack," and walked off in a huff!

I see that same kind of self-inflicted injury maim and destroy otherwise healthy, robust relationships and families. It doesn't only involve a spouse, it can just as easily involve a child or children. It will happen every time if we, as parents, nurture annoyances, trivialities, and incidental, inconsequential, age-typical, garden-variety weed behaviors to the point where they simply crowd out, suffocate, all other forms of life.

No matter who we live or work with, there will always be someone or something that will bug us. Always! If we wait for all these someones or somethings to shape up so we can be happy, we will wait in miserable anticipation until hell freezes over.

Parents, here is some counsel you would do well to abide as couples as you set the course for your family.

First, show your children that you love one another. Be appropriately affectionate in their company. A great American religious leader, David O. McKay, said, "The greatest gift a father can give his children is to love their mother." (Certainly, this is equally true for a wife to her husband.) Hold hands, kiss, sit close to each other. My mother- and father-in-law, well into their 90s, were young love birds at heart. At every meal, Dad would help Mom with her chair— "scooting" her up to the table. He would then kiss her and say, "I love you, Mother dear." Shortly before Dad's death, I walked into their house, unannounced. There, in the dimly lit living room, sitting close to each other on the couch, holding hands and talking, were Mom and Dad. What a model!

Second, verbally express appreciation and love for your spouse and the good things he/she does. I love the story of the old Scotsman who was burying his wife of 60 years. His friend said to him, "A good woman she was." To which the old man replied, "Aye, that she was, and I came near telling her so a time or two." You get the message. Louise and I have been married nearly 40 years. In that time I might have spoken to her harshly five or six times, and she's sick and tired of it! But I repeatedly and daily hug her, kiss her, and tell her I love her, and she hasn't begun to get enough of that yet.

Third, be happy. Smile, laugh, joke. Collect jokes and tell them to one another. Share humorous anecdotes. Let humor give spice to the relationship. Laughter is, indeed, an effective tonic.

Fourth, set some time aside to be alone. A night out, a weekend away, a stroll in the evening hand-in-hand. These quiet times together needn't be expensive. There probably isn't a marriage counselor on earth who doesn't have this one on his/her list of things couples should do to strengthen their love.

Fifth, never miss an opportunity to overlook your spouse's shortcomings. I've heard it said that when going into marriage we should keep our eyes wide open, but once married, we should keep them half closed. In saying this I realize that there are some behaviors that can't be ignored, in which case proper action should be taken. But for the most part, as I've noted already, it is the little things that we nurture into big things that are the greatest threats to happy marriages. I'm reminded of the mother who asked a wise man what advice she should give her son as he was about to enter marriage. He answered, "When he becomes unhappy with his wife, tell him to never miss an opportunity to keep his mouth shut."

Sixth, and last, be faithful to one another—*absolutely* faithful to one another. We are living in an age of sexual promiscuity that is killing our society by destroying families. Anyone who disputes that is either insufferably ignorant or forever "on the prowl." For the past 30 years, we have been bombarded with pronouncements of "the new morality," and "free love." Baloney! It is neither new nor moral; it is neither free nor love. No matter how it's sliced, no matter how it's portrayed, it is nothing short of a selfish, undisciplined, uncaring desire to satisfy the flesh. There is not one shred of scientifically sound data that speaks to the value of sexual promiscuity—in *or* out of marriage—as a means of strengthening a relationship. None! Zero! On this matter, it's time, folks, for society to take a look at what the social research has to say, not what some self-serving, ego-maniacal, TV or radio talk-show host or hostess has to say about fidelity in marriage. Science, indeed, is a wonderful thing, but it is such an awful shame that it is being so categorically ignored in this vitally important matter. For all intents and purposes the sexual behavior of humankind is not being driven by knowledge, logic, or even common sense. Its being driven by unbridled, raging hormones that have been unleashed by a titilating media barrage of "If it feels good, do it." And, along with coercive, aversive, and abusive human interactions, it is striking a lethal blow at the very heart of the family unit: the marital relationship! Is it any wonder society is in the mess it is—and getting worse by the minute!

One of my daughters-in-law told me recently about a conversation she had with several of her fellow nurses. She was defending sexual morality as the better way to behave, in or out of marriage. One of the nurses replied, "I certainly wouldn't buy a pair of shoes without first trying them on. Why should I be any less careful in choosing a husband?" She was serious, by the way. Is that the level of commitment with which people should enter marriage today? A commitment that regards marriage as something one will eventually grow tired of, something that will eventually go out of style and be thrown away, like an old pair of shoes?

While attending a gathering of high school students who were discussing courtship, a young lady gave a wonderful talk on self-control, values, and the importance of waiting until the "right time" (meaning in marriage) to express one's love sexually. She held before her audience a slice of bread, spread with jam. She licked her tongue across the jam, handed the bread to a girl in the audience, and said, "Have a bite." Of course, the girl refused. The thought of biting off a piece of bread that had been licked was

> *Sex is not a need, it's a drive. We must learn to satisfy our needs but control our drives.*

disgusting! She handed it to a boy and said, "Take a bite." He, too, refused, recoiling in disgust, saying "Yuck!" She offered it to the audience, asking, "Anyone here want a bite?" as she drew her tongue again across the bread. "Gross!" I heard one girl say. Someone else said, "This is making me sick!" This delightful young girl then said, "I am no more interested in marrying a man who has sullied himself sexually than I am in eating a piece of bread that has been licked by others," and she sat down. What a message. What a powerful, powerful message, the wisdom of which is supported by a mountain of research. Remember this: sex is a drive, not a need. Our personal responsibility to ourselves and to society is to satisfy our needs while controlling our drives. Society, at large, appears to have failed to make that important distinction and to deal with it responsibly.

Moms and Dads, teach this important value by living it. There is *no* better way. Turn off the TV when the trash comes on. Avoid literature and movies that glorify and create a desire for sexual gratification. You certainly wouldn't eat something that was laced with poison. Why, then, feed poison to your mind? If this shoe fits, wear it: clean up your life. It's never too late!

## NOW TO REVIEW

1. *Show* your children that you love one another.
2. Verbally express appreciation to one another.
3. Be happy, smile, laugh, and joke.
4. Spend quality time alone.
5. Never miss an opportunity to overlook your spouse's shortcomings.
6. Be absolutely faithful to one another.

*Research has shown that the most effective way to reduce problem behavior in children is to strengthen desirable behavior through positive reinforcement rather than trying to weakens undesirable behavior using aversive or negative processes.*
*S.W. Bijou*
*The International Encyclopedia of Education, 1988*

*We encourage...people to view every habit and custom with an eye to possible improvement. Solutions to problems of every sort follow almost miraculously."*
*B. F. Skinner*

# TWENTY-SEVEN
# Positive Parenting: Summary and Review

Raising children—particularly teenagers—is not always easy. We tend to overreact. We tend to do for our children what they can and need to do for themselves. We tend to stand between them and the instructive consequences of their own behaviors. Sometimes we forget that our children *are* children in the process of growing. As children grow, communication tends to break down, rules are not carefully and consistently enforced, and we wonder if and how we're going to make it as a family.

Good parenting requires good parenting skills.

It's been reported that over three-fourths of all American high school students have contemplated suicide as a reasonable solution to solving their problems. A third of these have actually tried taking their own lives. The majority of those said they couldn't get along with parents and suicide seemed like the best way out. It is terribly unfortunate that suicide would be considered a reasonable alternative to any of life's problems. It is doubly unfortunate that, at a time when we know so much about how to improve the relationship between parents and children, so many problems continue to exist. Research

> **Good parenting requires good parenting skills.**

367

in human behavior has taught us wonderfully helpful things. In this chapter, I review many of those things as they relate to important parenting skills. Particularly I focus on nine skills, drawn from the preceding pages of this book, parents should have that we know, when-applied correctly, *will* improve parent-child relationships. These skills *will* help parents and children get along better by creating a happier environment at home, or wherever parents and children are together; and should difficulties arise (as they always will!), the chances are great that problems will be handled in a positive, appropriate way.

Regarding "chance," remember human behavior can only be predicted in terms of probabilities, not certainties. Although we might want total rapport or a 100% perfect relationship with our children, the best we can hope for will always be something less than perfect. In nature some laws produce the exact same results every time, such as the law of gravity. Behavior seldom if ever works that way, but by using well-applied skills, we can greatly increase the probability that behavior *will* proceed in a desirable direction.

We must also accept the fact that risks are involved in raising children, and these risks increase with age. When working with infants and children, the risks tend to be low while the probabilities for success are high. As age increases so do the risks, and the probabilities for success decrease, as illustrated by Figure 6.2, pg. 140. Rather than be discouraged by this, we must be ready for it and be prepared to adapt our parenting behaviors accordingly.

Age isn't the only variable that affects risk. Emotional stability, life experiences, parent's experiences as children, and the quality of their own childhood environment all influence the level of risk. Nevertheless, despite these variables, it is possible to learn and to use a better way to understand and interact with children. When that is done, parents and their children *do* get along much better.

By appropriately and consistently using the nine skills discussed here, we as parents can create a "proactive" environment in the home. A proactive environment is a positive, supportive, reinforcing environment that is under parental control. This is in contrast to a "reactive" environment in which the mood of the home is vulnerable to every mood brought into it by whomever may enter. (See Chapter 4, On Being In Control, Figure 4.1, pg. 89.)

Think about your own home and ask yourself the question, "What sets the mood of this home?" I have asked this question of parents all across the United States. Usually, they describe their home environment as one which reflects the moods brought into it by members of the family. A child has had a bad day at school and comes home grumpy and upset. Other family members react to this in kind. The mood of the home is immediately negative; reactive. This isn't unusual. When children are upset and cranky, parents tend to react in an upset and cranky way. Data suggest that parents are 6 to 10 times as inclined to be negatively reactive than they are to be positive and proactive in responding to the behavior of others in the family.

It doesn't have to be that way. Reactive responding is a learned behavior, but parents can learn a better way. We can't expect our home to be pleasant if we are unpleasant, out of control, and reactive. We must also get one thing clear immediately: if we are

> *Giving children the responsibility to frame a happy, positive home environment is like putting the fox to guard the hen house.*

going to wait for our children to somehow naturally "shape-up" in order for things to get better, we will be waiting for ever! Giving children the responsibility to frame a happy, positive environment in the home is like putting the fox to guard the hen house. Creating a happy mood in the home is *our* responsibility as parents. By first controlling our own behaviors, then by effectively applying selected skills, we can have a remarkable effect on improving the quality of life at home.

Here is an example of what I mean. Several years ago, our 17-year-old daughter came home from school in what appeared to be a very good mood. Once inside the house, though, she slammed the door so hard it shook the whole front end of the house, she threw her books on the floor, and let out a scream of frustration and anger. I was in the family room and my first *reactive* inclination was to march right out there and tell that kid she wasn't going to get away with that junk in this house! As I moved stridently towards the hall, I reminded myself that I was reacting, that I was allowing an adolescent child to set the mood of the home and to dictate my behavior. I stopped, took a few deep breaths, regained my composure, and walked into the hall in complete control of my emotions. My daughter was standing there breathing heavily and obviously very upset. Ignoring the books and papers strewn all over the floor, I gently took her hand and in quiet, compassionate tones said, "You have had a bad day. I'm sorry." Still breathing heavily, and obviously out of control of her emotions, she responded, "Yeah. I had a rotten day!" I said, "Let's sit down on the couch in the living room." Sitting together, I put my arm around her and she began to relax immediately. Her head fell on my chest, and she began to sob. Tears cascaded down her face and onto my shirt. Her body quivered with emotion. After what seemed like a very long time, she caught her breath, her quivering and sobbing stopped, and she just lay there against me like a limp rag. I asked, "Would you like to talk about it?" "No," she replied, "I just needed someone to understand." She gave me a big hug and a kiss, told me she loved me, picked up her papers and books, and went downstairs to her bedroom. The rest of the day proceeded happily. A "reactive" response to that behavior would have destroyed the quality of the environment in the home for the remainder of the evening. A "reactive" response would have accomplished nothing except to damage the relationship between a daughter and her dad. It would have robbed me of a great opportunity to show compassion and concern to a lovely girl who was momentarily upset, and to strengthen the bonds between us.

Parents *can* learn a better way, as illustrated by this next situation (told to me by a father). The daughter, while in high school, had taken up with a group of kids whose life style was almost 100% opposed to the value system of the home. The parents behaved

> **Proact. Do not react.**

badly; that is, reactively. They scolded her for taking up with such an element of people. They moralized, preached, warned, chas-tised, threatened. It didn't do anything but make matters worse.

Before long, the daughter was coming home smelling of alcohol and tobacco. To her father that was the last straw. He had grown up in a home where alcohol had been abused, and where alcohol and tobacco had worked a severe economic and emotional hardship on the family. As a child, he had come to hate alcohol and tobacco with a boundless passion. Those feelings had lain dormant in him for many, many years. He never had any reason to be very annoyed about people using alcohol or tobacco because he could just leave situations where they were being consumed. He had protected himself. But now, this horrible influence, and memories of the past, were assaulting him again right in his own home! By one of his own children! He couldn't just leave! It all seemed so cruel and unfair to him. He began avoiding his daughter. He absolutely couldn't stand to be in her presence. He couldn't stand to touch her and hug her as he had done every day of her life. He didn't want to talk with her or to be with her or to have anything to do with her! It was terrible! Without a doubt, he was behaving worse than she was.

His wife hadn't grown up under these same conditions. Though distasteful, they didn't affect her the same way they did the father. Consequently, she was not as distracted from the needs of their daughter as he had been. She reminded her husband—sometimes gently, but not always!—of his responsibility to behave "proactively"; to use those skills the family was in such need of during such critical times. Although the mother had her bad moments too (they suffered together), the father finally learned a better way of responding to his daughter. He put together a plan. He anticipated those situations to which he would otherwise "react," then wrote out how he should behave (see Figure 7.1, page 153). He role played; he acted out this better response. He practiced what he would do in distasteful situations. He learned to replace his old, bad, *reactive* responses with new, good, *proactive* ones. IT WORKED!

Despite the appearance and smell of his daughter, despite her behaviors, and despite his own adverse feelings he began to be stable. He began greeting her warmly and affectionately when she came home, like he used to. Every day, he told her he loved her and let her know how valuable she was to him.

> **Practice proactive responsing.**

When her less-than-desirable friends came to the house, he greeted them with the same enthusiasm he greeted his other children's friends. He and his daughter talked about all the crazy and inconsequential things that kids like to talk about. This opened the way to talk about important things and to communicate feelings and concerns in a way that was acceptable.

The change was dramatic. In some areas it was immediate. Every time she entered the house, she went directly to her dad for a hug and a kiss and to tell him she loved him. She followed this same routine when leaving the house.

The quality of her life didn't change entirely to what her parents would have it be, but the quality of "their" life together couldn't have been better. Her problems remained her problems. Her dad felt bad for her because of them, but there was no longer a wedge between them.

Following a car accident, a policeman took her home crying and upset. Fumbling around for her cigarettes, she became distracted and ran into the back of another car, sustaining damage to both the other car and her car. She was so distraught. You can't imagine what a temptation it was to her dad to say, "I told you so." Billions of brain cells screamed out at him, "This is your chance to get even! This is your chance to tell her what's what!" And frankly, he wanted to! Fortunately, he had learned his proactive skills well. Instead of giving way to the idiot temptation that was flooding over him to be reactive, he gently and compassionately took his trembling, cigarette-smelling daughter into his arms, held her close, told her how sorry he was, and did everything he could to help relieve *her* suffering. Suddenly, he realized "he" was not suffering! She clung to him tightly with her arms fully extended around him. And cried. She then kissed him, told him she loved him, and said, "Thanks Dad. You helped me a lot and I appreciate it." The mood he wanted in the home prevailed: calm, understanding, loving, and compassionate.

The skills discussed in this chapter are all intended to help parents create that kind of proactive environment in the home, and to learn how to interact effectively with their children. If they are used consistently and effectively, that is *exactly* what will happen. Your children might not behave in every respect and in every situation exactly as you want them to (as was undoubtedly the case with you and your parents when you were a

> There is absolutely no substitute for positive and pleasant interactions between parents and their children.

kid!), but at least the environment in your home will be under your "proactive control", and you will have learned a better way, a wonderful way, to raise children. You will have acquired valuable parenting skills. Parent burnout occurs when parents struggle unsuccessfully—skill-less—with day-to-day problems. With skills, you will still get tired (parenting can be exhausting), but you won't burn out. "Burnout" refers to mental exhaustion, and mental exhaustion is largely a product of not knowing what to do. With skills, you know what to do.

Now let's discuss these nine skills. You've heard these before but read them carefully again for emphasis.

## Skill #1:
## The Ability to Seize Opportunities to Have Frequent Positive Interactions with Your Children

There is absolutely no substitute for positive and pleasant interactions between parents and their children! When children are in a good mood, playing nicely together, pleasant to be around, doing their chores as instructed, getting their homework completed, and generally behaving appropriately, these behaviors should be acknowledged. Acknowledge them in very natural ways, but don't feel you have to acknowledge every single appropriate behavior. Just make certain that your praise and acknowledgments are distributed evenly and sincerely among the children, and see that they are given without fanfare, done simply in just a few seconds, and with few words. Smiles, a pat on the back, and sincere verbal acknowledgment are all things you can do to positively acknowledge appropriate behaviors. Do this several times an hour when in the company of your children. If each interaction takes only 3 to 4 seconds, you could have 15 to 20 per hour and it would only take about a minute of your time. That certainly isn't too much to ask.

Positive acknowledgment of appropriate behavior is a skill all parents need to learn. Studies of parent/child interactions clearly show that parents are much more likely to pay attention to inappropriate behavior than they are to attend to appropriate behavior. We also know that many parents give little thought to the quality of their interactions with their children. To become more aware of how you interact with your children, I suggest that you take a few days and record the quality of your own interactions with your children. Make a note every time you have a positive interaction, and every time you have a negative one. You may even want to describe the interactions. Figure 27.1 gives you an idea about how to do this. For starters, I recommend there *never* be more than one negative interaction for every eight to ten positive interactions. When keeping such a record, it generally isn't necessary to keep it for more than a few days—a week at most. Usually, within a few days, behaviors reappear and parents soon come to realize how things really are. By doing this, they have also prepared the groundwork to make things better.

Even at best, family life has its ups and downs. After a while, if you notice the atmosphere in the home becoming tense and strained again, just keep a record for a few days and you will almost surely find out why. When my children were young, there were times when sibling rivalry would get so bad the entire mood in the home was negative. Those were the times I'd keep a record of my wife's and my interactions with our children. Invariably, after a day or two we were able to determine what the problem was and set things in order. It was almost always a case of our giving attention to inappropriate behavior rather than appropriate behavior.

Sometimes, we forget to praise good behaviors. A simple way to remember to praise is to tape reminder notes where you are sure to see them. A taped reminder on the bathroom mirror will prompt you to tell Billy how nice his room looked after he cleaned it up. A note taped to the kitchen cupboard will easily remind you to tell Mary how much you appreciated her getting her homework done. On pg. 85 is an example of such a reminder. Other reminders could be a picture tilted off level, a nickel in your shoe, or a knick-knack intentionally located out of place.

> *A dull pencil leaves a more lasting impression than does the sharpest memory.*

Since behavior is the product of its immediate environment, it is important that a measure be taken of the quality of the environment. One way of doing this is to keep track of the quality of the interactions between parents and their children, as illustrated in Figure 27.1. First, describe the interaction, and then indicate whether it is a positive or negative interaction. Keep the record for at least a few days, usually no more than a week, but don't let the children know what you are doing.

The things we do and say, and even the way we feel, are usually prompted by something that happens around us. Typically, we are more sensitive to negative behaviors: a child who acts out, children who fight, or a son/daughter who comes home too late. These are often dramatic and hard-to-ignore behaviors. They have a strong influence over our own behavior and prompt us to pay attention to them. This being the case, we need a counter-force, something to prompt us to pay attention to the great mass of appropriate behaviors generally left unnoticed.

I realize that with some children, particularly those in their mid-teenage years, it might be very difficult to behave in a positive way to some of their weird and obnoxious behaviors. We sometimes get the feeling that they *never* behave appropriately, when in fact there are usually only a few undesirable behaviors that regularly reoccur, and loom so large we can't see around them. But there are typically many more good behaviors and, if we look hard enough, we can find them.

While in her midteens, our youngest daughter wrote me the following note. It taught one of the greatest lessons of my life.

> Dear Dad:
> Yesterday I had all the dishes washed, dried, and put away. You didn't even notice. I wish you would pay more attention to the things we do correctly than the things we do wrong. You will see that the correct outnumber the incorrect. I love you, but I am not perfect. I need more compliments.

Out of the mouths of babes!

I recall an account of an interview with a major league baseball player who was asked to explain his remarkable recovery from a terrible slump of the year before. He credited his success to his new coach: "He got more out of me than anyone ever has. He is the greatest motivator I ever knew. He never says anything negative about you. He's completely positive."

## Skill #2:
## The Ability to Clearly Establish and Communicate Your Expectations

Make certain your children understand perfectly what you expect of them, how you expect them to behave. This can be taught most effectively through role playing where children repeat back to you your expectations until you are satisfied they know and understand perfectly what you expect. Here are a couple of examples, beginning with young children.

*Are you absolutely sure your children know exactly what you expect of them?*

## Figure 27.1—Assessing the Quality of Parent-to-Child Interactions

Beginning date_____ Ending date_____

| DESCRIPTION OF THE INTERACTION | + | - |
|---|---|---|
| Billy came to dinner when I called and I said, | | |
|    "Thanks, Billy, for coming to dinner so quickly." | 1 | |
| Mary left her room a mess and I scolded her. | | 1 |
| | | |

The setting is a parent and her child, Billy. The expected behavior is to have Billy hang up his coat.

Parent: "Billy, when you take your coat off, I expect you to hang it up in the closet. What do I expect you to do when you take you coat off?"

Billy: "You want me to hang it up in the closet."

Parent: "That's exactly correct, Billy. Good answer. I expect you to hang it up in the closet. Come over here to the closet and I will show you exactly what I expect."

*Note:* It is always good to teach the behavior in the setting where it is most likely to occur.

After saying this, go to the closet, take out a coat, put it on the child, take it off, put it on the hanger, and hang it up. Then say, "Now, you do that, Billy."

If the child performs correctly, acknowledge that by saying, "Good. That is exactly correct. You hung your coat up exactly as you are expected to do. Now, put it on again, go outside, come right back in, and show me what you are supposed to do with you coat."

As the child performs correctly, acknowledge that: "Very good. You hung up your coat exactly as you are expected to do. That's super."

Give the child the opportunity to practice the behavior that is being taught. With each successful practice, acknowledge that success both verbally and physically. A sincere hug is great.

This same approach can be used to teach children to come to dinner when called, do what they are told to do, clean up their toys, or whatever.

The key is that they actually show you by what they *do* that they understand your expectations. Too often, parents tell their children to do something and then ask, "Now, do you understand what I'm telling you!?" Anxious to get their parents off their backs, children will say "yes" to anything. This is not acceptable. It leaves the door open to too much interpretation and forgetting. You must first tell them, then demonstrate it, and then have them do it—repeatedly, until you are *absolutely sure* you know *they* know it, and are able to do it. By then, they also know that you know they *can* do it.

Now let's look at an older child.

The setting is a mother with her 16-year-old daughter who has recently gotten her driver's license and wants to use the car. The mother is instructing the girl about being responsible when using the car.

Mother:  "Mary, you are to be commended for having met all of the requirements to earn a driver's license. That's super.

"Using the family car is a heavy responsibility. It is also a desirable privilege."

*Note:* Stress that it is a *privilege*. And remember—privileges are earned!

Mother:  "Mary, this privilege is available to you so long as you meet certain expectations. I am concerned for your safety, and my expectations relate to your safety. What are some things we expect you to do as you drive the car that will help keep you safe?"

*Note:* Remember, never tell a child something he/she already knows. Let the child tell you.

Mary:  "Well, you want me to drive carefully and obey speed limits and traffic signs."

Mother:  "Absolutely correct! You are expected to operate the car safely and within the law. What does that mean to you?"

*Note:* The mother doesn't ask, "Do you understand?" She invites a substantive response. For purposes of clarification, she asks questions and creates situations, and then invites responses:

Mother:  "For example, suppose your friends want you to take the car to an out-of-the-way country road and do some drag racing. How will you respond? What will you say?"

*Note:* The mother would want to continue this type of questioning or probing until she was sure her expectations were thoroughly understood.

This procedure should be used in exploring all of the ramifications of using the car:

When and how often the car can be used,
who pays for the gas and upkeep,
how late at night can the car be used,
and so on.

The beginning of a child's driving career is the time to thoroughly cover these expectations. The child will gladly put up with this type of discussion given the desirable privilege at hand.

Let's suppose the daughter takes issue with the discussion or feels like she is being treated like a child. Parents needn't feel defeated, frustrated, or intimidated by such resistance. In fact, such resistance is to be expected! It is age-typical behavior. You'd handle that resistance this way:

| | |
|---|---|
| Mary: | "Mother! This is crazy. I know how to take care of myself and the car. I really resent this!" |
| Mother: | "Mary, I can appreciate that you might find this a little annoying. I'm sorry it upsets you, but this is super important to me. Now, think about it, what would you do if your friends began pressuring you to do something really inappropriate like drag racing with the car? Kids do that sort of thing— especially if it's someone else's car!" |
| Mary: | "I'm more than a *little* annoyed, Mother! I'm offended. I resent being treated like a baby!" |
| Mother: | "I still need to know what you'd do in the face of peer pressure, because you will certainly be the object of it sooner or later." |
| Mary: | (A bit disgusted!) "Oh, for heaven's sake, Mother. I'd just tell them no. After all, I'm no dummy. I'd just tell them I'm not going to do a stupid thing like that!" |
| Mother: | "Thanks, Mary. That assurance means a lot to me. Knowing what I can expect from you in a moment of crisis is very important and your mature response is very comforting, thanks." |

*Note:* You'll notice how the child tried to draw the mother off track, but she wouldn't allow that to happen. She completely ignored any mention of how "crazy" the mother's concern was, how annoyed or offended the girl was, or how unadult the girl was being treated.

The mother didn't argue, become upset, preach, moralize, resort to logic or reason, none of this junk. She directly, with compassion and understanding ("I can appreciate that you might find this a little annoying. I'm sorry it upsets you..."), pressed her need for the required information ("...but this is super important to me."). Though the girl resisted and balked twice, she finally came forth with an acceptable response. This is quite typical.

If parents remain proactive and on course, the chances are overwhelmingly positive that the children will come forth with an acceptable response. In coming forth with that response, the kid might be sullen, angry, disgusted, or caught up in any one of a dozen dumb-dumb demeanors. Just space it off. Respond as a highly civilized adult no matter how uncivilized the kid behaves. Why should you get upset? After all, it's your car. You can use it whenever you want!

Suppose the child gets so upset she simply won't cooperate. Just say:

Mother: "Mary, I can see you are really upset by this conversation. Let's drop it for now and revisit it again when you are more in control of your emotions. Once we've had this conversation thoroughly, the privilege of using the car will be yours."

Do not try to resolve problems when those involved are emotionally upset.

*Note:* The complete responsibility for the positive resolution of the problem is right where it should be—on the kid's shoulders. The parent has not tried to resolve the problem at a moment of emotional upset. *You never try to be therapeutic when a person is drunk, stoned, or emotionally enraged or distraught*! You wait until they sober up, dry out, or calm down.

> **Do not try to resolve problems when those involved are emotionally upset.**

Let's suppose that Mary really comes unglued:

Mary: (shouting) "What! Do you mean to tell me that I can't use the car until I've answered your stupid, lousy, #!!!*@, questions! I need the car, Mother, and I need it tonight. I have plans! I've passed drivers ed, I passed my driver's test, and I have my license. You have no right to do this to me, Mother! No right at all! I can't believe this!" (huff, puff)

Mother: (Calmly) "Mary, as soon as we've finished this discussion and I have the assurances I need, the privilege of using the car will be yours. It's up to you. Go to your room, cool down, think it over, then let's resume this discussion when you are ready to do so."

*Note:* The mother has not been drawn off course, has not allowed the daughter's rage to enrage her, has not been distracted by profanity (which might well be discussed later), and has reminded the girl that using *her* (the mother's) car is a privilege, not a right! She quietly and simply gave direction to the girl's behavior, and with that gave her the responsibility for the ultimate resolution of the problem: "Go to your room, cool down, think it over, then let's resume this discussion when *you* are ready to do so." By proceeding this way at the beginning, though sometimes distasteful and clouded with emotion, the child will come around *soon*; after all, you are managing a very powerful contingency. It usually proceeds something like this:

Setting: The girl returns and, though outwardly calm, is still obviously angry and seething inside. Mother has a faint, though obviously secure, smile on her face. She is in complete control. The daughter is likely a bit confused by this. Only a short time earlier she had pulled out all the stops in an effort to blow her mother away, but mother is still there, well anchored in complete control, unmoved, unruffled. By now the daughter must certainly be thinking, "What a brick!", as thoughts of the story of the "Three Little Pigs" cross her mind. She composes herself; she postures herself to be equal to the task:

Daughter: "Mother, I'm sorry you don't trust me. I feel like you are treating me like a baby. As you can tell, that really upsets me. Nevertheless, it is obvious to me that I'm going to have to endure this little charade of yours before you're going to let me use the car. So let's get this over with!"

*Note:* What an astounding victory for mother and daughter! The mother's strength as a calm and in-control leader in the home has been established, and even though the daughter (as children that age will typically do) doesn't *appear* to like it, she respects it, and at that age respect is more meaningful than love. Children that age understand respect a lot better than they understand love, let me tell you! In time, under such conditions, both love *and* respect will emerge.

Mother: "Thanks, Honey. I'm glad you're ready to proceed. Now, getting back to where we left off...."

*Note:* Mother cut through all the verbal smoke and smog and junk and got right back on task.

It is important to keep in mind that what people do, that is, how they behave, is put into action by some kind of prompt or cue. Parents' expectations and directives are types of prompts. If children have a clear, working understanding of their parents' expectations, and understand the consequences of meeting or not meeting them, they are more inclined to behave appropriately. Which brings us to the next important skill.

## Skill #3:
## The Ability to Clearly Establish and Dispense the Consequences for Compliance and Noncompliance

Children and parents alike all behave and perform better when they know exactly what the consequences of their behavior are. When we as parents have those consequences clearly understood, we are in a much better position to be in control of our own emotions and behavior while dealing with the out-of-control behavior of our children.

A common problem—perhaps the *most* common problem—we as parents get ourselves into is when in the heat of emotion, frustration, and anger we impose a consequence that we have neither the intention nor the ability to carry out. It is not unusual at all, in a moment of anger and frustration, for a parent to yell, "You're never going to use that car again as long as you live, so help me!!!!" Then the next day the kid is merrily driving off in the car and the parent is feeling more helpless than ever.

What has the child learned? "Let the old man spout off, lay low for a day or two, mind your manners, and everything will be okay." There is a better way. To illustrate that better way, we will build on the examples from Skill #2: Clearly establishing expectations.

In the first example, the child was being taught what was expected of him relative to hanging up his coat. The child had demonstrated to the parent's satisfaction that he knew what was expected of him when he took his coat off. The parent is now discussing consequences.

Parent: "You did really well. You showed me that you know exactly what to do with your coat.

"When you hang your coat up, I will put a happy face on this chart. See, like this." (Show a chart and a happy face.)

"See, Billy. I put a happy face in this square because you hung your coat up as you are expected to do.

"With those happy faces, you are going to be able to earn fun things. With two happy faces, you'll earn the privilege of riding your bicycle after school the next day."

*Note:* It's important to remember that appropriate behavior is more likely to be forthcoming if it has attached to it something the child really values. Billy loves bike riding; therefore, when he behaves appropriately, he earns that privilege. The key is to identify those things that are highly valued by a child, and make them available as a result of good behavior. We call it "Grandma's Law": Eat your potatoes and gravy, then you can have pie and ice cream.

Sometimes management systems become so complex and so miserable to manage they become more intolerable than the behavior being managed. When using this strategy, keep any reinforcement system as simple as possible. For example, in most instances *simply giving the child a hug or a kiss and a verbal acknowledgment of good behavior is all that is needed.* To a large extent, what is appropriate is a matter of judgement on the part of the parent, and depends on what the parent knows about the

child. If a parent knows the child will need a heavy reinforcement for compliance, then a more elaborate reward system like the one described above might be appropriate. It is a judgement call on the part of the parent, based in large measure on the effect the system is having on the behavior.

Just as a child is reinforced for doing what is asked of him, he must also know the consequences of not doing what he's told. For example:

Parent: "Billy, now that you know what to expect when you hang up your coat, here's what you can expect when you don't. If you fail to hang up your coat, we will put a frowny face on your sheet. For every frowny face, you will deny yourself the privilege of riding your bike for *one* day. What will happen, Billy, if you forget to hang your coat up?"

Billy: "I won't be able to ride my bike one day."

Parent: "Good listening, Billy. That's correct, you'll lose the privilege of riding your bike for one day."

*Note:* In this conversation, Billy must understand that he is denying himself this privilege because of his inappropriate behavior. Thus, in the event of non-compliance, if a child leaves his coat laying on the floor, *the child has denied himself* valuable privileges. You as a parent are not doing the denying. You have already demonstrated that you are ready and eager to give the child whatever he has earned, good or bad.

When employing such a strategy, stick to your plan. Don't allow yourself to be distracted by arguments, reason, or the emotions of the child. Show empathy and understanding but stay the course. If a child misbehaves and loses the privilege of riding his bike, and he is very upset, remain calm and say: "I'm sorry you lost the privilege of riding your bike. Hopefully, you'll have earned that privilege by tomorrow." Then leave it at that.

## Skill #4:
## The Ability to Ignore Behaviors Which Do Not Threaten the Basic Quality of Life, Limb, and Property (which include most age-typical behaviors)

As we study behavior in the home between siblings and parents, it is interesting to observe that the vast, vast majority of all inappropriate behaviors are benign. That is, they are really of no consequence in terms of being a threat to anyone or anything. They are garden variety, age-typical, weed behaviors. If left alone, they'll eventually "dry up" (as my dad would say) and go away. Unfortunately, as parents, we tend to irritate these behaviors by picking away at them. We become taken by the notion that we aren't fulfilling our responsibilities as parents unless we "nip these problems in the bud."

Unfortunately, in our efforts to nip these behaviors in the bud, we can actually make them worse. An important principle of behavior has taught us that behavior can be powerfully reinforced

> *Most annoying behavior will go away if left alone.*

by parental attention; consequently, if we pay attention to inappropriate behaviors, those behaviors will continue. But remember, the same is true for appropriate behavior! Most misbehaviors children display in the home are basically inconsequential in terms of normal growth and development. As parents, we have to be very careful we don't get uptight about these behaviors. We have to remember that they are just normal growing-up behaviors. In fact, most of us can look back over our own childhood at home with our brothers and sisters and recall a lot of fights, arguments, and rivalry we were involved in. It is very unlikely that any of it effected our healthy growth and development, or our long-term relationships with our brothers and sisters.

When we give such behaviors attention, children will misbehave just to get that attention. A major solution to this is to simply ignore such behavior. When I say ignore such behavior, I mean that literally in every sense of the word. We are well advised in such instances not to even look at the children with a scowl or a smile on our face. We shouldn't say a single word in response to such behaviors. We shouldn't make any gestures which would indicate we are paying any attention to it whatsoever. In fact, a very effective strategy is to simply turn and walk away. Just get up and walk out of the room where the behavior is taking place. (But when leaving, don't roll your eyes to the ceiling!) This is one of the simplest yet most difficult things for parents to do, mainly because it runs so contrary to how we typically respond in such instances. When children misbehave, our very first inclination is to react immediately to put a stop to that nonsense right now! Once and for all! What actually happens is that we reward it; hence, we reinforce the very behavior we want to get rid of, the very behavior that annoys us the most.

> You will never manage the behavior of others if you first don't manage your own behavior!

Again, as difficult and unlikely as it may sound, it is nevertheless correct that the single best way of dealing with benign inappropriate behaviors, typically referred to as sibling rivalry and annoying behaviors such a tantruming, whining, pleading, crying, grouchiness, and so on, is to simply ignore it. This is called putting the behavior on extinction.

## Skill #5:
## The Ability to Attend to an Inappropriate Behavior Unemotionally, Precisely, Directively, and Instructively

Some behavior is so serious as to be harmful to property, person, and normal growth and development. These behaviors include fighting where it is highly likely that a child will be harmed, breaking and destroying things, berating and putting a person down to the point that it affects one's image of self, demanding unearned privileges, and so on. When such behaviors occur, remain calm, and deal with them directly as illustrated by the following two examples.

In this first example, a child has become angry to the point of throwing things and hitting other children. Rather than angrily shouting at the child to "STOP THAT!" or hitting the child, calmly stand in front of him (one and a half to two feet away); put your hand softly on the child's shoulder (assuming that such a gesture will not invite physical retaliation); nonthreateningly raise your other hand, leaving the palm open with the fingers apart and slightly curled forward (this is a "soft" hand signal); look the child squarely in the eyes, and say, "That behavior must stop immediately. It is not allowed here." Rivet your gaze on the child's eyes for about 3 seconds (this invites emotions to cool down), then empathetically *redirect* the child's behavior:

Parent:     "I'm sorry you're so upset. Go to your room for 10 or 15 minutes. Lie down, relax, think about your soccer game tomorrow, and when you are feeling better, come see me."

            *Note*: It takes only a few seconds to calm an otherwise angry, aroused child if you the parent are calm and obviously in control of your emotions and behavior. Given this environment, you are then in a position to convincingly redirect the child's behavior. When doing so, be very precise, and move it in a direction that will likely be acceptable to the child: "Think about your soccer game tomorrow," or whatever pleasant thing the child is anticipating being involved in in the near future.

The child may argue or resist by saying something like, "It's her fault! I hate her guts! You always blame me. She starts all the trouble and never gets blamed for it! It isn't fair!!" and on and on and on. Do not, I repeat, DO NOT, answer or respond in any way to any of these charges, be they true or false or questionable. Rather, with empathy and understanding, say:

Parent:     "You'll be happier, Son, and feel a lot better, after you've calmed down. Things happen that can really upset us. I know the feeling. Let's visit about it in 10 or 15 minutes."

Gently put your hand on the child's back, midway between the shoulder blades and the small of the back, and begin walking together in the direction of the child's room (or the couch where he is to sit down, to a chair outside on the patio, or wherever he has been directed to go to calm down). After a few steps in that direction, pat the child on the back and with a very gentle forward nudge, prompt the child to proceed alone to his (as one parent put it) "think it over area."

When the child returns, say, "I'm glad you're feeling better. Would you like to talk about it?" If he does, proceed with empathy and understanding, but *do not* get sucked into a conversation about fault, fairness, or how terrible his sister is. Deal only with *his* feelings, not others' faults. And keep the visit short. As the child's behavior improves, reinforce that. This is called the stop, redirect, reinforce strategy. If necessary, go through the same procedure with the sister.

In this second example, let's suppose a child has behaved irresponsibly and has not gotten his assigned chore done. Let's further suppose that the child has been appropriately instructed about the chore: he knows exactly what is to be done, by when it is to be done, and how well it is to be done. The child also understands the consequences, both positive and negative, for getting the work done or not getting it done. Rather than "bug" the child repeatedly because he hasn't gotten the chore done, once the time for getting the chore done has past, be unemotional, precise, and direct in dealing with that failure to comply. Suppose the child knows he's allowed to go to the movie with his friends when his Saturday chore is done by 11:00 in the morning. He understands that. There is no doubt in his mind as to what is expected of him. One o'clock in the afternoon comes around, the chore hasn't been done and the child comes to you for permission to go to

> Children are reactive because they are not fully civilized—as is also the case with some adults!

the movie with his friends. You don't berate the child and go into a long sermon in which you remind the child about his lack of compliance and how it disappoints you that he didn't do what he was told to do, and on and on and on. Rather, unemotionally, precisely, and directly say,

Parent:  "I'm sorry that you aren't able to go to the show, that by not getting your chore done you deprived yourself of that privilege."

Of course, the child will react. He will desperately try to strike up an argument. He may question your love for him. He may give all kinds of convincing reasons why he didn't get his chore done. He will assure you that if he's able to go to the show, he will get his chore done as soon as he gets home. If he gets really angry, he will tell you what a stupid rule you've imposed upon his life, and so on. Listen to all of this calmly and empathetically, and respond by saying something like,

Parent:  "Yes, I can imagine you'd be upset. It would have been a lot of fun to have been able to go to the show with your friends."

This will likely spark the child's anger and he will become even more intense in his criticism and denial. Again, listen to all of that junk with a lot of empathy and when the kid is done, you say,

Parent:     "I can understand you'd be upset, and I am sorry for that. Nevertheless, it was your decision and these are the consequences you have earned."

Then look the child right in the eyes and calling him by name say,

Parent:     "This matter is settled. If you are so upset you are not pleasant to be with, go to your room and think it over."

If the child continues to behave badly and to carry on, you might have to remind him that other more serious consequences will result from his persisting with that behavior. If this reminder is given, then the related consequence *must* go into effect *immediately*! Otherwise, it is just an idle threat. If you don't want to deal with the matter any more at the moment, simply leave the room. Maybe you can go into your bedroom where you can lock the door. If he howls and carries on outside, just let him have at it. Typically it is short lived. The point is, you can have an immense effect on inappropriate behavior by simply dealing with it directly and unemotionally and precisely. Don't talk much. It's important to get your message across using only a few words, with as little time spent at it as possible.

In some instances, the child's behavior might, indeed, make you very upset. You might feel you can't proceed in an unemotional, precise, and direct manner. If that is the case, simply say to the child, "I need a moment to myself. We will discuss this matter later. I'll be back in fifteen minutes." Then just leave the room. In that fifteen minutes the child will have had a chance to cool down, and you will have had a chance to get your thoughts together and be prepared to deal with the matter as it should be.

To instruct or reinstruct a child about how to behave appropriately, use the teaching interaction strategy (also known as the Corrective Teaching Model) discussed at length in Chapter 3, pages 67-69. It is such a wonderful way to teach children how to behave.

Parents and teachers repeatedly say to me, "This kid just can not behave!;" "What's the matter with that kid?!;" "He just can't seem to learn;" and so on. There is a better, more positive, and mature way of assessing children's behavior, a way that focuses on learning, not on deficits. For example,

> *If a child can learn to behave inappropriately, he can learn to behave appropriately.*

| RATHER THAN SAY | SAY |
| --- | --- |
| "What's the matter with that kid?" | "What has that child not been taught?" |
| "That kid can't learn to behave!" | "What does the child need to learn so he can behave appropriately?" |

Note: If a child can learn to behave inappropriately, he can learn to behave appropriately.

In the first instance, the *blame* for the child's behavior is placed on the child. In the second instance, the *responsibility* for teaching the child is where it should be, on the parent or the teacher. Parents and teachers need to spend more time and effort concerned with teaching appropriate behaviors than with wringing their hands over, or punishing, inappropriate behavior.

The ability to remain calm in the company of a mouthy, outraged, bratty kid is not easy. It's much easier, in fact, to respond in-kind with mouthy, outraged, and other aversive behaviors. At the moment, being able to be calmly directive and instructive can be next to impossible. Still, you need not feel as though you are a prisoner of such a setting. You can always just walk away, buy some time, and return to the problem later when things have calmed down.

A single mother of a difficult 14-year-old boy was in my office recently and told me of a wonderful experience she had in this regard. She and her son were standing nose-to-nose as he spit out one ugly, vituperative expletive after another. Her mind was in a whirl; she felt completely disoriented as this uncivilized little creature unleashed his vile wrath all over her. She knew that to respond in-kind would only make matters worse, and to try reasoning with the boy would be just one notch above insanity. Then, on impulse, out of nowhere as the boy was carrying on, she leaned forward and gave him a great big kiss "right on the lips. I couldn't believe what I had done! He stopped immediately and we just stood there in dead silence looking at each other. I quietly told him I loved him. He just looked at me—kind of funny, kind of confused and he walked away and went into his bedroom. About half an hour later he came to me and said, 'I love you, too, Mom. I'm sorry for what I said,'" and he hugged her. With this new healthy "setting condition" in place, they were able to work out their problems. She was then able to be instructive in a positive way.

## Skill #6:

## The Ability to Not Question a Noncompliant Child About His Behavior

Asking a child to explain his inappropriate behavior is counterproductive. It simply calls attention to the very behavior you want to get rid of by inviting an extended verbal exchange about it. Also, when parents ask their noncompliant children to explain their behavior, the parents don't really want an answer, they want compliance, and an answer is no reasonable substitute for compliance. In fact, an answer might simply make things worse, especially if it's a smart-mouth answer that annoys the parent. For example, suppose the child has failed to get his homework done, and it is now time for him to leave for school. There is no time to do the homework. The parent asks the child,

> *A dumb question can hope for no more than a dumb answer.*

Parent:     "Why in the world didn't you get your homework done?! I have told you a hundred times that you have got to get that homework done. What are we going to do about this? Tell me, why didn't you get that homework done!?!!"

Child:     "I didn't get it done because I hate to do homework."

The child has answered the question, but he is still not in compliance. In the meantime, he has gotten a ton of attention for noncompliance. What has been accomplished? Nothing constructive, for sure. The child is still noncompliant. He's been the object of a great deal of attention for being noncompliant, and he isn't terribly upset about being noncompliant. It's the parent who's having a fit!

Parents, put this note on the mirror in your bathroom as an important reminder: "If what you are about to say or do does not have a high probability of improving things, don't say it and don't do it."

Rather than carrying on with a bunch of questions that only make matters worse, state your expectations, clarify consequences, then let those consequences do the talking for you. Ask questions *only* if you need information for problem solving. Otherwise, you're just blowing off steam (evidence of being full of a lot of hot air!).

## Skill #7:

## The Ability to Use the Inappropriate Behavior of One Child as a Prompt to You to Attend to the Appropriate Behavior of Other Children

As I have noted repeatedly, parents are inclined to immediately attend to inappropriate behavior, the consequence being that inappropriate behavior is strengthened by the attention that is given to it. Unwittingly, parents reinforce the very behavior they want to get rid of. To help us *not* pay attention to inappropriate behavior, use the inappropriate behavior of one child as a prompt to turn your attention to children who are behaving appropriately. For example, suppose two children are arguing with one another while another child is behaving very well. Rather than saying a word to the kids who are arguing, without fanfare go to the one that is behaving appropriately and quietly say, "I'm really glad to see you enjoying yourself so much. That looks like a fun book you're reading. When you are done with it, I'd love to have you tell me about it," then walk on. I recently had an experience with a mother of four young children that beautifully illustrates this point. She was concerned because one of her older sons had terribly poor table manners. Every time the boy behaved badly at the dinner table the mother would pay attention to him and say all kinds of things which, of course, did nothing but worsen the situation. Her other three children, on the other hand, were quite well mannered at the table. For that, they received no attention whatsoever. I suggested to the mother that when her son put his elbows on the table (which really annoyed the mother), she turn her attention to the other children and say things like, "I really appreciate the way Mary is sitting so nicely at the dinner table. Thank you, Mary." The mother tried it and was amazed to observe the immediate results. She said, "My son's elbows went off the table so fast, his face fell right into his plate!" She used the strategy consistently, though intermittently, from then on and literally eliminated the problem that had been upsetting her for so long.

> *So far as children's behavior is concerned, do not leave well enough alone!*

There is an old adage in our society that says, "Leave well enough alone." This is good advice in some settings, such as where dangerous animals and volatile explosives are concerned, but it is not appropriate when dealing with good behavior. We should attend to "well enough," and leave the other alone—whenever possible, which is certainly most of the time.

## Skill #8:
## The Ability to Smile and Laugh, Touch and Talk—a Lot!

An entire book could be written on the teaching and therapeutic value of smiling, laughing, touching, and talking. When a child gets out of line at the grocery store, rather than jerk the kid back with a scowl and a "Get over here! Now do what I tell you!" gently take the child by the hand, smile, draw him close to you, give him a hug or a pat on the back and gently say, "Thank you for standing close to me. I like having you close to me." Rather than berating a teenager for staying out too late, say, "I'm so glad you're home safe and sound. I've worried about you," then follow this with a hug and kiss and a sincere "Sleep tight. I love you." Let consequences do any remaining talking for you.

I have repeatedly stressed the importance of appropriate touching. It is a wonderful way for parents to bond with their children. There are studies which show that Americans touch each other less than do people in nearly any other country. One study showed, by comparison, that whereas Italians touch each other an average of 120 times an hour, Americans average only 2.8 times an hour. For emphasis, I reiterate that touching should be appropriate, and in families the more the better—as appropriate!

Leave your children notes of affection and appreciation. One night I forgot to leave a note on the pillow of our third daughter and she wrote a note back, "I missed the good-night note last night." What wonderful bonds can be formed with even a dull pencil and a scrap of paper.

## Skill #9:
## The Ability to Assess Behavior Analytically and to Treat It Clinically

In our efforts to raise our children well, we often become our own worst enemies by rushing into things, issuing ultimatums, and making decisions without being adequately prepared. Seldom do crises occur in homes that are of such a serious nature that they absolutely *must* be dealt with immediately, on the spot. We too often think that's what needs to be done; thus, we act hastily only to regret it. In the vast majority of instances when we must intervene, we are best advised to proceed cautiously, to be objective and calm, perhaps make a note of what is happening, then proceed carefully on the basis of the

> *Learn to gather data and let it help you solve problems. It beats having your feet planted squarely in mid air.*

information we have gathered. We should ask ourselves, "What are the consequences that are shaping and maintaining that behavior?" and, "What must we do to arrange the environment so that the behaviors that are in the children's best interest are properly taught and reinforced?"

One of my colleagues shared with me a wonderful experience he had with one of his teenage boys who resisted getting his homework done and turned in on time. Rather than getting upset, fussing and fuming, and bugging the boy with all kinds of verbal junk, he paused, quietly observed his son's behavior around home for a few days, kept cool, maintained an up-beat relationship with his son, and waited for the environment to suggest an answer to the problem. "Remember, behavior is largely a product of its immediate environment." Sure enough, only a few days passed and the solutions became apparent. He hadn't realized before how much his son enjoyed the privacy of his bedroom. What a great, positive consequence for compliance: privacy! (It turned out to be more valuable than money.) Of course, the boy had to earn it. But how? You guessed it, by getting his homework done and in on time. His father took the boy's bedroom door off and said to him quietly and kindly, even benevolently, "Son when your homework is done and in on time, you can have your bedroom door back." (In the science of human

**Indeed, science is a wonderful thing.**

behavior this is called a response cost.) The homework problem was solved in a very positive way; furthermore, as the timely completion of homework was paired with privacy and with Dad's verbal praise, the boy embraced learning as enjoyable and his outlook on school took on a whole new character. Pretty wonderful solution, wouldn't you say? (If you have had similar experiences with positive solutions to perplexing problems, please send them to me so I can share them with other parents. When you do so, please tell me something about your circumstances, e.g., whether you're a single parent, whether you live in a particularly difficult social setting, family size, and so on.)

For your interest and amusement, I have included at the end of this chapter a brief report a teacher submitted to me describing his experience with a behavior he was concerned about. It is a very nice illustration of a systematic and effective approach to problem solving that you would be well advised to use as the need exists. Figure 4.2, and an explanation of its use (pages 97–102) provide a valuable tool for systematically analyzing behavior.

When deciding on an intervention, we should always look for methods that are easy to apply and are solidly anchored in science. Avoid methods that are supported only be tradition, testimonial, conventional wisdom, logic, anecdotes, and past experiences. This kind of media-mentality and tabloid-reasoning will almost always result in disappointment, and even tragedy. Here are two examples of such mentality:

> "I spank my kids because that's how my parents raised me. I got what
> I deserved and because of it, I turned out okay. If I'd have been molly-
> coddled and allowed to get away with things like kids do nowadays,
> I'd have been as bad as they are." And,

"Don't give me that patience-and-kindness-all-the-time stuff. The parents next door just drip of that kind of stuff and every one of their kids is a curse to society."

It is true, human behavior being what it is, some children raised in abusive homes will turn out great, while some children raised in wonderful homes will turn out terrible. But *for the most part*, these are exceptions to the rule. In the field of research, we look for what are called measures of central tendency; that is, evidence of conditions or circumstances that are most frequently characteristic of whatever it is we are studying. For example, let's say that for some odd reason, in a neighborhood of middle-income people, there lives a family that is worth a billion dollars. Tabloid reasoning would seize upon the billionaire as evidence of the wealth of the neighborhood. The scientist, looking for a measure of central tendency, would report that with one unexplained exception, the neighborhood is made up of middle income families. That would be the measure of central tendency, the best indicator of the economics of the neighborhood.

When looking for methods to raise our children, we should avoid unexplainable exceptions and look for methods that are characteristic of those approaches which have proved to have the highest probability of producing the results we want. If you were going to invest your money, you would avoid unexplainable exceptions and look, rather, for investments that are supported by measures of central tendency. Granted, an investment in an exception might pay off big. Lotteries, sweepstakes, and other far-out risks and chances have been known to heap wealth on individuals. But no one in his right mind would bet his life against those odds.

In this book, I've addressed only methods that are characteristic of measures of central tendency, methods that provide you with the best chances of winning—where the odds are overwhelmingly in your favor. I've done here precisely what you would expect your physician to do when treating your body, what you'd expect the pilot to do when flying the plane on which you were a passenger, what you'd expect a plumber to do when fixing a leaky faucet, and what I expect you to do when raising your children: assess things analytically and treat them clinically, with precision, care, and tons of love.

Be eager to put science to work in your high responsibility to appropriately shape your children's behavior. It's the surest way to go. As noted by B. F. Skinner, "...a scientific view of man offers exciting possibilities. We have not yet seen what man can make of man."

## NOW TO REVIEW

1. Seize opportunities to have frequent positive interactions with your children.

2. Clearly establish your expectations.

3. Clearly establish the consequences for compliance and noncompliance.

4. Ignore behaviors which do not threaten the basic quality of life, limb and property (which include most unacceptable behaviors).

5. When it becomes necessary to attend to an inappropriate behavior, be unemotional, precise, and directive.

6. Do not question a noncompliant child about his behavior, or ask him to explain his inappropriate behavior.

7. Use the inappropriate behavior of one child as a cue to you to attend to the appropriate behavior of other children.

8. Smile and laugh, and touch and talk—a lot!

9. Assess behavior analytically and treat it clinically.

Using these skills effectively will have an immediate, remarkable, and long-term positive effect on the quality of the environment in your home and in your ability to establish and maintain a proactive environment. Remove the following page and display it in a prominent place as a prompt to *you* to behave well.

I end this book with a small but great bit of advice: Teach your children with love, never in anger; speak to your children with gentleness, never in anger; laugh and smile with your children, never at them; be a happy parent, be happy to be a parent, and that's what your children will learn!

> *Research has shown that the most effective way to reduce problem behavior in children is to strengthen desirable behavior through positive reinforcement rather than trying to weaken undesirable behavior using aversive or negative processes.*
> *S.W. Bijou*
> *The International Encyclopedia of Education, 1988*

# IMPORTANT RULES OF PARENTING TO KEEP IN MIND

1.  Seize opportunities to have frequent positive interactions with your children.

2.  Clearly establish and communicate your expectations.

3.  Clearly establish the consequences for compliance and noncompliance.

4.  Ignore behaviors which do not threaten the basic quality of life, limb, and property (which include most unacceptable behaviors).

5.  Attend to inappropriate behavior in an unemotional, precise, and directive way.

6.  Do not question a noncompliant child about his behavior, or ask him to explain his inappropriate behavior.

7.  Use the inappropriate behavior of one child as a cue to you to attend to the appropriate behavior of other children.

8.  Smile and laugh, talk and touch—a lot.

9.  Assess behavior analytically and treat it clinically.

# A Classroom Teacher's Approach to Problem Solving

## Problem

Chris had the unpleasant habit of sticking his finger up his nose during seatwork. He would sit at his desk busily doing his assignment, but almost without fail he would insert his left index finger into his nose.

## Baseline Data

I took data on how often he did this by keeping a record on a pad of paper which I carried in my pocket. That data looked like this:

Day 1: 16 times

Day 2: 18 times

Day 3: 17 times

I showed this data to his mother. She knew he had this problem and explained to me that I was the first teacher willing to tackle it.

## Procedure

*Target behavior.* To make Chris aware of this behavior and to eliminate it from Chris' life.

*Intervention.* Intervention had 5 parts, as follows:

1. Whenever Chris exhibited the target behavior, I said "Thank you Chris."

2. Chris kept a chart of the times he exhibited the behavior. (He self-managed.)

3. A string was tied around his index finger as a reminder.

4. A bandage was put on the end of his index finger.

5. A penny was placed in his shoe as a reminder not to put his finger in his nose.

## Result

The results were fantastic! Within a week he had extinguished the behavior. He was never seen thereafter putting his finger in his nose. Chris is happy, his mother is elated, and I feel pretty effective!

A sixth grade teacher

# INDEX

## INDEX OF TABLES

## INDEX OF FIGURES

## AUTHOR INDEX

Alexander, L., 326
Azrin, N.H., 259, 261, 262

Bijou, S., vii-viii, 24
    and at the close of each chapter
Bloom, B., 311 ,312, 318
Brook, J., 341
Burbank, L., 33

Coleman, J., 311
Cautela, J., 5
Chance, P., 111
Cheney, C., 259
Cherrington, D., 11

Epstein, R., 9
Ewing, C., 124

Faust-Campanile, J., 259, 260, 261
Foxx, R.M., 259, 261, 262
Friman, P., 250, 255

Goodlad, J., 309
Grant, C.D., 196, 197

Hickey, M., 3
Hyman, I., 195

Jensen, B., 110
Jenson, G., 360

Kenning, M., 259, 260, 261
Kerwin, M.L., 250
Kiester, E. and S., 304

Latham, L., 88

Morgan, D., 334
Mayer, G.R., 58, 325
McCoy, E., 181
McIntire, R. and C., 297
McKay, D., 362
Miller, B., 6
Morse, M., 79

Osborne, M., 250
Owens, M., 195

Rolider, A., 244
Rosemond, J.K., 180

Sidman, M., 24, 37
Skinner, B.F., 12, 391
Sloane, H., 110, 322
Sneed, T.J., 259

Sullivan, L., 4, 5
Sulzer-Azaroff, B., 58, 325

Taylor, Jane, 142
Taylor, Jill, 39

van der Post, L., 142

Walker, E., 261, 259
Werner, E.E., 11, 351
West, R., 13-14, 346
Wyatt, J., 251

Young, R., 67, 68, 110, 346

## Index of Organizations and Institutions

American Academy of Pediatrics, 3

Boys Town, 277
Brown University, 11

California Department of Education, 2
Center for the Study of Social Policy, 3
Centers for Disease Control, 331
Child Abuse Prevention Council of
    Ogden, 192

Fullerton California Police Department, 2

Girl Scouts of the U.S., 173

Harvard Medical School, 335, 336, 337

National PTA, 3
National Association of Secondary
    School Principals, 326
National Education Association, 195, 311
National Association of School
    Psychologists, 195

Sylvan Learning Centers, 326

U.S. Department of Commerce, 318
U.S. Surgeon General, 79, 331
U.S. Labor Commission
    Report, 307, 318
University of Pennsylvania, 360
University of Kansas Achievement
    Place, 277
University of Maryland, 360